T0322084

philosophers

who changed history

philosophers
who changed history

Foreword by SIMON BLACKBURN

SECOND EDITION
Toucan Books Ltd.
Editorial Director Ellen Dupont
Art Editor Thomas Keenes
Editor Dorothy Stannard
Picture Research Sharon Southren
Consultant on Second Edition Dr Sid Hansen
Additional text Joanne Bourne, Dr Sarah Bufkin, Jennifer Carter,
Sid Hansen, Johanna Meehan, Mike Robbins

DK London
Editor Kathryn Hill
Senior Art Editor Helen Spencer
Managing Editor Gareth Jones
Senior Managing Art Editor Lee Griffiths
Production Editor Jacqueline Street-Elkayam
Production Controller Nancy-Jane Maun
Senior Jacket Designer Surabhi Wadhwa-Gandhi
Jacket Design Development Manager Sophia MTT

DK Delhi
Senior Jacket Designer Suhita Dharamjit
Senior DTP Designer Harish Aggarwal
Senior Jackets Coordinator Priyanka Sharma Saddi

FIRST EDITION
Senior Editors Hugo Wilkinson, Chauney Dunford
Senior Art Editor Helen Spencer
Managing Editor Gareth Jones
Senior Managing Art Editor Lee Griffiths
Jacket Designer Surabhi Wadhwa-Gandhi
Design Development Manager Sophia MTT
Jacket Editor Emma Dawson
Pre-production Producer Gillian Reid
Senior Producer Rachel Ng
Associate Publishing Director Liz Wheeler
Publishing Director Jonathan Metcalf
Art Director Karen Self

Produced for DK by
cobaltid
www.cobaltid.co.uk

Art Editors Paul Reid, Darren Bland, Rebecca Johns
Editors Marek Walisiewicz, Diana Loxley,
Johnny Murray, Kirsty Seymour-Ure

This edition published in 2024
First published in Great Britain in 2019 by
Dorling Kindersley Limited
DK, One Embassy Gardens, 8 Viaduct Gardens,
London, SW11 7BW

The authorized representative in the EEA is
Dorling Kindersley Verlag GmbH. Arnulfstr. 124,
80636 Munich, Germany

Copyright © 2019, 2024 Dorling Kindersley Limited
A Penguin Random House Company
10 9 8 7 6 5 4 3 2
002–339250–Feb/2024

All rights reserved.
No part of this publication may be reproduced, stored in or
introduced into a retrieval system, or transmitted, in any form,
or by any means (electronic, mechanical, photocopying,
recording, or otherwise), without the prior written permission
of the copyright owner.

A CIP catalogue record for this book
is available from the British Library.
ISBN: 978-0-2416-5682-2

Printed in UAE

www.dk.com

This book was made with Forest
Stewardship Council™ certified
paper – one small step in DK's
commitment to a sustainable future.
**For more information go to
www.dk.com/our-green-pledge**

CONTRIBUTORS

Tony Allan
is a professional writer who has published more
than 30 titles, among them *The Mythic Bestiary*,
Archaeology of the Afterlife, and *The Symbol
Detective*. His book *Prophecies* has been
translated into 10 languages.

R.G. Grant
has written extensively in the fields of history,
biography, and culture. His recent works include
Sentinels of the Sea and contributions to *Writers
Who Changed History*.

Diana Loxley
is a freelance editor and writer, and a former
managing editor of a publishing company in
London. She has a doctorate in literature.

Kirsty Seymour-Ure
has a degree in English literature and Italian
from Durham University. Now living in Italy, she
is an experienced freelance writer and editor.

Marcus Weeks
is a writer and musician. He studied philosophy
and worked as a teacher before embarking on
a career as an author. He has written and
contributed to many books on philosophy,
literature, and the arts.

Iain Zaczek
studied French and history at Wadham College,
Oxford University. He has written more than
30 books on various aspects of culture, history,
and art.

CONTENT CONSULTANT
Will Buckingham
is a philosopher, novelist, and lecturer. He has
taught at De Montfort University, Sichuan
University, and the Parami Institute, Yangon. He
has a particular interest in the interplay between
philosophy and narrative, and has written
numerous academic works as well as
several novels.

FOREWORD
Simon Blackburn
is a Fellow of Trinity College, Cambridge,
the Emeritus Bertrand Russell Professor of
Philosophy at the University of Cambridge,
and the author of many books, including the
best-selling *Oxford Dictionary of Philosophy*
(1994), *Think* (1999), and *Being Good: A Short
Introduction to Ethics* (2001). OUP published *Lust*,
his contribution to their *Seven Deadly Sins* series,
in 2005. He was a Fellow and Tutor at Pembroke
College, Oxford, from 1969 to 1989, and from
1990 to 2000 an Edna J. Koury Distinguished
Professor of Philosophy at the University of
North Carolina, Chapel Hill. He edited the journal
Mind from 1984 to 1990.

◁◁◁ **PAGE 1 COPY OF** *THE THINKER*,
AUGUSTE RODIN, 1904

◁◁ **PAGE 2** *THE SCHOOL OF ATHENS*
FRESCO, RAPHAEL, 1509–11

◁ **PAGE 3 16TH-CENTURY ETCHING OF A**
PHILOSOPHER STUDYING AT HIS DESK

▷ *ARISTOTLE WITH A BUST OF HOMER*,
REMBRANDT HARMENSZOON VAN RIJN, 1653

CONTENTS

Foreword

There are many academic pursuits we use to investigate ourselves and our world. Sciences such as biology, chemistry, and physics do this; likewise humanities such as classics or history, linguistics or archaeology. Philosophy can also be said to do it, but in a different way. Its focus is not on our material or physical nature, nor on our wars or politics or artefacts, but on the ways in which we think about ourselves and our world, and the implications of these ways of thinking for our everyday lives.

Human consciousness forces us to think and reason, to use strategies of trial and error, to draw inferences and make predictions, and so to sift truth from falsity. These processes tell us who we are and where we are in the universe, and so we need to understand their inner workings, their scope, and their limits. We also need to set ourselves ways of living in the world as we understand it. We choose and act, evaluate options, and consider our aims and priorities. Some philosophers have concentrated more on the first – theoretical – set of issues. Others, moral and political philosophers, have thought more about the second set of issues – the practical problems of life. The great philosophers, whose lives and works are considered in this book, thus provide us with the means to understand ourselves and our world, and provide wisdom in how to apply that understanding.

As this book illustrates, it seems remarkable that the earliest writings we now recognize as philosophical works began to flourish in very different places, but around the same time. In China, India, and Classical Greece, about 500 years before the Common Era, there emerged – independently – literature concerned with reflection, inquiry, and self-understanding. There was thought and intelligence long before this, of course, and literature, religions, and codes of conduct. But it was as if human beings had simultaneously heard and tried to answer a call to revisit and interrogate their blueprints for living. Naturally Confucius, the Buddha, and Plato answered that call in different ways and with different emphases. But once this self-consciousness had seeded itself, the long march of philosophical reflection began in earnest.

As different periods threw up different economic, social, scientific, and political questions, so the topics that consumed the most philosophical energy also changed. In religious periods, such as the Middle Ages in the West, the relations between God and man occupied the sharpest minds. When science began to challenge the authority of the Church, the nature of scientific inquiry and the understandings it gave us of our physical environment became the priority. With the rise of the commercial world, the monarch's monopoly over political power came under scrutiny; and with industrialization, the relation between capital and labour began to occupy more attention. Copernicus, Newton, and Darwin each shook our sense of our place in nature, and so reflecting on how to adapt old ways of thought to these new understandings became urgent. In this book, we see how the greatest philosophical minds rose to these challenges.

Scientific advances set new philosophical agendas, but so too do rising dissatisfactions and anxieties. Where hope binds people together in cooperation and trust, fear splits them apart in suspicion and mistrust. Perhaps we have entered an age in which people fear apocalypse rather than hope for nirvana. Yet difficult times are hospitable to philosophy. Whenever old blueprints for the conduct of life begin to fade and lose their authority, there is no finding new ones except through the hard philosophical work of confronting ourselves and our world with truth and reason.

The men and women illustrated in this volume have had very different understandings of the world, of ourselves, and of the wisest ways of conducting our lives. They have constructed systems of thought, some of which endure, and some of which have suffered at the hands of time, or in the light of new experience, or further

reasoning. However, they all shared a conviction of the importance of the task. Even sceptics who doubted the very possibility of philosophical understanding, found it important to persuade people to live their lives aware of the void this leaves.

To appreciate fully the different ways in which even a few of these thinkers have pursued the truth would be a long task. But just to browse through the gallery of their names and achievements is a reassurance and a revelation. We are not alone in the world, and we are not the first to have found in philosophy a kind of salvation. We can thank history for the great men and women who were curious enough to struggle with the problems thrown at us by the world and our place in it, who spent their lives trying to leave it better than they found it, and who left us words with which to voice thoughts that would otherwise never have risen to the light of day.

Simon Blackburn

ANCIENT

CHAPTER 1

▷ **LAOZI AS A DAOIST DEITY**
In religious Daoism, Laozi is often portrayed as a supreme Daoist deity, as in this illustration, where he is shown enthroned, flanked by attendants, and holding the yin-yang symbol, which in Daoist metaphysics represents the complementary but opposing forces of the universe.

Laozi

6TH CENTURY BCE, CHINESE

Laozi is traditionally said to have been the author of the *Daodejing*, or *The Classic of the Way and of Virtue*, and the founder of the philosophical system later known as Daoism.

"**The way** is constantly **without action**, yet there is **nothing** that is **not done**."

DAODEJING

According to legend, the sage Laozi ("Old Master") was an older contemporary of Confucius, and lived in the 6th century BCE. The historian Sima Qian (see p.19) claims that Laozi worked as the keeper of archives in the Zhou court, where he was once visited by Confucius, who consulted him about *li* (ceremonies and rituals).

Towards the end of his life, it is said that Laozi became weary of the corruption and political machinations of the court, and left for the western frontier, riding a water buffalo. At the gate, he was stopped by a guard, who persuaded him to write down his words of wisdom. Laozi obliged – the result was his book the *Daodejing*, or *The Classic of the Way and of Virtue*. The aged sage then mounted his water buffalo and rode westward, never to be seen again.

The *Daodejing*

Details of the actual Laozi – if indeed he existed at all – are almost entirely lost to history, and many scholars now believe that the *Daodejing* is not the work of one hand but instead a compilation of sayings and oral teachings by a number of writers, and that it that reached its final form some time in the 4th century BCE.

◁ **LAOZI AND THE WATER BUFFALO**
This Song dynasty statue depicts Laozi – dressed as a farmer and disenchanted with corruption at the Zhou court – riding westward on a water buffalo.

The *Daodejing* is short: the Chinese text is just over 5,000 characters long. It is a paradoxical work and, like its legendary author, hard to pin down. Written in a series of brief, fragmentary verses that hint at meaning rather than presenting clear, logical arguments, it has been interpreted in many ways: as a guidebook for political leaders; as a book of mystical insights; and as a treatise on self-cultivation.

Following the Daoist path

At the centre of the *Daodejing* is the metaphor of the *dao*, which can be translated as "road", "path" or "way" (see box, below). The *Daodejing* is concerned with how we might optimally make our way through the world; and it emphasizes repeatedly that the best strategy is often to minimize our action, and draw power from the ebb and flow of the universe. Forcing how we act is, according to the *Daodejing*, not advisable. Instead, we should seek natural ways of acting so that things can take place more spontaneously.

In Chinese, this idea is called *wuwei*, usually translated as "non-action" or "doing nothing". The profound insight here is that trying too hard can be the very worst strategy. "If you act through non-action," the text advises, "there is nothing that is not well-governed." Non-action is not the absence of action, but rather acting with the least possible effort.

The *Daodejing* is one of the most translated texts in history. In the 7th century it was translated into Sanskrit and spread far beyond China. In recent years, hundreds of editions have been printed in a number of European languages.

△ **DELIVERING THE *DAODEJING***
This 16th-century illustration (ink on paper), traditionally attributed to the artist Li Gonglin, shows the great sage Laozi delivering his text the *Daodejing* to the gatekeeper who requested that he write down his words of wisdom. The sacred text recommends finding one's pace in the natural rhythm of the universe and learning to practise *wuwei*, or "non-action".

IN CONTEXT
Daoism

Daoism is a Chinese system of philosophy and practice that traces its roots to Laozi and the philosopher Zhuangzi. The principal concern of Daoism is the idea of "the *dao*" or "the way", the primordial and eternal aspect of the universe, the underlying ordering principle of everything that exists. The first use of the Chinese term *daojia*, which corresponds to "Daoist", was in the 2nd century BCE, during the Han dynasty.

THE DAOIST YIN-YANG SYMBOL FORMS A PATHWAY IN A BAMBOO FOREST, CHINA

Confucius

551–479 BCE, CHINESE

Confucius was arguably the most influential teacher in Chinese history. A humanist, he was concerned with how to live a virtuous life, and how to establish a society built upon that virtue.

The name by which Confucius is known in the West is the Latinized version of the Chinese Kong Fuzi, or Master Kong. He was born in the state of Lu in the northeast of China, in present-day Shandong province, and lived in what is known as the Spring and Autumn period of Chinese history. This period, which is named after the ancient history book called the *Chunqiu*, or *Spring and Autumn Annals* (see box, right), stretched from 770 BCE to 481 BCE. It was a time of political upheaval and uncertainty during which a number of small states competed for supremacy. Confucius regretted this fragmentation and his philosophy continually looked back to the earlier Western Zhou dynasty (c.1046–771 BCE) as a time of unity and stability, and sought to recover this past to restore what he saw as the virtue of former times.

Family and early life

According to the historian Sima Qian (145–86 BCE), who wrote *Records of the Grand Historian*, a monumental history of ancient China (see box, p.19), Confucius's family was descended from a branch of the royal house of the ancient Shang dynasty. This may or may not be the case, but it is known that the family had lost any wealth they may have possessed by the time

of his birth. Their struggles only increased. When Confucius was three years old, his father died, leaving the boy to be brought up by his mother.

Voracious learning

Confucius clearly had an appetite for learning. He attended a school for commoners, where he mastered the Six Arts – consisting of rites, music, archery, chariot racing, calligraphy, and mathematics – that were the basis of Chinese education, and he also

gained a good knowledge of the classical traditions. In his late teens Confucius began the first of a succession of low-ranking government jobs and then started teaching in his thirties, soon gathering a group of followers impressed by his views on how learning, justice, virtue, and benevolence might encourage a harmonious social and political system.

In about 502 BCE he secured more steady employment, first as the governor of the small town of

△ **WESTERN ZHOU WINE VESSEL**
Bronze vessels, such as this ornate 10th-century wine bucket, played a key role in the ritual banquets in family temples or over ceremonial tombs.

▷ **CONFUCIUS, c.1770**
According to the historian Sima Qian, Confucius did not contest an observation that was made about his appearance – that he was sad and forlorn, and resembled a stray dog.

IN CONTEXT
The Spring and Autumn Annals

The chronicle that gives its name to the period associated with Confucius is a month-by-month account of events in the state of Lu over the 241 years between 722 and 481 BCE. It is believed to have been compiled by Confucius from the chronicles of the state of Lu; Confucius's additions and omissions to the revised text are thought to be highly significant because they subtly present his moral judgements on the events and people it describes. Many prominent Chinese scholars have written commentaries on the *Annals*, attempting to reveal these meanings.

A REPLICA OF THE SCHOLAR DU YU'S 3RD-CENTURY ANNOTATED *ANNALS*

> **"Learning** without **reflection** is a **waste;** **reflecting** without **learning** is **dangerous**."
>
> CONFUCIUS, *ANALECTS*

▷ **THE TEACHER OF TEACHERS**
This Qing dynasty (1644–1912) image shows Confucius with his students. He was willing to instruct anyone, and refused all payments and gifts.

Zhongdu, and then minister for crime in the state of Lu. However, Confucius soon became disillusioned with the reality of politics. According to the collection of his teachings known as the *Analects* (*Lunyu* in Chinese – see box, below), he was disgusted when the rival state of Qi sent the Lu court a gift of dancing and singing girls. On receipt of the gift, the chief minister locked himself away for three days of carousing. For Confucius, this was no way to run a state. He left Lu soon afterwards, and began a period of wandering in exile, seeking the ear of a ruler who might be willing to put his ethical teachings into practice.

His quest was unsuccessful and he returned to the state of Lu in 484 BCE to live out his last few years. Although he was hugely respected as a teacher by thousands of followers, he was frustrated by his lack of success as a political adviser. He died believing that he had failed in his lifelong task to restore the world to the order of the Western Zhou dynasty.

Confucius the teacher

The *Analects* not only is an account of Confucius's teachings but also provides fascinating glimpses of how he taught, tailoring his lessons to individual students, with a keen awareness of their strengths and weaknesses. He led his students patiently – it was more important that they progressed steadily than rapidly, and he believed that a good teacher "should not teach a student anything before he becomes strongly interested in it" because once he becomes motivated, he can "understand three times more than what was taught". Confucius saw every experience and every observation of others as an opportunity to learn. In one famous passage from the *Analects*, he says: "If there are three people walking together, one will be my teacher. I will take their goodness and follow it; I will take their badness and correct it."

Ren and *zhi*

A central concept in the *Analects*, and one of foundational virtues of Confucianism, is *ren*, an idea that has its roots in earlier Chinese texts. It is often translated as "humaneness", "benevolence", or "humanity", although

IN CONTEXT
The *Analects*

The closest that remains of Confucius's own words is the book known in English as the *Analects* (*Lunyu* in Chinese), which was compiled by his disciples (and perhaps also by their disciples), which means that it cannot be taken as an entirely reliable guide to his actual words and actions.
Despite the fact that the sayings in the book are second-hand, the Song dynasty philosopher Zhu Xi (1130–1200) argued that the study of the *Analects* was the most direct way of grasping Confucius's intentions.

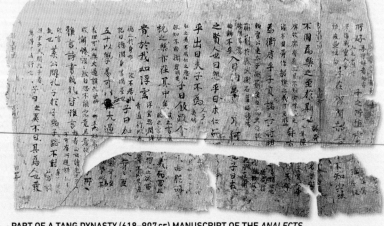

PART OF A TANG DYNASTY (618–907 CE) MANUSCRIPT OF THE *ANALECTS*

> "I am **not bothered** that I am **not understood**. I am **bothered** when I do not know **others**."

CONFUCIUS, *ANALECTS*

its true meaning is more nuanced and better understood through the Chinese character for *ren*. This has two graphical components: on the left-hand side stands the character for "person", and on the right-hand side the character for "two". Putting these together, the resulting character could be interpreted to mean the optimal way of connecting to – or relating to – others.

The *Analects* makes clear that *ren* is not just a property of individuals: it is thoroughly interpersonal: "The person who has *ren*, wanting to establish themselves, helps others to establish themselves; wanting their own achievement, they help others to achieve." One cannot have *ren* without its affecting one's relationships with others. *Ren* is a social virtue, and Confucius views humans as social

beings who derive their identities through interaction with the broader human community.

In a particularly enigmatic passage in the *Analects*, Confucius also talks about the relationship between *ren* and knowledge, or *zhi*. "Those with *zhi* delight in water," Confucius says. "Those with *ren* delight in mountains." One interpretation of this passage is that *ren* is something that is consistent

△ *REN* CHARACTER
Ren has many interpretations and nuances but it was defined by Confucius himself through the Chinese word for love, *ai*; he explained that its meaning was to "love others".

▽ **MOUNTAINS AND WATER**
Confucius made extensive use of analogy, such as the mountains and water of *ren* and *zhi*, in his teachings to make his students delve deeper into a subject.

> # "Without knowing the proper rituals, there is no way you can establish yourself."
>
> CONFUCIUS, *ANALECTS*

and still, like a mountain. It should not change according to specific situations. But *ren* alone is not enough. It needs to be coupled with a knowledge of the changeability of the world (also described as the ability to see what is right and wrong). A fulfilled life demands that the two are maintained together: the mountain-like stillness and consistency of *ren* or benevolence, and the fluidity of *zhi* or knowledge.

Improvement through ritual

The dimensions of stillness and movement described by the terms *ren* and *zhi* are brought together in another important aspect of Confucius's thought: *li*, which is usually translated as "ritual" or "proper conduct". In Confucius's terms, ritual is not a set of rigid rules and regulations, but deeply felt, flexible, and creative. The significance of *li* can perhaps be best explained by considering

the ritual of music. (Confucius himself was not only a skilled musician, composer, and singer, but also a master of music education.)

A group of musicians needs to have a shared understanding of what is appropriate for the genre they are playing; they need to understand at least some basic musical rules, such as chord progressions, key changes and so on; it is also important that they are able to listen attentively

▽ **VIRTUE, MUSIC, AND HARMONY**
Traditional *yayue* music that Confucius would have known is still performed in China. Confucius wrote that "personal cultivation begins with poetry, is made firm by rules of ceremonials, and is perfected by music".

◁ **TRANSLATED TEXT**
These pages are from *Confucius, the Philosopher of the Chinese*, a 1687 translation of Confucius's work into Latin. On the left is an engraving of Confucius.

the Confucian classics. This helped to put Confucius's thought at the heart of Chinese intellectual life for the next 2,000 years.

Confucianism has had an influence not only in China, but also on the development of philosophy in Korea, Japan, and beyond. In the 17th century, Jesuit scholars translated Confucius into Latin (and Latinized his name), and his works became known in the West, impressing such philosophers as Voltaire and Leibniz. Today, not only is Confucianism – a political tradition that is uniquely Chinese – enjoying a revival in China, but it is also of increasing influence in the field of comparative philosophy.

Contemporary relevance

One area in which Confucius's thought is of particular contemporary importance is in the approach in moral philosophy known as virtue ethics. The central question in virtue ethics is not "What is the nature of goodness?", or "What ought I do?", but instead, "How does a virtuous person act?" Confucius's response to this question, that a virtuous person acts with *ren*, and regulates their action according to *li*, continues to fascinate and challenge present-day thinkers.

IN PROFILE
Sima Qian

Sima Qian (c.145 BCE–87 BCE), was an astronomer, historian, and writer who lived in the Han dynasty. He is most famous for his book the *Shiji* or *Records of History*, an account of the previous 2,500 years of Chinese history. The *Shiji* contains biographies of Confucius, Laozi, Mengzi, and other philosophers; although it is not an entirely reliable source, Sima Qian's genius for telling a compelling story and organizing his material makes it a riveting read.

TITLE PAGE OF A 19TH-CENTURY EDITION OF THE *SHIJI*

to one another; and they need to be creative and imaginative in how they interpret the music.

These ideas can be extended more broadly to social rituals. To create social harmony, it is necessary to have an understanding of what is appropriate in any given setting. Participants need to understand some basic social rules. They need to be attentive to each other and must also be creative in how they act within these frameworks. If all this is in place, then the end result is not just social and political harmony, but also mutual pleasure and a depth of shared feeling. All interactions between people, objects, and nature – and the principles of proper government – should be guided by *li*. This concept of civility was later codified in the Confucian classic the *Liji* (*Record of Rites*).

An official philosophy

Confucius's thoughts went on to influence the lives of billions of people. In the fourth and third centuries BCE, the philosophers Mencius (see pp.44–45) and Zhuangzi (see pp.46–49) developed and systematized

Confucian thought. Then in the Han dynasty, beginning in 206 BCE, Confucianism quickly became established as a central pillar of the official philosophy of government. In the middle of the 2nd century BCE, a new examination system was introduced for recruitment to the growing imperial bureaucracy, and at the heart of this system were

◁ **TOMB OF CONFUCIUS**
A stone stele and burial mound mark the tomb of Confucius in Qufu, Shandong province. The cemetery is the burial site for thousands of the sage's descendants.

"How could **benevolence** be **far-off**? If **I wish** for **benevolence**, then it is right **here**."

CONFUCIUS, *ANALECTS*

Siddhartha Gautama

c.480–c.400 BCE, INDIAN

Siddhartha Gautama, also known as the Buddha, or "awakened one", was an Indian philosopher who was born in the 5th century BCE. His teaching focuses on overcoming dissatisfaction with everyday life.

Contemporary scholarship suggests that Siddhartha Gautama, who was later known as the Buddha, was born in the 5th century BCE and died at the age of 80. The precise dates of his life remain somewhat controversial, but there is little disagreement about the fact that he was a member of the Shakya clan, who lived on what is now a border between India and Nepal, and that he was brought up in relative wealth and comfort.

At that time, India was a centre of philosophical and religious activity. The region was also undergoing urbanization, with rapid increases in trade and travel, and the emergence of large and very powerful states. Following Siddhartha's death, this culminated in the rise of the Mauryan Empire (see box, right). The period starting in the 7th century BCE also saw a notable growth in groups of religious practitioners and *sramanas*, or wandering philosophers.

◁ **HEAD OF THE BUDDHA**
This magnificent sandstone Buddha head is entwined in the roots of a sacred banyan tree at Wat Mahathat temple, Ayutthaya, central Thailand.

◁ **THE BIRTH OF THE BUDDHA**
This scene from an 18th-century Tibetan painting depicts the Buddha's birth and "first seven steps". According to legend, he was born from his mother's side.

It is hard to disentangle history and legend, but it is generally agreed that Siddhartha left his home and family to become a *sramana*, and that he apprenticed himself to a number of teachers. Eventually, he had an experience of *bodhi*, or "awakening", which he described as a liberation from suffering or dissatisfaction with life. Following this experience, he spent the rest of his life teaching. After his death, he left behind many thousands of followers.

The legend of the Buddha

The various Buddhist traditions have supplemented this basic biography with elaborate myths concerning Siddhartha's life. According to these accounts, he was raised in the palace of his father, King Shuddhodana, and was surrounded by every pleasure imaginable. Fearful that he might tire of the palace, the king ensured that his son should have no awareness of sickness, old age, and death.

The young prince spent his early life immersed in sensual pleasures, unaware of these existential dangers.

IN CONTEXT
Ashoka and the Mauryan Empire

Between 322 BCE and 187 BCE, the mighty Mauryan Empire rose to become one of the largest political entities in the world. The empire was established by Chandragupta, who ruled until 297 BCE. His grandson, Ashoka, came to power in 268 BCE. Following a brutal victory in battle over the eastern coastal region of Kalinga (modern-day Odisha), Ashoka converted to Buddhism. After this, although he did not renounce violence altogether, he put in place a series of reforms that were, for his day, remarkably enlightened.

LION EMBLEM ON THE ASHOKA PILLAR AT THE HANGING GARDENS IN INDIA

" I am born for **supreme knowledge,** for the **welfare of the world**, thus this is my **last birth**. "

ASHVAGHOSHA, *BUDDHACHARITA*

IN CONTEXT
Mahavira and Jainism

One of Siddhartha Gautama's contemporaries was the teacher Mahavira, who is associated with the Jain school of philosophy. The legend of Mahavira's life to some extent mirrors that of Siddhartha's, but the teachings of the two schools are very different. Jainism puts a strong emphasis on *ahimsa*, or non-harming, and, unlike Buddhism, asserts the existence of a soul. It claims that in causing harm to others, the soul is polluted and cannot attain its natural state of bliss. The aim within Jainism is to abstain from harm, so that the soul may eventually be liberated.

STONE STATUE DEPICTING A SEATED MAHAVIRA, INDIA, 12TH CENTURY

> " **Birth** is **suffering**, **ageing** is suffering, **sickness** is suffering, **death** is suffering... **grief** and **despair** are suffering. "

"ACCESS TO INSIGHT", IN THE *DHAMMACAKKAPPAVATTANA SUTTA*

However, when travelling outside the palace, he witnessed three things that impressed on him the reality of human suffering: a sick person, an old person, and a corpse. The sights plunged the young man into despair. On a subsequent trip he had another experience, seeing a *sramana* whose noble bearing filled him with hope. Siddhartha reasoned that it may be possible to find release from human suffering through the example of these wandering philosophers. Soon after this experience, Siddhartha left the palace – helped, in many versions of the legends, by a host of friendly gods – and renounced the life of luxury to become a wanderer.

Despite its inherent implausibility, this legend has endured because of its ability to present a clear dramatization of the existential problem of suffering, which lies at the heart of Buddhist philosophy.

Teachings

Thanks to the large body of texts preserved by his followers, scholars know that Siddhartha was a teacher. Of particular importance in this respect are a number of texts written in Pali – an ancient Indian language that is related to Sanskrit – that were compiled several generations after Siddhartha's death.

The key problem identified in these texts is that of *dukkha*. Although this term is most often translated as

"suffering", a more accurate translation might be "unsatisfactoriness". The concept refers to the fact that everyday human experience, or mundane life, is both fundamentally unsatisfactory and painful. *Dukkha* refers to a wide range of unsatisfactory experiences, ranging from extreme agony to frustration and a general sense of dissatisfaction with existence.

Pain without suffering

An understanding of the precise nature of *dukkha* is crucial to Buddhism. This is explained in the Pali texts by way of an example: when Siddhartha was very old, his body was often racked with pain – but this was physical pain, without the anguish of suffering. Siddhartha argued that people habitually add suffering on top of pain in many different ways: for example, by trying to push away the pain, or by asking "why me?" – but in so doing, they subject themselves to intense anguish and distress.

Siddhartha maintained that his experience of *bodhi* placed him beyond the reach of *dukkha*, and that

his teachings could show others the way beyond this unsatisfactoriness. He used the analogy of a man who has been struck by an arrow, and is then immediately struck by a second arrow. The first arrow is the physical pain: this is an inescapable part of having a body. But the second arrow is the mental distress that is a response to pain, which is something that can be eradicated. When this happens, people can experience the ebb and flow of unpleasant or pleasant sensations without the push-and-pull that so often accompanies them.

In addition to *dukkha*, there are two other characteristics of human experience that are emphasized in Buddhism: the first is that it is always changing; and the second is that there is no underlying soul or substance (no fundamental essence of "me") that is doing the experiencing.

▽ **PAGES FROM THE PALI CANON**
The Pali Canon is the standard scripture of the Theravada tradition. Originally transmitted orally, the scriptures were first written down in Sri Lanka c.29 BCE.

A practical system

The philosophy that was proposed by Siddhartha was not merely a system of thought, but a practical template for living differently. The system is sometimes divided into three aspects. The first aspect is *sila* – translated as morality or ethics. The fundamental concept behind Buddhist ethics is that all actions bear fruit in consequences: certain actions inevitably lead to results. Therefore, if someone wishes to transform their life and their experience, they must begin by changing how they act in the world.

The second aspect of the system is *samadhi*, or concentration. This covers a range of meditation and concentration practices that help the practitioner to develop a sense of calmness and focus. However, *samadhi* alone is not enough to completely transform experience. In order for this to take place, *panna*, or wisdom – the third and final aspect of the system – is required. This practice involves close and detailed analysis of our minds, as well as of the world of our experience, to see the patterns at work, so that we might eventually transform this experience.

The spread of Buddhism

Siddhartha was just one of a number of travelling teachers in the India of his day – he himself was, for example, a contemporary of the great Jain teacher Mahavira (see box, opposite). However, the system of philosophy and practice that Siddhartha put in place assumed immense significance. This was in part due to the patronage of Ashoka, an emperor of the Mauryan dynasty (see box, p.21).

Buddhism spread widely, adapting as it went. It entered into China during the Han dynasty (206 BCE–220 CE) and moved into Korea and Japan. It also spread throughout South and Central Asia, and as far as Afghanistan and parts of what is now Russia. The religion went into decline following the rise of Islam, but saw a revival after the 19th century, when it attracted the attention of Westerners – in particular the Theosophy movement in the US.

In the modern day, there has been a tremendous resurgence of interest in Buddhist psychology and the practice of meditation. Major research has also been undertaken into the crossovers between Buddhist practices and neuroscientific studies of the mind. Meanwhile, mindfulness practices that are drawn from Buddhism are now used in contexts far removed from their Buddhist origins.

△ **BUDDHIST MONKS, THAILAND**
Buddhist monks are shown here in meditation, wearing their distinctive saffron-coloured robes, at Wat Phra Dhammakaya Temple, Bangkok, Thailand. The robes are traditionally wrapped around the left shoulder, leaving the right shoulder bare, as here.

" **So hard to see**, so very, very **subtle**, alighting wherever it likes: the mind... **The mind protected brings ease**. "

"THE MIND", IN THE *DHAMMAPADA*

▷ **DIOTEMA**
Depictions of Diotema are necessarily works of the imagination because there are no contemporary records of her appearance. Here, she appears in a work by Franc Kavčič, a Neoclassical painter of Slovenian origin who was active around the end of the 18th century.

Diotima of Mantinea

5TH CENTURY BCE, GREEK

One of the very few female philosophers to achieve recognition in classical Greece, Diotima of Mantinea is credited with inspiring Socrates and providing Plato with the basis for his concept of "Platonic love".

"**Love** is neither **wise** nor **beautiful,** but is rather the **desire** for **wisdom** and **beauty**."

DIOTIMA OF MANTINEA, QUOTED BY SOCRATES IN PLATO'S *SYMPOSIUM*

What little is known of Diotima's life comes from Socrates' description of his discussion with her, as recounted by Plato in the *Symposium*. While some scholars have doubted Diotima's existence as an actual historical person, almost all of the characters in Plato's dialogues represent well-known people in contemporary Athens, and it is highly unlikely that Diotima is an exception; other later writers also refer to Diotima as a historical rather than a fictional character.

Socrates probably met Diotima in around 450–440 BCE, when he was in his 20s. He describes her as a priestess of Mantinea, a town in Arcadia, who was renowned for her wisdom and powers of prophecy. Socrates, however, was struck more by Diotima's intellect than by her prophetic abilities: like most Greek philosophers of the time, he was interested primarily in the scientific nature of the world around him, but his conversation with Diotima persuaded him to turn his attention from the outside world to human concerns – in particular, to the concepts of love and beauty.

The meeting with Diotima had a life-changing impact on Socrates, since it determined the philosophical path that he was to take, which in turn set the agenda for subsequent Greek thinkers.

Love and beauty

Plato portrays Socrates as speaking passionately about Diotima's ideas. This would certainly have caused consternation among Socrates' male companions because at the time women were not regarded as worthy of intellectual consideration. In classical Greece, a woman's place was in the home, attending to the needs of her husband or father.

However, there were a few exceptions: one sure route to independence and respect was to become a *hetaira* – a high-class courtesan who provided intellectual as well as physical stimulation; another was to take on the role of a priestess, as Diotima had done. Even given her status as a priestess, Socrates' admiration for her arguments is testimony to Diotima's exceptional intellect.

The only comparable female character in Plato's dialogues is that of Aspasia, a *hetaira* who was famous for entertaining some of the most prominent thinkers in Athens (see box, below). In the *Menexenus*, Plato portrays Aspasia as an intellectual in her own right, and as a teacher of rhetoric and oratory.

However, it is only Diotima who is credited with having original ideas and arguments, and these are in marked contrast to those of Aspasia. Whereas Aspasia is characterized by her advocacy of sensual pleasure and erotic love, Diotima argues for a deeper understanding of love and beauty. Socrates recalls her description of a "ladder of love", leading from physical attraction to appreciation of a person's inner qualities, and then to a love of beauty itself – the ideal "Form" of beauty as Plato describes it.

△ **EROS, GOD OF LOVE**
Socrates delivered his lessons about love via his dialogue with Diotima. The main argument is that the energy of erotic attraction (personified by the god Eros) can be used in a spiritual and philosophical exercise that eventually leads to the contemplation of God.

IN CONTEXT
Women philosophers in Ancient Greece

Women had almost no legal or political rights in Ancient Greece. Despite their low status in society, some women were accepted and respected by their male peers. Pythagoras, for example, treated women (including the philosopher Theano) as equals to men in his school; and Plato is known to have had two female students, Lasthenia of Mantinea and Axiothea of Philesia (who dressed as a man when she attended the Academy to avoid being considered a *hetaira*).

THE PHILOSOPHER ASPASIA BY MICHEL CORNEILLE THE YOUNGER, c.1685

▷ **SOCRATES SEATED ON A BENCH**
This Roman fresco found in a private house in Ephesus, Turkey, dates from the 1st century CE. Socrates' squat physique here is true to descriptions of his appearance in Plato's *Symposium*.

Socrates

c. 469–399 BCE, GREEK

Plato described Socrates as the "gadfly" of Athens, a persistent irritant challenging the customs of the city-state. Derided for his teachings, he was sentenced to death for impiety and corrupting the city's youth.

Socrates was born in Alopece, a suburb of Athens, around 469 BCE. Over his lifetime, Socrates saw the Athenian Empire defeated by Sparta in the Peloponnesian War and subjected to cruelty and oppression by the oligarchs who followed.

The Athenian agora

Socrates' father, Sophroniscus, was a stonemason, and his mother, Phaenarete, a midwife. Despite their humble status they ensured that their son received a good education that included the study of poetry, music, and athletics. Sophroniscus also taught him the family trade, but Socrates showed more interest in talking to people in the *agora* – the main meeting place – in Athens.

As he grew up, Socrates became a well-known figure in the city, and at the age of 18 took on the duties of a male citizen, which included membership of the democratic governing assembly and making himself available for military service.

Around this time, it is believed that Socrates sought guidance in philosophy from teachers including Parmenides, Anaxagoras, and the priestess Diotima.

Through his discussions in the *agora*, Socrates developed his reputation as a philosopher and gradually gained a following, largely composed of young men from the upper class of Athenian society. Beyond his followers, however, he drew little respect as a citizen, and was even seen by much of the public as a figure of fun.

Athenian culture valued beauty – especially male physical beauty – and Socrates did not meet the classical criteria. He was short and squat, with a snub nose, bulging eyes, and a pot belly, and took no interest whatsoever in personal grooming or clothing. This led to his portrayal by the playwright Aristophanes as a comical character with his head in the clouds – a figure who was immediately recognizable to theatre audiences.

◁ **PARMENIDES OF ELEA**
According to Plato, the young Socrates was influenced by Parmenides, who lived in the mid-5th century BCE, and was among the first philosophers to champion the primacy of deductive reasoning to justify his arguments.

The historical Socrates, however, is far removed from such satirical portrayals. Various sources, including references in Thucydides' *History of the Peloponnesian War*, indicate that he served valiantly in several campaigns against Sparta. He fought in the battles of Potidaea, Delium, and Amphipolis, and was decorated for his courage in action. At Potidaea, he saved the life of his close companion Alcibiades, and then declined the decoration recommended for him, instead urging that it should be given to Alcibiades.

Socrates made no secret of his love for Alcibiades, nor of his physical attraction to young men, as this was accepted custom in Athenian society. He insisted that his relationship with Alcibiades was built on a concern for his soul rather than sexual desire.

◁ **SOCRATES AND ALCIBIADES**
This bas relief made by Neoclassical sculptor Antonio Canova shows Socrates as a muscular warrior, heroically rescuing his wounded friend Alcibiades at the battle of Potidaea.

> **IN PROFILE**
> **The Sophists**
>
> Athens arose as a wealthy city-state with an emergent democracy in the 5th century BCE. Those involved in the rule of the city recognized the importance of political as well as military skills. A class of teachers emerged – the Sophists – who taught the arts of rhetoric and debate, alongside other subjects deemed suitable for the noble classes, such as mathematics, philosophy, music, and athletics. Socrates was scornful of the Sophists, partly because they worked for money rather than in a search for knowledge or wisdom, but also because their primary aim in debate was to win the argument rather than uncover the truth.

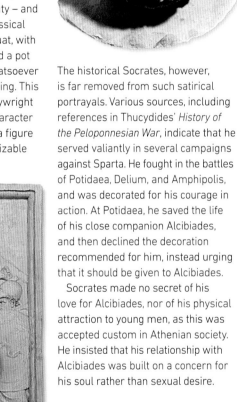

> **"The unexamined life is not worth living."**
> SOCRATES, IN PLATO'S *APOLOGY*

"There is only one **good**, **knowledge**, and one **evil**, **ignorance**. "

SOCRATES, IN DIOGENES LAERTIUS'S *THE LIVES OF EMINENT PHILOSOPHERS*

IN CONTEXT

The first moral philosopher?

Socrates is often contrasted with all the Greek philosophers who preceded his influence, collectively known as the pre-Socratics. These philosophers were primarily concerned with finding the underlying principles of the natural world – the metaphysical nature of the universe. Socrates chose instead to focus his attention on examining the very human concerns of justice, virtue, beauty, and so on. It is, however, an oversimplification to state that the pre-Socratic philosophers took no interest whatsoever in moral and political philosophy.

▽ **THE AGORA OF ATHENS**
The *agora* was a gathering place and market – the social and commercial heart of the city of Athens. Today, it is an archaeological site below the Acropolis.

Life and marriage

Socrates married late in life. His wife, Xanthippe, with whom he had three sons, Lamprocles, Sophroniscus, and Menexenus, was as much as 40 years his junior. She was reputedly a formidable woman, whom Socrates considered a foil to his intellect, but some men also called her a nag and a scold – her name even entered common use as a synonym for shrew.

An apocryphal story is told of her losing patience with her day-dreaming spouse, and emptying the contents of a chamber pot over his head. However, she may well have had good reason for her anger and frustration: Socrates, as far as is known, had no regular work or inherited wealth and, as well as spending his time philosophizing in the *agora*, had a reputation in Athens as a bon viveur – a legendary drinker who frequently enjoyed drink-talking sessions with his male companions. There is also evidence that Socrates had a second wife, Myrto, perhaps bigamously, or that she was a mistress he paid an allowance to when she was widowed.

Although some details of Socrates' life can be gleaned from contemporary sources, it is more difficult to gain an accurate picture of his philosophical ideas. Much of what is known about his thinking comes from the writings of his disciples, in particular Xenophon and Plato, and the much less reliable accounts of later authors, such as Diogenes Laertius. Xenophon gives a historian's perspective of Socrates, but provides only a sketchy account

◁ **SOCRATES AND XANTHIPPE**
This 16th-century painting illustrates an incident reported by Diogenes Laertius, a 3rd-century biographer of Socrates: Xanthippe, in a rage, tips a chamber pot over the philosopher's head.

of his teachings; Plato, meanwhile, presents Socrates as a didactic character in his dramatic dialogues and scholars are uncertain to what extent he uses Socrates as a mouthpiece for his own ideas.

Trial and sentence

In his discussions with citizens in the *agora*, Socrates purposely set about challenging their preconceptions and opinions, earning his reputation as an argumentative "gadfly" who held little respect for the institutions of the city. This impertinence gained him enemies, and eventually led to his trial and death sentence. However, this was only part of the story of Socrates' indictment.

After Athens had been defeated by Sparta in the Peloponnesian War, its democracy was replaced – for a period of around eight months – by the rule of the Thirty Tyrants, a group of ruthless oligarchs who ran Athens as a puppet Spartan state. During their rule, many native Athenians fled the city, although Socrates remained there – it was known that he admired some aspects of Spartan rule, and a number of the Tyrants had been his students. Moreover, his great

companion Alcibiades was associated with the Spartans, and had even temporarily defected to their side.

When democracy was re-established in Athens, an amnesty was proclaimed to prevent reprisals against those who had held Spartan sympathies. However, the court was persuaded to prosecute Socrates on the non-political, but no less serious, charges of disrespect of the city's gods and the criminal corruption of young people. For this, Socrates was sentenced to death but was given an opportunity to escape punishment. As a believer in due process, however, and on principle not willing to give up his philosophical investigations, he famously chose to accept the verdict of his fellow citizens and carry out the execution by drinking a toxic potion containing hemlock. Plato attended Socrates' trial and subsequently wrote the *Apology*,

an apparently faithful account of the defence that his teacher presented to his accusers in court. It provides a fascinating insight into the methods that Socrates used to examine philosophical concepts.

The Socratic method

According to the *Apology*, Socrates related that his friend Chaerephon had once asked the Oracle at Delphi if there was anyone who was wiser than Socrates; Chaerephon reported back that the answer was no. Being a modest man, Socrates found this difficult to accept, and insisted that he actually had little knowledge other than of his own ignorance.

This premise – that of feigned ignorance – became the starting point for his philosophical investigations. He would engage people in discussion, leading them to believe they knew

far more than he. Having drawn out their illogical opinions, he would gleefully dissect the flaws in their arguments one by one. This was the crux of the so-called Socratic method, also known as *elenchus*, a technique for examining a point of view to expose its weaknesses, but also to reveal essential truths.

Legacy and influence

Socrates amassed a loyal following of disciples, including Plato, Xenophon, and Antisthenes, but established no school and left no written legacy. His influence, however, was vast, shifting the emphasis in Greek philosophy from the metaphysics of the natural world to the examination of human concerns, and providing a method of philosophical debate with which to challenge accepted wisdom and elicit the truth.

△ **THE DEATH OF SOCRATES,** 1787
In this work by the French Neoclassical painter Jacques-Louis David, Socrates (centre) is shown sitting up in his bed, his hand hovering over the chalice of hemlock. He is flanked by his distraught followers. Plato – represented here as an old man – sits at the foot of the bed with his head down, suggesting resignation to his mentor's impending death.

" **The hour** of **departure** has **arrived**, and we go our ways – **I** to **die** and **you** to **live**. Which is the **better**, only **God knows**. "

SOCRATES, IN PLATO'S *THEAETETUS*

Diogenes of Sinope

412/404–323 BCE, GREEK

Diogenes was well known in Athens for his often outrageous challenging of conventions, and for conspicuously living the austere and virtuous life advocated in his Cynic philosophy.

It is not known if Diogenes committed any of his ideas to writing, as no texts by him have been discovered. What has survived, however, is his reputation, together with a collection of anecdotes about his life and work, recounted by later biographers, such as Diogenes Laertius and Stobaeus. These paint a picture of a man who lived strictly according to his principles, did not suffer fools gladly, and often made his philosophical points with mischievous wit.

◁ **ANTISTHENES**
This 2nd-century Roman marble sculpture depicts Antisthenes of Athens, one of the founders of the Cynic school of philosophy.

coins and sent into exile. Diogenes, still a young man, fled to Athens, and it was there that his passion for philosophy began. He was especially struck by Antisthenes, a former disciple of Socrates, who had developed his own interpretation of what it meant to live virtuously; Diogenes is said to have begged him to take him on as a student.

Diogenes was among the thinkers who became known as the "Cynics"– from the Greek *kynikos*, meaning "dog-like" – who rejected social convention and etiquette in favour of living a more simple and natural existence (see box, right). There are

Flight to Athens

Diogenes was born and brought up in the Greek colony of Sinope, on the Black Sea coast of what is now Turkey. His father Hicesias was in charge of minting the currency, and it seems that Diogenes became his assistant, as they were both implicated in a scandal involving adulteration of the

numerous anecdotes of Diogenes' life of poverty and his dog-like behaviour: most agree that he made his home in a *pithos* – a large ceramic jar – in or near the *agora* (public meeting place) and had few, if any, possessions. One story tells how he saw a child drinking water from its cupped hand – a sight that prompted him to discard his own wooden bowl as a luxury. Athenians were outraged by his behaviour, not least because he satisfied all his natural urges in public, wherever and whenever he needed – this at a time when it was socially unacceptable even to eat in the marketplace.

Final years

Diogenes eventually left Athens and settled in Corinth. His fate is the subject of legend: he was abducted by pirates and sold as an enslaved person in Crete; a prospective buyer, Xeniades of Corinth, asked what his trade was, and Diogenes replied that he wanted to be sold to someone who needed a master. Impressed, Xeniades bought him and took him to Corinth as tutor to his children, and apparently to live as a free man. Some accounts state that he died from a dog bite, or from eating a bad octopus, but it is more likely that Diogenes died peacefully of old age, probably while still a guest in the house of Xeniades.

> IN CONTEXT
> ## The Cynics
>
> Diogenes was the epitome of the school of philosophical thought that came to be known as Cynicism; indeed his epithet, *Kynikos*, provided its name. Its basic principle – that virtue and happiness can be achieved by living an ascetic life in accord with nature – was set out by Antisthenes, but Diogenes' uncompromising interpretation of the principle marked the start of the philosophical movement. Many other philosophers were attracted to Cynicism, including Diogenes' disciple Crates of Thebes, whose student Zeno of Citium developed the Stoic philosophy.

A 1ST-CENTURY WALL PAINTING DEPICTING CRATES OF THEBES

◁ **THE RUINS OF CORINTH**
Diogenes spent the later part of his life in Corinth, in the Peloponnese. Some legends relate that the king Alexander the Great sought out his counsel in the city.

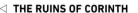

▷ **DIOGENES WITH A LAMP**
In this 1673 work by the leading Spanish painter Jusepe de Ribera, Diogenes is shown holding a lamp. According to some stories, the philosopher would stroll around the *agora* in broad daylight holding his lamp; when asked why, he would reply that he was "just looking for an honest man".

Plato

c.428– c.348 BCE, GREEK

Plato's impact on the development of Western philosophy is virtually unrivalled. He set out his ideas in the form of around 30 dialogues, which present and contrast a range of philosophical viewpoints.

IN PROFILE
Pre-Socratic influences

Socrates was Plato's mentor and the formative influence on his philosophy. Before meeting Socrates, Plato studied with Cratylus, a disciple of Heraclitus. He was familiar with Heraclitus's theory that everything is in a state of flux (change is central to the universe) but also with Parmenides' opposite view that the universe is unchanging and eternal. One of Plato's major achievements was to reconcile these two ideas in his theory of Forms. Pythagoras, too, was an inspiration to Plato, both for his sometimes mystical vision of an ordered universe governed by the ideal laws of mathematics, and for the philosophical "commune" he established.

Along with his mentor, Socrates, and his pupil Aristotle, Plato is generally regarded as representing the apex of Greek philosophy.

In his lifetime, Athens was the cultural and intellectual capital of the Eastern Mediterranean, but it was also the centre of severe political upheaval. Plato was born shortly after the beginning of the Peloponnesian War (431–404 BCE), which saw conflict between Athens and Sparta threaten the Athenian democracy.

◁ **PLATO BY RAPHAEL**
Raphael's masterpiece *The School of Athens* (1509–11) in the Vatican shows an impossible gathering of classical thinkers, including Plato (detail seen here).

Plato's family was one of the wealthiest in Athens and boasted an ancestry of famous statesmen and nobles. His father, Ariston, claimed to be descended from the kings of Athens and Messenia, and his mother, Perictione, came from the family of Solon, the architect of the first democratic constitution of Athens. One of four children, Plato received the education typical of an Athenian aristocrat, taking lessons in grammar, mathematics, music, and athletics with the finest tutors Athens could offer. He was a keen and exceptionally able student, and is said to have been especially proficient in wrestling. According to some sources, it was his wrestling teacher who gave him the

△ **STELE FROM KERAMEIKOS**
This relief from c.510 BCE depicts a wrestling competition. Wrestling was a popular sport at the time, and was taught in schools known as palaestras.

nickname "Platon" (from the Greek word for "broad") on account of his physique; other stories say that he earned the alias because of his facial features, or even the breadth of his knowledge and skills. Whatever the origin, the name Platon (anglicized to Plato) stuck so firmly that we cannot now be certain of his given name – possibly Aristocles.

As he grew up, he took an interest in philosophy, and no doubt came across the ideas of the great pre-Socratic

BRONZE BUST OF HERACLITUS OF EPHESUS (c.535–c.475 BCE)

" Until **philosophers** are **kings**, or **kings**... have the **spirit** and **power** of **philosophy**... **cities** will **never** have **rest** from their **evils**. "

PLATO, *REPUBLIC*

"Isn't **anyone** who **holds** a **true opinion without understanding** like a **blind man** on the **right road**?"

PLATO, *REPUBLIC*

△ **SPARTAN BRONZE HELMET**
The Spartan army that occupied Athens was legendary for its discipline and determination; every Spartan was trained in warfare from an early age.

philosophers Pythagoras, Parmenides, and especially Heraclitus, who had taught his tutor Cratylus.

Theatrical career

Plato's ambitions initially lay in the theatre rather than in philosophy and he set out to make his name as a tragedian, following in the footsteps of Aeschylus, Euripides, and Sophocles. First, however, having come of age at 18, he had to fulfil his duties as an Athenian citizen, serving as a soldier in the war with Sparta, and becoming actively involved in politics as befitted a man of his noble descent.

At the age of about 20, Plato fell in with a group that followed Socrates, whose regular challenges to the status quo appealed to rebellious youths. Socrates was already a

well-known philosopher in Athens, notorious for accosting citizens in the *agora* (central square) and questioning them about their beliefs. Plato fell under his spell, and became his most loyal and brilliant disciple. He soon abandoned his nascent career as a playwright and instead spent his spare time in the company of Socrates in discussion and debate. He also gradually extricated himself from the government of the city, finding himself in sympathy with Socrates' scepticism of the establishment.

The death of Socrates

Soon after Plato met Socrates, Athens was defeated by the Spartans, who installed a government of "Thirty Tyrants" (among them Plato's uncles Charmides and Critias) to replace the

democratic government. Plato's loyalties were thus divided, and when the democracy was restored a year later, he felt uneasy with the way that Athens was being governed.

An amnesty was declared to prevent political reprisals against sympathizers of the Spartan occupiers, but within a few years spurious charges were brought against Socrates, who was seen as a threat to the state. Plato attended the trial, and was devastated when his mentor was sentenced to death for impiety and corrupting the youth of the city. It was a turning point in Plato's career: he set about writing a dramatic transcription of Socrates' passionate defence in the trial, the *Apology*, which was to be the first of his series of dialogues featuring

IN CONTEXT
Democracy in Athens

In 594 BCE, the statesman Solon created a constitution for the city-state of Athens. This laid the foundation for a form of democracy that was later reinforced by reforms introduced by Cleisthenes and Ephialtes. Free male citizens were given the opportunity to participate in the political process through membership of the Assembly, and the power of the aristocracy was gradually weakened. The system was not universally popular, and in its first century there were times when Athenian democracy faltered. The most significant threat, however, came with the Peloponnesian War (431–404 BCE), which culminated in Athens' defeat by Sparta and the installation of the "Thirty Tyrants". Nevertheless, democracy was restored the following year.

THE BEMA (PODIUM) OF PNYX, SITE OF ASSEMBLIES IN ANCIENT ATHENS

Socrates as the main protagonist. The trial also helped to clarify his political opinions, and it is likely that he began work on the *Republic* around this time.

Dramatic dialogues

Plato drew on his experience as a dramatist when writing the dialogues. In them, he found the ideal medium for presenting philosophical ideas in the way Socrates had done – as a dialectic process, rather than as a treatise that set out a single argument. The dialogues were made all the more readable by the theatrical manner in which he presented his characters as participants in a discussion.

▽ **TEMPLE OF APOLLO, SYRACUSE**
Plato spent several years in Syracuse, a Greek colony in Sicily that for a long time rivalled Athens as the most important city of the Greek world.

Travels to Syracuse

Plato's association with Socrates, and his perceived anti-democratic leanings, as well as his family's connection with the Spartan regime made him an object of suspicion in Athens. A fellow disciple of Socrates, Euclides of Megara, offered him refuge at his home in Corinth, which had been an ally of Sparta during the war. Plato stayed there for several years, mixing with like-minded thinkers without fear of persecution, before deciding to travel to some of the more remote Greek colonies around the area of the Mediterranean. He visited North Africa, spending time in Cyrene (in present-day Libya) with the mathematician Theodorus, and probably also stopped off in Egypt. From there he journeyed to southern Italy, where he came across the remnants of the Pythagorean community.

Aged around 40, Plato travelled to Syracuse in Sicily, which was ruled by the tyrant Dionysius I. He was asked to tutor Dionysius' brother-in-law Dion, and the two formed a friendship. However, the unpredictable Dionysius fell out with the philosopher and threatened to have him sold as an enslaved person. Judging that he would now be safer in Athens, Plato returned home.

The Academy

Perhaps inspired by his experience of the Pythagorean community, and of teaching Dion in Syracuse, Plato began to establish a school in Athens. He had inherited a plot of land just outside the city walls in the Grove of Hecademus

△ **EUCLID OF MEGARA**
Euclid established his own school of philosophy (in Megara, on the Isthmus of Corinth) based on the teachings of Socrates. He became a friend – and an intellectual sparring partner – of Plato.

(or Academus), next to a gymnasium, which he felt was ideal for informal gatherings of students. His school, later known as the Academy, was run like a private club. Membership was open to all those (including women) suitably qualified in the disciplines of mathematics and philosophy. It was not a school in the sense of a place of instruction, nor did it promote a specific doctrine; it was an institution for the exchange of ideas, with Plato and senior members guiding the debate.

The Theory of Forms

Now comfortably settled in Athens, and stimulated through interactions with his students at the Academy, Plato embarked on what is considered by many scholars to be the "middle period" of his writings. In these, it is possible to see a gradual change in the substance of the arguments propounded by the Socrates character; Plato moves away from merely reporting his mentor's ideas to developing a philosophy of his own.

The best known and most influential of the dialogues of this period is the *Republic*, in which Plato presents his concept of an ideal society and how it should be governed. This idea is – perhaps understandably – coloured by the philosopher's aristocratic background and also by his own experience of democracy, which, it should not be forgotten, had executed his hero, Socrates.

Plato advocates a form of benign monarchy or oligarchy, a rule by "philosopher-kings"; but just as importantly, the arguments that he presents in support of this form of governance provide a description of the Theory of Forms, a core

△ **CLASSICAL ATHENS: THE CRADLE OF WESTERN CIVILIZATION**
During the 5th and 4th centuries BCE (the Classical period), Athens was the centre for the arts and philosophy. Its culture had a profound influence on the development of the Roman Empire.

element of Platonic philosophy. He illustrates the Theory of Forms in a famous section of the *Republic*, known as the "Allegory of the Cave".

Plato asks his readers to imagine a dark cave, in which prisoners are tied up facing the back wall; behind them is a fire. Unseen by the prisoners, people parade with various objects so that their shadows are cast on the wall. The prisoners take the shadows to be reality because they are ignorant of their existence as objects. In the same way, the world that we perceive with our senses is illusory, and the things we take to be reality are in fact merely "shadows" of ideal Forms that we perceive not with our senses, but with our intellect.

The ideal state, argues Plato, should be founded on justice and virtue, and governed by rulers who understand such concepts. What we know of them in the world is a shadow of the Forms of ideal virtue and justice, which can only be apprehended by philosophical investigation. So, the only people with the knowledge to rule an ideal state are those versed in philosophy.

IN CONTEXT
The "Socratic problem"

Plato presented his ideas in the form of dialogues, in which the character leading the discussion was usually Socrates. A pertinent question is how much Plato is reporting the ideas of Socrates, and how much the Socrates character is a mouthpiece for his own thoughts. It is generally accepted that in the *Apology* and other early works, Plato records Socrates' views; he then begins to elaborate on these in a series of transitional writings, while the later works present original ideas.

SOCRATES TEACHES ALCIBIADES, A CHARACTER IN THE DIALOGUES

KEY WORKS

407 BCE
Plato meets Socrates, and abandons his aspiration to be a tragedian.

399–390 BCE
Begins writing his dialogues, which include *Apology* and *Euthyphro*, with Socrates as their main protagonist.

388–367 BCE
Embarks upon the "middle period" of his writing, expounding his own ideas in texts that include *Meno* and *Republic*.

c.387 BCE
Founds the Academy just outside the city of Athens.

360 BCE
Uses a complex and unresolved form of dialogue in *Theaetetus*, which explores the nature of knowledge.

360–348 BCE
Begins his late-period dialogues, which include *Timaeus*, *Critias*, and *Laws*.

"Wonder is the feeling of a philosopher, and philosophy begins in wonder."

PLATO, *THEAETETUS*

Late years

Plato's settled life at the Academy was interrupted in 367 BCE, when Dionysius I was succeeded by his son Dionysius II. Dion asked Plato to return to Syracuse to tutor the young ruler; Plato agreed, but was placed under house arrest in Sicily. With some persuasion, Dionysius released Plato, who returned to Athens. A few years later, now an old man, Plato was invited back to Syracuse; shortly after his arrival he was again arrested, but managed to escape. Dion was furious, and launched an attack on Sicily, taking control until he was assassinated.

Not surprisingly, Plato became disillusioned with politics; he devoted the last years of his life to the Academy and his writing, including the more reflective dialogues of his "late period", in which the Socrates character is either often reduced to a minor role, or omitted completely.

There are various accounts of Plato's death – for example, with a girl playing a flute for him by his deathbed – but all that is reliably known is that he died in Athens, aged around 80.

◁ **PLATO'S ACADEMY**
This mosaic floor from Pompeii depicts Plato's Academy: the philosopher sits beneath a tree in a grove, teaching a group of disciples.

Aristotle

384–322 BCE, MACEDONIAN

Aristotle presented a style of philosophy in distinct contrast to that of his mentor Plato, and established an empirical approach that has influenced philosophers and scientists to the present day.

◁ **MACEDONIAN BIRTHPLACE**
Aristotle was born in Stagira in Macedon. In 349 BCE, the city was destroyed by Philip II of Macedon; Philip refounded Stagira years later as an apology to Aristotle.

Aristotle thrived in the Academy's atmosphere of scholarship, and proved himself the most brilliant of Plato's students. Plato encouraged debate and original thinking, and Aristotle gradually discovered that he was not always in agreement with his mentor's theories. Despite their differences of opinion, however, the two must have established a good working relationship – and probably a close friendship – because Aristotle remained at the Academy until Plato died, some twenty years after Aristotle first arrived.

Sanctuary in Assos

As the foremost philosopher at the Academy, Aristotle might appear to have been the most obvious successor to Plato as its head. However, it was Plato's nephew, Speusippus, who was appointed. There are various theories as to why Aristotle was overlooked: some hold that it was because his philosophy had become so contrary to Plato's teachings; others that it was due to his connections with Macedon, at a

Unlike the other two great Athenian philosophers, Socrates and Plato, Aristotle was not born in Athens itself, but was a native of Macedon in the northwest of Greece. His father, Nicomachus, was the physician of King Amyntas of Macedon, and Aristotle was born in Stagira on the Halkidiki peninsula, not far from the royal court. It is likely that he spent some time in the palace with his father, and was known to the royal family; this connection with the Macedon rulers was to figure largely in his later life.

Aristotle's mother and father died when he was in his teens, and the boy's education was then overseen by his guardian, Proxenus of Atarneus, a family friend who was married to Aristotle's elder sister. Proxenus realized that the young man was an exceptional scholar, and when he reached the age of about 17, sent him to Athens to continue his studies at Plato's Academy (see pp.35–36), which by then had established itself as the foremost school in Greece for mathematics and philosophy.

IN CONTEXT
Athens and Macedon

Athens became the leading power in Greece in the 6th century BCE, and the practice of democracy in the city-state brought it domestic stability. It battled continually, however, to maintain supremacy, most notably against Sparta in the Peloponnesian War (431–404 BCE). After Sparta was defeated in 371 BCE, Athens faced a new threat, from the northern Greek state of Macedon. Philip II of Macedon conquered much of Greece in the 4th century BCE, and Macedonian influence on Athens increased until it was also taken over. The political centre of Greece shifted to Macedon, and the formerly independent city-states, including Athens, lost their status.

GOLD COINS STRUCK WITH THE IMAGE OF PHILIP II OF MACEDON

◁ **ARISTOTLE IN URBINO, c.1476**
This painting by Justus of Ghent was part of a commission to decorate the study of the lord of Urbino in the Palazzo Ducale, Urbino, Italy.

"All men by nature desire knowledge."
ARISTOTLE, *METAPHYSICS*

△ **ATHENA TEMPLE, ASSOS**

Pictured here are the magnificent Doric columns in the ruins of Athena Temple, Assos, Turkey. In 350 BCE, Assos came under the control of a Hermias, a person who had formerly been enslaved to the city's previous ruler, Eubolos. Hermias, who studied in Plato's Academy, invited a number of his fellow students to the city to help establish an academy there. After Plato's death, Aristotle spent three years in Assos.

time when anti-Macedonian sentiment was running high in Athens (see box, p.39). Whatever the reason, he left the Academy. Feeling uncomfortable as a Macedonian in Athens, he went with his colleague Xenocrates to the court of their friend Hermias of Atarneus in Assos, along the coast of what is now Turkey. The three men had studied together at the Academy, and Hermias offered Aristotle a place to continue his studies.

Studies of life

While in Assos, Aristotle developed an interest in biology, and especially the study of marine life; his research

in this area reinforced his idea that knowledge is acquired through empirical observation. His stay was ended when the Macedonian king, Philip II, withdrew his armies from the area, leaving Hermias at the mercy of the invading Persian army. Aristotle was furious with Philip, and not for the first time; soon after ascending to the throne, Philip had razed Stagira, Aristotle's home town, to the ground.

▷ **ON ANIMALS**

Aristotle was a pioneer of biology. His works on the subject are grouped together in *De animalibus* (*On animals*), here in a 15th-century Latin translation.

Aristotle fled from Assos to the island of Lesbos accompanied by his friend Theophrastus, another Academy alumnus. Together they made an exhaustive classification of the wildlife of the island and the sea creatures and plants in the Gulf of Kalloni.

"In **all things** of **nature** there is something of the **marvellous**."

ARISTOTLE, *PARTS OF ANIMALS*

"Man is by nature a political animal."

ARISTOTLE, *PARTS OF ANIMALS*

Hermias's adopted daughter, Pythias, had also fled to Lesbos, and soon after arriving on the island she and Aristotle married, and had a daughter, also named Pythias.

Aristotle and Alexander

Philip of Macedon was anxious to repair relations with Aristotle, and in 343 BCE invited him to his court to become the head of the royal academy, whose students included his son Alexander, as well as children of other royal families. The philosopher was eventually persuaded, but only after Philip agreed to completely rebuild the town of Stagira.

Aristotle remained in Macedon for the following eight years and, for about two of those years, taught the young prince, who was later to become known throughout the world as Alexander the Great (see box, below).

Aristotle was a formative influence on the young man, who continued to value his advice when he became king. Their relationship, however, was not straightforward. Aristotle continued to harbour resentment against Philip and his family for the destruction of Stagira and also for the betrayal of Hermias; and the two later divided over the issue of the Persians.

Aristotle regarded the Persians as barbarians and encouraged Alexander to adopt this view. When Alexander succeeded to the Macedonian throne in 336 BCE after the death of Philip, he set out – with Aristotle's support – to conquer all of Persia. Over the next decade he crushed his enemies in a series of decisive battles.

Later, however, Alexander made the decision to try and establish better relations with the Persians and even took steps to integrate some of their customs into the royal court and army – acts that Aristotle could not reconcile with his own contempt for the Persians. As time went on, Alexander became increasingly suspicious of his teacher's counsel, and Aristotle felt disappointed and let down by his protégé.

The Lyceum

Alexander's first mission when he came to the throne was to extend his rule over the whole of Greece, and therefore Athens soon came under Macedonian control. Aristotle judged that it was now safe to return to Athens and – as he now had little to do at the royal court – left Macedon.

△ **KALLONI LAGOON, LESBOS**
Accompanied by his wife, Pythias, and his botanist friend, Theophrastus, Aristotle stayed for two years on the island of Lesbos in the northeastern Aegean Sea. It was on the island that he carried out many of his observations and dissections of sea creatures.

IN PROFILE
Alexander the Great

In Aristotle's lifetime, Greek history was dominated by the extraordinary expansion of the empire under the Macedonian ruler Alexander the Great (356–323 BCE). By the time he came to power at the age of 20, Alexander's father Philip II had already extended Macedonian influence across much of Greece, and Alexander swiftly completed the process. In place of the warring city-states of Greece, there was now a unified Hellenistic state, from which he extended his empire across Persia into India, and into North Africa. By the time he was in his thirties, Alexander ruled the most powerful empire in the world. At the height of his success he developed a fever and died in Babylon, aged 32.

1ST-CENTURY ROMAN MOSAIC OF
ALEXANDER AT THE BATTLE OF ISSUS

IN CONTEXT
Plato and Aristotle

The contrasting philosophies of Aristotle and his mentor Plato are widely regarded as the "prototypes" of two different approaches that run through the history of philosophy – empiricism and rationalism. Where Plato posited a separate realm of ideal Forms, Aristotle insisted there is only one world, the world we live in; Plato believed that knowledge is innate and accessed by reason alone, Aristotle that it is learned through experience. Although there was obviously a great deal of mutual respect, the two men had very different temperaments, which shaped their thinking. Plato was a theorist, a mathematical thinker, with a penchant for the mystical, while Aristotle was down to earth, practical, and methodical.

THE SCHOOL OF ARISTOTLE, GUSTAV ADOLPH SPANGENBERG, 1883/88

With Alexander's encouragement he set up his own school in Athens, a rival to the Academy.

Aristotle chose to locate the school on a plot of land in the public area next to the temple of Apollo Lykeios (Apollo the wolf-god), which gave the school its name, Lyceum. The land had been a gymnasium (or exercise ground), and lent itself well to his purposes because it provided a space where he could conduct his classes in the open air and debate with his students as they walked around the grounds. It was because of this habit of his – holding lessons and discussions

◁ **NICOMACHEAN ETHICS**
Aristotle's work on ethics (dedicated to his son Nicomachus) appears here in a 10th-century manuscript. The text explores how people should best live.

on the *peripatos*, or ambulatory – that the members of the school became known as the "Peripatetics".

In a similar manner to a modern university, the Lyceum was not only a teaching institution but also a centre for research, and members of the school collectively amassed a huge collection of texts, which were stored in its library.

Philosophical texts
Aristotle himself contributed numerous manuscripts to the Lyceum. These were written on scrolls of papyrus, some of which he classified as "exoteric", or for a general public readership, and others as "esoteric", or intended for use within the Lyceum. Unfortunately, the exoteric texts have not survived, and what is known of Aristotle's philosophy is taken from

the esoteric texts, which are in the form of sometimes obscure and densely written essays, perhaps designed as lecture notes. These notes were collected by scholars and arranged by subject into the volumes as we are familiar with them today, such as the *Physics*, *Metaphysics*, *Nicomachean Ethics*, *Politics*, and *Poetics*.

This was undoubtedly the most productive period in Aristotle's life – a time when he consolidated all his philosophical ideas and put them into writing and, through the Lyceum, established an Aristotelean school of thought.

At the same time, however, Aristotle's personal life was in considerable turmoil. Not long after returning to Athens, his wife, Pythias, died. He later married again – this

> "**None** of the **moral virtues** arises in us by nature; for **nothing that exists** by nature can **form a habit** contrary to its nature."
> ARISTOTLE, *NICOMACHEAN ETHICS*

"Only an **utterly senseless person** can **fail** to **know** that **our characters** are the **result** of our **conduct**."

ARISTOTLE, *NICOMACHEAN ETHICS*

was being prepared, but before he could be charged, he fled to his mother's estate in Chalcis, on the island of Euboea in 322 BCE. His reported parting shot – in which he referenced Athens' treatment of Socrates – was that he would not give Athens the opportunity to sin twice against philosophy. That same year, he died of a stomach illness, having requested in his will to be buried next to his wife.

As arguably the first true scientist in history, and also the first to teach students systematically – his status as a philosopher and teacher is without equal.

◁ **TEACHING THE PRINCE**
Aristotle taught Alexander at the school at Mieza in Macedon. He encouraged the young man's interest in the art of healing as well as philosophy.

time to a Stagiran woman called Herpyllis, who some scholars believe may possibly have been enslaved to him, and with whom he had a son, named Nicomachus.

Meanwhile, his relationship with Alexander was deteriorating rapidly: Aristotle was losing patience with the emperor's unbridled arrogance and his bizarre delusions of divinity; Alexander, on the other hand, was growing increasingly paranoid and suspected plots against him – he even accused Aristotle of conspiring to have him assassinated.

Later years

When Alexander died suddenly in 323 BCE, far from feeling more secure, Aristotle found himself even more threatened. The pro-Macedonian government of Athens was overthrown, and widespread anti-Macedonian feeling grew. It was well known that Aristotle was a Macedonian, and that he had connections with the Macedonian royal family (and with Alexander in particular), making him an obvious target for persecution. A case against him on trumped-up charges of impiety

▷ **THE FOUR ELEMENTS**
Aristotle thought that matter could adopt four forms – fire, earth, water, or air – and also developed a cosmology based on the spheres of the heavenly bodies. This idea was taken up later, including in Peter Apian's 16th-century view of the universe, which saw Aristotle's elements surrounded by the fixed stars, spheres of the planets, and the abode of God.

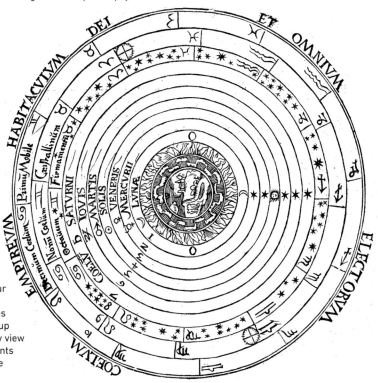

This Chinese painting depicts the great philosopher Mencius, whose work focused on, among other things, ethical ideas and practices, the importance of a good education, and the concept of innate goodness.

Mencius

c.371–c.289 BCE, CHINESE

Mencius, or Mengzi, is one of the foremost Confucian philosophers. He is particularly famous for his emphasis on innate goodness and the role of the environment in the formation of character.

Mencius, known in China as Mengzi, lived at a time of great political upheaval referred to as the Warring States period (see box, right). As had been the case with Confucius (see pp.14–19), Mencius's father died when he was young, and he was brought up in poverty by his mother.

According to legend, Mencius and his mother first lived near a graveyard, where the young boy took to imitating the paid mourners who were lamenting at funerals. They then took up residence near the market, where Mencius ran around imitating the cries of the traders. Eventually, the pair moved next to a school, where Mencius, ever the imitator, took to studying. His mother decided that this was a good place to settle. This story, although partly fanciful, dramatizes one of Mencius's central concepts: that environment is of paramount importance in the formation of character.

Innate goodness

Human nature, according to Mencius, is innately good. He illustrates this idea with the example of someone who witnesses a child falling down a well. The natural response to this situation, he argues, is alarm and distress – it would be inhuman to feel otherwise. But if we are innately good, this then raises the question of why people behave badly.

Ox Mountain

Mencius uses another striking image to argue that environmental factors can destroy this innate goodness. He talks of a beautiful mountain called Ox Mountain that was once covered in trees; but the trees were cut down, and sheep and cattle were brought to graze on it, so that all new growth was stripped away. The mountain might appear inherently desolate, but if you remove the negative environmental factors, the sprouts will regrow.

For Mencius, Ox Mountain is a powerful image of what can go wrong in life. We all have the "sprouts" of virtue: *ren*, or benevolence; *li*, or ritual propriety; *yi*, or righteousness; and *zhi*, or wisdom. However, environmental factors – such as poverty, or political misrule – undermine these factors. The idea of Ox Mountain suggests not only that environmental factors can deplete our innate goodness, but that they can also prevent the regrowth of this goodness once it has been depleted.

Travelling counsellor

Mencius spent much of his life, like Confucius, as a travelling counsellor, offering advice to princes and rulers. He advocated humane government, good stewardship of natural resources, light taxation, and the institution of systems of welfare to protect those who are disadvantaged. In the context of Mencius's time, these ideas were considered radical: certainly too radical for the power-hungry courts of Warring States China.

In his old age, Mencius, like Confucius, was disappointed that his ideas had not transformed the brutal politics of his day. Nevertheless, his thoughts continue to exert a strong influence in the fields of virtue ethics and environmental philosophy.

▽ **COMMEMORATING MENCIUS**
A traditional sacrificial ceremony to commemorate Mencius is being held here, during the winter solstice, at his temple and family mansion in Zoucheng City, Shandong Province.

IN CONTEXT
Warring States Period

The era of Chinese history that is known as the Warring States period (475–221 BCE) began when many individual feudal states were consolidated into seven major rival powers. New technologies, including crossbows and the large-scale production of bronze, iron, and steel swords, fuelled multiple bloody conflicts between the various contenders. However, the period was also one of tremendous intellectual achievement and of administrative development. The Warring States period effectively came to an end with the final victory of the Qin kingdom in the northwest, which was then followed by the establishment of the empire of Qin.

A BRONZE CAST SWORD FROM THE WARRING STATES PERIOD

Zhuangzi

c.370–c.290 BCE, CHINESE

"Master Zhuang" was the author of a number of Daoist parables and dialogues. Together with other works by his followers, known collectively as the *Zhuangzi*, they became a classic text of Chinese philosophy.

Very little is known of the life of the philosopher honoured with the title "Master" Zhuang, and credited as author of at least part of the anthology that bears his name. There is some anecdotal information from historians, often writing centuries after his death, and from references to incidents in his life in the *Zhuangzi* itself, which were added to the collection by his followers.

It is known that Zhuangzi was active in the 4th century BCE, at the height of the Chinese Classical period, when philosophy had reached a peak of sophistication, producing the so-called "Hundred Schools of Thought" (see box, right). His given name was Zhuang Zhou, and tradition has it that he was born in the town of Meng, in the Song region of China, and worked as a minor official, possibly managing a warehouse for lacquerware.

A simple life in nature

In the *Zhuangzi*, the philosopher is portrayed as living the life of a hermit, choosing to distance himself from society and retreat with his wife to the remote countryside. This was in keeping with the central theme of his philosophy – the Daoist principle of living a simple life in accord with nature, and following the *dao*, "the Way". Nevertheless, he was apparently well known for his wisdom, and

probably had a small number of students or disciples. His reputation spread beyond the local region too; according to a story in the *Zhuangzi*, King Wei of Chu was so impressed by what he had heard of him, that he sent messengers to offer him the post of chief minister in the Chu court. Zhuang Zhou replied to the offer by pointing out that King Wei kept a sacred turtle, dead for 3,000 years, in a box in a temple. He asked the messengers whether the turtle would prefer to be in that place of honour, or alive and in the mud; he himself preferred, he said, to remain alive in the mud.

Debate with the logicians

Despite the solitary lifestyle described in the *Zhuangzi* and the rejection of conventional status, it is clear that Zhuang Zhou was a highly educated man, and had quite likely studied literature and philosophy with some

of the foremost figures of the time. He was roughly contemporary with Mencius and the logicians of the School of Names, and their influence can be seen in much of the *Zhuangzi*. Although his Daoist philosophy often contradicted the logicians, he had close friends among them, including Gongsun Long and in particular Hui Shi, known as Huizi (Master Hui), both of whom appear as characters in dialogues in the *Zhuangzi*.

However, his logician friends are more often than not presented as foils for his own ideas, unwitting stooges in his witty demolition of their rational arguments. Many of the stories in the book are in the form of dialogues between Zhang Zhou and one or other of his companions – most often Hui Shi, the butt of much of Zhang Zhou's good-natured banter. With clever wordplay and humour, he points out the inconsistencies and absurdities

IN CONTEXT
The Hundred Schools of Thought

The Warring States period (475–221 BCE), was a time of conflict, reform, and administrative turmoil in ancient China that required rapid innovation in social and political thought. Many different philosophical approaches emerged, centred on the ideas of scholars and itinerant teachers. The most influential of these so-called "Hundred Schools of Thought" were Daoism and Confucianism, and the smaller Mohist and Yin–Yang groups (which tried to explain the world in terms of the opposing forces of yin and yang). These schools were all effectively quashed by the adoption of Legalism, an authoritarian political philosophy, by the Qin dynasty, which replaced the Zhou in 221 BCE.

A YIN-YANG SYMBOL DATING FROM THE WARRING STATES PERIOD

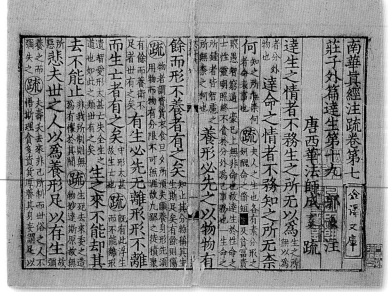

◁ **THE *ZHUANGZI***
Written fragments of the *Zhuangzi* have been found in tombs from the Han dynasty (206 BCE–220 CE). This copy dates from the Song dynasty (960–1279).

像 子 莊

◁ **ZHUANGZI, OR ZHUANG ZHOU**
For Daoists like Zhuangzi, the rational mind led away from the *dao*, the path of intuition. By laughing and holding ideas up to ridicule, he could free himself from the tyranny of the rational mind.

IN PROFILE
Guo Xiang

Little is known of the life of the scholar Guo Xiang, but his legacy in the form of the authoritative edition of the *Zhuangzi* has established him as a pioneer of the Neo-Daoist *xuanxue* ("mysterious learning") movement, which had begun with Wang Bi's commentaries on the *Dao De Jing*. What Guo Xiang achieved, however, was more than merely editing the text of the *Zhuangzi* and arranging it according to its presumed sources; he also added a commentary introducing original ideas – in particular reconciling the Daoist nature of the text with the predominant Confucian moral code of the time.

of conventional, rational argument. In one celebrated tale, for example, Zhuang Zhou comments on how happy the fish are, swimming in the river. Hui Shi asks him how he knows what the fish enjoy, to which Zhaung Zhou replies: "You are not me, so how do you know that I do not know what fish enjoy?" In characteristically logical fashion, Hui Shi thinks he can win the argument by responding: "No, I am not you, so I do not know what you know. But you are not a fish, so that proves you do not know what fish enjoy." "Let's go back to your original question," Zhuang Zhou suggests. "You asked how I know what fish enjoy, so you knew then that I did know."

Dialogues and anecdotes

Serious points are made in a light-hearted way in the *Zhuangzi*, and in a style that appeals as much for its literary value as its philosophical content. Simple anecdotes, elegantly told, led to its immediate and enduring popularity. Perhaps the best known of these is the tale of Zhuang Zhou dreaming that he was a butterfly and forgetting he was Zhuang Zhou, then

▷ **DOI GOGA CALLIGRAPHY**
The first two sentences of the *Zhuangzi* are beautifully rendered by Confucian scholar, intellectual, and celebrated artist Doi Goga 1817–80).

waking and no longer knowing whether he was Zhuang Zhou who had dreamed he was a butterfly, or a butterfly dreaming he is Zhuang Zhou.

Several of these parables are written in the first person, suggesting that they were indeed the work of Zhuang Zhou, while others, which differ stylistically and philosophically, refer more obliquely to events in the life of Master Zhuang, including accounts of his death, and are presumed to have been written by members of his following.

Evolution of the text

Despite its multiple authors, the collection of works became widely known in China as the *Zhuangzi* within a century or so of Master Zhuang's death. Many different versions of the text evolved and until the 3rd century CE the accepted version was a 52-chapter collection.

This changed when Guo Xiang (see box, above) compiled an authoritative edition of the work, compressing it into 33 chapters, and adding an explanatory commentary. He also arranged the chapters to reflect what he considered to be their authorship: the first seven chapters, which he called the "Inner Chapters", were

◁ **THE PLEASURES OF FISHES**
This Yuan dynasty (1271–1368) painting by Zhou Dongqing was inspired by a passage in the *Zhuangzi* concerned with recognizing the feelings of joy in others.

KEY WORKS

c.350–300 BCE	300– c.100 BCE	111 CE	c.300 CE	742 CE
Writes the anecdotes and parables now collectively known as the Inner Chapters (chapters 1–7) of the *Zhuangzi*.	Followers of Zhuang Zhou expand the *Zhuangzi* with more of his stories, and some original material.	In the history of the Western dynasty the *Han Shu* (*The Book of Han*), the *Zhuangzi* is described as having 52 chapters.	Chinese scholar Guo Xiang edits the text of the *Zhuangzi*, reducing it from 52 chapters to the now standard 33.	Emperor Xuanzong of Tang proclaims the *Zhuangzi* a classic of the Chinese canon.

attributed to Zhuang Zhou; the next 14, the "Outer Chapters", were assumed to have been written by his followers, as they either recount the teachings of the Master or provide stories in the same style; and the final "Miscellaneous Chapters" were of unknown origin.

A key work of Daoism

Although appreciated as an exquisite work of literature, the *Zhuangzi* was treated suspiciously by philosophers because it mocked the rational arguments of the logicians and Mohists, and dismissed the mundane nature of Confucianism (although Guo Xiang's annotated edition did much to help its acceptance). The core message of the book, the idea of *dao*, stressed the oneness of everything, and that peace and contentment can be achieved through *wu wei* – through not striving, but simply being in accord with nature, and accepting life and death as natural processes of transformation. Daoism, which had been eclipsed by other schools of thought, especially Confucianism and Legalism for several centuries, gradually experienced a resurgence thanks in large part to Guo Xiang's edition of the *Zhuangzi*. Its naturalist sentiments, expressed in a quirky, non-rational way, appealed in particular to the growing Buddhist movement in China, which developed its distinctive branch, Chan Buddhism, by incorporating elements of Daoism of the *Zhuangzi*. Today, the *Zhuangzi* is revered as a masterpiece of classical Chinese literature, and a seminal text of Daoist philosophy.

△ **DREAMING OF A BUTTERFLY**
This 18th-century ink drawing by Ike no Taiga depicts the anecdote of Zhuangzi dreaming that he was a butterfly. His philosophical questioning of what it is to be real recurs in Western philosophy with Descartes, who declared there to be "no certain indications by which we may clearly distinguish wakefulness from sleep".

"Now **I do not know** whether it was **then** I **dreamed** I was a **butterfly**, or whether I am **now** a **butterfly dreaming** I am a **man**."

ZHUANGZI

Epicurus

c.341–270 BCE, GREEK

Epicurus's liberal materialism has been widely misunderstood as a brand of self-indulgent pleasure seeking. This is quite contrary to the philosophy he advocated in his school known as "the Garden".

Epicurus was born on the island of Samos, where his parents had settled 10 years earlier. He was educated in the Athenian colony there, studying under the Platonist philosopher Pamphilus until called to Athens to do his military service, aged 18. It is likely that he spent some of his time in the city attending lectures at Plato's Academy and Aristotle's Lyceum.

After the death of Alexander the Great in 323 BCE, the Athenians were expelled from Samos and Epicurus's family settled in Colophon, Asia Minor. He visited them there before deciding to continue his studies, first with the Aristotelean Praxiphanes, then with Nausiphanes of Teos, who was a disciple of the atomist Democritus.

Epicurus eventually fell out with his tutors, developing his own distinctive philosophy. In around 310 BCE he took up a teaching post at Mytilene, capital of Lesbos, but soon found himself in trouble for promoting heretical and impious ideas, and made a perilous sea-crossing to escape censure.

▷ **PLEASURE SEEKERS**
Epicurus's philosophy is mistakenly equated with the pleasure of the flesh embodied in the god of wine and fertility, Dionysus, shown here in a replica of a 4th-century Roman sculpture.

In the more liberally minded town of Lampsacus he founded his own school, assisted by Hermarchus, a colleague from Mytilene. The school quickly gained a reputation as a seat of learning, and on the strength of its success – and in the knowledge that attitudes to new ideas were softening – Epicurus decided to move his operations to Athens. In 306 BCE he bought a house and land in the city and established a sort of philosophical community, which because of its beautiful grounds was known by everyone simply as "the Garden". Epicurus spent the rest of his life teaching and putting into practice the lifestyle he advocated, which was summed up by the inscription reportedly above the entrance to the Garden: "Stranger, here you will do well to tarry; here our highest good is pleasure."

Epicurianism

For Epicurus, the object of life was to live happily. But rather than the pursuit of physical pleasure, he advocated moderation and tranquillity; true pleasure, he argued, is freedom from pain and fear, and in particular the fear of death.

Like Democritus, he believed that there is nothing in the cosmos except atoms and empty space, and so denied the existence of an immaterial, immortal soul; from this he concluded that "When we are, death is not come, and, when death is come, we are not"– so death is nothing, and is nothing to be feared.

After his death, his popularity gradually waned. Epicureanism came to be seen as shallowly hedonistic by the Romans, and denounced by Christianity for its materialist, atheist, humanism, but was rediscovered during the Scientific Revolution of the Renaissance and Enlightenment, and exerted an influence on modern scientific liberalism.

IN CONTEXT
Philosophy in Hellenistic Greece

The death of Alexander the Great in 323 BCE marked the beginning of the Hellenistic period in Greece, a high point of Greek cultural influence. This turning point was also signalled by the death of Aristotle, the third of the trio of great Athenian philosophers after Socrates and Plato. New schools of thought emerged to match the spirit of the age. Pyrrho of Elis (365–275 BCE) founded the movement that became known as Scepticism at much the same time as Epicurus established his school; however, the most influential of these movements was Stoicism, founded by Zeno of Citium (333–263 BCE), and inspired by Diogenes the Cynic, which became the predominant philosophy of the Roman Empire.

▷ **EPICURUS, ROMAN BUST**
Friendship and simple pleasures were, for Epicurus, the key ingredients of happiness. True to his beliefs, he remained cheerful and friendly even through the excruciating pain from the kidney stones that eventually killed him in about 270 BCE.

◁ **PHILOSOPHER'S GARDEN, 1834**
The painter Antal Strohmayer imagines Epicurus's school in this image. Epicurus deliberately sited his school half way between the Academy and the Stoa, where Zeno of Citium had established his Stoic school of philosophy.

▷ **MARCUS AURELIUS**
Marcus Aurelius is represented wearing a helmet and in his role as a military leader in this detail from a 17th-century wool and silk tapestry, after a drawing by the accomplished Flemish painter Abraham van Diepenbeeck (1596–1675).

Marcus Aurelius

121–180 CE, ROMAN

When Marcus Aurelius became Roman emperor in 161 CE, he was known for his scholarship in Stoic philosophy, was nicknamed "the Philosopher", and hailed as the fulfilment of Plato's ideal of a philosopher-king.

◁ **BATTLE SCENE**
The walls of a 2nd-century sarcophagus are decorated with a relief showing a battle between Roman horsemen and Barbarians during the Germanic Wars under Emperor Marcus Aurelius.

IN PROFILE
Epictetus

The Stoic school of philosophy was founded in Greece in the 2nd century BCE but, largely thanks to the work of Epictetus (c.55–c.135 CE), became the predominant philosophy of the Roman Empire. Epictetus (which means "acquired" in Greek) was born in Hierapolis, Phrygia, and in boyhood was taken to Rome and enslaved. His owner, a freedman, allowed him to study and eventually gave him his freedom. When philosophers were banished by the emperor Domitian, he moved to Nicopolis in Greece, where he established his own school. His teachings were collected by his student Arrian as the *Discourses* and the *Enchiridion* (*Handbook*). As a Stoic, he led a simple life, and lived to the age of about 80.

Marcus Aurelius was born Marcus Annius Verus in Rome in 121 CE (only when he became emperor did he take the name Marcus Aurelius Antoninus Augustus). When his father – Marcus Annius Verus III – died the younger Marcus was about three years old, and was brought up by his mother, Lucilla, and his grandfather. He was taught at home by private tutors and was especially inspired by Diognetus, who introduced him to Stoic philosophy. He also showed an aptitude for literature, but philosophy was his main interest from then on, often to the detriment of his studies in law and oratory.

Ascent to emperor

In 138 CE, Hadrian, the Roman emperor, nominated Aurelius Antoninus, Marcus's uncle, as his successor, specifying that Antoninus should adopt Marcus and another boy, Lucius Verus. After Hadrian's death in 138 CE, Antoninus became emperor, and conferred on Marcus the name Aelius Aurelius Verus Caesar, effectively selecting him as his heir.

Under Antoninus, Marcus became prominent in public affairs, serving as quaestor and consul, and in 145 CE sealed his connection with the emperor by marrying his daughter Faustina. The following years were largely occupied with his official duties and bringing up their young family.

Antoninus died in 161 CE and Marcus took up the office of emperor only reluctantly, and on condition that he ruled jointly with his adoptive brother, Verus. Surprisingly, the senate agreed to his request, and for the first time Rome had two co-emperors.

The arrangement worked well, not least because the empire was facing attacks on two fronts – from the Parthians in the east, and the Germans in the North. Verus was sent to lead the campaign in Parthia, leaving Marcus to oversee domestic affairs and co-ordinate the northern defences. War was compounded by plague, which struck the army in Parthia and made its way to Rome. About a quarter of the Roman population died, among them Verus, leaving Marcus as sole leader in 169 CE. Marcus abandoned the Parthian War to concentrate on Rome's northern borders. He spent much of his time at the battlefront, and in 175 CE travelled to Syria to quell the revolt of his governor there.

Despite the commitments of empire, Marcus still made time for his philosophical studies. From about 170 CE until his death in 180 CE, he wrote a series of essays, later collectively known as the *Meditations*, in which he elaborated on the Stoic philosophy (see box, right), emphasizing the importance of living in accordance with nature, and recognizing the difference between the things we have the power to change and those we must learn to accept.

Historical legacy

The war in Germany dragged on, and Marcus returned to oversee operations, but in 180 CE he died in Vindobona (now Vienna). His death marked the end of the Pax Romana, a stable, peaceful era within the Roman Empire, despite the wars at its borders. Marcus Aurelius is considered the last of the "Five Good Emperors", a just and respected ruler, more concerned with maintaining the peace and prosperity of his people and protecting them from aggression than waging war to expand his empire.

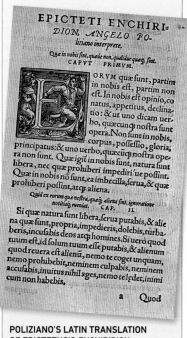

POLIZIANO'S LATIN TRANSLATION OF EPICTETUS'S *ENCHIRIDION*

▷ **LUCIUS VERUS**
In this statue, the head of Lucius Verus (made c.165 CE) has been mounted on the body of a soldier. Verus was equal in status and power to Marcus Aurelius, but lacked his authority and his ability to shoulder the responsibilities of state.

Nagarjuna

c.150–c.250ce, INDIAN

Nagarjuna was one of the most important and influential philosophers in the Buddhist tradition. He was the founder of the Madhyamaka or "Middle Way" school, which developed from commentaries on his works.

As is fitting for a philosopher who dedicated himself to exploring the Buddhist idea of *sunnata* (emptiness, or non-self), very little is known about Nagarjuna's life other than that he lived in the 2nd–3rd centuries ce in South India, where he was a Buddhist monk and a prolific writer. Of the vast body of works he left behind, the best known is *Mulamadhyamakakarika*, or *Fundamental Verses on the Middle Way*, in which he provides the most complete and succinct exploration of his philosophy of emptiness – the idea that everything lacks (or is "empty" of) inherent existence. In other words, things do not exist inherently in and of themselves, independent of other things.

The Middle Way

Nagarjuna took seriously the Buddha's exhortation to find a "middle way" between extremes – an idea that, over the years, has had many interpretations. It has been taken variously as a call to behave moderately in everyday life,

◁ **NAGARJUNA**
In this Tibetan painting dating from the 18th century, Nagarjuna (the large figure at the centre) is pictured surrounded by the Mahasiddha, characters who embody mystical perfection.

to embrace spiritualism as well as materialism, and to reconcile the duality that pervades most thinking.

Translating the Buddha's demand into the philosophical realm, Nagarjuna argued that there are two positions that we can take in relation to existence. On the one hand, he pointed out that things have an inherent existence – they exist autonomously, independent of other things. However, in this scenario, it is difficult to account for change, for how one thing can transform or affect other things. He also explored the opposite extreme, that nothing at all exists, which is also unsatisfactory because there is evidently something happening. When we look out of a window, we see trees and birds, so there must be some sense in which we, the birds, and the trees exist. Nagarjuna claimed to have found a middle way between these two extreme positions.

Two truths

Nagarjuna found the solution in his doctrine of "two truths". He argued that things are empty of inherent existence, or self-essence – this is "ultimate truth". But that is not to say that they do not exist at all. Things like trees, birds, and people exist in that they are vividly present to us – this is

"conventional truth". So things exist, but their existence is to some extent dependent on other things, including our perception of them. Nagarjuna did not claim that the nature of things is emptiness, but made a more subtle claim – that all things (including emptiness) are empty of inherent existence. His philosophy maintains this double vision of simultaneously seeing both conventional and ultimate truths; but, for consistency, he also argued that the distinction between these two truths is itself empty.

IN CONTEXT
The Madhyamaka school

Nagarjuna stands at the forefront of a tradition in Buddhist philosophy known as the Madhyamaka (Middle Way) school. This school developed through various commentaries that elaborated on Nagarjuna's writings, especially those by the 7th-century Indian scholar Candrakirti. The Madhyamaka school became very influential in Tibet, where its enigmatic, metaphysical character placed it at the heart of Buddhist philosophy there. Contemporary philosophers continue to debate the implications of Nagarjuna's work.

ANCIENT GILDED BRONZE BUDDHA SCULPTURE, TIBET

"Neither from **itself** nor from **another**, nor from **both**, nor **without a cause**, does **anything** whatever, **anywhere** arise."
NAGARJUNA, *MULAMADHYAMAKAKARIKA*

Augustine of Hippo

354–430 CE, ROMAN AFRICAN

A hugely influential Christian philosopher and theologian in his time, Augustine remained an inspirational figure throughout the Middle Ages, when two religious orders were named after him.

Augustine was born at Thagaste (now Souk Ahras in Algeria) in the Roman province of Numidia. He was named Aurelius Augustinus, indicating the Roman origins of his family. His father, Patricius, was a pagan, working as an official in the local government, but his mother was a devout Christian, later canonized as St Monica.

Augustine went to a local school in Madaura before moving to Carthage, the most important Roman city in North Africa, in 371 CE. Latin was his native tongue and he gained a solid grounding in classical literature, but, unlike most of the other ancient philosophers, he never attained much proficiency in Greek. When residing in Carthage, he read *Hortensius* by the Roman orator Cicero (106–43 BCE), a book that helped to shape his career. In his *Confessions*, Augustine related how it inspired him to devote his life to the pursuit of wisdom and to his intensive studies of the Scriptures.

Dualistic beliefs

Augustine's studies of the Scriptures did not lead directly to his conversion. He had been raised as a Christian, but he had not been baptized; in addition, he was living at a time and in a part of the Roman Empire where there were many other competing religions. Much to the despair of his mother, Augustine joined one of these – a Gnostic sect known as Manichaeism. The Manichees believed in a dualistic system, in which the world was a battleground between goodness and evil, darkness and light. They shared some values with Christianity, but denied the Virgin Birth and the redeeming power of the Crucifixion. Later, in his *Confessions*, he would condemn the Manichaean preachers as "men with glib tongues who... had the snares of the devil in their mouths", but Augustine remained firmly committed to their cause for almost 10 years.

At this time, Augustine was a teacher. Briefly a schoolmaster at Thagaste, he returned in 376 CE to Carthage to teach rhetoric. There, he indulged in the life of sin that he later described in his autobiography. He took a mistress and had a child with her – a boy named Adeodatus. Writing with hindsight in *Confessions*, Augustine admitted that the

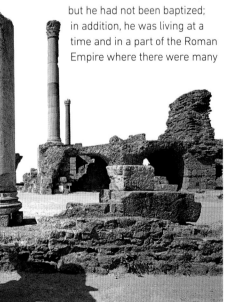

◁ **RUINS OF CARTHAGE**
Carthage, where Augustine studied and taught, was the pre-eminent Roman city in Africa. By the 1st century CE its population was over 500,000. It was also an early centre of Christianity.

IN PROFILE
St Ambrose

In his autobiographical work, *Confessions*, Augustine credited Ambrose – then the bishop of Milan – as the major inspiration for his conversion. Like Augustine, Ambrose came from a secular background. His father was a praetorian prefect of Gaul and, for a brief spell, he himself served as the consul of Milan. He was appointed bishop in 374 CE and gained renown for his campaigns against Arian heretics and for the quality of his sermons. It was these that influenced Augustine. Paraphrasing verses from the Psalms, Augustine wrote of Ambrose: "his golden tongue never tired of dispensing the richness of your corn, the joy of your oil, and the sober intoxication of your wine" (*Confessions*, Book V).

15TH-CENTURY DEPICTION OF ST AMBROSE IN HIS STUDY

"I went to **Carthage**, where **I found myself** in the midst of a **hissing cauldron** of **lust**."

AUGUSTINE OF HIPPO, *CONFESSIONS*

▷ **ST AUGUSTINE IN HIS STUDY**, 1480
This painting by Sandro Botticelli depicts a specific moment in Augustine's life. The theologian is pictured experiencing a vision of St Jerome at the precise moment of Jerome's death.

IN CONTEXT
The Sack of Rome

At the end of the 4th century CE, the Roman Empire in the West was in deep crisis. Barbarian tribes were overrunning Roman imperial territories and the capital was transferred to Ravenna in 402 CE. The greatest threat came from the Visigoths, who ravaged Italy and sacked Rome in 410 CE – the first time the city had been captured since 390 BCE. The Visigoths looted for three days, before moving on to attack other targets. This event shook the civilized world. Some blamed the disaster on the rise of Christianity and the abandonment of the old, pagan gods. Augustine wrote *The City of God* specifically to refute this.

SACRED OBJECTS BEING HIDDEN FROM THE ADVANCING VISIGOTHS

relationship was the result of his own "restless passions". He also made a pointed distinction between marriage, which was contracted for the purpose of having children, and more lustful associations, where the birth of children was "begrudged", although as he wrote, "we cannot help but love them" if they come along.

Augustine's relationship with his mistress was clearly stronger than he cared to admit. They remained together for 15 years and he gave her up very reluctantly, under pressure from his mother, writing how his heart was "crushed and bleeding" when the woman was "torn from his side". This drastic action was taken because Monica had arranged a more suitable match for him. However, there was a delay of two years, because the girl was still too young. During this time, Augustine's resolve weakened again and he took on another mistress. In the end, the arranged marriage never took place.

The road to conversion

In 384 CE, Augustine gained a prestigious promotion when he was appointed as a professor of rhetoric at Milan. This was to be a key period in his spiritual development. The influence of the Manichees was waning while, at the same time, he was becoming more interested in Neoplatonism. Ironically, this pagan-inspired philosophy helped to smooth the path to his conversion. His interest stemmed mainly from his reading of the Greek philosopher Plotinus. In the *Enneads*, his collection of essays, Plotinus outlined his concept of the universe as an emanation of the One, an omnipresent manifestation of

supreme goodness. This seemed more convincing than the dualism of the Manichees, helping Augustine to a far better understanding of the spiritual nature of God.

While in Milan, Augustine began attending the sermons of Bishop Ambrose. Initially, he was attracted by the bishop's reputation as a fine speaker, but as he listened to this "holy oracle", he gradually began to look at the Scriptures in a different way. He learned how to understand the spiritual sense behind their literal meaning. As a result, both Augustine and his son were baptized by Ambrose on Easter Saturday in 387 CE.

△ **AUGUSTINE IN ART**
As one of the four doctors (teachers) of the Western Church, Augustine often features in Christian art. This painting by 15th-century artist Ottaviano Nelli shows him being taken to school by St Monica.

Augustine renounced the secular life and returned to Africa the following year with the intention of founding a monastery. He settled in his family home at Thagaste, which he turned into a base for the new community. However, he did not remain a monk for long. In 391 CE, during a visit to the Numidian port of Hippo (now Annaba, Algeria), Bishop Valerius persuaded

KEY WORKS

396–397 CE
Writes *On Christian Teaching*, a guide that shows Christian teachers how to use the Scriptures in their work.

c.397–400 CE
Divided into 13 books, the *Confessions* charts Augustine's gradual route from a life of sin to his conversion to Christianity.

400–416 CE
After many years spent ruminating on the controversial subject, Augustine writes *On the Trinity*.

413–424 CE
Writes *The City of God*, his most important text on Christian philosophy, in response to the fall of Rome.

426–427 CE
Towards the end of his life, Augustine revisits and revises some of his earlier works in *Retractions*.

"O God... **where were you** all this time? **Where were you hiding** from me?"

AUGUSTINE OF HIPPO, *CONFESSIONS*

him to become ordained as a priest. Augustine quickly gained a reputation as a fine preacher and, in 396 CE, succeeded Valerius as the bishop of Hippo. He remained there for the rest of his life, writing, and carrying out his pastoral duties.

Augustine left a huge legacy. He was a prolific writer, producing more than 90 books, along with hundreds of letters and sermons. He also had an immense impact on monastic life, lending his name to an order of canons and an order of friars. His books, the *Confessions* and *The City of God*, have become classics. The *Confessions* broke new ground in the field of biography. At a time when saints'

lives tended towards hagiography, dominated by miraculous events and virtuous behaviour, Augustine went out of his way to highlight his early sins and misdemeanours. This made him seem much more human to his readers, never more so than when he uttered his famous plea to God – to make him pure, but not yet. The biography was interspersed with philosophical meditations, such as ruminations on the nature of time.

Christian philosophy

Augustine's most important text on Christian philosophy, *The City of God*, was intended primarily as an attack on pagan culture and values, but it also contained his ideas on original sin, predestination, and free will. These views were to resonate down the centuries, when they were taken up by the Protestant reformers John Calvin and Martin Luther (who was an

Augustinian friar). They and their colleagues regarded Augustine as a precursor of their movement.

Among his theological works, the masterpiece was *On the Trinity*. He meditated on the question of the Trinity for many years and in the dedicatory letter, he admitted: "I was young when I began this, an old man when I published it." The exact nature of the Trinity was a highly controversial issue in the early Christian Church, but Augustine brought clarity and authority to the subject.

Augustine died in 430 CE, at a time when the Vandals had invaded North Africa and were besieging Hippo. His remains were later transported to Italy, initially to Sardinia and subsequently to a shrine in Pavia.

△ **THEOLOGICAL WORKS**
Augustine was one of the most prolific and important scholars of the early Church. This copy of selected works by St Augustine was produced in the 12th century in Britain.

▽ **RUINS OF HIPPO REGIUS**
Hippo was besieged by the Vandals in 430 CE. Augustine prayed for deliverance but died three months into the siege; the city fell to the Vandals soon after.

▷ **THE PHILOSOPHERS OF ALEXANDRIA**
This fresco depicting Hypatia addressing the philosophers of Alexandria decorates a wall in San Clemente in Rome. The fresco was created between 1425 and 1431 by Masolino da Panicale, one of the masters of the early Italian Renaissance.

Hypatia

c.355/370–415/416 CE, ALEXANDRIAN GREEK

Hypatia was the foremost astronomer and mathematician of her day. She was also a recognized Neoplatonist philosopher and teacher, known for her philanthropy, charisma, and love of learning.

In a sense, there are two Hypatias, one a real woman, the other a glamorous figure whose legend has evolved over the centuries. The second Hypatia was beautiful, virtuous, and a lifelong virgin; she was the last great thinker of antiquity, the last pagan; and her violent death resembled the martyrdom of a saint. In Charles Kingsley's novel (*Hypatia, Or New Foes with an Old Face*, 1853) her killing was a pretext for anti-Catholic sentiment; in a recent film (*Agora*, 2009) the target was Christian fundamentalism.

The historical Hypatia is a more shadowy figure. Her traditional date of birth is c.370 CE, although some authorities suggest it was considerably earlier, perhaps by as much as 16 years or more, so she may not have been a young woman at the time of her death.

Teaching in the academy

Hypatia grew up in Alexandria, where her father, Theon, ran an academy. Geographically, Alexandria lies in Egypt but, at the time, it was part of the eastern half of the Roman Empire (the empire had been divided earlier in the century). In cultural terms, it was predominantly Greek. Theon was a distinguished but unexceptional mathematician who edited and produced commentaries on the works of Euclid and Ptolemy. It has been suggested that Hypatia collaborated with him on some of these, but this

> "We have **seen** with **our own eyes...** the **lady** who **truly presides** over the **mysteries** of **philosophy.**"
>
> SYNESIUS OF CYRENE ON HYPATIA, LETTER TO HERCULIAN

▷ **THEON'S COMMENTARY**
Hypatia's father, Theon, was known for his observations of lunar eclipses. He is the author of this commentary on Ptolemy's *Canones manuales* (a collection of astronomical tables).

cannot be proved. Theon undoubtedly trained his daughter and she succeeded him at the academy, where she taught mathematics, philosophy, and astronomy. Although none of her writings survives, she is known to have produced commentaries on the *Arithmetica* by Diophantus and *Conic Sections* by Apollonius of Perga, as well as a work on astronomical tables.

On Neoplatonism

Despite considerable speculation, it is unclear whether Hypatia wrote anything on philosophy. However, she was certainly acclaimed as a highly gifted Neoplatonist teacher. The main source of information about

this comes from the letters of Synesius of Cyrene (see box, right), Hypatia's pupil.

Neoplatonism was the dominant religious philosophy of later pagan antiquity (once people had stopped believing in the old gods of the classical world). Primarily, it was filtered through the teachings of Plotinus (c.205–270 CE), whose beliefs provided a synthesis of rationalism and a route to salvation – by accepting the One, the transcendent form of Goodness – that carried faint echoes of Christianity.

Although a Neoplatonist herself, Hypatia was tolerant of other faiths. Despite this, she was murdered by Christian zealots, who dragged her from her carriage and flayed her alive with shells (or possibly roof tiles – the Greek term is ambiguous). It seems, however, that political as well as religious differences were the cause of her death. Alexandria was a violent place, riven by warring factions, and Hypatia fell foul of a feud between Cyril, the local bishop, and Orestes, the Roman governor. She supported Orestes, which probably sealed her fate. Her murder shocked the Christian world, and Cyril was generally blamed for it, though it did not prevent him from later being canonized.

IN PROFILE
Synesius of Cyrene

Synesius was Hypatia's most famous student at the academy in Alexandria. Born into a wealthy family, he was a man of many parts. Among other things, he became a poet, a military commander, and a bishop, although he was always happiest living the life of a country gentleman. While studying with Hypatia, Synesius was a Neoplatonist. He later became a Christian, although perhaps not a very committed one. When he was offered the bishopric of Ptolemais, he accepted with reluctance, concerned that he might have to relinquish his wife. Synesius was a varied and talented writer, producing sensitive Neoplatonic hymns, spirited letters, and a treatise on dog breeding.

SYNESIUS, BISHOP OF PTOLEMAIS

◁ **RUINS OF ROMAN ALEXANDRIA**
Alexandria had been under formal Roman rule since the 1st century BCE. During Hypatia's life, it was part of the Eastern Roman Empire. Life in the city was turbulent, being beset by fighting among Christians, Jews, and pagans.

Directory

Thales of Miletus

c.624–546 BCE, GREEK

Regarded as the first philosopher and scientist in Western civilization, Thales is known only through fragmentary and often contradictory accounts of his life and thought as represented in the works of other writers.

Born in Miletus, a prosperous Greek city on the Aegean coast of Anatolia, Thales may have travelled widely in his younger years, for he is said to have learned geometry from Egyptian priests and probably picked up his knowledge of astronomy from the Babylonians. His most well-attested feat was the prediction of a solar eclipse in 585 BCE. Thales asserted that the basic substance of the world was water, and believed that the Earth was a flat disc floating on an ocean.

Thales founded the Milesian school of philosophy, which sought to account for the natural world by means of observable, scientific principles. Thales is said to have died of heat stroke while watching the Olympic Games. None of his written works has survived, but he is believed to have written two treatises on astronomy.

▷ Mahavira

c.497–425 BCE or c.599–527 BCE, INDIAN

Followers of the Jain faith consider Mahavira to be the 24th *tirthankara*, an enlightened guide showing the path to escape from the cycle of death and rebirth. As a historical figure, he was born into a royal family in present-day Bihar, northeast India. Around the age of 30 he left his princely home to become a wandering ascetic. After 12 years of suffering and indignity he attained enlightenment, and began teaching a group of disciples. Unlike his contemporary Gautama Buddha, Mahavira believed in a soul separate from the body, which through many incarnations could rise towards bliss or sink towards hell. His major ethical principle was non-injury (*ahimsa*), the duty to avoid harming any creature. He regarded reality as too complex and multifaceted to be grasped as a whole or adequately expressed in language.

His teachings, transmitted orally through his chief disciple, Gautama Swami, formed the basis for the sacred texts of Jainism, the Agamas.

△ A MARBLE STATUE OF MAHAVIRA, JAISALMER FORT, RAJASTHAN, INDIA

Kanada

c.6TH–2ND CENTURY BCE, INDIAN

So little is known about Kanada that not even the century in which he lived can be decided with any certainty. He was the founder of Vaisheshika, one of the six orthodox schools of Hindu philosophy, and was the author of at least one major text that expressed his thoughts. This text – the *Vaishesika Sutra* – dates from the early 2nd century BCE, but Kanada himself may have lived during a much earlier period.

Kanada has attracted attention for his theory that matter is composed of eternal indestructible atoms, which combine temporarily to form observable objects and phenomena. These atoms are of four kinds: earth, air, water, and light. Three atoms joined together form the smallest possible observable entity.

Kanada asserts that humans can gain knowledge of the world through perception and inference. His work includes empirical observations of a range of natural phenomena, including magnetism and the flow of liquids, for which he tries to provide causal explanations.

Kanada's account of the spiritual struggle to escape the cycle of birth and death is relatively conventional.

KEY WORKS: *Vaisheshika Sutra*, c.200 BCE

Pythagoras

c.570–c.495 BCE, GREEK

A mathematician and mystic, Pythagoras was born on the island of Samos in the eastern Aegean Sea. At some time around 530 BCE he moved to Croton, a Greek colony in southern Italy, where he established a religious community obeying a strict code of behaviour. Known as the *mathematikoi*, adherents were sworn to secrecy. They lived ascetically, were forbidden to eat meat or wear animal skins, and had to avoid the consumption of beans. Men and women were admitted on an equal basis and property was held in common.

Pythagoras taught a doctrine of reincarnation and transmigration of the soul (in Greek, *metempsychosis*), and believed that numbers (numerical ratios and mathematical axioms) were the basic constituents of the universe. According to him, the Earth was a sphere surrounded by heavenly bodies, which move in wider spheres that are related numerically, like the notes of harmonious music.

Pythagoras is credited with inventing mathematical deduction, in which new truths are evolved from self-evident principles. He may have died in a violent attack on his community by the people of Croton.

▷ Heraclitus

c.535–475 BCE, GREEK

The Greek thinker Heraclitus lived in the city of Ephesus, now in Turkey. He is known to have written a book of philosophy that was widely read in the ancient world, but only fragments of which – quoted by other writers – have survived to the present day.

Born into an aristocratic family, Heraclitus was melancholy and misanthropic, observing that "most men are bad". He believed that fire was the fundamental element. The world, which was eternal and had been created 'neither by gods nor men", existed in a state of perpetual flux. "You can never step into the same river twice," he stated, because the river was never the same between any two instants. He also held that the fusion of opposites was the essence of the world – "the way up and the way down are one and the same".

Heraclitus viewed war and strife as a necessary coming together of opposites and praised the use of punishment to force men to behave better. But no one could really change: "Character is destiny." It is said that he died after covering himself with cow dung to cure an illness.

△ **HERACLITUS, DETAIL FROM** *THE SCHOOL OF ATHENS*, **RAPHAEL, 1509–11**

Parmenides

c.515–445 BCE, GREEK

The philosopher Parmenides lived in the Greek colony of Elea in southern Italy. He was probably a pupil of Xenophanes (c.570–475 BCE), who became best known for nurturing the idea of monotheism.

The only work Parmenides is known to have written is a long poem, *On Nature*. Of its 800 verses, about 160 are known today through being quoted by other authors. The poem consists of two parts: "The Way of Truth" and "The Way of Opinion". The first part argues that the world is an unchanging whole, an indivisible One – nothing comes into being or passes away. The second part describes the illusory world that can be perceived. Parmenides founded the Eleatic school whose members included Zeno of Elea. Plato wrote a dialogue describing a fictional encounter between Zeno, Parmenides, and Socrates, but it is unclear whether Parmenides and Socrates ever actually met.

KEY WORKS: *On Nature*, c.475 BCE

Zeno of Elea

c.490–c.430 BCE, GREEK

According to Plato, the young Zeno travelled to Athens with Parmenides and engaged in debate with Socrates. Zeno's paradoxes, cited in the works of Aristotle, were intended to defend Parmenides' view that motion and change were an illusion. Zeno's paradox of Achilles and the tortoise claims to prove that in a race the fleet-footed hero could never overtake the slow-moving reptile. His paradox of the arrow demonstrates that an arrow in flight never moves, because at each instant it is still. Zeno allegedly conspired against Nearchus, the ruler of Elea. Arrested and tortured, Zeno succeeded in biting off the tyrant's ear before his captors killed him.

Mozi

470–430 BCE, CHINESE

Born in the kingdom of Lu in northern China, Mozi may have been a convict or enslaved. He trained as a carpenter and was later employed as a military engineer. His lowly origins and practical inclination led him to abandon Confucianism, with its emphasis on ritual, in favour of beliefs that were more appealing to China's artisan class. Mozi argued that conforming to traditional practices did not make a person's actions morally correct, and he sought an objective and pragmatic route to the setting of moral values.

Rejecting the Confucianist devotion to family and clan, Mozi advocated love for all humankind, teaching that "universal love is the way of heaven". His pragmatic ethics were based on advancing the general welfare of society. Whatever actions promoted social order, wealth, and population growth were virtuous. He urged rulers to show benevolence and avoid war.

Mozi attracted a large following and his teachings were collected in the eponymous *Mozi*, a book of 71 chapters, 53 of which survive. Initially a rival to Confucianism and Daoism, Mohism was repressed in the Qin dynasty (221–206 BCE) and never recovered.

▷ Democritus

c.460–c.370 BCE, GREEK

The philosopher and scientist Democritus was born at Abdera in Thrace, northern Greece. He belonged to a wealthy family, which reputedly hosted Persian King Xerxes during his retreat from an invasion of Greece in 480–479 BCE. This brought the young Democritus into contact with Persian *magi* (wise men) in Xerxes' entourage. He subsequently travelled widely in search of knowledge, studying mathematics in Egypt and voyaging as far as India. Returning to Abdera he studied natural phenomena and elaborated the atomic theory previously proposed by Leucippus, a philosopher from Miletus.

Democritus claimed that the universe consisted of an infinite number of varied atoms that were eternal, indestructible, and indivisible. He saw them as constantly in motion in a void, combining to form different substances. To him, there were many different worlds, each growing and decaying. Everything, Democritus claimed – including thought – "happens according to necessity" and is the result of physical causes. While this position was seemingly contrary to the notion of free will, Democritus wrote prodigiously on ethics and believed that people could make free choices, but within the parameters of his atomic determinism. Democritus wrote many works over his long life (some accounts indicate that he lived to the age of 104) but none has survived to the present day.

Yang Zhu

440–360 BCE, CHINESE

The thought of Yang Zhu, a philosopher of the Warring States period (475–221 BCE) in China, is known principally through a few anecdotes in the works of other philosophers – most of whom disapproved strongly of his ideas. Yang believed that each individual has a nature that it is his or her purpose

△ *THE CHEERFUL DEMOCRITUS*, CHARLES-ANTOINE COYPEL, 1746

to fulfil. In the face of inevitable death, the wise man would choose to seek pleasure and live life to the full. He thought that belief in duty to the state or the family was an error, and reportedly refused to perform military service himself.

The great Confucian sage Mencius said of Yang Zhu: "If by plucking one hair from his leg he might benefit the whole empire, he would not do it." Yang's motto was "Each for himself", meaning that an individual should avoid harming others but was under no moral obligation to act for others' benefit. His radical assertion of individualism posed a significant challenge to the mainstream of Chinese philosophy.

Sun Tzu

c.5TH–4TH CENTURY BCE, CHINESE

Sun Tzu is famous as the author of an ancient Chinese guide to military science and strategy, *The Art of War*, which embodies concepts that are akin to Daoism. Ancient Chinese historians described him as a general serving the kingdom of Wu in the 6th century BCE. However, recent analysis of military details in his famous book, for example its frequent mention of the use of crossbows, places its composition at a later date, during China's Warring States period (475–221 BCE), when skill in strategy and leadership was in high demand

as seven states fought for overall control of China. Sun Tzu advocates a subtle approach to warfare, in which knowledge of oneself and one's enemy is key and inaction is often preferable to action; he states that "to subdue the enemy without fighting is the acme of skill". Sun Tzu claims that the wise general, serene and capable of self-knowledge, will let his army flow around the enemy's strong points like water, only engaging in battle when the enemy's weakness makes victory certain.

Sun Tzu's thinking has been applied to business problems, such as how to gain market share while minimizing retaliation from competitors, and how to identify a competitor's weaknesses.

KEY WORKS: *The Art of War* (date uncertain)

Gongsun Long

c.325–c.250 BCE, CHINESE

Renowned for his teasing paradoxes, Gongsun Long is classified as a philosopher of the School of Names, a group of thinkers interested in logical and epistemological issues. A native of the kingdom of Zhao (now Shanxi province) in the Warring States period, he was an adviser at the royal court, who used his influence to aid peace. His anti-war stance suggests he may have been influenced by Mozi. His paradoxes appear in his collection of essays and dialogues the *Gongsun Longzi*. Six of its 14 chapters survive, including "On Pointing at Things", "On Hardness and Whiteness", "On Understanding Change", and "White Horses are not Horses".

Opinion is divided as to whether Gongsun was making serious philosophical points or simply sustaining apparently impossible propositions for amusement, as a demonstration of his skill in the manipulation of logic. He is cited as claiming proudly: "I confounded the wits of the hundred schools."

KEY WORKS: *Gongsun Longzi*, 300 BCE

▽ Xun Kuang

310–235 BCE, CHINESE

Xun Kuang, often known as Xunzi (meaning "Master Xun"), was a leading Confucian philosopher. Born in the kingdom of Zhao towards the end of the Warring States period, he travelled to the kingdom of Qi and studied at the prestigious Jixia academy, where he later became an influential teacher (his pupils included the Legalist philosopher Han Fei).

Unlike other Confucian thinkers, Xun Kuang believed humans were naturally bad in their behaviour and desires. Goodness could only be achieved through the practice of correct ritual and a conscious effort to follow the Way, the fixed moral path marked out by the ancients. He did not believe in the intervention of Heaven in human affairs. Humans made their own fortunes or misfortunes by choosing the right or wrong path. An erudite elite was needed to lead and educate ordinary people.

By the end of his life, Xunzi was considered the leading teacher of the Chinese world. He died in retirement in the kingdom of Chu. After his death his thoughts were collected in the *Xunzi*.

KEY WORKS: *Xunzi*, 1st century BCE

Han Fei

c.280–233 BCE, CHINESE

Han Fei was born into the ruling family of the kingdom of Han late in the Warring States period. After studying under Xun Kuang, he began to focus his thoughts on ending the existing disorder in China, applying his mind to the social and political problems that followed the collapse of the feudal system. A Legalist philosopher, he argued that appeals to personal morality or traditional wisdom could never create a strong, stable, and wealthy state. Instead he asserted that a ruler should exploit the self-interest of his immoral subjects, rigorously applying laws to force their selfishness to serve the state's interests, and severely punishing any disobedience.

In 234 BCE, Han Fei was sent to the kingdom of Qin, to dissuade its ruler King Zheng from attacking Han. Seeing Han Fei as a dangerous rival, Zheng's chief adviser Li Si had the king imprison him, then persuaded the incarcerated Han Fei to take poison. Zheng later became China's first emperor, using Han Fei's Legalist philosophy to guide his political innovations. Han Fei's collected writings, the *Han Feizi* (which run to 55 chapters), are among the most complete texts to survive from their period and are an important source for numerous anecdotes from the Warring States period.

KEY WORKS: *Han Feizi*, 3rd century BCE

Wang Chong

27–c.70 CE, CHINESE

Born into a modest family in modern-day Zhejiang province during the Han dynasty, philosopher Wang Chong was self-taught. Orphaned at an early age, he was sent to study at the Academy in Loyang. He was reportedly too poor to buy books and instead learned by reading texts in bookshops.

A quarrelsome anti-authoritarian character, he never held any official post for long. Invited late in life to become an adviser at the court of Emperor Zhang, he failed to turn up.

Wang Chong's major work consists of 80 essays collected as *Lunheng* (*Balanced Discussions*). Probably written between 60–70 CE, they cover topics ranging from astronomy and meteorology to government and morality. Wang's account of the world is mechanistic and materialist, and he provides a critique of Confucian texts and popular superstitions, refuting them through rational analysis and observation. He rejects the Confucian notion that virtue is the key to success for ordinary individuals or rulers, seeing luck and destiny as decisive in life. His writings gained a wider readership only after his death.

KEY WORKS: *Lunheng (Balanced Discussions)*, c.60–70 CE

Plotinus

204–270 CE, GREEK

The Neoplatonist philosopher Plotinus was born – according to the account of his student Porphyry – at Lycopolis in Egypt, which was then a province of the Roman Empire. His ethnicity is uncertain, but he spoke and wrote in Greek. He took up philosophy at the age of 27, and travelled to Alexandria, a great centre of learning, where he read the works of Plato and Aristotle. However, it was his introduction to the teacher Ammonias Saccas that shaped his philosophical thought and kindled an interest in Persian and Indian teachings.

In 243 Plotinus joined an expedition to Asia that was led by the Roman emperor Gordian III. After Gordian was killed in Mesopotamia, Plotinus abandoned his quest for the wisdom of the East and returned to Rome, teaching and writing philosophy.

Building on the works of Plato, Plotinus created a metaphysical hierarchy of three non-material realities: the unknowable One; Spirit or Intellect; and Soul. To him, the aim of life was to free oneself by contemplation of the delusory restraints of material existence. His thoughts became a major influence on Christian and Muslim philosophy.

KEY WORKS: *The Enneads*, c.270 CE

△ XUN KUANG

MEDIEVAL

CHAPTER 2

▷ **BOETHIUS PANEL**
A 15th-century panel, thought to be by the Spanish painter Pedro Berruguete, depicts a contemplative Boethius. He was the last Western scholar with first-hand knowledge of Greek philosophy until the rediscovery of ancient learning in the 12th century.

Boethius

c.475/480–c.525 CE, ROMAN

Boethius was one of the last great philosophers of the classical age. For centuries, his translations, commentaries, and writings provided scholars with an invaluable link to the learning of the ancient world.

> "In other **living things** to be **ignorant** of the **self** is **natural**; but in **man** it is **a defect**."
>
> BOETHIUS, *THE CONSOLATION OF PHILOSOPHY*

Boethius was born into the chaotic aftermath of the Fall of Rome. After the city itself was taken by the Barbarians in 476 CE, leadership of the remaining Roman territories passed to the emperor in the East, in Constantinople. Much of Italy was soon under the control of a Germanic tribe, the Ostrogoths (East Goths), whose leader, Theodoric the Great, was proclaimed king in 493 CE (see box, right). For many years, Theodoric maintained peaceful relations with the East, acting as a form of viceroy for the emperor, but their relationship was always an uneasy one.

Public office

Boethius came from an aristocratic Roman family that was accustomed to high office. His father had been a consul and Boethius followed in his footsteps; in addition, Theodoric appointed him as his *magister officiorum* (head of the civil service), and it is remarkable that Boethius was able to combine his political duties

with his philosophical research. After his father's death, Boethius was educated by his wealthy guardian, Memmius Symmachus. In common with most patrician families, Symmachus saw no contradiction in being a Christian and studying the philosophers of pagan antiquity and, as a result, Boethius became extremely well versed in classical Greek texts. His works included translations and commentaries on Plato and Aristotle, and philosophical attempts to reconcile their different viewpoints; he also wrote handbooks on the *quadrivium* – the four mathematical disciplines (arithmetic, geometry, music, astronomy) – that formed a major part of the teaching curriculum.

In around 522 CE, the political climate changed as growing tensions with the East made Theodoric suspicious of his Roman

◁ **COMMEMORATIVE DIPTYCH**
Elaborate ivory panels were often commissioned to honour Roman officials. This diptych shows Boethius's father, who became consul – a position later awarded to Boethius.

◁ **IMPRISONMENT IN PAVIA**
This illustration from a 1385 edition of Boethius's *The Consolation of Philosophy* shows the author in jail; he was later executed for conspiracy.

ministers. Boethius was arrested, imprisoned, and eventually executed. During his confinement, he wrote his masterpiece, *The Consolation of Philosophy*, in which the author bemoans his fate and is visited in prison by the personification of Philosophy. She chides him gently, reminding him that Fortune is an ever-turning wheel and that the earthly gifts she brings will not last long. The wise man can find true happiness only by searching for the ultimate Goodness, which she equates with God; this leads to an examination of the nature of God and time.

A classic work

The book was written in a classical format: Boethius speaks in prose and Philosophy answers in verse. It raises many questions, not least because the consolation provided by Philosophy is not exactly Christian, but closer to a form of pantheism. It may be that Boethius hoped this approach would attract a wide audience, or he may simply have been anxious to avoid antagonizing Theodoric. *The Consolation* proved a great success, spawning hundreds of manuscripts in most European languages. Alfred the Great and Geoffrey Chaucer were just two of its many translators.

IN PROFILE
Theodoric the Great

Theodoric was born in the Roman province of Pannonia (near the border of modern Austria and Hungary) in 454 CE, the son of an Ostrogothic chieftain. As a boy, he was taken to the city of Constantinople and held hostage to ensure the compliance of the Ostrogoths to Byzantine rule. His knowledge of Byzantine ways helped him to form good relations with the East and he was encouraged by the Eastern Roman emperor, Zeno, to supplant the troublesome Odoacer, then king of Italy. The alliance between Zeno and Theodoric was eventually undermined by religious differences. The Ostrogoths were Arians – Christian heretics – and when a later emperor began to persecute this sect, Theodoric retaliated by taking measures against the Christians in the West. Boethius was one of many who suffered.

CONTEMPORARY GOLD COIN STAMPED WITH AN IMAGE OF THEODORIC

Ibn Sīnā

980–1037, UZBEKISTAN

Ibn Sīnā was a philosopher and physician who lived at the turn of the 10th century during the Islamic Golden Age. He is acknowledged as one of the most important Islamic thinkers in history.

Ibn Sīnā, often known in the West as Avicenna (the Latinized version of his shorter name), was born Abū Alī al-Husayn ibn Abd Allāh in a village near Bukhara, in present-day Uzbekistan. He was the son of a governor of the Samanid Empire – a Sunni emirate that at its height encompassed much of modern Afghanistan, as well as areas of Iran, Tajikistan, Kyrgyzstan, Pakistan Turkmenistan, and Kazakhstan.

Ibn Sīnā became famous not only as one of the leading philosophers of the Arab tradition, but also as a physician and a natural scientist. A polymath, his extraordinary body of work ranges from astronomy and physics to geography, psychology, music, and mathematics.

A child prodigy

Ibn Sīnā's many biographies, as well as his autobiography – which he dictated to his student al-Jūzjanī – reveal him to be a person of many talents, with an insatiable appetite for learning. By the time he was 10 years old he had memorized the Koran in its entirety, and by his teenage years had begun his studies in philosophy, medicine, and jurisprudence.

While he is said to have found philosophy perplexing, the study of medicine apparently came easily

to him. By the age of 18, Ibn Sīnā had become so well respected for his medical expertise that he was called upon to treat Nuh ibn Mansur, the sultan of Bukhara, whose ailment had baffled his physicians.

His successful treatment of the sultan gained Ibn Sīnā access to the magnificent Samanid court and its extraordinarily rich library. It was here that he read Arabic translations of Greek and Indian philosophy, as well as Babylonian texts, early Islamic commentaries and textual criticism, and works on engineering, physics, logic, psychology, engineering, and

mathematics. He thrived in this scholarly environment and wrote his first work at the age of just 21.

Departure from Bukhara

Political upheaval led to the decline of Samanid rule and the rise of the Ghaznavid dynasty. In around 1004, Ibn Sīnā left Bukhara and travelled westwards in search of sympathetic patronage. Even without access to a library, his remarkable memory allowed him to continue to think and write on the move, until he finally settled in Isfahan, where he remained until his death.

▷ **IBN SINA**
This portrait of Ibn Sīnā from a 14th-century illuminated manuscript shows the physician-philosopher crowned, in his later years. The script above his head reads "Avicenna" – the Latinized name by which he is best known in the West.

IN CONTEXT
The Islamic Golden Age

The Islamic Golden Age traditionally refers to the period from the 8th to the 13th centuries, from 762 CE – when Baghdad was established as the capital of the Abbasidic caliphate – to the Siege of Baghdad in 1258. This was a period of tremendous cultural and artistic richness and philosophical innovation. The work of philosophers and translators from the Islamic Golden Age also played a key role in helping to transmit Greek philosophy to the West.

MEDIEVAL ARABIC DEPICTION OF THE GREEK THINKER ARISTOTLE TEACHING

> "The **knowledge** of **anything**, since **all things** have **causes**, is **not acquired** or **complete** unless **it is known** by its **causes**."
>
> IBN SINA

Uicenna

Elementa sunt
quatuoz. ignis. aer.
aqua. terra. Ignis
caldus et hymidus.
aqua frigida et hu
mida. tra frigida et
sicca. Cominctiones
nonē sf. vm. eqles.
et vna equalis. de
equalibus. Uere
quatuoz simplices
si caldum et frig
vum. humoum et
siccum. et itu
oz ex his co
posita.

Dos belemens sob st
.s. lo foc z la er zlaygua
zla terra. lo foc es cart
et sec. lo aer es caut z
hunu. laigua es fie
da et humida. la ten
es freida et socca. lae
gnuxtion sob .iv. les
.vm. sut equals. z
vna egual. de aqude
sb'egual. les sob siph
.s. caut z freit hum
z sec z les autres. ii
sont opostes da qles.

"So **I continued** until I had made myself **master of all the sciences**; I now **comprehended them** to the **limits** of **human possibility**. "

IBN SINA

IN PROFILE
Galen

The physician and philosopher Galen, or Aelius Galenus (c.130–c.216 CE), had a significant influence on Ibn Sīnā's work. Galen was born in the Greek city of Pergamon, and later moved to Rome, where he worked for a while as physician to the emperor and philosopher Marcus Aurelius (see pp.52–53). Galen's medical works were translated into Arabic at the beginning of the Islamic Golden Age. Like Ibn Sīnā, Galen saw the roles of the physician (who cures the body) and the philosopher (who cures the soul) as intimately linked.

MINIATURE FROM GALEN'S *BOOK OF ANTIDOTES*, 1199

Major works

Of Ibn Sīnā's several hundred works, two are of particular significance in the history of thought: his epic, five-volume medical textbook, known as the *Canon of Medicine*, which was completed around 1025, and his major philosophical publication, *The Book of Healing* (often referred to as *The Cure*), which was published in 1027.

The first of these works, the *Canon*, drew together Ibn Sīnā's extensive experience as a physician and also his extensive knowledge of the medical tradition – in particular, the work of the Greek physician Galen (see box, left). The *Canon* was widely used in Europe until the 18th century, and is a testimony to the author's learning, as well as to his great powers of observation: not only is it the first text to clearly describe the symptoms of anthrax, but it is also one of the very first examples of evidence-based medicine.

This concern with health is also central to Ibn Sīnā's approach to philosophy, as outlined in his second major work, *The Book of Healing*. For him, philosophy was a therapeutic discipline, curing the ignorance of the soul in much the same way that medicine seeks to cure the sickness of the body. *The Book of Healing* drew together both Arabic and Greek philosophical sources, including Aristotle, Al-Kindī, and Al-Fārābī. It is

thought that Ibn Sīnā wrote much of this text from memory, without access to any books whatsoever.

The Floating Man

In one of his experiments, Ibn Sīnā set out to determine what we can know of ourselves if we are deprived of our senses. To do this he devised the idea of a man floating in mid-air: the man is blindfolded, with his arms out to either side so that he is not touching anything – he has no sensory input and therefore no perception whatsoever of his body, the outside world, or indeed of any physicality.

According to Ibn Sīnā, if we can imagine that the man retains a perception of himself, despite this sensory deprivation, it follows that what we "are", our sense of self, exists independently of our bodies and our senses. This theory does not prove the existence of the soul, but it does suggest that the self or the "I" may conceivably be distinct from, and exist independently of, the body.

Ibn Sīnā's Floating Man resembles Descartes' "mind/body dualism", as expressed some 600 years later in Descartes' famous assertion, "I think, therefore I am" (see p.120).

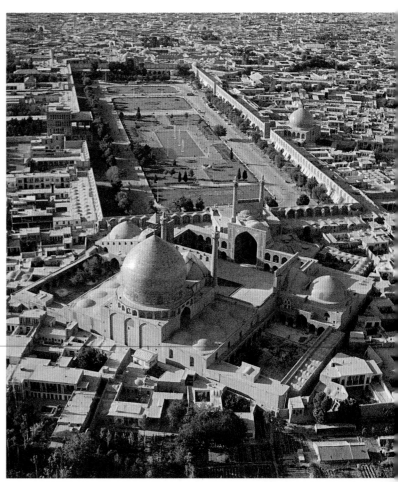

▷ **AERIAL VIEW OF ISFAHAN**
In 1021, following political turmoil in Bukhara, Ibn Sīnā settled in Isfahan. The magnificent Shah Mosque, just one of the city's many architectural masterpieces, is shown here.

◁ **THOMAS AQUINAS**

◁ **THOMAS AQUINAS**
The medieval thinker Thomas Aquinas (1225–74), shown here in a painting by Andrea di Bartolo (1368–1428), was influenced by Ibn Sīnā's "contingency argument" concerning God's existence.

Contingency argument

According to Ibn Sīnā, God is at the centre of all things – everything emanates from God as a result of his self-willing – and he formulated an interesting and influential argument in support of the creator's existence.

Ibn Sīnā claimed that things can be impossible (a square circle, for example), or possible but contingent (they exist, but do not have to exist), or possible and necessary (they exist out of necessity). Things that exist but do not have to (because it is imaginable that things could have been otherwise) include Ibn Sīnā, you, me, my cat, Ibn Sīnā's cat, and so on. In other words, whether each of these things exists depends on the existence of other things. However, if everything exists only contingently, then nothing need exist at all. Therefore, when we trace back this chain of causes, we eventually arrive at a necessary existent upon which all others things depend – and that necessary existent is God.

Death and influence

Some of the traditional biographies suggest that Ibn Sīnā's death was caused by an obstruction in the large intestine (a condition that the philosopher had written about in his *Treatise on Colic*), brought on by an overindulgence in sex. It is true that Ibn Sīnā had an immense liking for sex, food, and wine (which helped him write long into the night), and that he hosted debauched drinking parties to round off a day of philosophical discussion. However, more recent scholarship maintains that the suggestion he died from too much sex is implausible, both medically and historically, and is doubtless the result of later writers tampering with the accounts of his life.

Ibn Sīnā is believed to have written more than 400 works in his lifetime; around 250 have survived, and of these some 100 are philosophical texts. He is known to have been read by Thomas Aquinas, among many others, and his work was important not only in the Islamic world, but also in the rediscovery of Aristotle and Greek philosophy and logic in the West, and in the shaping of Jewish and Christian philosophy. Many scholars consider Ibn Sīnā to be one of the most important medieval philosophers – a towering figure in Islamic thought.

△ *CANON OF MEDICINE*, **TITLE PAGE**
Ibn Sīnā's five-volume *Canon of Medicine*, which he completed in 1025, covers human anatomy and a wide range of symptoms and diseases; it also includes important compendia of medicines.

KEY WORKS

c.1003
Writes *Philosophy for the Prosodist*, which focuses on metaphysics and Aristotelian philosophy.

1025
Completes the five-volume *Canon of Medicine*, the most important of his medical publications.

1027
Publishes *The Book of Healing*, his epic philosophical text, which draws upon the work of Aristotle.

1030
His philosophical work *Pointers and Reminders* discusses both logic and metaphysics.

▷ **ANSELM OF CANTERBURY**
This 12th-century stained-glass window from Norwich Cathedral in Norfolk shows Henry I kneeling before Anselm of Canterbury. The two came into conflict when the king claimed the right to grant spiritual jurisdiction to the clergy.

St Anselm

1033–1109, ITALIAN

Anselm was an influential philosopher and theologian, widely known as "the Father of the Scholastic tradition". As archbishop of Canterbury, he was also a staunch defender of the rights of the Church.

IN PROFILE
Lanfranc

Lanfranc was Anselm's mentor and his predecessor at Canterbury. Born in the Italian town of Pavia, he studied in France and became prior of the monastery of Bec in around 1045. Lanfranc soon earned the patronage of Duke William (the Conqueror), who appointed him archbishop of Canterbury in 1070. It is possible that he presented the case for invading England to the pope. Lanfranc was primarily a theologian, asserting the superiority of faith over secular reasoning, but he also wrote a book on logic (now lost) and was one of the first to examine the links between philosophy and grammatical analysis.

LANFRANC, DEPICTED IN AN 18TH-CENTURY PAINTING

> " I do not **seek to understand** in order to **believe**, but **I believe** in order that **I might understand**. "

ANSELM, *PROSLOGION*

Born in Aosta, in present-day Italy, Anselm was of noble descent. He could have chosen a life of comfort managing the family estates, but decided instead to pursue a career in the Church. After a period of travelling, he entered the thriving Benedictine monastery of Bec, in Normandy.

Bec was garnering a reputation as a centre of learning, largely through the efforts of Lanfranc, its charismatic prior, who exerted a huge influence on the young Anselm. When Lanfranc left in 1063, Anselm succeeded him as prior and continued his work. After Lanfranc's death, Anselm took up his late mentor's prestigious post as archbishop of Canterbury.

Conflict with the Crown

Anselm became archbishop at a critical period in the history of the English Church. Its role and structure had been radically transformed after the Norman invasion of 1066, and he had to contend with the displeasure of the displaced early medieval clerics and with the ambitions of the new regime, which sought to control every aspect of the Church.

Throughout his career at Canterbury, there were frequent clashes with the Crown over matters of jurisdiction. These disputes became so bitter that Anselm had to endure two periods of exile (1097–1100 and 1103–1107). The quarrels continued long after his death, eventually leading to the murder of a future archbishop of Canterbury, Thomas Becket, in 1170.

Anselm's turbulent life in England disrupted his scholarly interests, and he produced his most important writings in the calmer surroundings of Bec. In these works, Anselm laid the foundations of the philosophical method that became known as Scholasticism – a teaching system adopted by Church schools and universities from the latter part of the 11th century. Students were educated through a combination of religious doctrine and the works on philosophy and logic by Aristotle and other ancient authors.

Anselm made it plain that he valued faith more highly than reason, but sought to buttress this faith with rational arguments. His key texts in this respect were the *Soliloquy* (1076) and the *Proslogion* (1077–78). In the former, he put forward his "cosmological" theory (the idea that all natural things depend on some greater external force for their existence), while the latter contained his celebrated "ontological argument". This states that if we can accept the idea of God as "something than which nothing greater can be conceived", then he must exist in reality; for, if God only existed in our understanding, then something greater could be conceived (the reality of God) and that would be a contradiction. This deceptively simple argument sparked off a philosophical debate that continued for centuries, and cemented Anselm's reputation as the most influential thinker of his age.

△ **WILLIAM II (RUFUS)**
Anselm was pressured into becoming archbishop of Canterbury by the king, William Rufus, pictured here in the 13th-century *Historia Anglorum*. Disagreements between the two soon escalated, and Anselm was effectively exiled to Rome and his revenues seized by the king.

▷ **BEC ABBEY, NORMANDY**
The Benedictine Abbey of Bec, where Anselm studied and became prior, was founded in 1034, at the time of William the Conqueror.

Héloïse

c.1101–1164, FRENCH

Although famed for her love affair with Peter Abelard, Héloïse was an influential thinker in her own right. Her celebrated letters reveal a fine scholar and philosopher, and a pioneer of feminist thought.

Héloïse was both niece and ward of Fulbert, a canon at Notre-Dame in Paris. Little is known of her parents, but some speculate that her mother may have been a nun. The girl was educated at a convent in Argenteuil, outside Paris, where she showed great promise in her studies of Latin, Greek, and Hebrew, prompting Fulbert to invite her into his home and hire Peter Abelard (1079–1142) as her tutor.

Abelard already had a considerable reputation in the Paris schools as a brilliant, if controversial, teacher. While living under Fulbert's roof, he began a clandestine affair with his star pupil (who may have been as young as 15). Their secret was revealed when Héloïse became pregnant.

Tragedy and separation

The consequences of the affair were dire. Héloïse gave birth to a boy called Astrolabe. Abelard agreed to Fulbert's demand that he marry her, but asked him to keep the wedding secret to protect his own reputation; Fulbert went back on his word and made the marriage public. Abelard sent his wife back to Argenteuil, still hoping to conceal the truth, but Fulbert mistakenly believed that the seducer was planning to abandon Héloïse, so he exacted a terrible revenge. One night, his henchmen broke into Abelard's room and castrated him.

After this, the lovers separated and retired into the Church; Héloïse became a nun at Argenteuil, while Abelard became a monk at the abbey of Saint-Denis.

Many accounts end their narrative at this point, but in fact the couple were later reunited for a time. In 1122, Abelard founded an oratory in Champagne, which he dedicated to the Holy Spirit. Seven years later, he invited Héloïse – by now a prioress – to establish a new community there, after she and her nuns were expelled from Argenteuil.

The couple's celebrated letters date from the early 1130s, when Abelard was back teaching in Paris. The correspondence demonstrates that their love for each other was as strong as ever, but it also offers an insight into Héloïse's strong-minded outlook. In the early letters, she expresses a feminist philosophy that was centuries ahead of its time, denouncing the institution of marriage as little more than a legalized form of sex work. In the later correspondence, she collaborated with Abelard in drawing up guidelines for the organization of her new community. Héloïse often took the lead in these discussions, demonstrating how the Benedictine Rule needed to be adapted to suit the needs of her women. Her arguments produced tangible results as the community thrived under her leadership, expanding into several new daughter-houses (dependencies).

◁ **HELOISE**
Héloïse has emerged as a woman of power and insight, as well as a tragic lover. Artists have reinterpreted her image over the centuries as a mirror for their own times.

◁ **THE LOVERS' TOMB**
A decorative canopy built in 1817 covers the tomb of Abelard and Héloïse in Paris's Père Lachaise cemetery. The tomb became a shrine for forlorn lovers.

IN CONTEXT
The legend of Abelard and Héloïse

Even though Abelard and Héloïse were among the most prominent intellectuals and religious thinkers of 12th-century France, they have been remembered as the archetypal tragic lovers, whose attempt to reconcile their emotions with their monastic duties is so touchingly recorded in their letters. This portrayal dates back to the 13th century, when Jean de Meun included them in his section of the *Romance of the Rose*. Since then, the couple's story has inspired poems, plays, novels, and films. These range from Alexander Pope's plaintive verse epistle *Eloisa to Abelard* (1717) to Jean-Jacques Rousseau's fictional bestseller *Julie, ou la nouvelle Héloïse* (1761); and from the biopic *Stealing Heaven* (1988) to the puppet sequence in the film *Being John Malkovich* (1999).

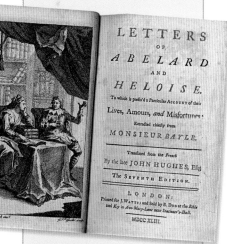

COPY OF THE *LETTERS OF ABELARD AND HELOÏSE*, 1743

Hildegard of Bingen

1098–1179, GERMAN

Hildegard was one of the most extraordinary women of her age. Dubbed "the Sibyl of the Rhine", she was a visionary, a mystic, a composer, and a writer on subjects ranging from cosmology to medicine.

Hildegard was probably born in Bermersheim, in the Rhineland. As the tenth child in her family, she was offered by her wealthy landowning parents to the Church – a common practice at the time. In 1106, she was placed in the care of a noblewoman, Jutta of Spanheim, who was entrusted with her religious education. They lived on Jutta's estate before becoming recluses at the monastery of Disibodenberg. A convent established there, and headed by Jutta, became Hildegard's home for many years.

From a very early age, Hildegard experienced visions. A fiery light possessed her, leaving her unable to move, but giving her moments of intense spiritual insight. She initially kept silent about these episodes, only revealing them later in her life.

Visionary works

On Jutta's death in 1136, Hildegard succeeded her as abbess and soon began recording her visions, aided by her secretary, a monk called Volmar. Three remarkable theological manuscripts resulted: *Scivias* (*Know the Way*, 1141–51); the *Book of Life's Merits* (1158–63); and the *Book of Divine Works* (1163–74).

Scivias is the best known of the three, partly because the original manuscript contained striking illustrations, possibly by Hildegard herself. It includes many passages of apocalyptic imagery and deals with the themes of creation, redemption, and salvation. *Life's Merits* is crafted as a dialogue between virtue and vice, while *Divine Works* includes Hildegard's highly controversial cosmological theories.

Hildegard wisely sought the approval of Bernard of Clairvaux – the most famous churchman of the day – before she published her visions. She soon became famous and attracted so many new converts that she founded another convent at Rupertsberg, near Bingen. She also took the unprecedented step of embarking on preaching tours in Germany.

Music and life

Hildegard was modest about her writings, insisting that she was barely educated and relied on Volmar to correct her work. This may have been a deliberate strategy to allow her voice to be heard in an overwhelmingly patriarchal organization.

The breadth of Hildegard's work is impressive. She was a pioneering composer who saw music as "the sacred sound through which all creation resounds". Her liturgical pieces are quite unlike contemporary plainchant and she even produced a kind of opera – *Ordo Virtutum*, a morality play set to music. In addition, she was fearless in her dealings with the outside world. She had no qualms about writing to the emperor, scolding him for his support of antipopes (see box, right), and she challenged an interdict (religious punishment) imposed by the bishop of Mainz.

IN CONTEXT
Political strife

Hildegard's career coincided with a period of bitter conflict between Germany and the papacy. The most divisive issue was lay investiture – the practice of secular figures controlling major ecclesiastical appointments. Pope Gregory VII clashed with the king, Henry IV, over this abuse in the late 11th century and the dispute persisted for decades. Ultimately, it prompted the German ruler, Frederick Barbarossa (1122–90), to invade Italy and to support a succession of antipopes (unofficial popes) during Pope Alexander III's term of office (1159–81). Hildegard took an active interest in these matters, writing a number of letters to Barbarossa.

RELIQUARY BUST OF FREDERICK BARBAROSSA, 12TH CENTURY

◁ **RECORDING THE DIVINE**
In this contemporary illustration, Hildegard is shown receiving a vision in the presence of her secretary, Volmar (who was the prior at the monastery of Disibodenberg), and her close friend and confidante, Richardis von Stade.

▷ **HILDEGARD**
Hildegard has been hailed as a proto-feminist. She challenged the inferior status of women in her time, and subverted the power of the patriarchy both in ecclesiatical matters and in her novel approach to musical composition.

Auerdys

Ego crç nõ gmedo niſi ut unuas

elt ouobç n
unuiſali
magıç h

ⁿ⊳ **IBN RUSHD IN DISCUSSION**
A detail from the 14th-century book *Liber de Herbis* by Monfredo de Monte Imperiali shows Ibn Rushd in an imaginary debate with Porphyry of Tyre, a 3rd-century CE Neoplatonic philosopher.

Ibn Rushd

1126–1198, SPANISH

Ibn Rushd was a philosopher from Córdoba who combined Greek and Islamic thought, arguing for harmony between reason and religion. He was instrumental in reintroducing Aristotle into European philosophy.

"Truth does not contradict truth but rather is consistent with it and testifies to it."

IBN RUSHD, *THE DECISIVE TREATISE*

The philosopher now known as Ibn Rushd (also Latinized to Averroës), was born in the Spanish city of Córdoba in the year 1126. His full name was Abu al-Walid Muhammad ibn Ahmad ibn Muhammad ibn Rushd. His father and grandfather were judges, and he continued the family tradition by training in Islamic jurisprudence while also studying both medicine and philosophy.

High office and exile

In the 12th century, much of Iberia was under the control of the Almohads, an Islamic revivalist dynasty. Ibn Rushd's family had close connections with the Almohad caliphs; these ties were cemented when Ibn Rushd moved to Marrakesh and was introduced to the second caliph, Abu Ya'qub Yusuf, by Ibn Tufayl (see box, right). The caliph, an accomplished scholar in his own right, was evidently impressed by his encounter with Ibn Rushd, appointing him to the position of judge in Seville and commissioning him to

IN PROFILE
Ibn Tufayl

Ibn Tufayl (c.1109–1185) was the philosopher, writer, and polymath who introduced Ibn Rushd to the Almohad caliph. He served the caliph and argued for Ibn Rushd to be his successor. His most famous work is the philosophical novel *Hayy ibn Yaqdhan*. It tells the story of a boy who is brought up alone on an equatorial island by an antelope. Through his close studies of the natural world, the boy becomes a philosopher. He is eventually rescued from the island, and goes on to teach others his deep knowledge of philosophy.

write extensive commentaries explaining the work of the renowned Ancient Greek philosopher Aristotle.

From 1169, Ibn Rushd began to produce a series of analyses of Aristotle's thinking. Their clarity made them hugely influential in the history of philosophy. They were translated into Latin and read by Thomas Aquinas, who was so impressed that he referred to Ibn Rushd simply as "the commentator" (even though he disagreed with him on many points).

Ibn Rushd was elevated to even higher office in 1182, when he was appointed as both court physician and chief judge in his home town of Córdoba – a position that put him at the very heart of the Almohad court.

However, when the second caliph died in 1184 and was succeeded by his son, Ibn Rushd gradually began to lose his standing. In 1195, at the urging of conservative figures in the court, he was sent into exile in the village of Lucena and all his books were burned. He was reinstated at the court two years later, but died in Marrakesh in 1198.

On philosophy

Ibn Rushd wrote widely on medicine, law, and theology, but some of his most original texts were those written in defence of philosophy. One such text is a response to the theologian Al-Ghazali's (c.1058–1111) critique of philosophy, *The Incoherence of the Philosophers*. Al-Ghazali argued for faith over reason, and attempted to systematically refute the work of Ibn Sīnā (see pp.70–73). In direct response, Ibn Rushd wrote *The Incoherence of the Incoherence*, arguing not only that religion and philosophy were complementary, but that the truths of philosophy and of scripture must be in harmony.

△ **IBN RUSHD COMMENTARY**
Ibn Rushd wrote numerous commentaries on philosophical and scientific tracts. This is the colophon (publisher's page) from his commentary on *Poem on Medicine*, an Arabic text from the Middle Ages that set out the principles and practices of medicine.

◁ **GREAT MOSQUE, CORDOBA**
Ibn Rushd worshipped at the Mezquita, Córdoba's magnificent 8th-century CE mosque. His grandfather, Abu al-Walid Muhammad, had been the imam there under the Almoravid dynasty.

Zhu Xi

1130–1200, CHINESE

Zhu Xi developed the hugely influential system of philosophy known in the West as Neo-Confucianism, and laid the groundwork for the traditional Chinese education system that remained in place until 1905.

△ **PALACE EXAMINATION**
This Song dynasty painting (960 BCE–1279 CE) shows students sitting imperial China's highly competitive civil service exams in the hope of eventually being appointed as administrative officials.

Zhu Xi is revered as one of the most important Chinese Confucian philosophers; some put him in second place only to Confucius. He lived during the Song dynasty (960 BCE–1279 CE), and was responsible for bringing together the far-reaching system of thought that is known in the West as Neo-Confucianism, but in China as *daoxue*. This term means "the Study of Dao", which might bring to mind the separate philosophical tradition of Daoism: however, the idea of "dao", meaning "way" or "path", is one that is shared between several Chinese schools of thought, among them Confucianism, and is not the sole property of the Daoist traditions.

Education and career

Zhu Xi, also known as Master Zhu, was born the son of a local official in Youxi, in what is now Fujian province. His family were not from Youxi, but his father had been exiled there in 1127, after the end of the Northern Song dynasty. Zhu Xi was initially educated by his father, and from the outset displayed an unusual intellectual

◁ **ZHU XI**
An active scholar and teacher, Zhu Xi made significant contributions not only to philosophy but also to history and literary criticism.

curiosity. At the age of five, he is said to have asked what lay beyond the heavens – a question that none of his elders or betters could answer to his satisfaction.

When Zhu Xi was just 13 years old, his father died, and a number of his father's friends took up the responsibility for continuing his education. The variety of teachers to whom he had access gave the young Zhu Xi an extremely broad range of intellectual influences, from all three of the great traditions of Chinese thought: Buddhism, Daoism, and Confucianism.

Zhu Xi passed the imperial scholars' examinations at the early age of 19. This was a staggering achievement because the average age for passing the exams was 35, and many candidates studied for their entire lives without ever succeeding. A scholar of Zhu Xi's evident talents could have risen to high office, but he held only two significant public posts –

IN CONTEXT
The Four Books and Five Classics

The Four Books and Five Classics are the major early canonical texts of Confucianism. They cover a wide range of topics, including philosophy, literature, economics, politics, art, science, and technology. The Four Books include edited conversations of Confucius and a collection of thoughts of the philosopher Mencius. Unlike some of his predecessors, Zhu Xi took the Four Books as the most important foundation of Confucian learning. The Five Classics are the *Odes*, the *Spring and Autumn Annals*, the *Documents*, the *Rites*, and the *Classic of Changes*. They initially formed part of the curriculum for the entrance exams to the Chinese imperial bureaucracy.

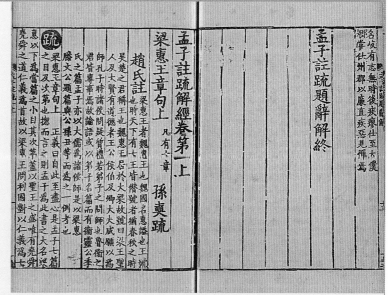

TITLE PAGE OF A COPY OF *MENCIUS* FROM c.1201–1204

" The **nature** [of mind] is **tranquil** while **feelings** are **active**, and the **mind involves** both **tranquillity** and **activity**. "

ZHU XI, IN WING-TSIT CHAN, "THE GREAT SYNTHESIS IN CHU HSI", *A SOURCE BOOK IN CHINESE PHILOSOPHY*

IN PROFILE
The Two Chengs

The brothers Cheng Hao (1032–85) and Cheng Yi (1033–1107) are often referred to as the "Two Chengs". They were two of the most important figures in the development of Neo-Confucianism, and had an enormous influence on Zhu Xi. The Cheng brothers were the first to argue for the fundamental role played by *li*, or principle. Of the two brothers, the younger Cheng Yi was more argumentative: his life was longer than that of Cheng Hao, but more turbulent. More than once, Cheng Yi found his teachings banned, although before his death he was eventually pardoned.

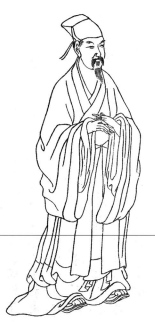

△ **LI TONG**
In 1160, Zhu Xi spent several months studying with the Neo-Confucian scholar Li Tong, who had a major influence on the development of his ideas.

first as subprefectural registrar of Tong'an (1153–56) and then as prefect of Nankang Military District (1179–82). His short tenures reflected his somewhat awkward character and his tendency to send letters to the emperor protesting about policies with which he disagreed.

From 1153, Zhu Xi studied under the Confucian philosopher Li Tong, and in 1160 formally became his student. Instead of continuing in public life, he opted to make a modest living as a temple guardian and devoted himself to becoming a sage through practising his philosophy.

Diverse writings
Free from the demands of his official post, Zhu Xi devoted himself entirely to writing and scholarship – his recorded sayings are no less than 300 scrolls long. As well as writing philosophical commentaries, strident letters, and a famous work called the *Jia Li*, or the *Book of Family Rituals* (a kind of Confucian etiquette guide for the family), Zhu Xi also wrote extensively on history, reworking a classic text, the *Zizhi tongjian*, so that it would better illustrate moral principles in government. He also left behind more than 1,400 poems on a wide range of subjects.

Towards the end of Zhu Xi's life, his outspokenness led to him being officially censured as a peddler of "false learning", and some even called for his execution. Nevertheless, this did not impact his popularity: when he died in 1200, almost 1,000 people attended his funeral.

Zhu Xi's reputation was rehabilitated soon after his death and he became a significant influence on Chinese thought and government in the 13th century. In 1313, the emperor Renzhong placed his system of

philosophy at the very heart of the imperial examination system, cementing Zhu Xi's legacy.

Neo-Confucianism
The term "Neo-Confucianism" was popularized by the philosopher Feng Youlan (1895–1990) in his influential history of Chinese philosophy, but its development can be traced back many hundreds of years.

Confucianism became the official state philosophy in China during the Han dynasty (206 BCE–220 CE), when thousands of academies were established to spread the ideology across the Chinese empire.

However, the disorderly decline of the Han helped to discredit their ideology too, and Confucianism became overshadowed by Daoism and Buddhism, both of which benefited from imperial patronage.

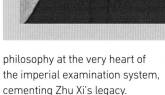

△ **EMPEROR NINGZONG**
After Zhu Xi's death, the Song emperor recognized his achievements and honoured him with the name Wen Gong ("Venerable gentleman of culture").

Confucianism began to re-emerge in a revitalized form centuries later, in the Song dynasty. The Confucian classics were revived, and Chinese thinkers rediscovered a doctrine dealing with the inner life of the mind, sagehood, and self-cultivation; Neo-Confucianism gradually began to supplant the "foreign" influence of Buddhism.

Zhu Xi was a key figure in the development of Neo-Confucian philosophy, and his great achievement was to draw together the work of five of his eminent predecessors: Shao Yong, Zhou Dunyi, Zhang Zai, and the two brothers Cheng Hao

"There is no **fixed shape** to the preservation of **perfect balance**. "
ZHU XI

"In the universe there has never been any material force (*qi*) without principle (*li*) or principle without material force."

ZHU XI, IN WING-TSIT CHAN, "THE GREAT SYNTHESIS IN CHU HSI", *A SOURCE BOOK IN CHINESE PHILOSOPHY*

and Cheng Yi (see box, opposite). He put the Confucian revival on a firm footing, making Confucianism the predominant Chinese philosophy for many centuries to come.

Li and *qi*
At the heart of Zhu Xi's philosophy is the relationship between two ideas: *li*, or principle, and *qi*, or vital energy. *Li* and *qi* refer to two aspects of all things. *Li* refers to the fundamental essence of things – their underlying logic – while *qi* is the vital force that coagulates and dissolves and, in so doing, gives form to these principles. Everything is made up of both *li* and *qi* and, says Zhu Xi, there is no *li* without *qi* and there is no *qi* without *li*.

Taking the example of a human being to illustrate these principles, the stuff we are made out of is *qi*, but this *qi* takes the particular form it does in accordance with *li*. Part of our *li*, our essence, is to have two arms, two legs, two eyes, and so on.

However, *li* refers not only to physical principles but also to moral principles. So part of our *li* is also to be humane, to act with ritual decorum, and to manifest wisdom. This is what makes the distinction between *li* and *qi* slightly different from the distinction between matter and form that is seen in Western philosophy. *Li* is both what something is, and what that thing ought to be. Human nature, or *xing*, is basically good, according to Zhu Xi; but

human beings can easily deviate from this goodness. Evil occurs when we deviate from our *li*, and take leave of our fundamental goodness.

Zhu Xi edited and wrote extensive commentaries on the classic texts of Confucianism, particularly the Four Books (see box, p.83). His commentaries were informed by his knowledge of history, current events, and personal reflection, and were notable not only for their breadth and insight, but also for the clarity of the writing. His scholarship refocused Confucianism on moral cultivation and away from its previous bureaucratic form. This is perhaps why Zhu Xi's work went on to be at the heart of Confucian learning from the 14th century up until the 20th century.

▽ **DAOIST TEMPLE, WUYI MOUNTAINS**
Zhu Xi was a renowned teacher and established an academy in the Wuyi mountains in 1183 to promote his philosophy. The area has been a heartland of Daoism for centuries and is home to many Daoist temples.

◁ **POETIC WORKS**
Despite denying that he was a poet, Zhu Xi left behind more than 1,400 verses, many of which drew on the natural world for inspiration. This calligraphic scroll illuminates his poem "Orchid".

▷ **PORTRAIT OF MAIMONIDES**
This medieval portrait of Maimonides shows him as a mature man, with a full beard and dressed in robes that suggest his high rank. As a young man, Maimonides had witnessed Spain's "Golden Age", when Jews and Christians lived in peace under Muslim rule and Córdoba was a centre of Jewish learning and Islamic culture.

Moses Maimonides

1135–1204, SPANISH (JEWISH)

A philosopher, physician, and jurist, Maimonides set out to reconcile Aristotelian doctrine with Judaic theology and became the most influential Jewish thinker of the Middle Ages.

"**Actions** are **divided** as regards their object into **four classes**; they are either **purposeless**, **unimportant**, or **vain**, or **good**."

MOSES MAIMONIDES, *THE GUIDE FOR THE PERPLEXED*

Moses Maimonides (meaning "son of Maimon") was born into a scholarly Jewish family in Córdoba, Spain, which was under Muslim rule at the time. The family's situation changed for the worse in 1148, when a new dynasty – the more radical Islamist Almohads – seized power. Unable to practise their religion openly, the family eventually left Spain for Morocco, where Almohad rule was less rigidly enforced. Meanwhile, Moses proved a precocious scholar, studying logic and metaphysics alongside the Jewish scriptures. His first work, published when he was just 16, was a treatise on philosophical terminology.

At the family's new home in Fez, Maimonides began to study medicine. However, when the head of the city's Jewish community was executed for practising the faith, the Maimon family fled again, first to Palestine and then to Egypt, which was under the rule of the more tolerant Fatimid dynasty. They settled in Fustat, close to Cairo, which would be Maimonides' home for the rest of his life.

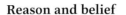

▷ **SALADIN**
This miniature shows the Sultan of Egypt and Syria, whom Maimonides served as physician. Saladin became famous for his campaigns against the Crusaders.

It was in Egypt that Maimonides compiled and published his first major work, the *Mishneh Torah* (a collection of Jewish oral traditions), but circumstances soon conspired to distract him from his studies. His brother drowned on a trading trip in the Indian Ocean, taking much of the family's wealth with him. As head of the household, Maimonides turned to medicine as a means to provide for his dependants. His practice flourished, and in time he was appointed court physician to Egypt's new ruler, the celebrated warrior Saladin. At the same time, he rose to prominence in the Jewish community, being recognized as its *nagid*, or religious leader.

Reason and belief
Despite his many commitments to family and community, Maimonides still found time to work on his magnum opus, *The Guide for the Perplexed*, which he completed in 1191. Addressed to people of a philosophical bent who had lost their faith, it sought to reconcile Jewish theology with the teachings of Aristotle (who at the time was seen as the chief authority on the terrestrial world).

Interpreting the scriptures
Maimonides maintained that the essence of God must always remain unknowable, being beyond human comprehension. Nevertheless, he saw the pursuit of truth as a religious duty, and believed that philosophy and revelation could jointly help in that task. More controversially for Jewish scholars, he also insisted that the Torah was not always to be taken literally: where its account seemed to conflict with reason, an allegorical interpretation should be sought.

Maimonides married late in life and fathered a son, Abraham, who also became a noted scholar. He died in 1204, widely respected as a pillar of the community; in accordance with his wishes, his body was buried at Tiberias in the Holy Land.

◁ **THE *MISHNEH TORAH***
This copy of the *Mishneh Torah*, now held at the Bodleian Library in Oxford, is signed by Maimonides. He declares in his own handwriting that this copy is the authorized version. It was compiled between 1170 and 1180.

IN CONTEXT
Life under the Almohads

The Almohad dynasty arose from a Berber tribe from the Atlas mountains. By the middle of the 12th century, they had conquered much of North Africa and Moorish Iberia, where they later built some extravagant mosques and palaces. The Almohads were Islamic revivalists, who demanded close observation of their religion's laws. Christians and Jews were persecuted and faced with the choice of death, exile, or conversion to Islam. When Maimonides settled in Egypt, outside the Almohad sphere of influence, his enemies maintained that he had feigned conversion to Islam at the time – a claim he denied.

ALMOHAD BANNER FROM THE BATTLE OF LAS NAVAS DE TOLOSA, 1212

ALBERTVS MAGNVS

Albertus Magnus

c.1200–1280, GERMAN

Known as *doctor universalis* ("the universal doctor") for the breadth of his learning, Albertus sought to reconcile Aristotle's ideas with Christian doctrine and left his mark as the teacher of the young Thomas Aquinas.

Albertus Magnus ("the Great") was born in the Bavarian town of Lauringen. An early learner, reputedly able to read and write fluently at the age of seven, he went on to study at the University of Padua. In his 20s, he became a monk, joining the recently founded Dominican order, and he continued his studies at Bologna and in Germany, moving naturally from studying to lecturing on theology and philosophy. In the 1240s, he moved to Paris, where as a lecturer at the university he encountered the young Thomas Aquinas.

Work with Aquinas

In 1248, when Albertus' superiors moved him to a new Dominican college in Cologne, his brilliant student Aquinas followed him. The two scholars were linked by a common fascination with the works of Aristotle, recently translated into Latin from Greek and Arabic versions. Albertus made it his life's work to expound the classical philosopher's ideas in the light of Christian doctrine. In time he was to write commentaries

on the entire Aristotelian canon, adding his own interpretations and speculations along the way. These reflected his intellectual interests, which included the natural sciences, astronomy, mineralogy, and music, as well as metaphysics and ethics.

Albertus came to Greek philosophy partly through the commentaries of Ibn Sina (see pp. 70–71) and Ibn Rushd (see pp. 80–81), and from them he borrowed a crucial concept regarding Platonic universals. These are the generic ideas underlying individual entities – for example, the concept "seat" underlies each of the separate objects that we sit on. He pursued their idea that Platonic universals take three forms: they exist prior to things, as part of the divine intelligence that shapes each individual example; they are within things; and they are also posterior to them as detected by

human intelligence, which seeks by reason and science to abstract them from the chaos of the particular.

Clerical duty and writings

In 1254, Albertus became a provincial of the Dominican order, supervising its activities over a whole province, and six years later he was appointed bishop of Regensburg in Germany. He left after three years to preach the Eighth Crusade at the request of Pope Urban IV. He continued to write voluminously, and when his collected works were finally published in 1899, they ran to some 38 volumes, treating topics as diverse as mineralogy and the nature of women. He outlived Aquinas by six years and died in 1280, by which time he and his great pupil had largely succeeded in their joint task of reconciling Greek philosophy with the teaching of the Christian Church.

△ **ON MINERALS**
Albertus wrote on a diverse range of subjects, including rocks and minerals. This woodcut is from a 1518 edition of his *De Mineralibus*, a five-volume tome that became a standard text on mining, mineralogy, chemistry, and metallurgy.

◁ **ALBERTUS MAGNUS**
This painting by an unknown artist shows Albertus is his Dominican monk's habit. In 1941 he was declared the patron saint of natural scientists by Pope Pius XII.

IN CONTEXT
Alchemy

In the years after his death, Albertus' name was linked with alchemy, the discipline that sought (unsuccessfully) to transmute base metals into gold. In reality, there is little evidence that Albertus ever took more than a passing interest in the subject, which at the time was considered a valid scientific pursuit. Albertus was the only thinker to be dubbed *magnus*, "the great", in his own lifetime – it is likely that proponents of alchemy used the prestige of his name to link it to pseudonymous works on the subject, claiming authorship by him.

AN ALCHEMIST AT WORK, ENGRAVING
AFTER STRADANUS (c.1570)

Thomas Aquinas

1225–1274, ITALIAN

Aquinas was the most influential thinker of the Middle Ages. He successfully reconciled the philosophy of Aristotle with the lessons of the Scriptures, becoming a major spokesman for the Catholic faith.

△ **COMMENTARY ON ARISTOTLE**
This edition of Aquinas's commentary on Aristotle was printed in 1575. The front page portrays Aristotle himself.

Thomas Aquinas was born near Naples, at the castle of Roccasecca, which belonged to his family. His father, Landulf, was the Count of Aquino, and his mother, Theodora, also came from a noble background. Thomas was the youngest of their nine children. At an early age, he was sent to school at the nearby Benedictine monastery of Monte Cassino, and while Aquinas's older brothers became soldiers, he was intent on a career in the Church.

This plan did not run smoothly. Aquinas grew up at a time of conflict between the Holy Roman Emperor, Frederick II (see box, p.93), and the papacy. Landulf was a loyal vassal of the emperor, but his lands were positioned awkwardly, near the border between Frederick's domains and the papal estates. As a result, his family's affairs were sometimes caught in the crossfire between the two warring factions. When Frederick's troops occupied Monte Cassino, Aquinas was sent to Naples, where he continued his education at the new university there.

Secular influences

At the impressionable age of 14, Aquinas entered a secular world that was very different to him. The university, founded by Frederick II in 1224 to train his administrative staff, was the first institution of its kind to have no links with the Church. Indeed, the university had a pronounced anti-papal atmosphere and possessed something of the exotic character of Frederick's court at Palermo, which was a melting pot of Latin, Jewish, and Muslim influences.

Among other things, the university taught Aristotle's natural philosophy (a subject banned in the colleges founded by the papacy), using some texts that had been introduced to the West through Arabic translations. Aquinas therefore became familiar with the intellectual traditions of several different cultures – a much broader training than he would have received at the monastery.

New orders

In Naples, Aquinas came into contact with the Dominicans, a recently established order of friars. Unlike the older monastic communities, who lived apart from the general populace,

IN CONTEXT
The Dominicans

The order was founded by a Spanish priest, Dominic de Guzmán, and was sanctioned by the papacy in 1216. In common with the recently founded Franciscans (1209), this was a mendicant ("begging") order. Its followers were not monks, who remained in their own, settled communities, but friars, who went out to preach on the streets. The order gained popularity quickly, particularly in towns and universities, attracting several major theologians to its ranks. The Dominicans' reputation for intellectual rigour made them a mainstay of the Inquisition when it was established in the 1230s.

MEETING OF SAINT FRANCIS AND SAINT DOMINIC, FRA ANGELICO, c.1429

▷ **THOMAS AQUINAS, 1476**
This image of Aquinas by Carlo Crivelli was part of an altarpiece made for San Domenico in Ascoli Piceno, east central Italy. Aquinas is pictured holding a book and a church (denoting scholarship and ecclesiastical status) and with his chest adorned with the Sun – a symbol of sacred learning.

" To **scorn** the **dictate** of **reason** is to **scorn** the **commandment** of **God**. "

THOMAS AQUINAS, *SUMMA THEOLOGIAE*

△ **CASTLE RUINS, ROCCASECCA**
Aquinas's family castle of Monte San Giovanni was in Roccasecca, a town that drew its importance from its proximity to the great Benedictine Abbey of Monte Cassino. Aquinas was held prisoner in the castle's tower when he determined to join the Dominican order.

the Dominicans founded their houses in towns and cities. They made direct contact with the faithful, preaching their Christian message on the streets. This active approach helped the order to gain many new followers and to grow rapidly. Aquinas, swept up in the fervour, decided that he wanted to join the Dominicans. However, whereas wealthy orders, such as the Benedictines, promised a secure career, the Dominicans seemed like a dangerous novelty, with their emphasis on poverty and begging. Aquinas's family were horrified: they

removed him from Naples and held him captive at Roccasecca for a year, hoping that he would change his mind, before finally relenting. It is not hard to understand the family's concerns.

A life in teaching

Aquinas continued his education in Paris, attaching himself to a fellow Dominican, Albertus Magnus – one of the greatest teachers of the day. He attended the master's lectures and followed him to Cologne to assist in establishing a study centre. Albertus forged his reputation through

his numerous commentaries on Aristotle, which also became the main focus of Aquinas's work.

Aquinas returned to Paris in 1252, completed his qualifications, and four years later gained his first major appointment as regent master of one of the chairs in theology. From this point on, he devoted himself to teaching, studying, and writing.

He wrote copiously; one estimate puts his output at over 8.5 million words, most of which was focused specifically on teaching. This was, it must be remembered, an age before

KEY WORKS

c.1252
Aquinas's first major work, *Commentary on the Sentences*, is an analysis of the Sentences (opinions) of Peter Lombard.

1256–1259
Produces "On the Truth", which takes the form of disputations (debates) with his students.

1259–1264
Writes *Against the Errors of the Infidels*, essentially a textbook for missionaries

1266–1273
Summa Theologiae (*Summary of Theology*) offers a definition of the theological system of the Catholic Church.

1270
Denounces the Averroist take on Aristotle's philosophy in *Against the Averroists: On There Being Only One Intellect*.

◁ **SUMMA THEOLOGIAE**
Aquinas's *Summa* is one of the most important texts in Western civilization. It appears here in an 18th-century codex.

printing, when books were not readily available for students, who instead attended lectures in which the master would read out a familiar text before analysing it, clarifying any difficult passages, and then expanding on it with ideas of his own. One of Aquinas's first major works was a commentary on the *The Four Books of Sentences* (1145–51) by Peter Lombard. This compilation of religious statements was one of the staple texts used in medieval theology courses of the day, and it was standard practice for teachers to produce their own commentaries on it.

Another popular teaching method was a structured form of debate known as a "disputation". The master would propose a topic – conflicting interpretations of a biblical passage, for example – and would then defend his chosen position against questions or objections from his students, supporting his arguments with

◁ SUMMA THEOLOGIAE
Aquinas's *Summa* is one of the most important texts in Western civilization. It appears here in an 18th-century codex.

citations from the Scriptures or texts by one of the Doctors (major theologians) of the Church. Aquinas compiled a number of books that were effectively edited versions of these disputations, the most influential of which were *De Veritate* (*On the Truth*), *De Potentia* (*On Divine Power*), and *De Malo* (*On Evil*).

Defence of Aristotle

A significant proportion of Aquinas's work stemmed from his study of Aristotle. Some of the latter's work had long been available – in the 6th century, for example, Boethius translated his works on logic – but the tremendous breadth of Aristotle's philosophy became far more apparent in the 13th century. Aquinas produced important commentaries on his works on ethics (the *Nicomachean Ethics*) and

▷ **PETER LOMBARD**
Born near Novara, Italy, Peter Lombard (1100–60) became bishop of Paris a year before his death. His theological writings were hugely influential.

metaphysics, and he was profoundly influenced by Aristotle's treatise on the soul (*De Anima*). He was also impressed with Aristotle's natural philosophy", finding that it was compatible with Christianity but that it clashed with the Averroists – the followers of the Muslim philosopher, Ibn Rushd (see pp.80–81) – because he felt that their interpretation of Aristotle posed a threat to Catholic orthodoxy. Aquinas outlined his objections in one of his most scathing, polemical works, *Against the Averroists: On there Being Only One Intellect* (1270).

Exposition of doctrine

Aquinas's great achievement was not only to provide a detailed exposition of Aristotle's ideas, but also to expand on them, bringing them into line with Catholic doctrine. By weaving the two so closely together he was, in a sense, creating a philosophy of religion, one in which reason and revelation could play an equal part. This found its clearest expression in his monumental masterpiece, the *Summa Theologiae*. In its introduction, Aquinas modestly described the work as an instructional guide for theology students, but it is far more than that. The work provides a comprehensive and systematic explanation of Christian doctrine – one that the Catholic Church still relies on heavily to this day.

Aquinas began writing the *Summa Theologiae* in Rome, but broke off abruptly in 1273 and never completed the work. During Mass on 6 December, he had a mystical experience – one that some modern commentators have interpreted as a stroke – and remarked to one of his colleagues that, "Everything I have written now seems to me as straw, in comparison with what I have just seen".

IN PROFILE
Frederick II

Frederick was the dominant political figure of his age. Contemporaries dubbed him *stupor mundi* ("the wonder of the world"), while modern commentators have likened him to the great princes of the Renaissance. Crowned Holy Roman Emperor in 1220, Frederick ruled vast territories, extending from Germany to Sicily, and was also king of Jerusalem. He was far more than just a soldier and administrator, however, with wide-ranging interests in science and the arts. Frederick promoted the Sicilian school of poetry, conducted strange but imaginative scientific experiments, and was an expert on falconry. His book on the latter subject, *On the Art of Hunting with Birds*, highlighted his considerable knowledge of ornithology.

BRONZE BUST OF FREDERICK II (1194–1250)

" The **highest perfection** of human life consists in the **mind of man** being **detached** from care, for the **sake of God**. "

THOMAS AQUINAS, *SUMMA CONTRA GENTILES*

▷ **WILLIAM OF OCKHAM**
This depiction of Ockham by the 20th-century stained-glass artist Lawrence Stanley Lee adorns All Saints Church in Ockham, Surrey, the philosopher's probable birthplace.

William of Ockham

1285–1347, ENGLISH

Ockham sought to cut through the abstraction of medieval thought by focusing attention on individual entities rather than on generalities. The philosophical tool he used to do this was logic.

"It is vain to do with more what can be done by fewer."

WILLIAM OF OCKHAM, *SUMMA TOTIUS LOGICAE*

William of Ockham lived in deeply troubled times. In an age in which the papacy had become embroiled in the growing tensions between the rulers of France and the Holy Roman Empire, he involved himself in heated theological disputes that ultimately led to his excommunication, although he avoided the even greater danger of being labelled a heretic.

Ockham is thought to have been born in the small village of Ockham in Surrey, and joined the Franciscan order at an early age. He studied theology at the University of Oxford; however, he left there without a formal graduation, leading to later disciples labelling him *Inceptor Venerabilis*, (Venerable Bachelor), because he never acquired a master's degree.

Controversy and exile

In 1324, Ockham left England for the papal court at Avignon in France. After his arrival, ideas that he had expressed in his Oxford days came under the scrutiny of a theological commission there; at the same

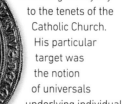

▷ **EMPEROR LOUIS IV**
This gold seal dating from c.1340 carries an image of the Holy Roman Emperor who gave refuge to Ockham and other theologians who had fallen foul of the Pope.

time, he became embroiled in another controversy, siding with the principal of his order who was in dispute with Pope John XXII about the morality of owning property (which the Franciscans eschewed). Fearing reprisal, he fled Avignon in 1328, seeking refuge with the Holy Roman Emperor, Louis IV of Bavaria. This act led to his excommunication, and Ockham spent the rest of his life under the protection of the emperor and his court in Munich.

Ockham contested the philosophical status quo. He sought to cut back the narrow-minded reliance on dogma and tradition in favour of the clear

logic of Aristotle, while at the same time affirming his loyalty to the tenets of the Catholic Church. His particular target was the notion of universals underlying individual things – the idea, for example, that all people have a common human nature with an existence of its own that can be directly perceived outside of its separate manifestations. In this respect, Ockham was a Nominalist – a proponent of the theory that the various objects to which a single general term applies (for example, "table") have nothing whatsoever in common other than their name.

Theological consequences

Ockham's Nominalism dictated that God – a universal – could never be known directly, so God's divine nature must always remain unintelligible to human beings. Unlike Thomas Aquinas, Ockham did not accept that people could determine the existence of God by reason alone; instead, an act of faith was required. In this respect, he cleared the way for agnosticism, while himself remaining firmly within the Catholic fold. Similarly, his insistence on the possibility of studying the world without recourse to theology or metaphysics opened a path for scientific research.

IN CONTEXT
Ockham's razor

Few people talk of William of Ockham today without referring to Ockham's razor – even though the idea that is embodied in the phrase was already old when he took it up, and can be traced all the way back to Aristotle. The principle, often summarized as "Entities are not to be multiplied without necessity" (a phrase Ockham never in fact employed), refers to his urge to cut through the abstruse complexities of earlier Scholastic philosophers. Today it is most often used to mean "All things being equal, the simplest solution is the best".

◁ **PALACE OF THE POPES, AVIGNON**
In the years 1309–77, the papacy was based in the city of Avignon in the South of France, following the refusal of the newly elected French pope, Clement V, to move to Rome.

Directory

Vasubandhu

4TH–5TH CENTURY CE, INDIAN

Born in Gandhara, now in Pakistan, the Buddhist monk and scholar Vasubandhu lived during the Mauryan Empire. After studying the Abhidharma interpretations of Buddhism with masters in Kashmir, he wrote the *Verses on the Treasury of the Abhidharma*, a work that has been influential in Tibetan and East Asian Buddhism, though he later grew critical of the Abhidharma.

Settling at Ayodhya in northern India, he associated with his half-brother Asanga in establishing the Yogacara philosophy, claiming to return to the original teachings of the Buddha in denying the existence of a permanent self or external objects. Visubandhu also wrote commentaries on sacred texts and a treatise on logic, *A Method for Argumentation*.

He is said to have been awarded 300,000 gold coins for winning a debating contest in front of a king, money he used to endow monasteries and hospitals. The Yogacara philosophy has been a major influence in Indian Mahayana Buddhism.

KEY WORKS: *Verses on the Treasury of the Abhidharma*; *The Treatise in Twenty Stanzas on Representation-Only*; *A Method for Argumentation*

▷ Shantideva

685–763 CE, INDIAN

Little is known for certain about the life of Shantideva, a celebrated thinker in the Mahayana Buddhist tradition. He is said to have been the son of a king in western India, with the birth name Shantivarman. When his father died he was advised by his spiritual guide, the celestial bodhisattva Manjushri, to renounce the throne and become a Buddhist monk. He attended the Nalanda monastery, a celebrated centre of Buddhist learning.

According to legend, Shantideva annoyed his fellow students by his laziness – they said he did nothing but eat, sleep, and relieve himself – so his masters instructed him to publicly recite a text. Shantideva recited his own description of the path to Enlightenment, *The Way of the Bodhisattva*, levitating and vanishing at the climax of the recital. *The Way of the Bodhisattva* remains an important text in Mahayana Buddhism, and is particularly admired for its reflections on ethics. Shantideva's text *Training Anthology* consists of a series of commentaries on the Mahayana sutras. His two works are admired as much for their poetic qualities as for their contribution to Tibetan tradition.

KEY WORKS: *The Way of the Bodhisattva*; *Training Anthology*

Kūkai

774–835 CE, JAPANESE

The founder of *Shingon* (True Word) Buddhism, Kūkai was born into an aristocratic family on the island of Shikoku. Sent to Nara, then the Japanese imperial capital, to study Confucianism and Daoism in preparation for a bureaucratic career, he instead adopted Buddhism and became a wandering monk. In 804 CE he travelled to China as part of a government-sponsored cultural mission. At Ximing temple in Xian he was initiated into the beliefs of Tantric Buddhism by the master Hui Guo (746–805 CE). Returning to Japan in 806 CE, he won recognition for his esoteric brand of Buddhism and became a leading figure in Japan's religious establishment.

Kūkai built numerous temples, founded a school, and devoted tireless efforts to creating a monastic complex at Mount Koya. His writings, culminating in the *Ten Stages of the Development of Mind*, focus on the attainment of Enlightenment in a single lifetime through a variety of meditative practices.

KEY WORKS: *Sango shiki* (*The Goals of the Three Teachings*), 797; *Shojijissogi* (*The Meaning of Word, Sound, Reality*), 817; *Jujushinron* (*The Ten Stages of the Development of Mind*), c.830

△ **SHANTIDEVA, 19TH-CENTURY PAINTING**

Shankara

788–820 CE, INDIAN

A pivotal figure in the development of Hindu thought, Adi Shankara was born into the landowning elite in Kerala, India. At an early age he left home to become a disciple of the guru Govinda Bhagavatpadan and travelled widely in India, engaging in debates, attracting disciples, and founding monasteries.

His thoughts have been preserved in numerous commentaries on sacred texts and in the *Upadesasaharsi* (*A Thousand Teachings*). Clarifying and strengthening the ideas of the Advaita Vedanta school of Hindu philosophy, he asserted that the individual Atman (Self) was identical to the Brahman (Supreme Being) and that all gods were aspects of the Brahman. He taught that the study of sacred texts was insufficient for full knowledge, which required the use of reason and attention to experience. Shankara died at the age of 32, probably at Kedarnath in the Himalayas.

KEY WORKS: *Commentary on the Brahma Sutra*; *A Thousand Teachings*

Al-Kindi

c.801–873 CE, ARABIC

Known as the "father of Arab philosophy", Abu Yusuf Yaq'ub ibn Ishak al-Kindi was born into a prominent Arab family at Kufa, in what is now Iraq. As a young man he moved to Baghdad, which was then the capital of the Islamic Abbasid caliphate. Working at the House of Wisdom – a library and intellectual centre established by the caliphs – he supervised the translation of thousands of ancient Greek manuscripts into Arabic, including works on philosophy, science, medicine, mathematics, geography, and astronomy.

Al-Kindi's own wide-ranging writings sought to reconcile the Greek learning inherited from the pre-Islamic world with Muslim theology, fusing ideas drawn from Aristotle, Plotinus, and other Neo-Platonists into an Islamic philosophy. His influence was at its height under Caliph Al-Mu'tasim (reigned 833–842 CE), but declined under al-Mu'tasim's successors, who reaffirmed an intolerant Islamic orthodoxy. Staying in Baghdad to the end of his life, by some accounts al-Kindi died in solitude and poverty.

KEY WORKS: *On First Philosophy*; *On the Intellect*; *On Sleep and Dreams*; *On Dispelling Sorrow*

Al-Farabi

c.872–c.950 CE, PERSIAN OR TURKIC

A leading thinker of the Islamic Golden Age, Abu Nasr Muhammad ibn Muhammad al-Farabi was known as "the Second Teacher", Aristotle being the first. Neither his birthplace nor his ethnicity is certain, but he probably came from central Asia. He lived most of his life in Baghdad but left the city in around 943 CE to escape political disturbances accompanying the decline of the Abbasid caliphate. He spent his final years in Egypt and in Syria, where he died in 950 or 951 CE.

△ MURASAKI SHIKIBU, TOSA MITSUOKI

Al-Farabi's writings cover a wide range of topics, from philosophy and logic to music and the sciences, adapting Ancient Greek thought to an Islamic context. Most notable among his surviving works is *The Virtuous City*. Influenced by Plato's *Republic*, it contrasts an ideal society, in which people collaborate harmoniously to achieve happiness, with the consequences of various forms of misgovernment. Al-Farabi's writings exerted a large influence on later Muslim philosophers, including Ibn Sina and Ibn Rushd.

KEY WORKS: *Al-Madina al-fadila* (*The Virtuous City*); *Kitab al-huruf* (*The Book of Letters*); *Kitab al-musiqa al-kabir* (*The Great Book of Music*)

△ Murasaki Shikibu

c.970–c.1014 CE, JAPANESE

Admired as the author of *The Tale of Genji*, sometimes considered the world's first novel, Murasaki Shikabu was the daughter of a minor member of the dominant Fujiwara clan. She numbered among her ancestors notable poets and scholars. Married in 998 CE but widowed three years later, she took a position as a lady-in-waiting to the empress Shoshi in Kyoto. Her experience of life at the imperial court, minutely observed, provided material for the fictional *Tale of Genji*, as well as for the non-fictional fragments known as *The Diary of Lady Murasaki*.

Written in the Japanese *kana* syllabic script, her works are notable for their refinement and psychological insight. Murasaki left the imperial court in 1011 and probably died in 1014, although some sources suggest she lived until 1031. Neglected for many centuries, since the 1700s, *The Tale of Genji* has become a key reference point for ideas of a distinctive Japanese aesthetic and style of thought.

KEY WORKS: *The Tale of Genji*, c.1000–1012; *The Diary of Lady Murasaki*, c.1010

Cheng Hao

1032–1085, CHINESE

Cheng Hao was born in Huangpi, Hubei province. Along with his brother Cheng Yi, he was sent to study under philosopher Zhou Dunyi (1017–1073) before attending the Imperial Academy in the Song dynasty capital Kaifeng. He had a successful career in the civil service, but from around 1070 devoted himself to the study of the Confucian classics and to teaching, mostly in association with Cheng Yi. Their thoughts and sayings are known from notes made by their pupils, which frequently do not distinguish between the "Two Chengs". Cheng Hao taught that *li*, "principle", infuses the universe and unites all things. Human nature is essentially good but only introspection can uncover the true Way. His brand of Neo-Confucianism would become the official doctrine of the Chinese state.

KEY WORKS: *Chengs' Surviving Sayings* (*Yishu*), 1168; *Chengs' Commentary on Classics*

Al-Ghazālī

1058–1111, PERSIAN

Sunni Muslim philosopher and theologian Abu Hamid Al-Ghazālī was born in Tus in Khorasan, then part of the Seljuk Empire. After studying under theologian Al-Juwayni (1028–1085) in Nishapur, in 1085 he was summoned to the court of Seljuk vizier Nizam al-Mulk in Isfahan. Recognized as the leading scholar of his day, he was appointed head of the prestigious Nizamiyya madrasa (school) in Baghdad in 1091.

In 1095, however, Al-Ghazālī renounced all official positions to pursue an ascetic life. After lengthy travels to Damascus, Jerusalem, and Mecca he lived in seclusion in Tus, only returning to public teaching late in his life. Muslims regard Al-Gazhali as a *mujaddid* – a renewer of faith.

He attacked elements of Arab philosophy based on Aristotle, asserting that all relations of cause and effect are a result of the will of God. His later works brought the Sufi tradition of ascetic mysticism into the mainstream of Sunni faith.

KEY WORKS: *Ihya 'ulum al-din* (*The Revival of the Religious Sciences*); *Tahafut al-Falasifa* (*Incoherence of the Philosophers*); *Mishkat al-Anwar* (*The Niche of Lights*)

Rāmānuja

c.1077–c.1157, INDIAN

Hindu philosopher Rāmānuja was born into a learned Brahmin family at Shriperumbudur, in what is now Tamil Nadu. As a youth he underwent an arranged marriage but offended his family by mixing with people of a lower caste. After breaking with his first teacher, Yadavaprakasa, and renouncing his caste-conscious wife, he became an ascetic devoted to Vishnu, travelling widely across India, gathering disciples, and founding a number of temples before settling on Shrirangam island.

Although Rāmānuja's native language was Tamil he wrote in Sanskrit when expressing his philosophy through his commentaries on the sacred texts. In his writings, he affirmed the importance of devotion to a personal God and adopted a subtle position on the relationship between Atman (Self) and Brahman (Supreme Being), described as "qualified non-dualism". His thought is especially admired for offering a philosophical basis for the rites and prayers of popular Hinduism.

Tradition claims that Rāmānuja lived to the age of 120, from 1017 to 1137. Modern scholars, however, believe that he died aged 80 in around 1157.

KEY WORKS: *Vedarthasangraha* (*Summary of the Meaning of the Vedas*); *Sri Bhasya* (*Commentary on the Brahma Sutra*); *Bhagavad Gita Bhasya* (*Commentary on the Bhagavad Gita*)

◁ ## Peter Abelard

1079–1142, FRENCH

Philosopher and theologian Peter Abelard was born into the minor nobility in Brittany. Preferring learning to knighthood, he studied under the best scholars in France, engaging in public disputes with several of his teachers, notably William of Champeaux (1070–1121), who thought his pupil arrogant.

From 1115 Abelard was master of Notre-Dame cathedral school in Paris, where his lively teaching style earned him a popular following. A love affair with the scholar and abbess Héloïse, niece of a Parisian canon, Fulbert, brought his undoing. Castrated on Fulbert's orders, he entered the monastery of St Denis.

The rest of his life alternated between monastic asceticism and teaching. Abelard's writings led to conflict with the religious authorities. In 1122 he was forced to burn *Theologia Summi Boni* (*History of the Supreme Good*) and in 1141 was excommunicated for heresy. As a scholastic philosopher, Abelard believed logic was the only path to truth apart from divine revelation. The letters between him and Héloïse are a literary classic.

KEY WORKS: *Sic et Non* (*Yes and No*), c.1121; *Theologia Summi Boni* (*History of the Supreme Good*), c.1121; *Historia Calamitatum* (*The Story of My Troubles*), c.1135; *Ethica seu Scito te Ipsum* (*Ethics or Know Yourself*), c.1140

Dōgen

c.1200–1253, JAPANESE

The founder of the Soto school of Zen Buddhism, Dōgen was born into the Minamoto clan at the imperial court in Kyoto. An orphan by the age of eight, he left Kyoto in 1213 to become a monk at the Buddhist temple on Mount Hiei. Dissatisfied with the Tendai school of Buddhism that was then dominant in Japan, in 1223 he travelled to China, where the monk Rujing (1162–1228) initiated him into Chan (in Japanese, Zen) Buddhism.

Returning to Japan in 1227, Dōgen promoted the practice of seated meditation (*zazen*) as a means to "cast off the body and mind". His ideas initially met a hostile response from traditional Tendai Buddhists, but his influence gradually spread.

He built a temple in the mountains at Eihei-ji, which became a permanent centre for Soto Zen. Dogen's teachings over 30 years, brought together in the *Shobogenzo*, focused on the belief that "practice is enlightenment". He is also admired as a poet.

KEY WORKS: *Fukan zazengi* (*General Advice on Zazen*), c.1227; *Bendowa* (*On the Endeavour of the Way*), 1231; *Shobogenzo* (*Treasury of the True Dharma Eye*), 1231–53

△ PETER ABELARD. ILLUSTRATION BY EDMOND MENNECHET, 1836

Duns Scotus

c.1266–1308, SCOTTISH

John Duns, known as Duns Scotus, was a leading philosopher and theologian of the scholastic era. Born in southern Scotland, he joined the Franciscan order in his youth and was educated at the order's study house at the University of Oxford.

In around 1301, Duns Scotus was sent to teach at the prestigious University of Paris, but was exiled from France two years later because he was one of a group of Franciscans who sided with the pope in a dispute with French king Philip IV. He was allowed to return the following year and resumed his teaching. Critical of the ideas of Thomas Aquinas, his lectures offered fresh arguments on issues such as the relationship between existence and essence, free will, and the proofs of the existence of God. His advocacy of the Immaculate Conception of the Virgin was considered potentially heretical. In 1307 the Franciscans moved him to Cologne, where he died the following year. He was beatified in 1993.

KEY WORKS: *Ordinatio*, 1300–04; *Collationes Parisienses* (*Parisian lectures*), 1302–07; *Tractatus Primo Principio* (*Treatise on the First Principle*), c.1307

Christine de Pizan

1364–c.1430, ITALIAN/FRENCH

Celebrated for her writings on the status of women, Christine de Pizan was born in Venice but brought up in Paris, where her father served as astrologer at the French royal court. Aged 15 she married a court official, Etienne du Castel, with whom she had three children. After his death in 1389, with a family to support, she began to write for money, gaining the patronage of the French royalty and aristocracy.

Her writings included a treatise on war and works on government and politics, but her main subject was the defence of women against their male detractors. Most notably in *The Book of the City of Ladies*, she argued that women were the equal of men in virtue, citing examples of great women from history and myth.

With France ravaged by war, Christine sought refuge in a convent for her final years. Her last work was a poem in praise of Joan of Arc.

KEY WORKS: *Le Livre de la cité des dames* (*The Book of the City of Ladies*), 1405; *Le Livre des trois vertus* (*The Book of the Three Virtues*), 1405; *Livre de paix* (*Book of Peace*), 1413

Nicolas of Cusa

1401–1464, GERMAN

A prominent ecclesiastic and innovative thinker, Nicolas of Cusa was born Nikolaus Cryfftz at Kues on the Moselle River. He studied at the University of Padua, where he encountered Renaissance humanism. After ordination he attended the ecumenical council of Basel from 1432 as an expert in canon law.

In 1437 he was sent as a papal legate to Constantinople, seeking reconciliation between Rome and the Greek Orthodox Church. As bishop of Brixen in the Tyrol from 1450 he engaged in efforts at Church reform that brought him into conflict with the secular authorities. He eventually fled his bishopric, ending his days as a papal adviser in the Vatican. His treatises and sermons offer an original Neoplatonist interpretation of Christianity, expressed through vivid metaphors. He argued that the Earth was neither fixed nor at the centre of the universe, that political authority required the consent of the governed, and that all faiths worshipped the same God with different rites.

KEY WORKS: *De concordantia catholica* (*The Catholic Concordance*), 1433–34; *De docta ignorantia* (*On Learned Ignorance*), 1440; *De coniecturis* (*On Conjectures*), 1442; *De pace fidei* (*On the Peace of Faith*), 1453

▽ Marsilio Ficino

1433–1499, ITALIAN

Renaissance humanist Marsilio Ficino was born outside Florence, the son of a doctor. A polymath, he was a doctor, priest, and musician, but gained fame as a philosopher and translator of classic works.

From an early age Ficino enjoyed the patronage of Florence's ruler, Cosimo de' Medici, who employed him as tutor to his grandson Lorenzo. Around 1460 Cosimo selected Ficino to head a Platonic Academy, dedicated to the recovery of the learning of the Ancient Greeks. Ficino undertook the daunting task of translating and commenting on the works of Plato and Plotinus, making them accessible to the educated elite of Western Europe. He also translated the *Corpus Hermeticum*, writings from the Hellenistic period that are believed to contain arcane wisdom attributed to Hermes Trismegistus (Thrice-Great), a character who was identified with the Greek god Hermes.

Ficino's own works encompassed subjects as diverse as mathematics, geometry, magic, and astrology. His philosophical writings, inspired by Neoplatonism, argued the case for the immortality of the soul and introduced the notion of Platonic love into Western culture.

Ordained in 1473, Marsilio Ficino became canon of Florence cathedral. In 1489 he had to defend himself against an accusation of heresy because of his interest in astrology and natural magic.

KEY WORKS: *Theologia Platonica* (*Platonic Theology*), 1474; *De Amore* (*On Love*), 1484; *De Vita libri tres* (*Three Books on Life*), 1489

△ **MARSILIO FICINO, UNKNOWN ARTIST**

EARLY MODERN

CHAPTER 3

Desiderius Erasmus

c.1466/69–1536, DUTCH

Erasmus was an important humanist scholar and a voice of moderation during the bitter disputes of the Reformation. In his most famous work, *In Praise of Folly*, he satirized the ills of the day.

Desiderius Erasmus was the illegitimate son of a priest and a physician's daughter. Orphaned at an early age, he and his brother went to school at Deventer, which became the cradle of Dutch humanism. Erasmus was pressurized by his guardian to enter the Augustinian priory of Steyn, and was ordained in 1492. He had no vocation for the monastic life, but it allowed him at least to pursue his studies of ancient classical literature. While at Steyn, Erasmus became emotionally involved with a fellow monk, Servatius. He also wrote his first treatises, which would not be published until many years later.

In 1493, a chance to escape the monastery arose when the bishop of Cambrai took Erasmus into his service. An eagerly anticipated trip to Italy did not materialize, but the bishop allowed him to complete his studies in Paris, at the Collège de Montaigu. However, this was also disappointing, as the place was still dominated by the Scholastic form of learning, which emphasized tradition and dogma and which Erasmus loathed.

Erasmus became a travelling scholar, moving from country to country in search of patrons – a life that allowed him to make contact with other notable humanists. He supplemented his income by teaching, translating, and writing – an activity that had become profitable since the recent invention of printing.

Translation and writing

Erasmus's Latin translation of the New Testament was used as the standard version of the text until the 19th century, and several of his other works also found success: *The Adages* (1500), a collection of Greek and Latin proverbs, became a bestseller, while his *Colloquies* (1519) was published in dozens of editions. Most famous of all, was *In Praise of Folly*, which Erasmus wrote to amuse Thomas More (see box, right) when he arrived in England in 1509. He produced the first version in a week, but expanded the text considerably before publishing it two years later. In the book, which was modelled on the satires by the

◁ **THE NEW TESTAMENT**
Erasmus believed that the new age of humanism demanded a fresh translation of the New Testament. This edition dates from 1548.

2nd-century classical author Lucian, Erasmus mocked a wide range of contemporary targets through the personification of Folly. She was a goddess of his invention, the daughter of Wealth and Youth, attended by the nymphs Ignorance and Drunkenness. Some of the humour was light-hearted, jesting about gamblers and cuckolds, but Erasmus also aired more serious criticisms about Scholastic monks and theologians.

Erasmus was writing at a dangerous time, when the obvious divisions of the Reformation were becoming more acute, so the notion of using Folly as a mouthpiece for his criticisms was both prudent and inspired. Erasmus's own views were probably closer to those of the Protestant reformers – he favoured a personal relationship with God via the Scriptures rather than through the organized, ritual practices of the Church – but he was cautious enough to condemn the more extreme views of Martin Luther in print.

◁ **ERASMUS'S STUDY**
In 1521, Erasmus stayed with his friend Pieter Wychman in a former schoolhouse in Anderlecht. The house is now preserved as a museum of Erasmus's life and works.

IN PROFILE
Thomas More

The lawyer, statesman, and renowned humanist Sir Thomas More (1478–1535) was Erasmus's closest friend in England. Erasmus dedicated *In Praise of Folly* to him and the title is a pun on his name (its Latin form is *Moriae Encomium*, which could also be translated as "In Praise of More"). Both men admired the satires of Lucian, and More himself wrote the famous satirical work *Utopia* (1516). Unlike Erasmus, however, More became dangerously involved in politics. He served for a time as Henry VIII's lord chancellor, but his refusal to acknowledge the Act of Supremacy – the bill that made the king head of the Church of England – led him to be convicted of treason and beheaded in May 1535.

COVER OF A FRENCH EDITION OF MORE'S *UTOPIA*, 1643

▷ **ERASMUS BY HOLBEIN**
This image was produced by the great German portraitist Hans Holbein the Younger, who spent two periods in England painting members of the royal court. Both he and Erasmus were leading figures of the Northern Renaissance.

▷ **NICCOLO MACHIAVELLI**
This portrait dating from the late 16th century was made by the Florentine artist Santi di Tito (1536-1603) long after the philosopher's death. The artist is thought to have exaggerated Machiavelli's features to make him appear more devious.

Niccolò Machiavelli

1469–1527, ITALIAN

Machiavelli was a statesman, philosopher, historian, and playwright, but is best known for his adroitness as a ruthless political theorist, epitomized by his masterpiece, *The Prince*, which still retains its power to shock.

◁ **THE WRITER'S DESK**
Machiavelli wrote at this desk in L'Albergaccio, his home in San Casciano, during his exile from Florence. The house is still owned by members of his family.

Niccolò Machiavelli's career coincided with the high point of the Renaissance, the most glorious period in Italy's cultural history. At that time, Italy was not a nation but a collection of city-states ruled by ambitious, violent families – the Medici, the Borgias, and the Sforzas. Their bitter rivalries were complicated by invading French and Spanish armies, as well as by the manipulative policies of the papacy. Machiavelli was able to observe their jockeying for power at close quarters, and his writings reveal the dark underbelly of Renaissance Italy.

Power and diplomacy
Machiavelli was born in Florence, the son of an attorney. His family appear to have had a noble ancestry, but they were poor. Virtually nothing is known of his early years and his life only comes into sharp focus in 1498, when he became a clerk in the second chancery of the Florentine Republic.

At that point, the city of Florence was in crisis. The rule of the Medici had ended after the French invasion of 1494, and the turbulent regime of the firebrand preacher Girolamo Savonarola was drawing to a close. Stability returned only with the election of Piero Soderini as ruler in 1502 (see box, right).

With Soderini in power in Florence, Machiavelli gained in status and, even though he never reached the top rank of diplomats, he was involved in several key missions. He was sent to visit Cesare Borgia, apparently to check if he was plotting against Florence; and in 1503, he was dispatched to Rome to gauge the capabilities of the new pope, Julius II.

In 1512, a political twist brought about the end of the Republic and the return of the Medici. Machiavelli was dismissed from his duties, tortured, and briefly imprisoned. After his

release, he was exiled to San Casciano, just outside Florence, where he soon became bored, missing the excitement of political life. To fill his time, he began to write. He penned comic plays – which were very popular during his lifetime – and histories. He also wrote three texts that related more to his working life – *The Prince*, *Discourses on Livy*, and *The Art of War*.

Political philosophy
The Prince – the most notorious of Machiavelli's works – was not published in his lifetime, the first edition appearing in 1532. The book took the form of a treatise advising an imaginary prince how best to govern. There was nothing new about texts of this kind (they dated back to antiquity), but instead of the usual catalogue of princely virtues, Machiavelli preached a political morality that was based entirely on expediency, rather than on conventional ethics.

His prince should not "flinch from being blamed for vices which are necessary for safeguarding the state". Sometimes meanness was better than generosity, cruelty more effective than mercy, and breaking faith more beneficial than honesty. Machiavelli's emphasis on realpolitik earned him scorn in some quarters, but he has since been hailed as the father of modern political philosophy.

◁ **THE PRINCE, MANUSCRIPT**
Machiavelli's *The Prince* shocked readers on its posthumous publication, with some commentators accusing its author of being in league with the devil.

IN PROFILE
Piero Soderini

Machiavelli's employer in Florence was the statesman Piero Soderini (1450–1522), the scion of an old, distinguished family; one of his brothers became a bishop, another an envoy to Venice. Soderini was elected *Gonfaloniere* (ruler) of Florence in 1502 after serving as the city's ambassador to France. He was elected for life (the Florentines wishing to stabilize their governance), but ruled for only a decade before he was driven out of office during the War of the Holy League in 1512. Machiavelli admired Soderini as a leader, but lost respect for him after his timid fall from power. Soderini spent his final years exiled in Rome, unable to return to the city he loved.

"It is **far better** to be **feared** than **loved** if you cannot be **both**."

MACHIAVELLI, *THE PRINCE*

Michel de Montaigne

1533–1592, FRENCH

In a time of religious intolerance and strife, Montaigne brought a spirit of sceptical enquiry and self-questioning to the exploration of knowledge, and a search for meaning to the minutiae of his own life.

△ **TITLE PAGE OF *ESSAIS*, 1725**
First published in 1580, Montaigne's essays span three volumes in 107 chapters. The author repeatedly re-edited the work over many years.

Michel de Montaigne grew up during a period of intense sectarian division. By the time he reached adulthood, the Reformation was underway and northern Europe was riven between Catholic and Protestant factions vying for power. In an age of murderous antagonisms, his was a voice of reason and forbearance. As a writer, he pioneered the essay form, a genre that would prove enduringly popular across Europe and beyond as a medium for expressing complex ideas.

He was born Michel Eyquem de Montaigne to a wealthy and well-connected family in the Bordeaux region of southwest France (another branch of the family would later be responsible for developing the celebrated Chateau d'Yquem wines). Michel, however, chose to be known simply as Michel de Montaigne, the name of the family estate 50km (30 miles) east of the city, which his father had served as mayor. His mother was descended from Sephardic Jews who had emigrated from Spain and converted to Roman Catholicism.

Childhood and education

Montaigne received an extraordinary education. For the first year or two of his life, he was sent to live with a local peasant family to link him to the common people. When he eventually returned home, he was put in the care of a tutor who brought him up in an entirely Latin-speaking environment; he was six years old before he learned to speak French. In other respects, his father treated him kindly, giving orders that he should be woken up every morning to the sound of a lute.

Montaigne's eccentric childhood no doubt influenced his own ideas on education. He was strongly opposed to the notion of rote learning, believing instead that knowledge should be acquired through a dialogue between teacher and pupil. He thought that learning should be a pleasure, not a pain, and need not come through books alone. Above all, it should go with the grain of the child's personality, for "there is no-one who, if he listens to himself, does not find a pattern all his own, a ruling pattern, that struggles against education". By the age of 23, Montaigne had

IN CONTEXT
Montaigne the diplomat

Montaigne's France was divided along religious lines between Protestant Huguenots and those loyal to the Catholic Church. Montaigne himself stayed in the latter camp, but also maintained good relations with the Protestants and their leader, Henry of Navarre. When the warring factions clashed on the edge of his own estate, he tried to act as a mediator, dealing directly both with Navarre and with Catherine de Medici, mother of the Catholic king Henry III. On one occasion, he went on a secret mission to the king in Paris, bearing a message from Henry of Navarre. The deputation came to nothing, but Montaigne paid a price for his efforts when he was briefly imprisoned in the Bastille by Catholic extremists fearful of his contacts with the Protestant leader.

FRANÇOIS DUBOIS' PAINTING DEPICTS THE MASSACRE OF HUGUENOTS ON ST BARTHOLOMEW'S DAY, 1572, A KEY EVENT IN THE FRENCH WARS OF RELIGION

> "It should be noted that **children's games** are **not games**; they should be viewed rather as their **most serious activities**."
>
> MICHEL DE MONTAIGNE, *ESSAYS*

▷ **MONTAIGNE**
This anonymous portrait shows the face of Montaigne, a man who spent more than two decades in pursuit of the character he called "Myself".

IN CONTEXT
Montaigne's cat

Unlike his successor René Descartes, who took a mechanistic view of animals, Montaigne viewed them with empathy. Descartes thought that, because of their perceived lack of rational cogitation, they were little more than bundles of conditioned reflexes. Montaigne, though, saw human contact with his pets as a two-way process. "When I play with my cat," he wrote, "who knows if it is not rather she who plays with me?" His sympathy extended to dogs: "By nature I am so tender and childlike that I cannot bring myself not to play with my dog when he so wishes, even outside the allotted time."

ETCHING SHOWING MONTAIGNE WITH HIS CAT, c.1866–68

qualified to serve as a magistrate, and based himself in Bordeaux for almost the entirety of his legal career. His job had a political dimension that sometimes took him to the royal court in Paris, yet it failed to catch his imagination or fulfil his ambitions.

In 1571, at the age of 38, he made the momentous decision to retire to his estate to pursue his studies and to write. He was led to do so partly by the death of his father two years earlier, which left him master of the estate, but also by the passing of his dearest friend, the poet Etienne de La Boétie, who had worked with him in the *parlement* (judicial council) of Bordeaux. By this time, Montaigne had published his first work – a translation of a Spanish theological tome entrusted to him by his father.

The *Essays*
Over the next nine years, Montaigne worked on his *Essays*, in the process creating an entirely new literary form – the *essai*. In the sense that he used the word, an *essai* was an inner exploration – an attempt to probe his own thoughts on a given subject. His first *essais* were short and full of allusions and quotations; he was particularly drawn to the Stoic philosophers, notably Seneca, as well as to the biographer Plutarch. Soon, though, he proved eager to challenge received opinions, not least his own. The result was an approach of a very individual kind: sceptical, enquiring, humane, and surprisingly modern to today's readers. His self-doubt expressed itself strikingly in his personal motto: *Que sais-je?* (What Do I Know?).

Montaigne's guiding principle was the injunction to "Know thyself", and he used the essay format to draw an intimate portrait of the inner

workings of his own mind. In doing so, he provided his readers with what some commentators regard as an entirely new concept of the Self. Rather than presenting a consolidated version of the Self, Montaigne chose to emphasize its inconsistencies, claiming that "We are all patchwork, and so shapeless and diverse in composition that each bit, each moment, plays its own game". For him, instead of a single, immutable identity, there was a fluid persona that could be fleetingly captured in prose through rigorous self-analysis but never permanently pinned down.

Scepticism and hardship
Self-questioning also underpinned Montaigne's moral judgements. At a time of theological dogmatism and rigid rules of personal conduct, he was sceptical of certainties, choosing to see shades of grey where others insisted on a stark black-and-white. His relativism attracted criticism at the time, but in recent years has led him to be seen as a precursor of Modernism.

The quest for peace that had driven Montaigne to seek refuge in the tower of his chateau was soon to be challenged. He had married in 1565 and had six daughters, but only one survived beyond infancy. In 1578, he was afflicted by kidney stones, an ailment that was inherited from his father and that plagued him

▷ **HENRY III**
Montaigne earned the respect of the French king Henry III, who is depicted here c.1588 by the court artist François Quesnel.

sporadically for the rest of his life. The pain the stones caused was sometimes so intense as to make him faint. Nevertheless, he struggled on, analysing his own sufferings as clear-sightedly as he observed any other phenomenon.

Political strife
The first edition of the *Essays* was published in 1580. The book was well received, and Montaigne travelled to Paris to present a copy to France's Henry III. He then set off with his family on a year's journey through Germany, Switzerland, and Austria to Italy, partly in search of a cure for his ailment. He was summoned back unexpectedly 15 months later by news that he had been elected mayor of Bordeaux. He returned to France to serve two terms of two years each in the post – a poisoned chalice for a man who cherished his independence and calm. A worsening political situation made the task even harder: before his second term was up, he had to face a threatened coup by the extreme Catholic faction in the city.

> " A man who **fears suffering** is **already suffering** from **what he fears**. "

MICHEL DE MONTAIGNE, *ESSAYS*

△ CHATEAU DE MONTAIGNE
This tower on Montaigne's estate –
which the writer had rebuilt to his
own precise specifications – contains
his library and study.

The last years of Montaigne's life
were troubled by renewed civil war in
France, accompanied by an outbreak
of plague. He continued to revise and
expand the *Essays*, bringing out an
enlarged edition in 1588. Meanwhile
his health was deteriorating. Another
attack of kidney stones brought on

a throat infection as a side effect that
gradually suffocated him. He died in
his chateau – surrounded by family,
friends, and servants – in September
1592 at the age of 59.

A continuing reputation

Montaigne's reputation continued
to grow after his death. In England,
Francis Bacon's *Essays*, published
in 1597, were written very much in
the manner of Montaigne; in 1603, the
English scholar John Florio published
a translation of Montaigne's *Essays*

that made an impression on Florio's
acquaintance, the English playwright
William Shakespeare.

In later centuries, writers as
diverse as Ralph Waldo Emerson
and Friedrich Nietzsche expressed
admiration for Montaigne's work.
Few thinkers, in fact, have inspired so
much personal affection, a common
theme of their admiration being well
expressed by Emerson: "It seemed to
me as if I had myself written the book,
in some former life, so sincerely it
spoke to my thought and experience."

△ MARIE DE GOURNAY
Montaigne met the writer Marie de
Gournay in Paris in 1588 and the
two struck up a close friendship. She
became his "adopted daughter" and
later acted as his literary executor.

KEY WORKS

1568	**1570**	**1571**	**1580**	**1588**	**1595**
Publishes a translation of Raymond Sebond's *Theologia naturalis*.	Publishes the works of his friend Etienne de La Boétie, a philosopher, who had died in 1563.	Retires to his estate at the age of 38 and begins work on the *Essays*.	The first edition of the *Essays* is published. It sells out; a second edition follows two years later.	A Parisian printer brings out an expanded edition of Montaigne's *Essays*.	Marie de Gournay edits a further, posthumous, edition of the *Essays*; it becomes the definitive text.

Francis Bacon

1561–1626, ENGLISH

Bacon was a controversial statesman, lawyer, and literary figure. Above all, he is hailed as the father of empiricism whose methodology formed the basis of modern scientific enquiry.

Francis Bacon was born in London in 1561 and grew up around the court of Elizabeth I. Poor health plagued his life and he was educated privately at home until the age of 12, when he was sent to Trinity College, Cambridge. He briefly studied law at Gray's Inn, but interrupted his studies to travel through France and Italy with the English ambassador in Paris. On his return to England, he qualified as a barrister in 1582.

Rise and fall

Bacon was a member of parliament from 1584, but it was not until the accession of James I in 1603 – the year in which Bacon was knighted – that his career soared: he became solicitor-general, keeper of the royal seal, and in 1618, lord chancellor. He was a spendthrift and often in debt, despite his status. Considered to be a ruthlessly ambitious and scheming politician who sought favour with the king to advance himself, Bacon attracted enemies. In 1621, he was made viscount of St Albans, but in the same year he was convicted of accepting a bribe, imprisoned briefly, and fined a substantial amount.

After this scandal, Bacon immersed himself in science. Moving away from the Renaissance preoccupation with reviving the achievements of the ancients, he was the first philosopher to develop a post-Aristotelian method of empirical investigation – and it is for this that he is remembered.

Bacon's best-known works are *The Advancement of Learning* (1605), which discusses the state of scientific knowledge at the time, obstacles to progress, and his ideas for revitalizing secondary and further education; and his seminal text, *Novum Organum* (1620). It was here that he set out his ideas of a scientific method based on inductive reasoning. In keeping with the spirit of the modern age, Bacon wanted to acquire new forms of knowledge that could be used to improve the quality of human life, and to create new technologies, subsidized by the state, using strictly scientific methods grounded in observation and experiment, rather than simply in logical deduction. He reworked these ideas in fictional form in his utopian novel *The New Atlantis* (see box, below).

Death and legacy

Bacon's life was surrounded by controversy and rumour: some claimed he had an affair with Marguerite de Valois, the sister of the French king, others that he was homosexual. There was speculation that Bacon was the illegitimate son of Elizabeth I and even that he was the real author of some of Shakespeare's plays. Bacon's death was no less bizarre. He succumbed to bronchitis after stuffing a chicken with snow in an experiment to test the preservation of bodies. Some suggested that he faked his own death, a story that was never substantiated. It is undisputed, however, that many of the giants of philosophy, including Thomas Hobbes, John Locke, and David Hume, were influenced by Bacon. He remains a key figure in scientific methodology, one of the first thinkers to integrate scientific and philosophical reasoning, and a founder of modern science.

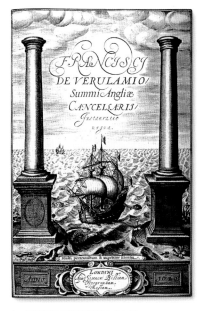

△ *NOVUM ORGANUM*, 1620
The title page of Bacon's *Novum Organum* (New Scientific Method) shows a galleon passing through the Pillars of Hercules (which symbolize the old-style system of logic) and into the Atlantic (which represents a new world of thought).

◁ **SIR FRANCIS BACON**
This portrait of Bacon was made by Paul van Somer, a Flemish artist who lived in England and became a leading painter of the royal court.

IN CONTEXT
The quest for utopia

From ancient myths of an original golden age and religious creation myths such as the Garden of Eden, through Thomas More's seminal text *Utopia* (1516), to the present, every culture has offered imaginary versions of an ideal society. Bacon's utopia appeared in his unfinished novel *The New Atlantis* (1624). It was a world based on progressive scientific improvement set on the mythical island of Bensalem in the state-sponsored research institute of Salomon's House. The work is a clear expression of Bacon's philosophical ideas in fictional form.

THE GARDEN OF EDEN WITH THE FALL OF MAN, JAN BRUEGHEL THE ELDER AND PETER PAUL RUBENS, c.1615

▷ **THOMAS HOBBES**
This portrait by (or possibly after) the English painter John Michael Wright (1617–94) shows the philosopher in his later years.

Thomas Hobbes

1588–1679, ENGLISH

Hobbes is best known for the political philosophy of *Leviathan*. A pessimistic materialist, he believed that only authoritarian government could save humans from the dire consequences of their own nature.

Thomas Hobbes was born in 1588, the year that Elizabethan England was threatened with invasion by the Spanish Armada. He later wrote that his mother "was filled with such fear that she brought twins to birth, myself and fear at the same time". Whether or not it was determined at the moment of his birth, Hobbes certainly grew up with a strong fear of war and a desire for stability. His own family provided an example of the damage caused by disorder. His father was a minor cleric serving at a country parish near Malmesbury, Wiltshire. In 1603, Hobbes senior was found guilty of verbal abuse and physical assault against a fellow clergyman, and disappeared from Malmesbury and from Hobbes's life. Hobbes then came under the protection of an uncle, who funded his education.

Hobbes showed precocious intelligence. Educated in the classics by a scholar in Malmesbury, he produced a translation of Euripedes' Greek drama *Medea* into Latin at the age of 14. Shortly afterwards he was admitted to university at Magdalen Hall, Oxford. He was not impressed by the university, developing an abiding aversion to Aristotle, whose works were regarded at Oxford as the sole source of authority in philosophy and the natural sciences. According to his first biographer, John Aubrey, Hobbes was "even in his youth... temperate both as to wine and women". He did not fit in with other students, whom he later described as "debauched to drunkenness, wantonness, gaming, and other vices".

A breakthrough

It may have been his reputation for good morals that earned Hobbes the breakthrough that changed his life. In 1608, aged only 20, he was appointed as tutor to the 18-year-old William Cavendish. The Cavendish family were wealthy aristocrats, possessing the dukedoms of Devonshire and Newcastle and owning the great country houses of Hardwick Hall and Chatsworth. They became his patrons for the rest of his life. Through this association, he was introduced to men of learning, including Francis Bacon. Hobbes also travelled, staying for long periods in Europe with his pupil, William, and later with other Cavendish offspring in need of a tutor.

Radical materialism

In the 1630s, Hobbes developed his general philosophical views, largely influenced by the physical sciences and mathematics. Inspired by the work of the ancient Greek mathematician Euclid on geometry, he adopted a method based on deduction from a few initial axioms. He was also guided by contemporary European thinkers engaged in what would later be called the Scientific Revolution. The French

△ **HOBBES'S *DE CIVE***
Originally published in 1642 in Latin as *De Cive* (*On the Citizen*), Hobbes's book later appeared in English as *Philosophicall Rudiments Concerning Government and Society*. It deals with the themes of liberty, dominion, and religion.

IN CONTEXT
The English Civil War

In 1642, war broke out between royalists led by Charles I (whom Hobbes supported) and the English parliament, which was defying royal authority over taxation and religious matters. The conflict that followed, also involving the Scots and Irish, was immensely destructive. As many as one in 10 of Britain's adult male population may have died in the fighting. Parliament was victorious and the king was executed in 1649. The most successful parliamentary general, Oliver Cromwell, established a military dictatorship as protector from 1653. After his death, the monarchy was restored under the executed king's son, Charles II.

CHARLES I BEING LED TO EXECUTION; 19TH-CENTURY ILLUSTRATION

"The **condition of man...** is a **condition** of **war** of **everyone** against **everyone**."
THOMAS HOBBES, *LEVIATHAN*

IN PROFILE
Galileo Galilei

A major influence on Hobbes, the Italian physicist Galileo Galilei was born in Pisa, Italy, in 1564. While teaching at Pisa and Padua universities, he investigated such phenomena as gravity, velocity, and relativity using the experimental method. Turning to astronomy, he developed a telescope with which he identified the moons of Jupiter. Denying that the Earth was the centre of the universe brought him into conflict with the Catholic Church. Condemned by the Inquisition, in 1633 he was forced to publicly recant his views. He died in 1642.

PORTRAIT OF GALILEO GALILEI, GIUSTO SUSTERMANS, 1636

astronomer and mathematician Pierre Gassendi became a close acquaintance, and Hobbes also met the Italian physicist Galileo Galilei. It was under Galileo's influence that he became convinced there was nothing in the universe but physical matter in motion. "Every part of the universe is body," he wrote, "and that which is not body is no part of the universe." He rejected the concept of any "incorporeal substance" such as mind or soul as an absurd contradiction. Thoughts were a motion in the brain.

This radical materialism would bring Hobbes into conflict not only with the religious authorities but also with his great contemporary René Descartes, whom he met in Paris in the 1640s. Descartes wrote, in response to Hobbes, that asserting thoughts could be matter in motion was as ridiculous as saying the earth was the sky.

Political philosophy

Hobbes's political philosophy grew in response to the turbulent events of his time. The Stuart kings, rulers of England from 1603, faced opposition from parliament, which sought to limit the powers of the monarch. In 1628, when parliament issued a Petition of Rights in protest against alleged abuses of royal authority, Hobbes published a translation of the work of the ancient Greek historian Thucydides that he intended as a criticism of democracy.

By the time Hobbes's treatise *The Elements of Law* appeared in May 1640, confrontation between Charles I and parliament had become acute. Hobbes sided with the king, commending "severe punishments" for those who raised factions that undermined obedience to his rule. But the tide was turning against Charles. In November 1640 he was forced to

summon what became the Long Parliament, and several prominent royalists were arrested. Fearing that he might be imprisoned for his views, Hobbes prudently moved to France.

As England descended into civil war, Hobbes did little to aid the royalist cause, other than acting as a maths tutor to the Prince of Wales – the future King Charles II – in exile in Paris. But the spectacle of war and regicide confirmed his belief that only horrors would result from the breakdown of order. At the height of

△ **CHATSWORTH HOUSE**
As the private tutor of the 2nd earl of Devonshire, Hobbes lived at Chatsworth House in Derbyshire for many years. The main collection of his papers is today held at the stately home.

his intellectual powers, he produced the most complete statement of his philosophy in *Leviathan* (1651). *Leviathan* links Hobbes's materialist view of human beings to a vision of society and government. He sees humans as naturally driven by their desires and fears to a ruthless conflict "of every man, against every man", in which "force and fraud" are virtues because they aid individual survival. To escape from this fearful anarchy, humans must agree to subject themselves to the absolute authority of a ruler, who will impose laws and guarantee internal peace and security.

The publication of *Leviathan* made Hobbes unpopular in Paris. It offended exiled royalists because it denied that kings ruled by divine right – Hobbes's absolute ruler could as well be a

◁ **LEVIATHAN, TITLE PAGE, 1651**
The title page identifies this work as Hobbes's masterpiece, *Leviathan or The Matter, Forme, and Power of A Commonwealth Ecclesiastical and Civil.*

> " The **life** of **man, solitary, poor, nasty, brutish** and **short.** "
>
> THOMAS HOBBES, *LEVIATHAN*

KEY WORKS

1640
Publishes *The Elements of Law*, which upholds royal authority against the claims of parliament.

1642
Presents his radical views on freedom, power, and religion in the treatise *De Cive*.

1651
Argues the need for the absolute authority of a ruler to maintain stability and prevent anarchy in *Leviathan*.

1654
Argues against the existence of free will in *Of Liberty and Necessity*.

1655
Presents his ideas on geometry, mathematics, and physics in *De Corpore*, a follow-up to *De Cive*.

1668
Writes *Behemoth*, a study of the origins of the English Civil War. It is published posthumously in 1681.

parliament as a king. Catholics were scandalized by its attacks on the Church and insistence that religion should be subject to the secular ruler. Once more fearing for his safety, in 1652 Hobbes returned to England, now a republic under Oliver Cromwell. Though he abstained from further political activity, he argued powerfully against the existence of free will and in favour of strict determinism in a debate with Bishop John Bramhall. Less effectively, he engaged in a dispute with the distinguished mathematician John Wallis, who convincingly refuted Hobbes's claim to have "squared the circle".

Life after the Restoration

The restoration of the monarchy under Charles II in 1661 brought Hobbes a pension but not the security he craved. Despite royal protection, he was threatened by parliament with prosecution for upholding atheism, an allegation he denied. He escaped legal action, but was no longer able to publish potentially controversial works such as *Behemoth*, his study of the origins of the Civil War. In his final years he returned to his love of the Greek classics, translating the *Iliad* and *Odyssey* into English.

Hobbes died in 1679, aged 91. His final words were: "I am about to take a great leap in the dark."

▷ **CHARLES II**
This painting of 1642 by William Dobson shows the Prince of Wales, the future king, Charles II. From 1646 to 1648, Charles was tutored by Hobbes when they were both in exile in France.

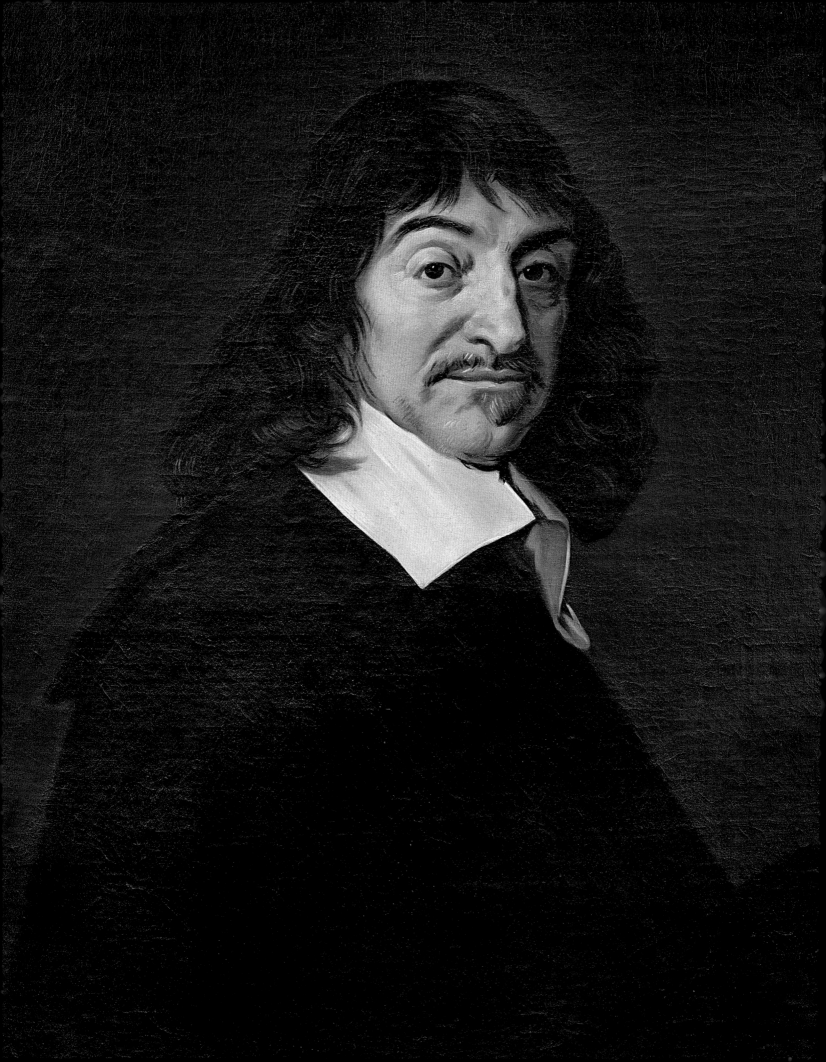

René Descartes

1596–1650, FRENCH

The "father of modern philosophy", Descartes was a ground-breaking mathematician and scientist. He founded the rationalist tradition, believing the use of reason was the key to knowledge of the world.

René Descartes was born in 1596 in the town of La Haye en Touraine, central France. His family belonged to the privileged class of lawyers and administrators – servants of the French state – who ranked beneath the aristocracy but were of solid wealth and status. His father was a member of the regional *parlement* (judicial council) of Brittany. Descartes' mother died about a year after his birth and he was brought up by a wet nurse and his grandmother. He formed no bond with his father, who lived mostly in distant Brittany and soon remarried.

Childhood and schooling

Descartes was, by his own account, a somewhat sickly child. He later wrote that he had inherited from his mother "a dry cough and a pale complexion, which stayed with me until I was more than 20", causing pessimistic doctors to predict an early death. In the tradition of his family, he was destined for a career as a lawyer and – eventually – entry into

△ **DESCARTES' BIRTHPLACE**
Descartes was born at his maternal grandmother's house in La Haye en Touraine. The village is now called Descartes in honour of its famous son.

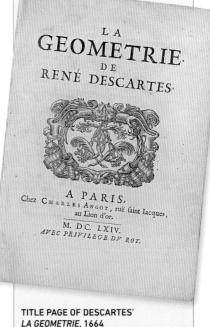

◁ **DESCARTES, 1649**
This painting, thought to be a copy of a lost 1649 work by Frans Hals, is probably a portrait of Descartes. He wears a large, starched white collar and a black coat – a style typical of a Dutch burgher.

parlement like his father. At the age of 11 he was sent to the newly founded La Flèche college, a prestigious school patronized by the French king Henri IV and run by the Jesuits. There, for eight years, he received a rigorous education in Aristotelian philosophy, Latin, Greek, and a little mathematics.

After a further year at the University of Poitiers he was qualified to begin a career in law. However, he had become deeply dissatisfied with his education. "I found myself so overcome by doubts and errors", he later wrote, "I seemed to have gained nothing from studying, apart from becoming gradually more conscious of my ignorance." Disillusioned with

IN CONTEXT
Descartes' geometry

Descartes was almost as influential a mathematician as a philosopher. He was an innovator in the application of algebra to geometry and in the use of coordinates – determining the position of a point by its relation to two fixed lines. Cartesian coordinates, as they are called, are still essential tools for astronomers, engineers, physicists, and designers of computer graphics today. Descartes first published his ideas on geometry as an addendum to *Discourse on Method* in 1637. In the introduction to its 100 pages, he boasted: "Any problem in geometry can easily be reduced to such terms that a knowledge of the length of certain straight lines is sufficient for construction."

**TITLE PAGE OF DESCARTES'
LA GEOMETRIE, 1664**

> " **I think,** therefore **I am.** "

RENE DESCARTES, *DISCOURSE ON METHOD*

"A **real seeker** after **truth** must, **at least once** in a **lifetime**, **doubt** as far as possible of **all things**. "

RENE DESCARTES, *PRINCIPLES OF PHILOSOPHY*

books, he resolved to travel and garner experiences, learning from observation of "what could be found in myself or the great book of the world".

For a young man of Descartes' status, the obvious alternative to a career in law was employment as an army officer. During travels that lasted 10 years, he served in the armies of the United Provinces (the Netherlands) and of Bavaria. He seems to have seen little action, although he may have been present in the Bavarian ranks at the battle of White Mountain near Prague in 1620. After his return to France in 1627, Descartes participated in the siege of La Rochelle, an episode of France's ugly civil conflict between the Catholic authorities and the Protestant Huguenots.

He never took his military career seriously, and at the age of 23 he embarked on the intellectual project that was to occupy the rest of his life.

Dreams of truth

On military service in Bavaria in November 1619, Descartes experienced a kind of revelation. Sleeping in a stove room on a freezing cold night, he had a series of dreams that, he claimed, showed him the path he should follow in life. He awoke convinced that he must seek a solid ground for truth through inner reflection, building on the logic of "clear and certain arguments".

Through the 1620s Descartes felt his way towards what he called "a completely new science" in which all questions would be solved by "a general method". Through a friendship with Dutch scholar Isaac Beeckman, he had been introduced to sophisticated mathematics. While developing original ideas on geometry that were among his most important

▽ **THE SIEGE OF LA ROCHELLE**
This engraving shows an episode in the siege of the French Atlantic port, 1627–28. Descartes visited the conflict to study the trajectories of projectiles and to observe the construction of a dike to block off the harbour entrance.

Fol. 118 *Fig. LIII.*

B

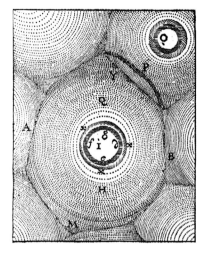

◁ **STRUCTURE OF THE BRAIN**
An illustration from the 1662 edition of Descartes' *Treatise on Man* reflects his interest in the relationship between body and soul, which he believed was mediated by the brain.

However, the treatise offered an impressive mechanistic vision of the natural world as composed purely of matter in motion. Around the same, time, Descartes wrote *Treatise on Man*, which inserted humans into this scheme. Chiefly a study in physiology, it describes the bodies of humans and animals functioning as sophisticated automata – machines analogous to clocks or mills – with physical causality creating the illusion of voluntary self-controlled action. But humans, Descartes argued, also have a "rational soul" of a different non-physical nature, "joined and united" with the body.

△ **THEORY OF VORTICES**
This illustration from a 1668 edition of Descartes' *Epistolae* shows a vortex – a circling band containing planets, comets, and other particles. He postulated that the universe consists of a network of interlocking vortices.

Philosophical fables

Neither of Descartes' treatises was published. Even though he presented them as "fables" about a hypothetical world and a hypothetical man, this could not disguise their radical divergence from established religious doctrine. The persecution of the Italian scientist Galileo Galilei by the Inquisition in 1633 showed that such revolutionary ideas were not acceptable to the Catholic Church.

work, he sought to formulate a way of applying the same form of rigorous thinking found in mathematics to all areas of philosophy and science.

Move to the Netherlands

From 1629, Descartes based himself in the United Provinces, because the Netherlands was the only place in mainland Europe where freedom of thought was broadly respected. An inheritance allowed him to live without material concerns, and so devote himself to his writings.

Itinerant by nature, he resided in a variety of different towns around the country and never married. He did, however, have a daughter, Francine, by a Dutch servant, Helena Jans van der Strom, in 1635. It is recorded that when the child died of scarlet fever

at the age of five, Descartes wept. He later provided Helena with a dowry so she could marry the son of an innkeeper.

Through the 1630s, Descartes attempted nothing less than a complete description of the universe and humans' place in it. The *Treatise on the World*, completed by 1633, covered such topics as the nature of heat, light, and matter, the Copernican heliocentric view of the solar system, and the operation of the senses. Some of its science was misguided – denying the existence of a vacuum required Descartes to invent "vortices" to explain the movement of the planets and comets, a theory that would hold sway in France long after the English scientist Isaac Newton had provided the correct explanation.

IN PROFILE
Elizabeth of Bohemia

Elizabeth of Bohemia (1618–80) was the granddaughter of England's James I. Educated in science, theology, and mathematics, at the age of 24 she began a correspondence with Descartes in which she challenged his theory of mind–body dualism, questioning how a "thinking substance" could act on matter to make a body move. Their letters, which displayed the warmth of close friendship, continued until his death in 1650. In later life Elizabeth became abbess of a Lutheran monastery at Herford in Germany.

PORTRAIT OF ELIZABETH, STUDIO OF GERRIT VAN HONTHORST, c.1650

△ **DISCOURSE ON METHOD**
Unusually, Descartes wrote this work in French rather than Latin, hoping to spread his belief in the primacy of reason to the largest number of readers.

Protestants were equally hostile to any hint of atheism – even though Descartes was always careful to allot God a necessary place in his universe. Eventually he prudently chose to publish three less controversial sections of the *Treatise of the World*, on geometry, optics, and meteorology, with an explanatory preface, the *Discourse on Method*.

Doubt as a tool

Along with the *Meditations* – published four years later, and which elaborates the same arguments – the *Discourse* proved to be Descartes' most durable contribution to philosophy.

Using a method that was to become known as Cartesian Doubt ("Cartesian" is the adjective from Descartes), he applied systematic scepticism to his beliefs in search of a certainty – something that he could not doubt and that must be true.

What we believe we know through the senses is unreliable, he argued, because it may be a hallucination.

▷ **THE PINEAL GLAND**
This sketch from *Treatise on Man* depicts the pineal gland (labelled H), which Descartes proposed as the link between vision and resulting action.

We cannot even be certain whether we are asleep or awake, as dreams can often seem like reality to the sleeper. We could be suffering the delusions of the insane, or be deceived by evil demons without being aware of it. But the one thing that cannot be doubted is that the doubter exists – hence Descartes' famous assertion: "I think, therefore I am." Urging his readers to meditate on their own thought processes, he claimed that inner reflection revealed the human mind as "a substance whose whole essence or nature consists only in thinking" and was wholly distinct from the body. He claimed that certain proof of God's existence could equally be found by introspection.

The outside world

The publication of the *Discourse* and the *Meditations* made Descartes a renowned thinker. Although he was living a reclusive life in the Netherlands, he corresponded with a diverse range of learned people throughout Europe, including Elizabeth of Bohemia and the French mathematician Marin Mersenne.

Descartes spent much of his time attempting to refute criticism of his ideas, in particular concerning the highly problematic relationship between the incorporeal, thinking mind and the mechanical body,

and on thorny questions of religious belief, where he was often required to display a defensive evasiveness.

He also carried out numerous dissections of live animals, experiments with barometers, and other scientific investigations. Twice, in 1647 and 1648, he emerged from his solitude to visit Paris – and it was here that he encountered the French mathematician and theologian Blaise Pascal, among many others. However, Descartes found that the world outside the Netherlands was torn by wars and political disputes, and he soon returned to his haven of peace.

Physiology of the emotions

In 1649, Descartes published his treatise *The Passions of the Soul*, dedicated to Elizabeth of Bohemia. Attempting to give an account of the emotions in physiological terms, it addressed directly the problem of

IN PROFILE
Christina of Sweden

Christina (1626–89) was one of the most extraordinary people of their age. Succeeding to the Swedish throne aged six, they were educated like a prince and crowned king, although they have been called queen. Christina developed a wide range of cultural and intellectual interests. Inviting Descartes to Stockholm was part of a project to make their court "the Athens of the north". In 1654, having converted to Catholicism, Christina abdicated and moved to Rome. There they acted as patron to the sculptor and architect Giovanni Bernini and the composer Alessandro Scarlatti, while causing scandal through wearing masculine clothes and conducting passionate relationships with women.

**CHRISTINA OF SWEDEN,
DAVID BECK, c.1650**

" To be **possessed** of a **vigorous mind** is **not enough**; the **prime requisite** is rightly to **apply it**. "

RENE DESCARTES, *DISCOURSE ON METHOD*

the connection between the mind and the body, locating the link – so he claimed – in the pineal gland.

In the meantime, his writings had attracted the attention of the culturally ambitious Queen Christina of Sweden. With the French ambassador to Sweden, Pierre Chanut, acting as intermediary between the philosopher and the queen, Descartes agreed to travel to Christina's court, sailing on

a Swedish warship sent to serve as his personal transport. The winter weather in Stockholm was brutally cold and the queen insisted on receiving lessons in philosophy at five o'clock in the morning. Probably weakened by this tough regime, Descartes succumbed to a fever in February 1650, dying at the age of 54. His last words were reportedly: "My soul, you have been held captive a

long time. This is the time for you to leave the prison and to relinquish the burden of this body."

As a Catholic who had died in a Protestant country, Descartes was initially buried in a cemetery for orphans and plague victims. In 1666 his body was exhumed and taken to Paris; his remains found a final resting place in the former monastery of Saint-Germain-des-Prés in 1819.

△ **DESCARTES AT THE COURT OF CHRISTINA OF SWEDEN**
In this 18th-century painting by French artist Pierre Louis Dumesnil, Christina of Sweden sits in debate with Descartes at the table on the right of the image (the queen is seated opposite the philosopher).

KEY WORKS

1628
Advocates deduction from one certain truth to another in *The Rules for the Direction of the Mind*, an unfinished treatise.

1633
Attempts a scientific description of light, heat, matter, the solar system, and tides in *Treatise on the World*, an unpublished work.

1637
Publishes *Discourse on Method*, which contains a basic statement of his innovative approach to philosophy.

1641
Writes a detailed exposition of his metaphysical system in *Meditations on First Philosophy*; it is written in Latin for a learned audience.

1644
Summarizes his views on philosophical method and the mechanistic universe in *Principles of Philosophy*.

1649
Dissects the mind–body relationship, the nature of the emotions, and questions of ethics in *Passions of the Soul*.

1664
Describes the human body as a machine in *Treatise on Man*, published posthumously.

Blaise Pascal

1623–1662, FRENCH

Pascal was a man of extraordinary talent in fields from mathematics to practical invention. However, the central focus of his life was his spiritual quest, which he described memorably in his unique prose style.

Blaise Pascal was born in Clermont-Ferrand, central France, in 1623. His mother died when he was three, and five years later the family moved to Paris, where his father focused on his children's education. A child prodigy, Blaise published a work on projective geometry at the age of 17, but he also had practical skills, evident in his development of the Pascaline. This device is now regarded by some as the world's first digital calculator.

Grace and invention

In 1646 Pascal came into contact with Jansenists – followers of an austere Catholicism that accepted divine grace as the key to salvation. Increasingly absorbed by religious concerns, he nonetheless continued his scientific work, testing Galileo's theories, building instruments to measure air pressure, and studying the nature of a vacuum. In the course of his experiments, he incidentally invented an improved syringe and established the theoretical basis for the hydraulic press.

After the spiritual trauma of his "night of fire" in 1654 (see box, right), his thoughts turned increasingly to religion. In 1655 he went on retreat to the convent of Port-Royal-des-Champs, the Jansenist headquarters outside Paris, and over the next four years divided his time between this

sanctuary and the French capital. It was in this period that he wrote his two best-known works, the *Lettres Provinciales* (*Provincial Letters*) and the *Pensées* (*Thoughts*). The first took the form of letters in defence of a Jansenist on trial by a theological court, criticizing the Jesuits (rivals of Jansenists) for their misleading logic. The work gained a wide audience, in part for the clarity of its style – later critics have acclaimed it as "the beginning of modern French prose".

The *Pensées*, written in 1657–58, were originally composed as notes for a proposed book, *The Defence of the Christian Religion*, which was left unfinished at Pascal's death. Reflecting the author's mental struggles, they focus on the spiritual inadequacy of human beings, who are racked by aspirations that remain unattainable without God's presence. This Supreme Being can only ever be approached

through Jesus Christ, who – by taking on Man's fallen state – made himself an intermediary through which to approach God.

Thereafter Pascal returned to science and studies of geometry with the encouragement of his superiors at Port-Royal. However, ill health, to which he had always been prone, intervened, and for the last three years of his short life, he devoted himself entirely to good works and the care of his own soul. He died in great pain in 1662 at the age of 39, probably as a result of stomach cancer.

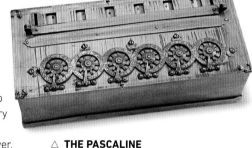

△ **THE PASCALINE**
This machine is an exact replica of Pascal's calculator, which he designed in 1642 to calculate addition and subtraction. The device won Pascal fame in his life, but it could not be mass-produced.

▽ **PORT-ROYAL-DES-CHAMPS**
Pascal's younger sister Jacqueline joined the Abbey of Port-Royal-des-Champs as a nun in 1651. Her influence helped to draw Pascal closer to Jansenism, which had taken root at the Abbey.

◁ **BLAISE PASCAL**
Pascal, depicted here by the French painter Augustin Quesnel, was a true polymath, but was best known in his lifetime for his sometimes controversial writings on faith and religion.

IN CONTEXT
Pascal's night of fire

Already religiously minded, Pascal had an intense supernatural experience that lasted for around two hours on the evening of 23 November 1654. It was to transform his life, redirecting his thoughts to spiritual matters. Pascal wrote down the revelation on a scrap of paper. Beginning "Fire. God of Abraham, God of Isaac, God of Jacob, not of the philosophers and scholars. Certainty, certainty, heartfelt, joy, peace...", the account suggests a very personal illumination. For the rest of his life Pascal kept the paper sewed into the lining of his coat, where it was eventually discovered after his death.

▷ **SPINOZA AT STUDY, 1664**
This portrait of Spinoza is by Franz Wulfhagen, a student of Rembrandt's. The work is believed to have been commissioned by Johann Eberhard Schwelling, a German-born scholar of science and law.

Baruch Spinoza

1632–1677, DUTCH

Condemned in his day as a heretic and a freethinker, Spinoza has come to be seen as a champion of intellectual integrity, fighting all forms of dogmatism and seeking a firm rational foundation for religion and ethics.

"In the **state of nature**, **wrong-doing** is **impossible**; or, if **anyone** does **wrong**, it is to **himself**, not to **another**."

BARUCH SPINOZA, *TRACTATUS POLITICUS*

△ **HOUSE IN RIJNSBURG**
From 1661 to 1663, Spinoza lived in this house in Rijnsburg, near Leiden, depicted by the Dutch artist Antonie Louis Koster. In Rijnsburg, Spinoza joined the study groups of the Collegiants (a liberal Christian association), becoming an important though divisive member of the organization.

Baruch Spinoza – who later took to Latinizing his Hebrew first name as Benedictus – was born in Amsterdam to a wealthy Jewish family who had previously fled from persecution in Portugal (see box, below). He was schooled in Hebrew studies, but his enquiring mind and his unwillingness to passively accept received ideas got him into trouble with the religious authorities, and eventually led to his excommunication from his own community. After this, he earned his living mainly as a lens grinder, supplying the growing market for spectacles, microscopes, and telescopes in the Netherlands at that time. The powdered glass he inhaled over the years may have contributed to his death from a lung complaint in 1677, at the relatively early age of 45.

Response to dualism
From his youth, Spinoza showed an intense intellectual curiosity that expressed itself in many forms. He was deeply versed in Hebraic monotheism, but equally immersed in the new philosophy of René Descartes and Thomas Hobbes – contemporaries of his, though of an earlier generation.

Descartes had proposed the existence of three substances in the universe – God, mind, and matter. Spinoza, however, could not accept the absolute distinction between the mental and the physical. His solution to Descartes' dualism was to propose

absolute monism: for him, mind and body and all their manifestations were only temporary modifications of a single substance making up the universe, and that substance was God. This pantheistic vision implied complete determinism: if every thought and action is part of a single entity that stretches infinitely beyond human comprehension, then there is no room for religious ideas of sin and righteousness, or indeed even of good or evil.

Spinoza was reviled by some as a renegade and atheist for expressing these ideas, but he also gained admirers who relished the scope of his intellectual ambition and

his commitment to freedom of thought – a commitment that was exemplified by his refusal in 1673 to take up the prestigious post of professor of philosophy at Heidelberg, Germany's oldest university, lest it compromise his ability to pursue his own vision.

Scientific methods
Spinoza's interest extended beyond philosophy into science, especially into the recent advances in astronomy and optics made by Nicolaus Copernicus, Johannes Kepler, and Galileo; indeed, his scientific leanings probably influenced his choice of lens-grinding

IN CONTEXT
City of freedom

In the 17th century, Amsterdam was an important haven for religious dissidents. Spinoza's family had moved there from their native Portugal to take advantage of the religious tolerance it offered to Jews. The city was also the publishing centre for philosophical works that were too contentious to be printed in France or England. The environment gave Spinoza the space to develop his ideas, which posed a challenge to traditional authority, paving the way for Enlightenment thinkers. However, the young philosopher attracted the hostility of synagogue elders by his willingness to challenge the authority of the Scriptures, and at the age of 23 he found himself the subject of a *herem*, or writ of excommunication. Citing his "abominable heresies" and "monstrous deeds", the document formally cursed him. As a result he was expelled for a time from the city, taking up residence in an outlying village.

SPINOZA IN AMSTERDAM OSTRACIZED BY THE LOCAL JEWISH COMMUNITY

"All excellent things are as difficult as they are rare."

BARUCH SPINOZA, *ETHICA*

as a profession. In his metaphysics too, he sought to achieve the objective certainty of physics and mathematics, taking the Greek geometer Euclid as his model. In his great work the *Ethica*, Spinoza borrowed from Euclid's format of numbered axioms, definitions, and propositions, each with an attached demonstration, to bolster his arguments in the belief that a geometric presentation of his ideas would be clearer than a conventional narrative

To modern eyes, his attempt to claim scientific certainty for imprecise concepts such as substance and thought might seem unconvincing, but Spinoza's dedication to the pursuit of verifiable truth in philosophy continues to inspire respect and admiration.

Bible studies

Spinoza held radical views on religion, arguing in the *Tractatus Theologico-Politicus* that readers of the Scriptures should interpret them on their own terms, without relying on the existing doctrine. He analysed the Torah (or Pentateuch, the first five books of the Bible) with the same clear-sighted, scholarly eye that he brought to all other subjects, an approach that led him to question the dates traditionally given for their authorship (he thought they were more recent than the accepted view) and to seek rational explanations for biblical miracles.

Spinoza also challenged the authority of the prophets, seeing them as fallible humans whose strength lay in their moral and ethical insights rather than their factual assumptions, which were only those of people of their time. In doing so, he launched what would come to be called the "higher criticism" of biblical texts. Although widely practised today, this approach drew much criticism from the religious establishment at the time.

◁ **ANONYMOUS TEXT**
Spinoza's work on politics was published anonymously (in Latin rather than Dutch) to protect him from his vociferous critics.

Political analysis

Spinoza also turned his mind to politics (particularly in the unfinished *Tractatus Politicus*). In this field he was greatly influenced by Hobbes: like Hobbes, he accepted the existence of a social contract that bound individuals to the state as the price of avoiding the perils of anarchy. As such, he opposed all forms of rebellion. In other respects, however, he took a more liberal view, rejecting Hobbes's insistence on autocracy as the only realistic model of government and instead proposing democracy as a natural form of social organization. Additionally, he always held that certain rights must be sacrosanct – most notably, freedom of thought.

Ethical thinking

Spinoza's most enduring work was in the field of ethics, where he examined how individuals can best adapt their lives to the totality of existence. He set out his position in the first part of his *Ethica* (*Ethics* or, in full, *Ethics, Demonstrated in Geometrical Order*). Spinoza argued that the acceptance of his monist view – that all is One,

IN CONTEXT
Spinoza the linguist

Spinoza came from a Hebrew-speaking family and is thought to have attended a school serving Amsterdam's prosperous Jewish community. There he would have studied the Hebrew Bible and the Talmud, the written version of the Jewish oral law, as well as earlier Jewish philosophers such as Maimonides. Outside school hours, Spinoza was taught Latin by a German scholar, and that was the language in

which he chose to write his major works. He had some knowledge of most major European languages, notably Spanish and Portuguese, and wrote his first, unpublished work – released in English translation in 1910 as *Short Treatise on God, Man and his Well-Being* – in Dutch. Latin, however, enabled him to address a wider audience; one modern commentator has referred to the *Ethica* as "the last indisputable Latin masterpiece".

SPINOZA'S *SHORT TREATISE ON GOD, MAN, AND HIS WELL-BEING*

◁ **SPINOZA'S STUDY**
It was in the house in Rijnsburg (now preserved as a museum) that Spinoza began work on his masterpiece, *Ethica*, in which he derives a cosmology from first principles and provides a guide to the meaning of an ethical life.

and that One is what we know as God – has moral implications. If there is only one substance (God) in which everything else exists as a mode, then everything that happens is merely a temporary modification of that substance, one that can be conceived as an attribute of either of Descartes' two categories of thought or extension – that is, as mental or physical. God, then, is always infinitely beyond our comprehension, representing complete knowledge, whereas our knowledge can never be more than profoundly limited and partial.

Crucially, however, Spinoza did not draw a defeatist conclusion from his insights. Instead he argued that our goal as humans should be to increase our knowledge as far as possible, thereby coming as close to God as our intellects can take us. The way to do this is to view the universe not as a passing show but as God sees it. Spinoza even coined a phrase to describe this viewpoint – *sub specie aeternitatis*, meaning "from the perspective of the eternal".

An enlightened life

The last two sections of the *Ethica* are entitled "Of Human Bondage, or the Strength of the Emotions" (Somerset Maugham would later borrow the first phrase as the title of a famous novel) and "Of the Power of the Understanding, or of Human Freedom". In these sections of the text, he argued that freedom lies in expanding intellectual comprehension, which brings us closer to God.

This aspect of Spinoza's thought won him many followers, but he was also admired for his personal qualities: his humility and dedication in the search for truth continue to inspire esteem. He lived modestly, did not seek honour or advancement, and maintained a courteous demeanour in the face of criticism and abuse. The British philosopher Bertrand Russell described him as "the noblest and most lovable of the great philosophers", adding "intellectually, some others have surpassed him, but ethically he is supreme".

KEY WORKS

1661	1663	1665	1670	1675	1677
Spinoza's *Treatise on the Correction of the Understanding*, gives his motives for the study of philosophy.	Completes the first part of his *Ethica*: *De Deo* (*Concerning God*), which sees God as identical with the universe.	Starts work on the *Tractatus Politicus*, which analyses various forms of government; it is unfinished at his death.	*Tractatus Theologico-Politicus* is published. It is officially banned in the Netherlands.	Completes work on the *Ethica* but delays its publication, fearing that it will bring about persecution.	The final, five-part version of the *Ethica* is published after Spinoza's death.

John Locke

1632–1704, ENGLISH

Locke's works formed the basis of political liberalism and philosophical empiricism, and influenced everything from the American Constitution to the thinking of George Berkeley and David Hume.

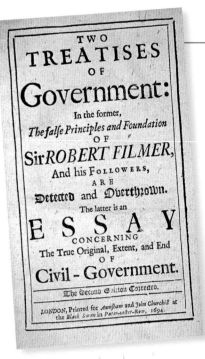

△ **POLITICAL POLEMIC**
This edition of Locke's *Two Treatises of Government* dates from 1694. The principles expressed in this work went on to be of fundamental importance to the Founding Fathers of the US.

Born in Wrington, Somerset, John Locke grew up in turbulent times. The English Civil War broke out when he was 10 years old, and in 1649 the king, Charles I, was beheaded and England became a republic under Oliver Cromwell.

From 1652, Locke studied at Christ Church College, Oxford. Finding the standard curriculum of classical philosophy unstimulating, in his spare time he read the ideas of recent thinkers such as Francis Bacon and René Descartes and attended lectures in science, mixing with rising stars of the new scientific age such as Robert Boyle and Robert Hooke. Locke also studied medicine, and when Anthony Ashley Cooper (later the earl of Shaftesbury) asked him to become his personal physician, he accepted and moved into Cooper's household in London. After the restoration of the monarchy in 1660, his patron's activism helped to shape Locke's political ideas.

Locke's empiricism

From 1675 to 1679, while living in France, Locke worked on what would become one of his most famous texts, *An Essay Concerning Human Understanding*, in which he set out his ideas on the mind and on knowledge. Rejecting the position of rationalists such as Descartes, he argued that humans are not born with innate knowledge, but that understanding is acquired through direct experience – a view known as empiricism. At birth, we are merely "white paper", or a *tabula rasa*, empty but receptive to the experiences that occur to us through life. The knowledge gained from sensory experience, or "sensation", is then complemented by "reflection".

Monarchy and exile

On his return from France, Locke composed his major political work, *Two Treatises of Government* (1689). In it he argued against absolute monarchy and also set out his ideas on the social contract, the will of the majority, the equality of human beings, and the duties and limits of legitimate government. At this time, the English royal succession was in turmoil, with the Whigs (a major political faction) rejecting the idea of a Catholic king. Suspected conspiracies led to arrests and executions, and in 1681 Shaftesbury, a Whig leader, fled to Holland; sensibly, Locke followed in 1683. During five years of exile, he continued work on *An Essay Concerning Human Understanding*, and wrote *Letter Concerning Toleration*, which contained his thoughts on the importance of religious tolerance.

Locke returned to England in 1689, a year after the Glorious Revolution that deposed the Catholic James II and installed the Protestant William of Orange on the throne. In his final years, Locke lived at the house of Lady Masham, in Essex (see box, below), where he entertained various friends, including Isaac Newton, and continued to write about politics, philosophy, economics, religion, and education.

▷ **LOCKE IN LATER LIFE**
This portrait of Locke made by Sir Godfrey Kneller in 1697 shows the philosopher in the last years of his life, by which time he had removed himself from society and settled in the country estate of his friend Lady Masham.

IN PROFILE
Lady Masham

Damaris Cudworth, Lady Masham (1659–1708), was the daughter of the Cambridge Platonist Ralph Cudworth, growing up in academic circles that allowed her intellect to flourish. She met Locke some time before 1682 and he encouraged her in her philosophical writings, praising her "original mind" and "clearness of thought". The two corresponded on a range of philosophical subjects, mutually influencing one another. She published two books, *A Discourse Concerning the Love of God* (1696) and *Occasional Thoughts in Reference to a Vertuous or Christian Life* (1705). She also corresponded with Gottfried Wilhelm Leibniz and was an early advocate of women's education.

THE MANOR OF OATES, THE RESIDENCE OF LADY MASHAM IN ESSEX

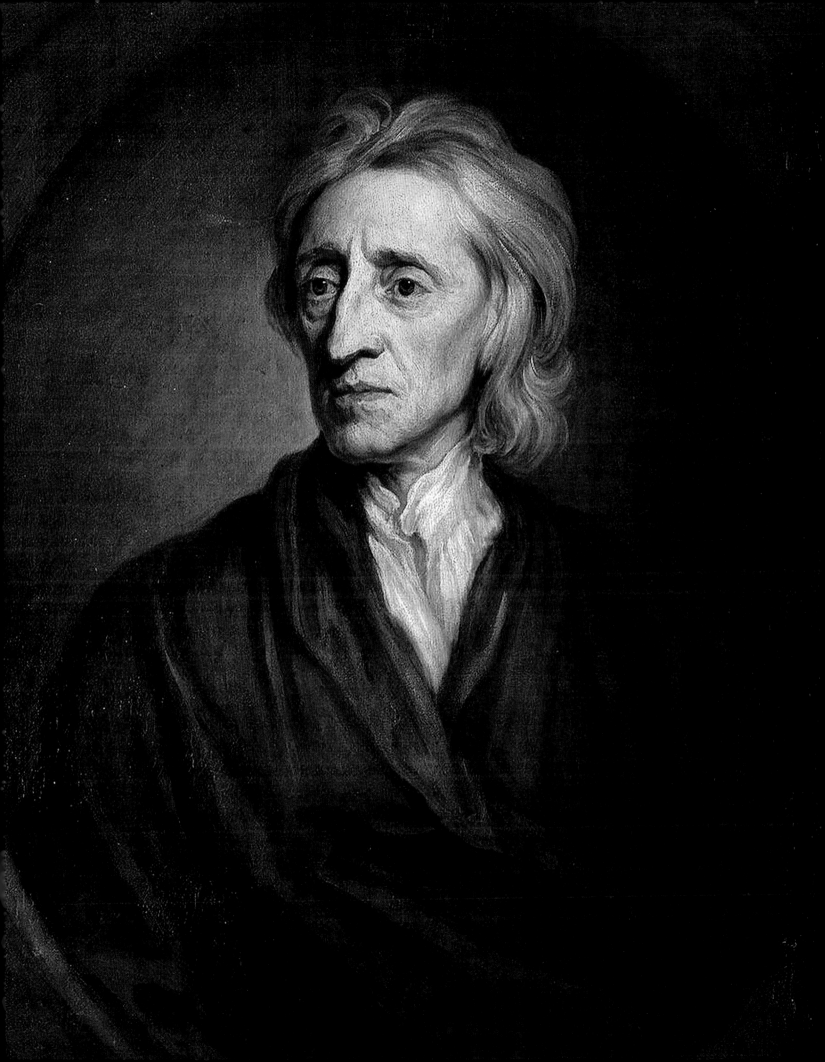

Gottfried Leibniz

1646–1716, GERMAN

Leibniz has been called "the Aristotle of the modern world". As a thinker, he sought to bridge the gap between the God-centred world of the Scholastics and the rationalism of the Scientific Revolution.

Gottfried Wilhelm Leibniz was the son of a professor of moral philosophy at the University of Leipzig. He followed in his father's footsteps as a student at the same institution, completing his bachelor's degree at the age of just 16 and his master's a year later. Leibniz then studied law, and was awarded a doctorate from the University of Altdorf in 1666.

Early years

Leibniz's precocity and his academic background pointed to a future as a thinker and teacher, but he rejected such a career on the grounds that "my thoughts were turned in an entirely different direction". The path he chose to follow instead was a worldly one, in which he sought advancement through placements with the nobility. He soon found a patron in the shape of the Baron von Boyneburg, a former chief minister of the elector of Mainz.

In the elector's service, Leibniz was able to travel on diplomatic missions: in Paris, he soon became acquainted with the philosophers Antoine Arnauld (see box, right) and Nicolas Malebranche, and the mathematician Christiaan Huygens; and on a later mission to London, he met the scientists and advocates of experimentation Robert Hooke and Robert Boyle.

In 1676 Leibniz transferred to the service of the duchy of Hanover, spending most of the rest of his life in that city. His principal employers were its ruling family, whom he served as a counsellor, librarian, and court historian. As such, he spent many years toiling on a history of the House of Guelph, from which they claimed descent, reaching the year 1009 by the time of his own death.

Leibniz's official duties in Hanover left him plenty of time to devote to his real interests, which included theology, ethics, and, above all, mathematics. In this field he was one of the great innovators, coming up with the discovery of calculus independently of Isaac Newton, who was working on the problem at the same time. Although Newton may have had precedence in formulating some of the key ideas, Leibniz was

IN CONTEXT
The Arnauld/Leibniz correspondence

During his time in Paris (1672–76), Leibniz was introduced to the eminent philosopher Antoine Arnauld (1612–94). Arnauld's intellectual interests were mainly in religion and theology. He was also a notable Cartesian scholar and the author of the *Fourth Objections to Descartes' Meditations on First Philosophy* (1641). In the mid-1680s Leibniz began a lengthy correspondence with Arnauld, which Leibniz described as being on "grace, God's concurrence with creatures, the nature of miracles, the cause of sin and the origin of evil, the immortality of the soul, ideas". What followed was an immensely rich exchange between the two thinkers, consisting of some 28 letters on metaphysics, ontology, and methodology, which influenced a short but important work by Leibniz, *Discourse on Metaphysics* (1686).

◁ **GOTTFRIED LEIBNIZ**
This portrait of the philosopher was made c.1700 by Christoph Bernhard Francke, a former military officer who was official painter in a north German court.

◁ **CALCULATING MACHINES**
Leibniz made four of his calculating machines. Only one survives, having been discovered in the attic of the University Church of Göttingen.

" If there were not **the best** among **all possible worlds, God** would not have produced **any**. "
GOTTFRIED LEIBNIZ, *THEODICY*

the first to publish on the subject, and some of his notations are used to this day. He is also credited with the invention of mathematical logic (although he remained publicly silent on the subject and it would be another 150 years before it became a recognized discipline) and carried out pioneering work on binary numbers – a subject that would become central to the computing revolution of the 20th century. In addition, he put his ideas to tremendous practical use by devising a stepped reckoner, a calculating machine (see p.131).

Suppressed ideas

Even though Leibniz's official duties at court were not onerous, they had an unfortunate effect on his philosophy. Always aware of the risk of offending his employers, he was cautious about publishing ideas that might have been seen as dangerously innovative or subversive. He published relatively little in his lifetime and much of his output took the form of short essays. He kept his thoughts largely for his correspondence with other thinkers, who would sometimes encourage him in his caution. Leibniz's friend the Jansenist (puritan Catholic) Antoine Arnauld at one point warned him: "I find so many things that alarm me in these thoughts, which almost all men, if I am not mistaken, will find shocking, that I do not see the use in writing down what all the world must seemingly reject."

Perhaps as a result, the ideas with which he became associated in his lifetime were those that he knew

◁ **LEIBNIZ'S HOUSE, HANOVER**
Leibniz lived and worked on the first floor of this grand house in Hanover. The house was destroyed by British bombs in World War II, but rebuilt in the 1980s.

> " **Music** is a hidden **arithmetic exercise** of the **soul**, which **does not know** that it is counting. "

GOTTFRIED LEIBNIZ, LETTER TO CHRISTIAN GOLDBACH, 17 APRIL 1712

KEY WORKS

1686
Writes *Discourse on Metaphysics*, a short treatise partly inspired by his correspondence with the French philosopher Antoine Arnauld.

1695
Publishes his *New System of Nature* as an essay in a French philosophical journal.

1704
Completes *New Essays on Human Understanding*, written as a rebuttal of John Locke's *Essay Concerning Human Understanding*.

1710
Publishes the *Theodicy*, the only one of his works to appear in book form during his lifetime.

1714
Writes *Monadology*, a short text outlining the concept of monads. It is published only after his death.

IN CONTEXT
Leibniz and Voltaire

Leibniz is best, but rather unfairly, remembered in literary circles as the inspiration for Dr Pangloss, a character in Voltaire's 1759 satire *Candide*. In the book, Pangloss's worldview is one of unbridled optimism, summed up in the phrase "All is for the best in the best of all possible worlds". The French thinker was taking aim at the argument used by Leibniz in his *Theodicy* (subtitled "On God's Goodness"), in which he argued that a rational and benevolent deity could not have created an imperfect world. Voltaire took issue with this view, using the calamitous 1755 Lisbon earthquake to cast doubt on Leibniz's reasoning.

would not cause outrage. In his theological tract, the *Theodicy* (1710), for example, he argued of all the infinite number of worlds that could have been created, God, as a perfect being, chose the best possible one. To explain the fact that evil nonetheless exists in the universe, Leibniz claimed that a world with free will is better than a deterministic one without free will, even if it enables wrong-doing. This optimistic viewpoint endeared him to the authorities, but drew the ridicule of later thinkers (see box, right).

Sufficient reason

Leibniz's more radical ideas emerged later. He distinguished, for example, between two types of truth: of reason, and of fact. Truths of reason (analytic truths) could, he argued, be assessed solely on their own merits by the exercise of logic. Such, for example, are mathematical formulae that are susceptible to direct verification; like all analytic truths, they cannot logically be denied, because the act of denial would involve a contradiction. But the other class, synthetic truths, require further investigation into the facts underlying them before they can be classed as true; they are not self-contained. This distinction became central to philosophical discourse over the next three centuries, being taken up by Kant in the 18th century and by the logical positivists 200 years later.

An addendum to the concept of the two types of truth lay in the principle of sufficient reason. Leibniz argued that every truth must have a reason why it is so. Analytic truths contain their own reasons that can be puzzled out by logic. For synthetic truths, though, the sufficient reasons must be sought in the physical causes that necessarily brought them. This line of thought provides a methodology for the logical examination of causality.

A far more controversial part of Leibniz's thinking was set out in *Monadology* (1714), which was an attempt to address the fundamental elements of existence, which he termed *monads* (from the Greek word *monas*, or "unit").

A universe of monads

According to Leibniz, an infinite number of monads makes up the universe. Modern readers inevitably associate these monads with atoms, but Leibniz conceived each one as a microcosmic world apart, self-sufficient and "windowless", while in itself reflecting the whole macrocosm.

More significantly still, Leibniz considered that although the monads might have some of the properties of physical entities, each one of them was in fact a soul; in their totality they made up the giant spiritual whole that is God's universe. In one respect this line of thinking looks back to the God-centred universe of the Middle Ages, but it also lends itself to a more contemporary interpretation.

Among Leibniz's pioneering concepts was what he called *vis viva*, or "living force" (now called kinetic energy), an attempt to describe the quantity of motion. Such radical thoughts – and the philosophical and mathematical debates that they inspired – were the ideas that connected the world that thinkers such as Thomas Aquinas would have understood with that of modern physics.

19TH-CENTURY FRENCH ENGRAVING IMAGINING VOLTAIRE'S DR PANGLOSS

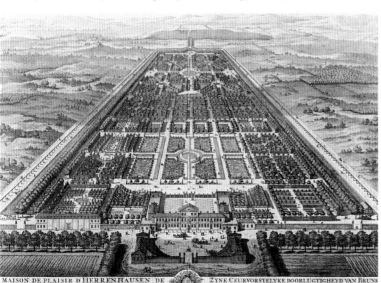

MAISON DE PLAISIR D'HERRENHAUSEN DE S.A. ELECTORALE DE BRUNSWIC LUNEBURG &c. &c. &c.

ZYNE CEURVORSTELYKE DOORLUGTIGHEYD VAN BRUNS WIC LUNENBURG VOORTREFFELYKE LUSTPLAATS GENAAMT HERRENHAUSEN

◁ **HERRENHAUSEN GARDENS**
One of Leibniz's favoured pastimes was strolling in the magnificent Baroque gardens of Herrenhausen Palace. Their centrepiece – a fountain capable of sending water to a height of 35m (115ft) – was designed by Leibniz.

Sor Juana Inés de la Cruz

1648–1695, MEXICAN

Scholar, poet, playwright, and nun, Sor (Sister) Juana devoted her life to philosophical and scientific study, and the production of a stream of literary works. In recent years she has been adopted as a feminist icon.

Born Juana de Asbaje y Ramírez in San Miguel Nepantla, a hamlet southeast of Mexico City, Juana was a child prodigy. She learned to read at the age of three and by the time she was eight she had composed a poem in honour of the Holy Sacrament. In 1660, she moved to live with her grandfather in Mexico City, where she is said to have learned Latin in just 20 lessons. Her reputation for wit and learning spread, and she was invited to the court of the Spanish viceroy and his wife, who became her patrons.

The service of God

In her teens, Juana determined to join a convent – where she could devote herself to study. After a three-month period as a postulant (candidate) with the Discalced Carmelites, an ascetic offshoot of the Carmelite Order, she settled for the slightly less strict Hieronymites, entering the Convent of San Jeronimo and Santa Paula when she was just 17. She was to remain there for the rest of her life, helped with her worldly needs for the first 15 years by an enslaved girl provided for her by her mother.

Over the next two decades Sor Juana assembled a library said to have contained 4,000 volumes and wrote the lyrical poems and plays on which her reputation rests. Her thoughts on gender and the relations between men and women have proved of particular interest to modern feminists. In this respect, one of her most admired

texts is her *Respuesta a Sor Filotea* (*Reply to Sister Filotea*), written in response to the bishop of Puebla, who had chosen that female pseudonym to criticize Sor Juana's secular pursuits. In response she argued that there is nothing whatsoever in Scripture that prohibits the education of women and that learning can only enhance their understanding of the sacred texts.

Nevertheless, the Church authorities took a critical view of her activities and the archbishop of Mexico – an opponent of plays and playhouses – accused her of waywardness. Perhaps as a result of this pressure, Sor Juana decided to give up all her worldly interests, signing a document of penance in her own blood and selling all her books and scientific instruments to give the money to the poor. She died in 1695 in an epidemic of the plague, which she caught while ministering to infected sisters in the convent.

◁ **COLLECTED EULOGIES**
The tributes written about Sor Juana by some 60 of Spain's pre-eminent poets were collected into this volume, which was first published five years after her death.

◁ **SAN JERONIMO**
This convent in Mexico City was the home of Sor Juana for more than 25 years. The convent closed in the 19th century.

> **IN CONTEXT**
>
> **Sor Juana the playwright**
>
> Part of Sor Juana's literary output consisted of plays that seem surprisingly worldly given that they were written by a nun. *Pawns of a House* is a comedy involving star-crossed lovers separated by a jealous rival, only to be reunited happily. *The Real Labyrinth is Love* adapts the story of Theseus and the Minotaur from Greek myth to reflect on the hero's subsequent relationship with Ariadne. The play partly inspired the Ballet Rambert's production *Labyrinth of Love*, while Juana's own life was the subject of British playwright Helen Edmundson's *The Heresy of Love*, premiered by the Royal Shakespeare Company in 2012.

▷ **SOR JUANA, c.1772**
In this posthumous portrait made by Andrés de Islas in c.1772, Sor Juana wears the habit of her order and an exaggerated nun's badge (*escudo de monja*) depicting the Annunciation. The surrounding books, inkwells, and quills signal her intellectual pursuits.

> "**Who** has **forbidden women** to **engage** in **private** and **individual studies**? Have they not a **rational soul** as **men** do?"
>
> SOR JUANA, *AUTODEFENSA ESPIRITUAL*

George Berkeley

1685–1753, IRISH

Berkeley was a churchman and philosopher. He propounded the concept of subjective idealism, maintaining that it is only in the act of perception that material objects exist.

George Berkeley was born in Kilkenny, Ireland, in 1685, and grew up in the grounds of Dysart Castle, where the family home lay. He attended Trinity College Dublin from the age of 15 and completed his education there, gaining a degree in 1704 and becoming a fellow in 1707. Two years later he was ordained into the (Protestant) Church of Ireland, and he remained a churchman for the rest of his life. He was appointed dean of Derry in 1724 and then bishop of Cloyne in County Cork 10 years later.

Early writings

Much of Berkeley's most original philosophical work was completed in Dublin by the time he was 28. *An Essay towards a New Theory of Vision*, his first significant text, was published in 1709, when he was just 24. Four years later, with three books already published, he travelled to England, where he attracted considerable attention. Jonathan Swift, who was an influential figure in political circles, introduced him at court (see box, right). Over the next few years

Berkeley travelled, serving as a chaplain and a tutor to aristocrats and their children on the Grand Tour. He settled for a while in Sicily and then spent almost four years in Italy.

On his return to Britain he became obsessed with a project to set up a college in Bermuda, then a British colony. Its function was to prepare indigenous Americans and British settlers for the ministry and for missionary work. Berkeley used his persuasive powers to obtain a royal charter for the scheme and he also received the promise of a substantial grant from the British government.

In 1728 he travelled to America with his newly-wed wife, and bought an estate in Rhode Island. By 1731, it was clear that funds from the British government would not be forthcoming, and Berkeley returned to London. A major beneficiary of his visit was Yale University, founded 30 years earlier, to which he left his library and his house.

Berkeley then spent three more years in London before receiving the appointment to Cloyne. He lived there for the next 18 years, moving with his family to Oxford only in

△ **ARMS OF CLOYNE CATHEDRAL**
Berkeley was bishop of Cloyne from 1734 until his death in 1753. The cathedral church is still in use today in Cloyne.

◁ **BERKELEY BY SMIBERT, 1727**
This portrait was made by John Smibert, a Scottish artist who accompanied Berkeley to America, hoping to become a professor at Berkeley's college.

IN PROFILE
JONATHAN SWIFT

The writer and cleric Jonathan Swift (1667–1745) was 18 years older than his countryman George Berkeley. Both men had attended Kilkenny College, a Church of Ireland school. It was Swift who presented Berkeley to the court of Queen Anne and gave him the chance to contribute to his journal *The Guardian.* Swift was a brilliant prose satirist and a fierce opponent of war and imperialism; he is best known for his parodic fantasy *Gulliver's Travels* (1726).

GULLIVER IN LILLIPUT, A SCENE FROM AN EDITION OF *GULLIVER'S TRAVELS*

> " In the **pursuit of truth** we must beware of being **misled by terms** which we do not rightly **understand**. "
>
> GEORGE BERKELEY, *DE MOTU*

△ **THE BERMUDA GROUP, 1728**
Berkeley (standing far right) is pictured here with the backers of his project to found a seminary and college in the New World. The artist, John Smibert, included himself in the painting (far left).

1752 to oversee his son George's matriculation into the university. He died in Oxford the following year, and is buried in the city's Christ Church Cathedral.

Response to Locke
As an idealistic young man, Berkeley had been distressed by the materialist implications of John Locke's empirical philosophy. Locke had proposed a mechanistic world in which bodies composed of matter interacted in space according to laws of science. Locke argued that these bodies enter consciousness through our sense organs; and when this stimulation reaches the brain, it generates ideas in the mind. Berkeley recoiled from this machine-like logic, which he saw as undermining the arguments for God's existence. He saw Locke's universe as one that ran entirely of its own accord without the need for divine intervention.

If God was taken out of the equation, Berkeley thought all morality was put at risk. In response, he chose to attack Locke's logic in its weakest part. In his *Treatise Concerning the Principles of Human Knowledge*, published when he was 25, and in the *Three Dialogues between Hylas and Philonous*, which appeared three years later, he argued that the only reality of which we can be sure is that within our own minds. The mental images we form are – for us – the real world. To be, in Berkeley's view, is to be perceived.

Berkeley followed through the logic of this position to the point of denying the existence of material objects when they are not directly perceived, at least from a human perspective. If pressed to state whether he believed that a table (for example) ceased to exist when there was nobody in the room to view it, he would have argued that it was indeed always there, because it was observed by an omnipresent God.

Refutation and admiration
Berkeley won admirers for the clear-sightedness of his ideas, but he also attracted a degree of ridicule from other thinkers of the time. A story that has entered the annals of philosophical history concerns the

" I might as well **doubt** of my own being, as of the being of those things **I actually see and feel**."

GEORGE BERKELEY, *THREE DIALOGUES BETWEEN HYLAS AND PHILONOUS*

KEY WORKS

1709
Writes *An Essay towards a New Theory of Vision*, which locates the existence of objects within the mind.

1710
Confronts John Locke's theories of human perception in *A Treatise Concerning the Principles of Human Knowledge*.

1713
Three Dialogues between Hylas and Philonous continues the arguments outlined by Berkeley in the 1710 *Treatise*.

1721
De Motu challenges Newton's doctrine of absolute space and motion.

1732
Publishes *Alciphron*, a series of philosophical dialogues attacking freethinkers

1744
Publishes *Siris*, a chain of arguments concerning the virtues of tar-water.

response of writer Samuel Johnson to being told that Berkeley's argument for the immateriality of things was hard to refute. Johnson reportedly aimed a hefty kick at a large stone, saying, "I refute it thus!"

Changing status

With advances in empirical science over the following decades, Locke's materialist view of the world came to prevail over Berkeley's subjective idealism. This position changed, to some extent, in the 20th century. Thinkers such as Ernst Mach and, later, Albert Einstein perceived the universe as relational (things were defined solely by their relations with other things), thus challenging the certainties of Newtonian physics. Philosophers looked again at Berkeley's earlier assault on the view – which by that time had been generally accepted – of the world as a gigantic machine.

When he was in his 30s, Berkeley had directly addressed Newton's views in his essay "On Motion", which he submitted unsuccessfully for a prize offered by the French Academy of Sciences. In it he proved willing to accept the laws of physics as useful tools in studying motion as long as they were not taken to be its causes. Bodies, being passive and inert, could not in themselves cause motion – only minds could, and that meant, ultimately, the mind of God.

From such arguments he drew a conclusion that some modern physicists have echoed – that even if the building blocks of the Newtonian system were actually fictions, they could nonetheless be helpful fictions insofar as they served a purpose in facilitating calculations and deducing formulae. Although their premises were very different, some relativists came to see Berkeley as a forerunner of their own critique of Newton. In

▷ **PRINCIPIA, 1687**
Isaac Newton's ideas, expounded in his three-volume *Principia*, helped to establish mechanistic materialism as the prevailing philosophy of the age.

a later work, *The Analyst* (playfully subtitled *A Discourse addressed to an Infidel Mathematician*), he took a similarly iconoclastic approach to the foundations of mathematics, styling himself a "free-thinker" in relation to the discipline's accepted truths.

Berkeley's taste for controversy in matters of the mind was tempered by wit and style, and throughout his life he showed a humane regard for the poor and disadvantaged. In London, he was active in the establishment of the Foundling Hospital for abandoned children, and was listed as one of its original governors. In America too he was remembered as a benefactor, and the city of Berkeley in California bears his name.

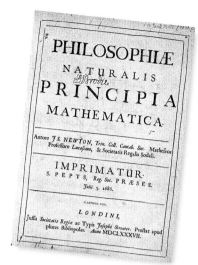

IN CONTEXT
Berkeley and tar-water

In the last decade of his life, Berkeley became obsessed with the supposedly healthy properties of tar-water, which is made by infusing pine- or fir-tar in water for 48 hours. He extolled the virtues of this bizarre concoction in *Siris*, published in 1744, returning to the subject eight years later in *Farther Thoughts on Tar-Water*. Despite the fact that the infusion – as is now recognized by medical authorities – had no therapeutic value, *Siris* sold more widely than any of Berkeley's previous works.

◁ **THE FOUNDLING HOSPITAL**
Established in 1739, the hospital soon moved to purpose-built premises in London's Holborn area. Its governors consisted of many nobles and luminaries of the age, including Berkeley and the artist William Hogarth.

Voltaire

1694–1778, FRENCH

A key figure in the rationalist Enlightenment era, Voltaire was one of the founders of the modern liberal tradition, committed to freedom of thought and expression, and critical of the authority of religion and the state.

François-Marie Arouet, known by his pen-name Voltaire, was born into the Parisian elite in 1694 and educated by Jesuits at the prestigious Collège Louis-le-Grand. Instead of following his father into the legal profession, he chose to become a writer. Although he built a reputation as a dramatist, his scurrilous wit led to trouble with the authorities. In 1717 he was locked up in the Bastille for 11 months and in 1727 he went into exile in Britain to escape further imprisonment. He returned to France two years later, enthused by the liberal philosophy of John Locke, the science of Isaac Newton, and British tolerance and freedom of speech.

Published in 1734, Voltaire's *Letters on the English* expressed admiration for religious dissidents, Locke's evidence-based theory of knowledge, and science freed from constraint by religious dogma. Denounced for its anti-Catholicism, the book was banned and burned in Paris. Voltaire escaped punishment by living in the French provinces with his mistress, the

Marquise du Châtelet (see box, right), who helped him produce *Elements of Newton's Philosophy* (1738), a work that did much to spread the Newtonian view of the universe in France.

Deism and freedom

Voltaire had no consistent political stance but remained unswerving in his opposition to abuses of authority by the Catholic Church. In 1763, he published an eloquent denunciation of religious fanaticism, the *Treatise on Tolerance*, in response to the Calas affair – the torture and execution of a French Protestant falsely accused of murder. In opposition to revealed religions he espoused deism, the view that a supreme being exists but does not interfere in human affairs.

Voltaire's legacy is that of a supremely gifted popularizer rather than an original thinker. His *Dictionnaire Philosophique*, published in 1764, brought the ideas of tolerance, freedom of speech, and deism to a wide public. One of his favourite genres was short fiction playing with philosophical ideas. In his 1759 novella *Candide*, the chief butt of his humour is the philosophy professor Pangloss, who constantly reaffirms Gottfried Leibniz's proposition that we live in "the best of all possible worlds", despite endless misfortunes.

Voltaire concludes that we would do best to "cultivate our garden" – that is, be busy and productive.

In his later years Voltaire settled at Ferney in southeast France, with his young niece Madame Denis as his mistress. By the time of his death in 1778, his fame as a fiction writer, dramatist, and campaigner against injustice was immense. By corroding respect for the authority of the Church and State among educated French people his thinking and writing contributed to the upheaval of the French Revolution in 1789.

IN PROFILE
Madame du Châtelet

Emilie du Châtelet (1706–1749) was a French mathematician, scientist, and philosopher. She translated Newton's *Principia* into French, including a commentary containing her own innovative ideas. Her treatise *Foundations of Physics* (1740) was a notable contribution to the philosophy of science. Voltaire's mistress for 15 years, she was in effect co-author of his *Elements of the Philosophy of Newton*. In 1748 she took a younger lover and in the following year she died in childbirth.

PORTRAIT OF MADAME DU CHATELET WORKING AT HER DESK

▽ **CANDIDE, 1759 EDITION**
Although written in a light, witty style, Voltaire's story presents a bleak view of the state of the world, with irrationality and cruelty on the rise everywhere.

◁ **VOLTAIRE READING FRERON**
In this portrait (c.1811) by Jacques-Augustin-Catherine Pajou, Voltaire smiles wryly while reading the journal of his great intellectual foe and critic Elie Catherine Fréron.

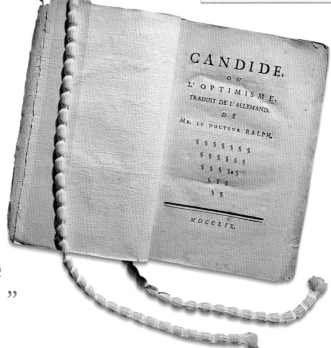

CANDIDE,
OU
L'OPTIMISME.
TRADUIT DE L'ALLEMAND,
DE
MR. LE DOCTEUR RALPH.

MDCCLIX.

" If **this** is **the best** of **possible worlds**, what are **the others**? "

VOLTAIRE, *CANDIDE*

David Hume

1711–1776, SCOTTISH

Hume was denied the academic career he had hoped for because of his barely disguised scepticism of religion, but his philosophical and historical writings made him a leading figure in the Scottish Enlightenment.

The foremost British philosopher of the 18th century, David Hume was better known by the public in his lifetime as a historian. However, his philosophical works were appreciated by his peers, most notably Immanuel Kant, who said that Hume had woken him from his "dogmatic slumber".

Studies and beliefs

Hume was born in Berwickshire, Scotland, just north of the border with England, on a small estate, where his father was laird. The family was prosperous, and David was raised in a somewhat conservative, religiously Calvinist atmosphere. He was only three when his father died, and his mother educated him at home, preparing him for university and the career in law that he was expected to follow. At the age of 11, he went to the University of Edinburgh, where he studied for four years. He soon realized that his interests lay not in law or commerce, but in literature and philosophy, and he sought private tuition in those subjects.

◁ **HUME BY RAMSAY, 1766**
This portrait was painted by Hume's good friend and fellow member of Edinburgh's Select Society, Allan Ramsay. He also painted a companion portrait of Swiss philosopher Jean-Jacques Rousseau.

There followed a period of intense study, which exacted a mental, and physical toll on Hume. In 1729 he suffered a nervous breakdown that was most likely precipitated by the subject of his research – his study of empiricist philosophy had made him question many of his beliefs, not least his religious faith.

As he regained his strength, Hume worked in Bristol in a merchant's office. However, he found that he needed more time for reflection and contemplation, and so in 1734 he took himself to La Flèche, on the Loire in France. In the peaceful atmosphere there, and with the opportunity of conversation with the Jesuits in the local monastery, be began to organize his philosophical thoughts. For the following three years he worked on *A Treatise of Human Nature*, which was published in two volumes in 1739–40.

In the *Treatise*, Hume cast a sceptic's eye over the way in which individuals experience and understand the world. As an empiricist, he dismissed the idea that reason alone reveals information about the world, making a distinction between what he called "relations of ideas" and matters of fact. He went further to argue that our assumptions about cause and effect, and the regularity and predictability of the world have no basis in reason.

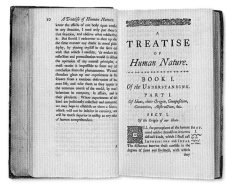

△ *A TREATISE OF HUMAN NATURE*
Hume's *Treatise*, which he published anonymously, was an attempt to devise a system of thought by which to appraise the basis of human nature. He argued against the rationalism of his day, that passion rather than reason moderated human behaviour.

IN CONTEXT
The Scottish Enlightenment

In the late 18th and early 19th centuries, Scotland underwent a period of intense intellectual activity, which became known as the Scottish Enlightenment. The four universities (St Andrews, Glasgow, Edinburgh, and Aberdeen) were major centres of learning, and Edinburgh in particular hosted a thriving culture of clubs and societies, including the Select Society and the Poker Club, where thinkers met for informal debate. Although it shared the same respect for reason as the European Enlightenment movement, the Scottish equivalent was a bastion of empiricism rather than rationalism, and included such figures as David Hume, Adam Smith, and James Boswell.

BRONZE STATUE OF ADAM SMITH, MARKET SQUARE, EDINBURGH

KEY WORKS

1739–40
Publishes *A Treatise of Human Nature*, later reworking it in *An Enquiry Concerning Human Understanding* (1748).

1741–42
Publishes the first edition of *Essays, Moral and Political*. He later adds to and republishes the collection.

1757
In *Four Dissertations*, Hume examines the psychology of "the passions" (feelings, emotions, and desires).

1760
Anonymously writes "Sister Peg", a satire concerned with the English parliament's distrust of the Scots.

1761
Publishes the last of the six volumes of *The History of England*, which becomes a bestseller.

1776
Writes a short autobiography, *My Own Life*, which summarizes his life and works.

1779
Dialogues Concerning Natural Religion is published posthumously by his nephew.

IN PROFILE
The Rousseau affair

While in Paris, Hume met the political philosopher Jean-Jacques Rousseau. Fleeing persecution in his native Geneva, Rousseau accompanied Hume back to England in 1766. At first Rousseau thrived in London society, but his demeanour soon soured and he became paranoid, accusing Hume of betraying him. Rousseau returned to Paris secretly, and Hume feared he would damage his reputation there. To pre-empt this, he published his own version of events, which had the opposite effect, turning the affair into the talk of the salons. Neither philosopher came out of it well.

LETTER FROM HUME IN JULY 1766 CONCERNING THE ROUSSEAU AFFAIR

Although regarded as a major work of philosophy today, and much admired for its clarity of style and often witty elegance, the *Treatise* was not well received at the time. Hume was disappointed, but not deterred; he felt, looking back later, that it was by no means perfect, and reworked it in a more accessible style as *An Enquiry Concerning Human Understanding* (1748) and *An Enquiry Concerning the Principles of Morals* (1751).

In pursuit of academe

In 1741, Hume published the first volume of *Essays, Moral, and Political*, which found a more appreciative readership than his first book, and over the next few years he established himself in the intellectual circles of Edinburgh society. It was time, he felt, to secure some kind of academic career for himself. In 1744, he applied for the position of chair of moral philosophy at the University of Edinburgh, a post for which he was admirably qualified. However, the appointment needed the approval of the notoriously conservative city council, which objected because of what it considered his "atheist" views. Rather than argue his case, Hume quietly withdrew his application and spent the next few years in a variety of unsatisfactory jobs. He left his beloved Edinburgh to work

as a private tutor to the marquess of Annandale in St Albans, but found his employer's eccentricity intolerable and left after a few months. He then became secretary to General James St Clair, seeing some military action in France, and then going with him as a diplomat to Vienna and Turin.

Historical writings

While Hume's reputation as both a philosophical and a literary writer continued to grow, he still hankered after an academic post, and applied for another professorship, this time at the University of Glasgow, in 1751. Again he was rebuffed and therefore took up a position as keeper of the Advocates' Library in Edinburgh. Even though this job provided little income, it gave him access to the books he needed for his next project – a history of Britain. Over the next nine years or so, he wrote his six-volume *History of England* (more of a history of Great

Britain), published between 1754 and 1761, which became a bestseller, making Hume a household name.

Controversy and feuds

At this time, Hume was best known to the public as a historical writer, but he remained committed to his philosophical essays, particularly on the subject of religion. He prepared a collection of dissertations in 1756, but word of their controversial content got out before their publication. The publisher was threatened with legal action, forcing Hume to rewrite the offending essay, "The Natural History of Religion", and to remove "Of Suicide" and "Of the Immortality of the Soul". The collection, *Four Dissertations*, emerged in 1757 but Hume heeded the advice of friends not to publish another of his works from this period. *Dialogues Concerning Natural Religion* accordingly appeared posthumously in 1779.

▷ **THE ADVOCATES' LIBRARY**
Hume was the keeper of Scotland's largest library in 1752–57. Now housing legal publications, it was originally Scotland's library of deposit.

Diplomatic travels

In 1763, Hume was persuaded to leave the Advocates' Library and go with the Earl of Hertford to the British Embassy in Paris. The move not only furthered his diplomatic career (he rose to the position of chargé d'affaires) but placed him into the heart of European Enlightenment society. He gained the friendship of such respected thinkers as Denis Diderot, Voltaire, and Jean le Rond D'Alembert, but had a disastrous relationship with Jean-Jacques Rousseau (see box, left).

Hume returned to Edinburgh, via London, in 1766, and apart from a short period in Paris the following year, spent the rest of his life there revising his works for further editions. He had become a wise and respected statesman and was appointed under secretary of state for the Northern Department in 1767.

In his 50s, Hume all but retired from public life to enjoy the social and literary life of Edinburgh, without the pressure of work. Although still pilloried by his critics, he maintained a wide circle of friends and colleagues

who admired his work and enjoyed his company: he was regarded as a kind man who possessed an optimistic disposition and enormous charm and wit. Although his life had not turned out exactly as he intended, Hume was never bitter and could look back on a varied and successful career, and a place as the leading philosopher of his generation.

In 1776, he died of a stomach complaint, possibly cancer, aged 65. He is buried in a tomb designed by his friend, the renowned architect Robert Adam, in Calton Cemetery, Edinburgh.

△ **ENLIGHTENMENT EDINBURGH**
In the 18th century, Edinburgh became one of the most vital intellectual hubs of the Western world. This view of the city was painted by the notable watercolourist Thomas Hearne in 1778.

" Generally speaking, the **errors** in **religion** are **dangerous**; those in **philosophy** only **ridiculous**. "

DAVID HUME, *A TREATISE OF HUMAN NATURE*

Directory

Wang Yangming

1472–1529, CHINESE

Neo-Confucian philosopher Wang Yangming was born in what is now Zhejiang province, the son of a distinguished government official. Wang studied the prescribed Confucian texts to pass China's civil service examination in 1499. The smooth progress of his bureaucratic career was interrupted in 1506, when a powerful eunuch at the Ming court ordered him to be flogged and exiled to a remote district of China for his protests against political corruption.

While in exile, Wang developed insights that formed the basis for a radical critique of the official Ming brand of Confucianism. Wang asserted that everyone had an intuitive knowledge of good and evil. Moral truth could be found by looking inside rather than outside. Knowledge was not a preparation for action; knowledge and action were one.

Recalled from exile in 1510, Wang shared his thoughts with a group of disciples, while also serving with distinction as a statesman and military leader, suppressing a number of revolts within the empire.

KEY WORKS: *Instructions for Practical Living*, c.1514; *Inquiry on the "Great Learning"*, c.1527

Francisco de Vitoria

c.1483–1546, SPANISH

The Spanish Catholic philosopher and theologian Francisco de Vitoria is famous for his work on the law and the rights of colonized peoples. Born into an aristocratic family in Burgos, he joined the Dominican order in 1504, and studied at the Sorbonne in Paris. Returning to Spain, he was elected to the chair of theology at the University of Salamanca in 1526. A much respected thinker, he advised Spain's rulers on a range of moral and theological issues.

De Vitoria's most famous arguments, presented in lectures in 1536–39, concerned international relations and Spain's rule over native peoples in its newly acquired American colonies. He argued that a *jus gentium*, or law of nations, should regulate the relations between states, guaranteeing freedom in commerce and also limiting the use of war. De Vitoria tentatively approved Spanish rule in the Americas but argued for the Indigenous people's natural right to their own land and to benevolent treatment. His views were highly influential in moderating Spain's behaviour towards the peoples whom they had conquered.

KEY WORKS: *On Civil Power*, 1528; *On Matrimony*, 1530; *On the American Indians*, 1539

Giordano Bruno

1548–1600, ITALIAN

Giordano Bruno was a mystic whose heretical opinions led to his execution. Born at Nola near Naples, the son of a soldier, he became a Dominican friar but, rebelling against the order's constraints, in 1576 embarked on an itinerant existence. Living in various European cities, he won renown as an inventor of mnemonic techniques. However, Bruno's prickly character and unorthodox ideas alienated secular and religious authorities.

Influenced by the Hermetic esoteric and philosophical tradition (based on the writings of Hermes Trismegistus), Bruno published works in the 1580s that ran counter to Christian teaching. He argued that space was infinite; that there was a multiplicity of inhabited

△ FRANCISCO SUAREZ, 17TH-CENTURY ENGRAVING

worlds; that God was spread through the universe; and that human souls would be reborn. In 1592 he was arrested in Venice for heresy and handed over to the Inquisition in Rome. Despite years of interrogation he refused to recant and was burned at the stake in Rome in 1600.

KEY WORKS: *The Shadows of Ideas*, 1582; *The Art of Memory*, 1582; *The Ash Wednesday Supper*, 1584; *On the Infinite Universe and Worlds*, 1584

△ Francisco Suárez

1548–1617, SPANISH

Born in Granada, Francisco Suárez was a philosopher in the scholastic tradition of Thomas Aquinas. Suárez joined the Jesuit order in 1564, and from 1570 he taught at Salamanca and various Jesuit colleges across Spain, also spending five years at the order's college in Rome.

In 1597, after having completed his *Disputationes metaphysicae* (*Metaphysical Disputations*), Suárez moved to the University of Coimbra in Portugal, remaining there for the rest of his career. His major work on law, *Tractatus de legibus* (*On Law*), argued against the divine right of kings, and asserted an oppressive ruler could be killed. The leading Catholic thinker of his day, in 1613 he was invited by Pope Paul V to refute the anti-Catholicism of James I of England. The resulting *Difensio fidei catholicae* (*Defence of the Catholic Faith*) was burned in England on the king's orders.

KEY WORKS: *De Incarnatione*, 1590–92; *Disputationes metaphysicae*, 1597; *Tractatus de legibus*, 1612; *Difensio fidei catholicae*, 1613

Mulla Sadrā

c.1571–c.1640, IRANIAN

Muslim philosopher and theologian Sadr ad-Din Muhammad Shirazi, known as Mulla Sadrā, was born into a wealthy family in Shiraz, Iran. At the time, the country was experiencing a cultural renaissance under the Shi'ite ruler Shah Abbas I.

Sadrā studied philosophy in Isfahan under two leading thinkers, Mir Damad and Shayk Bahai. In 1605 he withdrew to Kahak village near Qom, where he sought mystical insight through ascetic practices.

In 1612 the governor of Fars province invited Sadrā to return to Shiraz to run a *madrasa* (college). This became a major centre of learning, where Sadrā presided over his intellectual disciples and his large family. He produced numerous works, the most influential being *Transcendent Wisdom in the Four Journeys of the Intellect*, an extensive compendium of philosophical and theological thought. He sought to reconcile Ibn Sina's rationalism with Shi'ite theology and Sufi mystical intuition. An early existentialist, he asserted in a religious context that "existence precedes essence". Sadrā died at Basra while on a pilgrimage to Mecca, probably in 1640.

KEY WORKS: *Transcendent Wisdom in the Four Journeys of the Intellect; Inspired Recognitions; Keys to the Invisible World*

▷ Hugo Grotius

1583–1645, DUTCH

Known as the "Father of International Law", Hugo Grotius was born Huig de Groot in Delft, Holland. Prodigiously gifted, he attended Leiden University aged 11 and wrote his first book at 16. He rose to prominence as a legal adviser to the Dutch United Provinces, arguing for the freedom of the seas.

Involved in Dutch politics, Grotius supported the Arminians (Protestants who followed the theologian Jacobus Arminius) in a bitter controversy with the Calvinists (Protestant supporters of Jean Calvin). In 1619 the Calvinists triumphed and Grotius was imprisoned for life. After two years he escaped from Loevestein castle and fled to Paris. There he wrote his famous work *De Jure Belli ac Pacis (On the Law of War and Peace)*, discussing international law, the notion of just war, and the rules for the conduct of war. He also wrote on the need for religious tolerance.

From 1634 Grotius served as Sweden's ambassador to France, a key diplomatic post at a time of European conflict. He died in 1645 after being shipwrecked at Rostock on the German coast.

KEY WORKS: *The Free Sea*, 1609; *On the Power of Sovereigns concerning Religious Affairs*, 1609; *On the Law of War and Peace*, 1625; *The Way to Religious Peace*, 1642

△ **HUGO GROTIUS, MICHIEL JANSZ VAN MIEREVELT, 1631**

Pierre Gassendi

1592–1655, FRENCH

Philosopher and scientist Pierre Gassendi was born near Digne in Provence, southern France, and studied philosophy and theology at the universities of Aix-en-Provence and Avignon. He was ordained as a priest at the age of 24, but his intellectual interests drew him towards science. He published a critique of Aristotle's philosophy in 1624 and corresponded with leading figures in the Scientific Revolution, including Galileo Galilei and Johannes Kepler.

In 1631 Gassendi was the first astronomer to observe the transit of Mercury across the Sun. He carried out various scientific experiments and became professor of mathematics at the Collège Royale in Paris. Invited to comment on René Descartes' *Meditations* in 1643, he rejected the author's claim that knowledge could be based on reason, asserting that all knowledge must begin with the senses. Attracted by the philosophy of the Greek Epicurus, Gassendi attempted to reconcile an atomistic mechanistic view of the universe with Christian belief in the immortal soul.

KEY WORKS: *Exercitationes paradoxicae adversus Aristotelios*, 1624; *De motu impresso*, 1642; *Syntagma philosophiae Epicuri*, 1649; *Syntagma philosophicum*, 1658

Wang Fuzhi

1619–1692, CHINESE

Wang Fuzhi was the last major philosopher of Ming dynasty China. Born at Hengyang in Hunan province, he passed the country's civil service examination aged 24, but his career was disrupted by the invasion of China by Manchu nomads. The Manchu founded the Qing dynasty in Beijing but Wang sided with the Ming, who continued resistance in southern China. Serving for a time at the Ming court, he eventually took solitary refuge at the foot of the remote Chuanshan mountain.

In a series of commentaries on classic Chinese texts, Wang argued for a materialist vision in which humans created their own nature through their will and actions. Human emotions and desires were essentially good but needed to be tempered by judgement. History moved in cycles of growth and decay, but ultimately tended towards improvement. Many of his works were written under the pseudonym Chuanshan.

Wang lived well into old age – long enough to witness the final defeat of the Ming in the 1680s. However, the cause and the place of his death are not known for certain.

KEY WORKS: *Outer Commentary on the Book of Changes*, 1655; *Discourse on Commentaries on the Four Books*, 1655; *A Textual Annotation on the Book of Rites*, 1677

▷ Margaret Cavendish

1623–1673, ENGLISH

Born Margaret Lucas in Colchester, Essex, Cavendish was self-taught, benefitting from an aristocratic environment offering access to books. When the English Civil War broke out in 1642, her family fought for the Royalists and Margaret went into exile in France as a lady-in-waiting to the queen. In Paris she married William Cavendish, the future duke of Newcastle, who introduced her to philosophers such as René Descartes, Pierre Gassendi, and Thomas Hobbes.

On returning to England, she was the first woman to attend a meeting of the Royal Society. Cavendish wrote from an early age, producing poetry, drama, prose fiction, and philosophical works. Her status enabled her to overcome the prejudice against women philosophers. She was a materialist, although her notion of matter was complex and subtle. Her fantasy story *The Blazing World* (1666) expressed her views on government and society.

KEY WORKS: *Philosophical and Physical Opinions*, 1656; *Philosophical Letters*, 1664; *Observations upon Experimental Philosophy*, 1666; *Grounds of Natural Philosophy*, 1668

Anne Conway

1631–1679, ENGLISH

Sometimes referred to as "the first English feminist", Conway was born Anne Finch, a member of a prominent London family. She was taught philosophy by Cambridge Platonist Henry More. As a woman, she could not attend university: he therefore taught her by correspondence. In 1651 she married Edward, Viscount Conway, who shared her intellectual interests. From youth, Conway experienced terrible migraines for which she vainly tried radical treatments. One of her doctors, Flemish intellectual Francis Mercury van Helmont, introduced her to study of the Jewish Kabalah.

△ **MARGARET CAVENDISH, PETER LELY, 1665**

Profoundly religious, she sought to reconcile the pain she suffered with a benevolent deity, seeing suffering as a path to spiritual perfection. She rejected Cartesian dualism, denying the existence of lifeless matter.

KEY WORKS: *The Principles of the Most Ancient and Modern Philosophy*, 1690

Nicolas Malebranche

1638–1715, FRENCH

Malebranche was born into a high-status family in Paris. He suffered from a malformation of the spine and as a child was educated at home. After studying philosophy and theology at the University of Paris, he entered the Oratory, an Augustinian religious congregation. He was ordained in 1664. That year, reading Descartes' *Treatise on Man* inspired him to study Cartesian philosophy. The result was *Concerning the Search after Truth* (1674–75), which tried to reconcile the thoughts of Descartes and St Augustine, to show that God was active in every aspect of the world and the only source of causation, ideas, and perceptions. His work provoked controversy and his *Treatise of Nature and Grace* (1680) was placed on the Church's Index of Prohibited Books in 1690; it was joined by *Concerning the Search after Truth* in 1709.

KEY WORKS: *Concerning the Search after Truth*, 1674–75; *Treatise of Nature and Grace*, 1680; *Dialogues on Metaphysics and Religion*, 1688

Mary Astell

1666–1731, ENGLISH

Astell is best known for her advocacy of equal educational opportunities for women and hailed as one of England's first feminist philosophers. She was born to middle-class parents in Newcastle-upon-Tyne. Having lost both parents by the age of 22, she moved to Chelsea, then a village outside London, and joined a circle of gifted intellectual women, including Mary Chudleigh and Judith Drake.

Her book *A Serious Proposal to the Ladies for the Advancement of their True and Greatest Interest* proposed a detailed plan for the education of women. Basing her thoughts upon the distinction between the rational soul and the mortal body, she argued that society was responsible for the apparent inferiority of women's minds. Her other works covered matters ranging from God's perfection to the relationship between human and divine love, and the nature of marriage.

KEY WORKS: *A Serious Proposal to the Ladies*, 1694, 1697; *Letters Concerning the Love of God*, 1695; *Some Reflections upon Marriage*, 1700; *The Christian Religion*, 1705

Giambattista Vico

1668–1744, ITALIAN

A key thinker on the philosophical foundations of history and the humanities, Vico was the son of a poor bookseller in Naples. Largely self-taught in childhood, he graduated in law from the University of Naples in 1694, having supported himself during his studies by working as a tutor. In 1699 he was appointed professor of rhetoric at Naples. He held the post for the rest of his working life, despite efforts to attain the more prestigious and better paid chair in philosophy.

Vico's thought posited human creations – such as history, society, language, culture – as the true objects of human knowledge. His masterwork

Scienza Nuova (*New Science*) described history as the study of the evolution of societies and civilizations, which he believed exhibited regular, though not entirely predictable, cycles of growth and decline. Vico pioneered the study of language and myth as a way of understanding ancient societies.

KEY WORKS: *On the Most Ancient Wisdom of the Italians*, 1710; *The Universal Law*, 1720–22; *New Science*, 1725

Hakuin Ekaku

1686–1768, JAPANESE

Zen Buddhist teacher Ekaku was born in the village of Hara at the foot of Mount Fuji. His mother was a devout Buddhist, and at the age of 15 he entered the Zen temple of Shoin-ji as a novice. After studying at a number of temples, he returned to Hara in 1718 and became head of the Shoin-ji temple, with the title of "first monk".

Hakuin turned Shoin-ji into the foremost centre of the Rinzai school of Zen. He stressed that the search for personal enlightenment must be followed by a commitment to working for the good of all beings. His teaching method involved asking students to meditate on koans – paradoxical riddles such as his famous question: "You know the sound of two hands clapping; tell me, what is the sound of one hand clapping?"

KEY WORKS: *Idle Talk on a Night Boat*; *Goose Grass*; *Wild Ivy*

▷ Montesquieu

1689–1755, FRENCH

Enlightenment political philosopher Charles-Louis de Secondat, baron de Montesquieu, was born on his family's estates near Bordeaux. He studied law before inheriting the estate and title made him wealthy. The success of his *Persian Letters* – a satire on French society and religion, as seen through the eyes of two Persians – made him a sought-after figure in Parisian salons.

From 1728 to 1731 he travelled widely in Europe. His most important work, *The Spirit of the Laws*, was a comparative study of institutions, asserting that variations in laws and systems of government were shaped by factors such as climate, population, and the economy. He argued against despotism, advocating division of the executive, legislative, and judicial powers. His views were a major influence on the US Constitution.

KEY WORKS: *The Persian Letters*, 1721; *Considerations on the Causes of the Greatness of the Romans and their Decline*, 1734; *The Spirit of the Laws*,1748

Julien Offray de La Mettrie

1709–1751, FRENCH

Materialist philosopher La Mettrie was born at St Malo in Brittany. The son of prosperous parents, he studied medicine in Holland. Returning to France in 1742, he became an army doctor and accompanied the duke of Gramont to battle in the War of the Austrian Succession (1740–48). While suffering from a fever, he experienced hallucinations and made observations on their effect on his thoughts, concluding that mental activity must be the result of physical processes. His materialist view of the mind, *The Natural History of the Soul*, outraged Catholic opinion and the book was burned.

Fleeing persecution in 1746, he went to Leiden, where he wrote the atheistic *Machine Man* (1748) and *Penelope* (1750), which satirized the vanity of his profession. Prussian King Frederick II offered him sanctuary, making him a member of the Berlin Academy. His final works, advocating sensual pleasure, outraged even Voltaire.

KEY WORKS: *The Natural History of the Soul*, 1745; *Machine Man*, 1748; *Anti-Seneca*, 1748; *The Art of Pleasure*, 1751

Denis Diderot

1713–1784, FRENCH

Novelist, essayist, playwright, translator, and popular figure of Parisian café society, Denis Diderot was disinherited by his bourgeois father when he refused to enter the Church or study for a profession. Instead, he chose the life of a bohemian and writer, embracing the Enlightenment ideas that were sweeping Paris.

In 1747, Diderot joined forces with mathematician Jean Le Rond d'Alembert in an ambitious project to bring together all the world's knowledge in an encyclopedia – *Encyclopédie* (see p.152). The work took up much of his life and saw him impoverished, harassed, and at war with religious authorities who saw his theories on the origins of life without divine design as a dangerous attack on their authority.

A free-living, free-thinking intellectual, Diderot's philosophical beliefs moved from deism to atheism and ultimately to materialism, a view in which everything that exists in the world is made of matter and motion. He often employed imaginary conversations to present contending philosophical views. Many of his most famous works, such as the satirical novels *Jacques the Fatalist* and *Rameau's Nephew* were published after his death.

KEY WORKS: *Letter on the Blind*, 1749; *The Nun*, 1796; *Jacques the Fatalist and His Master*, 1796; *Encyclopédie*, 1751–1780; *Rameau's Nephew*, 1805

△ **MONTESQUIEU, AFTER JACQUES-ANTOINE DASSIER, c.1728**

MODERN

CHAPTER 4

Jean-Jacques Rousseau

1712–1778, SWISS

Rousseau was a thinker and writer whose radical ideas brought him into conflict with the authority of Church and State. He valued emotion over reason, nature over culture, and equality over social hierarchy.

Jean-Jacques Rousseau was born in Geneva in 1712, the son of a poor watchmaker. The experiences of his youth left him emotionally deprived and rootless. His mother died soon after his birth, and as a child he passed through the hands of various carers. He learned to read and was taught the Genevan Calvinist faith, but otherwise received little schooling. At the age of 12 he became apprenticed to a notary, then to an engraver. The discipline of an apprentice's life drove him to revolt, and at the age of 16 he ran away from Geneva to pursue an itinerant existence on the margins of society. Almost all that is known about this phase of Rousseau's life

comes from his autobiography, the *Confessions*, which is not necessarily reliable. He certainly experienced poverty and at times lived off menial jobs, but he was also befriended by a wealthy Swiss woman, Madame de Warens, who became both his mentor and his mistress – he always addressed her as "maman" (mummy). Under her influence he acquired an extensive education and always nurtured higher ambitions.

Move to Paris

Gifted in music, Rousseau went to Paris in the 1740s hoping to make his fortune with an unusual idea for a new system of musical notation.

Although this did not win acceptance, he established contact with Denis Diderot (see p.149) and other members of the Parisian intellectual elite, who at the time were advocating the application of reason to the cause of human progress.

Rousseau's breakthrough came in 1750, when the Academy of Dijon offered a prize for the best essay on the question of whether the sciences or the arts had contributed more to the moral advancement of humankind. By Rousseau's account, his decision to enter this competition was taken while walking from Paris to the fortress of Vincennes, where he was to visit Diderot, who had been imprisoned for criticizing religion. During the walk, Rousseau had a vision of people as naturally good but corrupted by society. This fundamental idea was to underlie all his subsequent works. Expressed in the "Discourse on the Sciences and the Arts", it won him the prize and established his reputation as a thinker. His follow-up essay, the "Discourse on the Origins and Foundations of Inequality", confirmed

IN CONTEXT

The *Encyclopédie*

Rousseau was one of the main contributors to the most ambitious literary project of his time, the *Encyclopédie*, which was published in 35 volumes from 1751–80. A great compendium of rational and secular knowledge, its creators – who included Denis Diderot (see p.149) – saw it as a new way of disseminating ideas. Diderot's subversive views on the Church and the monarchy caused the *Encyclopédie* to be banned in 1759, after which volumes were produced clandestinely. The volumes' Enlightenment text is credited with influencing attitudes that led to the French Revolution.

TITLE PAGE OF A 1751 EDITION OF THE *ENCYCLOPEDIE*

◁ **"LES CHARMETTES", ANNECY**
Rousseau stayed in this bedroom at the country house of his liberal mentor, Madame de Warens. He wrote about their relationship in his *Confessions*.

> " **Everything is good** as it leaves the **hands of the Author** of things; **everything degenerates** in the **hands of man**. "

JEAN-JACQUES ROUSSEAU, *EMILE*

▷ **JEAN-JACQUES ROUSSEAU**
This portrait was made by French painter Jean Édouard Lacretelle in 1843, long after Rousseau's death. The work was commissioned by the French king, Louis Philippe I.

KEY WORKS

1750
Expresses his belief that civilization corrupts natural humans in "Discourse on the Sciences and the Arts", his first important essay.

1754
Argues that wealth and status are a corruption of the natural state of humans in "Discourse on the Origins and Foundations of Inequality".

1762
Proposes a new style of education in *Emile* that will allow children to freely develop their natural talents and feelings.

1762
Argues for government based on the "general will" of the people in *The Social Contract*, his most influential political essay,

1782
Confessions, published posthumously, portrays the author as a romantic outcast at odds with society.

IN CONTEXT
Rousseau and the Revolution

During the French Revolution, which began in 1789, Rousseau's ideas were cited in support of direct democracy and the overthrow of the monarchy. The Cult of the Supreme Being, introduced by the revolutionaries to replace Catholicism in 1794, to some degree reflected Rousseau's belief in a "natural religion". The execution of alleged enemies of the revolution in the Reign of Terror was justified by reference to Rousseau's belief that individuals could have no rights in opposition to the popular will.

ROUSSEAU, DEPICTED WITH THE SYMBOLS OF THE REVOLUTION

his originality and the challenge he posed to established authority. Using an ideal "state of nature" as his yardstick, he condemned all hierarchies of wealth, status, and power as alienating consequences of a society based on property.

Truth in emotion

In the 1750s, Rousseau contributed to Diderot's *Encyclopédie*, but his major works published in 1761–62 showed a divergence from rationalism as he asserted the importance of feeling, rather than of the intellect. His epistolary novel *La Nouvelle Héloïse* was rapturously received, captivating the public with its lyrical descriptions of nature and the torments and ecstasies of its young lovers. As well as announcing the arrival of the new sensibility of the Romantic movement, the novel embodied its author's ideas on the supreme value of authenticity – truth to one's own emotions and instincts.

Emile, his treatise on education, proposed a revolution in attitudes to childhood. Instead of regarding children as tarred with original sin and needing strict discipline to suppress their evil tendencies, Rousseau said the aim of education should be to preserve a child's natural goodness. Children should be allowed to learn from the direct experience of nature

rather than from books and education and should be inspired to nurture their emotional development. He encouraged mothers to breastfeed their babies, instead of taking the usual route of employing a wet nurse.

Political philosophy

Rousseau's treatise *The Social Contract*, published in 1762, has remained a controversial work to the present day. Partly reflecting his experience of his native Geneva (a self-governing city) Rousseau advocated a type of direct democracy based on the active participation of all male citizens in political decision-making. He denied the right of kings to govern, because the people are sovereign. Where most Enlightenment thinkers emphasized individual freedom, Rousseau argued that once the will of the people had been determined, establishing the "General Will", no individual had the right to differ from it.

Official sanction

Before the 1760s, Rousseau had not suffered from official disapproval, and had even been offered a pension by France's King Louis XV after his opera *Le Devin du village* was performed at the royal court. But *Emile* provoked a hostile reaction from the authorities because it advocated the foundation of a "natural" religious belief based on the individual conscience and the feelings of the heart, rather than on revelation and doctrine. Denounced by the archbishop of Paris, the book was banned and burned. *The Social Contract* suffered the same fate. Rousseau fled France to escape imprisonment, eventually finding refuge in Britain, where he was a guest of the philosopher David Hume.

Despite his fame, Rousseau always remained a social outsider plagued by paranoia. He had formed an

▷ **EMILE, OR ON EDUCATION**
This is the title page of the original edition of Rousseau's book, published in May 1762. The work later inspired pioneers of child psychology such as Jean Piaget.

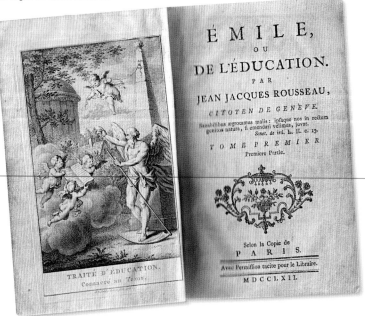

◁ **RESTING PLACE**
After a life of wandering, Rousseau found tranquillity in the gardens of Château d'Ermenonville, which belonged to his wealthy admirer Marquis René-Louis de Girardin. Rousseau wrote, "For a long time, my heart drew me here, and what my eyes see, make me want to stay here always." He died at Ermenonville and was buried on this island in the grounds.

▽ **LOUIS XV**
Rousseau declined the patronage of the French king Louis XV, depicted here in his royal splendour by the 18th-century artist Maurice Quentin Delatour. Louis was angered by the slight, declaring: "It might please me to send Monsieur Rousseau to the Bicêtre prison."

enduring liaison with an illiterate chambermaid, Thérèse Levasseur, who gave birth to five children, all of whom Rousseau deposited with a foundling hospital, a move that was at odds with his progressive intellectual views on child-rearing. Meanwhile, his paranoia increased, and his once-great friendship with Diderot descended into sour mutual abuse. In England, he became absurdly convinced Hume was plotting to kill him and decided to take a chance on returning secretly to France.

In the last decade of his life, Rousseau devoted himself chiefly to works of autobiography and introspection, including *Confessions* and *Reveries of a Solitary Walker*. In the *Confessions* he boldly claimed "to have entered on an enterprise that is without precedent... to show my fellows a man as nature made him...".

Whether Rousseau's honesty matched his ambition has been long debated, and the issue is unresolved. In 1776 he was knocked down by a large dog in a Parisian street and

suffered concussion, from which his health never fully recovered. He died two years later as a guest at Château d'Ermenonville in the Oise district of northern France.

Rousseau's grave at Ermenonville became a place of pilgrimage for a generation that had been inspired by the sentimental excesses of *La Nouvelle Héloïse*. During the French Revolution in 1794 the republicans, who claimed him as their precursor, moved his body to the Pantheon in Paris, where it now lies.

" **Nature made man happy** and **good...** but **society depraves him** and makes him **miserable.** "

JEAN-JACQUES ROUSSEAU, "DISCOURSE ON THE SCIENCES AND THE ARTS"

▷ **ADAM SMITH, c.1800**
This painting of Smith by an unknown artist is known as the "Muir portrait", after the family who once owned it. It was probably made posthumously, based on a medallion by James Tassie.

Adam Smith

1723–1790, SCOTTISH

Smith's best-known work, *The Wealth of Nations*, is regarded as the first book on modern economic theory, but Smith considered himself primarily a philosopher, deriving his "political economy" from his moral philosophy.

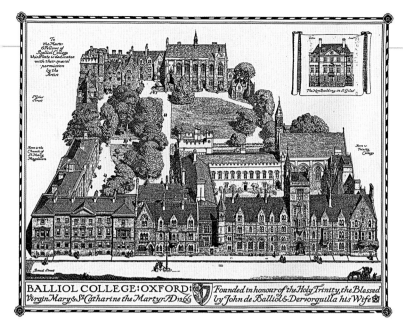

◁ **BALLIOL COLLEGE, OXFORD**
Smith's studies at Balliol gave him a contempt for elite English education. He said that his tutors there had "given up altogether even the pretence of teaching".

offered encouragement to explore new ideas, at Oxford Smith met with dogma and hostility towards original thought: on one occasion he was discovered reading Hume and the book was confiscated by university authorities. The little benefit he gained from his time at Oxford was through his access to the collections in the Bodleian Library. After five years of postgraduate study, he suffered a breakdown, and returned to Scotland without completing his scholarship.

Overcoming adversity

Since early childhood, Smith had always been something of a loner, awkward in company, and with a habit of talking to himself. His experience at

Along with his friend David Hume, Smith was a member of a group of Scottish intellectuals who met to socialize and debate philosophical issues in what became known as the Scottish Enlightenment (see box, p.143). The pair shared an interest in moral philosophy – in particular the idea of moral sense as a feature of human nature – which informed their work and resulted in some of the most influential philosophical books in English of the period.

Glasgow and Oxford

Adam Smith was born in Kirkcaldy, in eastern Scotland, in 1723. The exact date of his birth is unknown, but records show he was baptized on 5 June that year. His father, a lawyer and comptroller of customs, died around the time Adam was born, leaving his widow a comfortable sum to ensure the education of their son. Smith's childhood was largely uneventful, and he was sent to the local Burgh School, where he received a solid classical education. At the age of 14, he enrolled at the University of Glasgow, where he studied moral philosophy under professor Francis Hutcheson. Under the mentorship

of the great professor (who was later described as "the never-to-be-forgotten Hutcheson"), Smith graduated from Glasgow in 1740, and then earned a scholarship to continue his studies at Balliol College, Oxford. Here, the contrast with his time at Glasgow was stark. Whereas Hutcheson had always

> " **Nobody** ever saw **a dog** make a **fair** and **deliberate exchange** of **one bone** for **another** with **another dog**. "

ADAM SMITH, *THE WEALTH OF NATIONS*

IN PROFILE
Francis Hutcheson

Often referred to as the "Father of the Scottish Enlightenment", Hutcheson (1694–1746) was a Presbyterian minister as well as a philosopher, whose theories of human nature and moral sense were a significant influence on Adam Smith and David Hume. After teaching in Dublin, where he wrote *An Inquiry into the Original of our Ideas of Beauty and Virtue* and *An Essay on the Nature and Conduct of the Passions and Affections* (1725), he was appointed professor of moral philosophy at the University of Glasgow in 1729. In keeping with his down-to-earth approach to philosophy, he made a radical break with tradition by giving his lectures in English rather than in Latin.

FRANCIS HUTCHESON, ALLAN RAMSAY, c.1740–45

> "The **great affair**, we **always find**, is to get **money**."
>
> ADAM SMITH, *THE WEALTH OF NATIONS*

△ **FRANÇOIS QUESNAY**
Quesnay served as physician to the French king Louis XV before pursuing his study of economics. He became a leading light of the Physiocrats, a group of 18th-century thinkers who systematically analysed economic systems and who championed deregulation and a laissez-faire approach to trade. They believed that land was the basis of wealth.

Oxford further eroded his confidence. As he grew up, he became a rather eccentric character: absent-minded, obsessive, given to hypochondria, and with an idiosyncratic way of speaking. He was also self-conscious, especially about his appearance (in later life he said that "I am a beau in nothing but my books"), and he became known for his often distant smiling expression and his distinctive gait.

It must have taken courage, and conviction in his ideas, for Smith to agree to deliver a series of public lectures for the Philosophical Society of Edinburgh in 1748. Nevertheless, the lectures were well received and provided Smith with a means of entry into the intellectual circles of Edinburgh, where he met and began a lifelong friendship with one of his heroes, David Hume.

Sentiment over rationality

By 1751, Smith was held in high regard by his peers. He was offered a professorship in logic at his alma mater in Glasgow, and promoted to head of moral philosophy two years later. The post suited him well. He was more comfortable with the formality of academic life than public lectures

▷ **THE WEALTH OF NATIONS**
Smith's book, published in 1776, was instrumental in popularizing the ideas that underpin the school of thought that became known as classical economics.

or social gatherings – he found small talk difficult, and had few close friends other than Hume. It also gave him the opportunity to concentrate on writing, and in 1759 he published his first book, *The Theory of Moral Sentiments*.

This work was influenced by both Hutcheson and Hume and their ideas of a moral sense based on sentiment or emotion rather than pure rationality, but Smith went on to argue that human morality, and altruism in particular, has its roots in what he called "mutual sympathy of sentiments" – the empathy between the individual actor and wider society. He considered the book to be his major achievement, and the theory outlined in it underpins all

of his philosophical thinking, including the political economy described in the later *The Wealth of Nations* (1776).

Continental journeys

It seemed that Smith was set for a career at Glasgow University, but in 1763 he received an offer that he found difficult to refuse. A friend of Hume's, Charles Townshend, asked if Smith would become private tutor to his stepson Henry Scott, duke of Buccleuch, a post that carried a salary double that of his professorship. Smith accepted and accompanied Scott on a tour of the South of France that lasted almost two years, and then went with him to Geneva and Paris. The trip

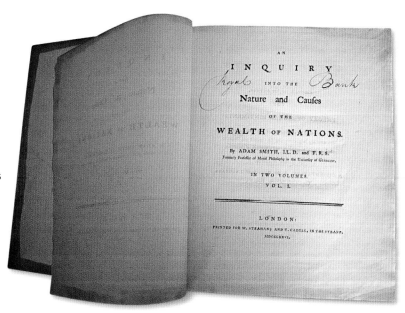

KEY WORKS

1748
Begins giving public lectures for the Philosophical Society of Edinburgh.

1751
Appointed professor of logic at Glasgow University, and the following year is made head of moral philosophy.

1759
Publishes his first book, *The Theory of Moral Sentiments*, which explores ideas such as morality and human sympathy.

1766
Retires from his academic career and spends the next 10 years on his great work, *The Wealth of Nations*.

1776
An Inquiry into the Nature and Causes of the Wealth of Nations consists of two volumes divided into five books.

1783
Becomes a founding member of the Royal Society of Edinburgh.

1787
Appointed to the honorary position of lord rector of the University of Glasgow.

IN CONTEXT
Mercantilism versus free trade

From the start of the Renaissance, economic theory was dominated by mercantilism, the view that a nation should aim for a positive balance of trade to accumulate wealth and to increase international influence in competition with rival states. This could be achieved by government regulation of imports, and a maximization of exports. The idea was enthusiastically followed by states such as Venice, and later by England and France. In the 18th century, however, economists such as Smith questioned the effectiveness of mercantilism, advocating instead a system of free trade, the international equivalent of the free market.

TRADE ON THE GRAND CANAL, VENICE, GASPARE VANVITELLI , c.1705

turned out to be inspirational, as it brought him into contact with some of the great thinkers on the continent, including Voltaire, Benjamin Franklin, and Jean D'Alembert. But it was the philosopher François Quesnay who impressed Smith most and prompted his interest in political economy.

Quesnay was the leader of the physiocratic school, which was challenging the prevailing mercantilist economic theory (see box, above), and instead advocating a policy of "laissez-faire" – a system of free trade.

Smith's time as Scott's tutor came to an end in 1766, and on returning to Kirkcaldy, he began work on a book setting out his own theory of political economy, a task that was to occupy him for the next 10 years. *An Inquiry into the Nature and Causes of the Wealth of Nations* (usually referred to simply as *The Wealth of Nations*) was published in 1776, and became a bestseller almost immediately. Regarded today as the first textbook of modern economics, it was far more than that: as well as describing

the principles of free markets, supply and demand, competition and self-interest in exchange, the division of labour, and government intervention, it put these ideas into the context of Smith's theory of morality and social interaction.

Smith never married, and the death of his friend Hume in 1776 was a heavy blow. After dealing with Hume's affairs as his executor, he found himself alone, and in 1778 he moved in with his mother at her home in Edinburgh, where he lived for the rest of his life. In his final years, he took a job as commissioner with the Scottish customs service and effectively rested on his laurels, gaining several honorary academic appointments, but producing little in the way of philosophical writings. His mother died in 1784, just six years before his own death on 17 July 1790, aged 67.

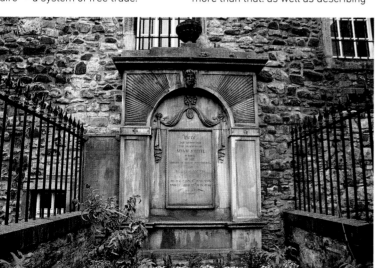

◁ **RESTING PLACE**
On his deathbed, Adam Smith reportedly expressed disappointment that he had not achieved more in his life. He was buried at Canongate Kirk on the Royal Mile in Edinburgh.

Immanuel Kant

1724–1804, GERMAN

Kant was the great reconciler of Enlightenment thought, seeking a synthesis between Descartes' rationalism and the empiricists' emphasis on experience. He was also heavily influenced by Newtonian physics.

Immanuel Kant was a hugely influential figure in the history of philosophy and the prototype of a new breed of professional philosopher. For much of his life he earned his living as a professor of logic and metaphysics but, remarkably for a man of learning, never travelled more than 100km (60 miles) from his place of birth.

Kant was born in 1724 into an impoverished family in what was then the East Prussian city of Königsberg; today it is Kaliningrad, the capital of the Baltic enclave of the same name that is administratively part of Russia. Both his parents were Lutherans.

The fourth of 11 children, he was the oldest to survive. At the age of eight he was sent to a school run by the pastor of his parents' church, where he learned Latin. In 1740 he entered the local university to study theology, but realized that his real interests were in mathematics and physics; he started writing his first book, on kinetic forces, at the age of 20.

Kant's father died in 1746, obliging him to find employment to support himself – he ended up working for nine years as a private tutor. This was the only period of his life in which he lived outside Königsberg – and even then, never moving far away. At the end of that time he managed, with the help of a friend, to complete his doctoral studies, qualifying him to return to the University of Königsberg as a lecturer. Although his writing is notoriously difficult, he was a popular teacher, and students flocked to study under him; for 30 years he even gave summer courses on geography that were always well attended.

A developing career

In 1770, having turned down the offer of prestigious posts at other institutions, he was finally offered the chair of logic and metaphysics at Königsberg, which he was to hold until ill health finally forced his retirement. By that time he had already published significant works on a variety of subjects, among them cosmogony, aesthetics, and even the spiritualist beliefs of Emanuel Swedenborg in a book entitled *Dreams of A Ghost-seer, Illustrated by the Dreams of Metaphysics* (1766). He had also started to refine his own philosophical beliefs, partly in reaction against

IN CONTEXT

Kant and the sciences

Kant showed a keen interest in the sciences throughout his life, but they were of particular importance to him during his early years. At the age of 24 – after having studied Newtonian physics as a student at the University of Königsberg – he wrote his *General Natural History and Theory of the Celestial Bodies* (which was not published until 1755). In this work he outlined the theory that suns and planets form from clouds of dispersed matter that are gravitationally attracted according to their differing specific densities and masses. Kant's nebular hypothesis of star formation is still generally accepted today.

COLUMN OF MOLECULAR HYDROGEN GAS, AN INCUBATOR FOR STARS

◁ **UNIVERSITY OF KÖNIGSBERG**
Kant enrolled as a student at Königsberg university at the age of 16; he was later appointed as a lecturer, and thereafter as professor of logic and metaphysics.

▷ **IMMANUEL KANT, 1791**
This celebrated portrait by the artist Gottlieb Doepler shows the influential philosopher in his late sixties, elegantly dressed and wearing a white wig.

"A **categorical imperative** [represents] an action as **objectively necessary** in itself, without reference to **any other purpose**."

IMMANUEL KANT, *CRITIQUE OF PRACTICAL REASON*

IN CONTEXT
The categorical imperative

Kant's work on ethics is most famously summed up in his concept of "the categorical imperative", which he formulated as: "Act only on that maxim through which you can, at the same time, will that it should become a universal law". The imperative is the requirement to behave in accordance with reason, from which all moral obligations arise. "Categorical" takes that duty out of the subjective realm, giving it the status of a universal law of nature that the person doing the act would wish all other people to obey – or, in layperson's terms, "Do as you would be done by".

◁ **CRITIQUE OF PRACTICAL REASON**
Title page of the 1797 edition of Kant's *Critique of Practical Reason*, first published in 1788, which highlighted the importance of freedom in moral philosophy.

Gottfried Leibniz's rationalism, which was the dominant intellectual mode at the time. He spelled out his views in his *Inaugural Dissertation* (1770), given on taking up his post; its full title, *On the Form and Principles of the Sensible and Intelligible World*, already addressed the dichotomy between the world of sensory experiences and of mental concepts that was to become central to his later concerns.

Knowledge and reason

Eleven years of silence followed, during which Kant distilled the ideas he finally expressed in mature form in his best-known work, *Critique of Pure Reason*, published in 1781. Its subject area was the philosophy of mind; its approach followed up the dualist arguments sketched out in the *Dissertation*. Knowledge, he argued, must involve both sensory awareness (the "experience" of the empiricists), and the cognitive concepts that rationalists like René Descartes meant by "reason". In doing so, he deliberately targeted Leibniz's view that we can attain knowledge of concepts like God or freedom, or other abstractions falling outside the realm of experience, simply by thought. In contrast, Kant insisted on a role for experience also.

Kant's approach starts from a distinction between two different sorts of reality. One the one hand, there is the totality of everything that exists, and on the other, all that we can apprehend, limited as that is by the

△ **KANT'S HOME AT KÖNIGSBERG**
Despite great success and international fame, Kant lived and worked his entire life in the Baltic port city of Königsberg, which in his day was part of Prussia.

constraints of our physiological apparatus – senses, brains, central nervous systems. The very nature of that apparatus shapes our experience of the world as one of "phenomena", things as they appear to us. But he also posits another kind of reality, that of things as they are in themselves, beyond our perception of them. This is the 'noumenal" world, which we have no way of accessing. It transcends our ability to perceive it.

Many things followed from this dualism. Knowledge – for Kant – involves a component provided by the senses (empirical experience), but also mental concepts (reason). These, he said, must include categories of understanding existing separately from, and in some cases *a priori* to, experience. This *a priori* knowledge

includes logic and the abstract laws of physics and mathematics. Kant concluded from this that, for example, there can be no intellectual proof for God's existence, which must rely on faith, and that space and time are both subjective, and part of humankind's general apparatus for making sense of the world.

The critical period

The 1780s are referred to as Kant's "critical" period – literally so, because during the decade he also produced two other influential "critiques". The first, the *Critique of Practical Reason*, appeared in 1788. In it he switched his attention to ethics, employing the same structure of a "Doctrine", an "Analytic" and a "Dialectic", followed by a "Methodology", to approach the subject. This work, which spelled out his concept of the categorical imperative (see box, left), set up a distinction between human inclination and moral reason. No such distinction would exist in a hypothetical "holy

KEY WORKS

"**Knowledge** begins with the **senses**, proceeds to the **understanding**, and ends with reason. There is **nothing higher than reason**."

IMMANUEL KANT, *CRITIQUE OF PURE REASON*

will", which would always act as it ought to and so would not require the concepts of duty and obligation, which are the expression of reason.

The *Critique of Judgement* followed two years later, addressing aesthetics. Kant wanted to know why we consider some objects beautiful but not others, and also why this judgement is often shared. He found the answer again in a joint mental process: the imagination delights in something; understanding then transfers this sensation to the cognitive faculties, which are shared with others, so moving the response outside the sphere of the subjective.

Final years

In his later years, Kant attained the status of a sage, famed across Europe and consulted by governments on matters of general interest, such as the suitability of vaccination. Yet he retained a modest lifestyle; famously, his neighbours in Königsberg could set their clocks by the regularity of his daily constitutional, taken along what became known as the Philosopher's Walk. After completing the critiques, his health began to deteriorate, and in 1799 he finally had to give up teaching. He died in 1804, during the Napoleonic Wars (1803–15); his last words are said to have been "*Es ist gut*", "It is good". After his death his influence continued to spread, and the Kantian legacy remained a significant element in philosophy well into the 20th century.

▽ **KANT AND HIS TABLE PARTNERS**
Kant (second from left) and his literary friends are shown in animated discussion in this early 20th-century painting by the German artist Emil Doerstling.

▷ **EDMUND BURKE**
English artist James Northcote shines
a flattering light on his sitter, Edmund
Burke, who was more often caricatured
as a beaky intellectual waving his
pamphlets at his political adversaries.

Edmund Burke

1729–1797, IRISH

Burke is often described as the father of modern conservatism. Most famous for his denunciation of the French Revolution, he argued for continuity and tradition, rejecting change based on abstract reasoning.

Promis'd Horrors of the French INVASION, —or — Forcible Reasons for negociating a Regicide PEACE. Vide. The Authority of Edmund Burke.

◁ **PROMIS'D HORRORS OF THE FRENCH INVASION, 1796**
This cartoon by James Gillray lampoons Edmund Burke's fears, showing French soldiers marching up St James' Street in London after invading Britain.

Born in Dublin, the son of a solicitor, Edmund Burke was educated at Trinity College Dublin. He moved to London to study law, but ended up becoming a writer and journalist. In 1757 he married a doctor's daughter, Jane Nugent, and published his first notable work, *A Philosophical Enquiry into the Origin of our Ideas of the Sublime and Beautiful*. Burke's only excursion into aesthetics, it anticipated the Romantic movement, contrasting the classical rationalist view of art based on clarity and proportion with the awe inspired by limitless grandeur.

Whig politics
Burke took up a political career in 1765, becoming a member of parliament and private secretary to a powerful figure in the Whig party, the marquess of Rockingham. The

▷ **MARQUESS OF ROCKINGHAM**
Burke's friend and political ally Charles Watson-Wentworth, the marquess of Rockingham, served two terms as the prime minister of Great Britain.

Whigs adopted a more liberal stance than their opponents, the Tories, and Burke's views were by no means conservative in his time. He called for an end to discrimination against Catholics and for compromise with the American colonies when they rebelled against British rule in 1775; he was also a fierce opponent of the extension of British control over India.

Earning a reputation as a notable orator and pamphleteer, Burke articulated his political philosophy as an active response to current issues. Rather than constructing a theory of politics and society from scratch, his starting point was acceptance of the complex reality of the world in which he lived. He saw a hierarchy based on property as the best guarantee of freedom and considered the running of affairs best entrusted to a responsible elite. Standing for election as MP for Bristol in 1774, he made a famous speech in which he maintained that an elected representative should not feel bound by the opinions of his electors, but should follow his own judgement and conscience to decide what was right.

Counter-revolutionary
The fullest statement of Burke's philosophy appeared in 1790 with his *Reflections on the Revolution in France*. Most Whigs had welcomed the French Revolution of 1789, but Burke denounced its radicalism as inevitably leading to tyranny. He argued against attempts to build an ideal society based on abstract theory, instead proposing gradual reform that respected tradition – "a disposition to preserve and an ability to improve". *Reflections* was a bestseller, providing inspiration for counter-revolutionaries but provoking a riposte from the radical Thomas Paine (see box, right)

Burke's final years were clouded by the death of his only son and his estrangement from his former colleagues. He died on his estate at Beaconsfield, Buckinghamshire.

IN PROFILE
Thomas Paine

Thomas Paine (1737–1809) was a British artisan who emigrated to Pennsylvania in 1774 and joined the American colonial revolt against British rule. His widely read pamphlet *Common Sense*, published in 1776, advocated democracy and attacked hereditary monarchy. In 1790, Paine moved to Paris to take part in the French Revolution. The following year he wrote *Rights of Man*, a scathing rebuttal of Burke's anti-revolutionary beliefs, which also proposed radical changes in Britain – namely, a written constitution and the abolition of aristocratic titles. In 1794, during the revolutionary Reign of Terror, Paine was imprisoned and narrowly escaped execution. His reputation in the US was ruined by publication of *The Age of Reason*, an attack on the Christian religion.

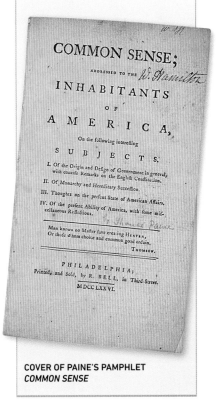

COVER OF PAINE'S PAMPHLET *COMMON SENSE*

"When **bad men combine**, the **good** must **associate**; else they will **fall one** by **one...**"

EDMUND BURKE, *THOUGHTS ON THE CAUSES OF THE PRESENT DISCONTENTS*

Jeremy Bentham

1748–1832, BRITISH

In his voluminous writings, Bentham analysed legal, educational, and constitutional matters, advocating a range of social and political reforms. However, he is chiefly remembered as the founder of utilitarianism.

Jeremy Bentham was born in London, the son of a wealthy attorney. His mother died when he was 11 and only one of his six siblings (his brother Samuel) survived infancy. Under his father's tutelage, Jeremy's childhood was dominated by a strict educational regime. He learned Latin and Greek at an early age and was accepted as a student at Oxford University when he was just 12 years old. He arrived there with 60 books, only 12 of which were in English (most were classical texts).

Bentham's father wanted Jeremy to follow him into the legal profession and the young man acceded to his wishes – up to a point. He gained his degree and was called to the bar in 1769 but never went into practice. Instead, he became more interested in examining the principles of the law itself. In part, this was inspired by his extracurricular studies at Oxford; while he was there, Bentham developed an interest in conducting chemistry experiments, which built up his analytical skills. His reading at university also strayed to encompass philosophical works such as those of Cesare Beccaria (1738–94). It was probably in Beccaria's groundbreaking *On Crimes and Punishments* (1764) that Bentham first came across the phrase "the greatest happiness of the greatest number".

An early rebuttal

Bentham's father was deeply disappointed by his son's refusal to choose a more conventional and profitable career path and deliberately kept him short of money. This had unfortunate consequences. In the mid-1770s, Jeremy fell in love with Mary Dunkley, the orphaned daughter of an Essex surgeon. The couple wanted to marry, but Bentham's father blocked their plans, refusing to increase Jeremy's allowance unless he took on a more secure job. The young man wavered but held firm to his principles, and the opportunity for marriage slipped away.

Legal writings

Bentham's plan was to support himself through his writing, but earning a living was a slow process because his chosen themes were vast, intractable subjects. To delay matters even further, he would often break off from these labyrinthine projects to write a topical pamphlet or a highly specialized digression.

Bentham's first major publication was one of these literary detours. His *Fragment on Government* was precisely that – a fragment of his *Comment on the Commentaries*. The "Commentaries" in question were *Blackstone's Commentaries on the Laws of England* – the definitive text on English law. Bentham's *Comment* turned out to be so long and unwieldy that he never finished it to his own satisfaction, and even those parts that were complete remained unpublished until 1928.

Fortunately, the *Fragment on Government* caught the eye of an influential patron. Lord Shelburne (see box, below) liked it so much that

△ **CESARE BECCARIA**
The writings of the Italian Enlightenment thinker Beccaria informed Bentham's views on the judicial system and the use of punishments such as torture and the death penalty.

▷ **JEREMY BENTHAM, c.1837**
This portrait is an early work by the noted English Symbolist painter and sculptor George Frederic Watts. It was created from the embalmed body of the sitter, which stood for many years in the entrance to University College London.

IN PROFILE
William Petty, 2nd earl of Shelburne

Bentham always regarded his meeting with Lord Shelburne in 1781 as a key factor in launching his career. Shelburne was already a major political figure: a former aide-de-camp to George III, a firm supporter of Pitt the Elder, and a future prime minister (1782–83). During their longstanding friendship, Bentham enjoyed many happy stays at Bowood, Shelburne's country estate in Wiltshire, mixing with leading political figures of the day.

BOWOOD PARK, WILTSHIRE, AFTER PAINTINGS BY BENJAMIN FAWCETT AND ALEXANDER FRANCIS

IN CONTEXT

Prison reform

During Bentham's lifetime, there were growing calls for prison reform. The impetus came from John Howard's report *The State of Prisons in England and Wales* (1777). Progress was also made by Elizabeth Fry – who introduced ladies' prison visiting and created a prisoners' aid society – as well as by the reforms outlined in Robert Peel's Prison Act (1823). A big problem in prisons was overcrowding after Britain stopped transporting prisoners, following the loss of its US colonies. Bentham's innovative Panopticon was designed to help address such issues.

A US PRISON BUILT FOLLOWING BENTHAM'S PANOPTICON DESIGN.

△ **ETIENNE DUMONT**
Swiss-born writer and editor Dumont was a great admirer of Bentham's work; he took on the challenge of translating and popularizing the philosopher's ideas.

he visited Bentham in his chambers in 1781 and invited him to come and stay at Bowood, his country retreat. Through Shelburne's circle, Bentham made connections that gave his ideas credence in the most influential legal and political spheres in the country. He also forged other critical connections, of which perhaps the most important was with Etienne Dumont, his Swiss editor and translator. Bentham was sometimes his own worst enemy when it came to writing. He embarked on ambitious projects, which he left unfinished; he sometimes had completed works printed, but delayed publishing them for years; and he wrote in a convoluted style that could be challenging. One pundit described his habit of putting "parenthesis within parenthesis, like a set of pill-boxes" as "the Sanskrit of modern legislation". Dumont turned his ideas into well-organized, readable prose.

Bentham's stays at Bowood also transformed his personal life, because it was there that he met and fell in love with Caroline Fox, the niece of the eminent statesman Charles James Fox, who briefly served as Britain's foreign secretary. The couple were close for a time, but Caroline politely turned down Bentham's offer of marriage. Even so, he never forgot her. When he was nearly 80, he wrote her a letter saying that she was still in his thoughts every day.

Journey to Russia

In reality, Bentham's closest friendship was with his brother, Samuel. Trained as a naval architect, Samuel was a brilliant engineer and polymath, who had travelled to Russia's Black Sea at the age of 23 in search of his fortune and had secured a position managing the estates of Prince Potemkin, an influential statesman and favourite

of the Russian empress, Catherine the Great. In 1785, Jeremy embarked on the arduous overland journey to join his brother, and remained in Russia for almost two years, hoping for a chance to propose his legal ideas to Catherine's court. The opportunity never arose, but while he was in Russia, one of Samuel's drawings gave Jeremy the idea for a major new project – the Panopticon.

The all-seeing eye

The Panopticon (Greek for "all-seeing") was the concept of a circular building with a central observation point that was designed to allow a single supervisor to monitor activities throughout the entire structure. Bentham believed that this idea could revolutionize working practices in Britain, and he envisaged prisons, workhouses, and factories based on this model. He persuaded the government to build a prison along these lines at Millbank in London, but the project was bedevilled by delays and eventually abandoned. Bentham received a generous financial settlement for his efforts, although this could never really compensate him for the 20-odd years that he had devoted to the idea.

The Panopticon's fate was typical of Bentham's projects. He drew up painstakingly detailed plans for new legal and constitutional systems, but found it hard to implement them. His ideas were well received by the administrations in post-revolutionary France, the newly independent US, and the fledgling states of Latin America, but these governments eventually opted for expediency rather than Bentham's idealistic schemes.

KEY WORKS

1776
Challenges the basis of English law in *A Fragment on Government*, which argues for a reliance on rational principles rather than precedent.

1786
Writes *Panopticon; or, The Inspection-House*. In the form of a series of letters, the work encapsulates Bentham's ideas for a model form of prison.

1789
Produces *Introduction to the Principles of Morals and Legislation* in which he outlines his doctrine of utilitarianism.

1817
Confirms his position as a radical, calling for electoral reform in the pamphlet *Plan of Parliamentary Reform*.

1830
Publishes the first volume of *Constitutional Code*, an ambitious scheme to provide an all-encompassing body of laws.

> " **Nature** has placed **mankind** under the **governance** of **two sovereign masters**, **pain** and **pleasure**. "

JEREMY BENTHAM, *AN INTRODUCTION TO THE PRINCIPLES OF MORALS AND LEGISLATION*

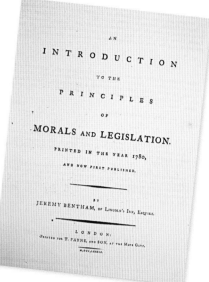

Utilitarianism

Bentham's greatest achievement was the philosophical and ethical framework that lay at the root of his reforms. He is hailed as the founder of utilitarianism, the doctrine that he outlined in his most important work, *An Introduction to the Principles of Morals and Legislation*. Human behaviour, he said, was governed by both pleasure and pain. The key to promoting one and avoiding the other was his "principle of utility", which he defined as "that property [which]... tends to produce benefit, advantage, pleasure, good, or happiness". The desirability of this "utility" could be reinforced by embedding it into the most fundamental notions of morality and the law. When applied to society at large, it inspired the mantra of utilitarianism – namely that the morally correct action was that which produced "the greatest happiness for the greatest number of people".

Bentham's central argument was gloriously simple, but the devil lay in the detail. He produced many acres of print trying to create an objective and comprehensive assessment of the diverse forms of happiness. He even devised a "felicific calculus" (happiness calculator) to measure their relative importance. This aspect of his work was more controversial and many of his ideas were later challenged by the other great champion of utilitarianism, John Stuart Mill.

Late years

Bentham continued working well into old age. He was a much respected figure, even though his eccentricities became more pronounced. He had a cat called the Reverend Dr John Langborn and a walking-stick named after Sancho Panza's mule in *Don Quixote*. Oddest of all, though, was his decision to have his corpse preserved as an "Auto-Icon". Bentham's skeleton survives to this day, padded out with straw and surmounted by a wax head. It is kept in the public atrium of the Student Centre at the University College London (UCL), which holds a large collection of Bentham's papers.

△ **ETHICAL CHOICE**
An Introduction to the Principles of Morals and Legislation (1780) set out Bentham's theory of utilitarianism – that the ethical course of action is the one that produces the greatest good for the greatest number.

▽ **FORD ABBEY**
Between 1814 and 1818, Bentham rented Ford Abbey in Devonshire as a country residence. His guests there included his great friend the philosopher James Mill, father of John Stuart Mill.

J.W. von Goethe

1749–1832, GERMAN

A towering figure in German cultural history, Goethe was a polymath whose works ranged from poetry to physics and biology. Although he was not a systematic philosopher, his thought had extensive influence.

Johann Wolfgang von Goethe was born in Frankfurt, a self-governing city in the Holy Roman Empire, where his father was a legal official. He studied law in Leipzig, then Strasbourg, where he met Johann Gottfried Herder (see box, right), who influenced him to adopt the anti-Rationalist attitudes of the *Sturm und Drang* (Storm and Stress) literary movement.

In 1774, Goethe published *The Sorrows of Young Werther*, a novel of doomed love and suicide that became a bestseller. Now famous across Europe, Goethe was invited by Duke Carl August of Saxe-Weimar-Eisenach to live at his court at Weimar. There he

became, for a while, the duke's principal minister and engaged in a wide range of civic activities. By the time he returned from a long stay in Italy his subjectivity and emotionalism had been tempered by notions of duty to society, and of order and proportion in aesthetics. Along with his close friend and associate the dramatist Friedrich Schiller, he led the movement known as "Weimar Classicism".

Science and philosophy

Schiller died in 1805, and the next year Goethe married Christiane Vulpius, his mistress since 1788. His major works after this time included *Theory of Colours* (1810), an attempt to refute Isaac Newton's work on light, and *On Morphology* (1817), a presentation of his views on botany and anatomy.

Although loosely influenced by Spinoza, Goethe's mature thought centred on

⊲ **FAUST**
Goethe's Faust explores the imperative to seek dynamic action and experience, while recognizing the perils of abandoning limits and restrictions.

the concept of organic development and of God as realized in nature, rather than standing outside it. The viewpoints that underpinned his theories on the evolution of plant structure informed his philosophy.

In his autobiographical *Dichtung und Wahrheit*, written between 1811 and 1814, he wished to show the stages of his early life developing "according to those laws that we observe in the metamorphosis of plants". Harmonious inner evolution, as exemplified by the growth of a plant, could ideally be matched by a human life that followed a path expressing the individual's inner essence.

The main preoccupation of Goethe's final years was the completion of his tragic play *Faust*, the first fragment of which had been published in 1790 but which was not finished until 1831. He died in Weimar, where he had lived most of his life, in 1832. His last recorded words were: "More light!"

⊲ **GOETHE IN THE ROMAN CAMPAGNA, 1786–88**
Goethe visited Italy in 1786, staying with the painter Johann Heinrich Tischbein, who made this portrait. The sojourn signalled a creative rebirth for the writer.

⊲ **GOETHE'S STUDY**
Goethe lived in the family home in Frankfurt until he was 16, and returned periodically. He wrote his breakthrough work, *The Sorrows of Young Werther*, at this desk in the house.

IN PROFILE
Johann Gottfried Herder

Johann Gottfried Herder (1744–1803) came to prominence as a literary critic who helped found the *Sturm und Drang* movement in German culture. He met Goethe in 1770 and became a major influence on the younger man, introducing him to the works of Shakespeare and promoting the aesthetics of Gothic medievalism against Greek classicism. In his later writings on history and folk poetry, Herder developed the idea of a nation as a racial group bound together by a shared language, culture, and traditions. He argued that adherence to the *Volk* (people) transcended class divisions and was more important than allegiance to a ruler. His influence is seen clearly in the ideas of Hegel and Nietzsche.

JOHANN GOTTFRIED HERDER, BY JOHANN LUDWIG STRECKER, 1775

Mary Wollstonecraft

1759–1797, ENGLISH

Wollstonecraft became a pioneering thinker of the British Enlightenment, producing a landmark text of feminist philosophy that paved the way for the suffragette and women's movements.

Mary Wollstonecraft was born in Spitalfields, London, to a middle-class family. In her childhood, she was witness to brutal attacks on her mother by her drunken, tyrannical father, and also learned that the family fortune was earmarked for her elder brother, with nothing for her or her sisters. These events shaped her views on gender inequality and underlined for her the importance of self-reliance and a good education, something she never received.

After a period working as a lady's companion and then caring for her dying mother, Wollstonecraft helped to establish a school for girls in north London in 1784. Although the school closed the following year, it inspired her first publication, *Thoughts on the Education of Daughters* (1787). She then worked briefly as a governess and also published a novel, a children's book, and, in 1790, an essay promoting republicanism and the ideals of the Enlightenment (see box, right).

A feminist manifesto

In 1792, aged just 33, she published her most important text, *A Vindication of the Rights of Woman*. In this political manifesto, Wollstonecraft suggested that women should be treated as equal citizens – a direct attack on Jean-Jacques Rousseau's advice in

Emile (1792) that girls should be educated differently from boys. Wollstonecraft considered their education to be fundamental to their rights as "human creatures" and challenged the prevailing view that women's biologically determined place was in the home.

Later that year, inspired by the egalitarian ideals of the French Revolution, she moved to Paris, where she had a relationship with US entrepreneur Gilbert Imlay; the couple were unmarried when, in 1794, she gave birth to a girl. Imlay deserted them the following year. Distraught, Wollstonecraft twice attempted suicide, but by 1796 she had recovered and published an account of her travels in Scandinavia. In 1797 she married William Godwin, a leading philosopher of the age.

A life reappraised

Wollstonecraft's life was cut tragically short at the age of 38, when she died giving birth to a daughter (who went on to become the author of *Frankenstein*, a classic work of English literature). For decades, Wollstonecraft was remembered more for her way of life than for her groundbreaking political theories, particularly following Godwin's biography of her, which caused unintended outrage for its revelation of her unconventional lifestyle – the politician Horace Walpole, for example, branded her a "hyena in petticoats".

From the early 20th century, Wollstonecraft's work began to receive the attention it deserved and since then has continued to inspire the global struggle for women's legal, social, and political rights.

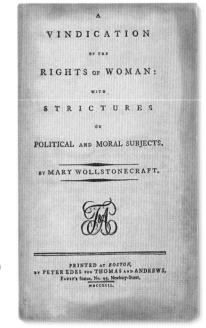

△ *A VINDICATION OF THE RIGHTS OF WOMAN*
This is the title page from the first (1792) American edition of Wollstonecraft's text. Its publication marked the origins of feminist philosophy and positioned the author as one of the major thinkers of the Enlightenment in Britain.

▷ **WOLLSTONECRAFT, c.1790–91**
This painting was made by John Opie. It shows Wollstonecraft in a pose and setting that were usually reserved at the time for men of letters, suggesting her intellectual equality with her peers.

IN CONTEXT
Enlightenment ideals

Wollstonecraft was one of the leading thinkers of the mid- to late 18th-century European movement known as the Enlightenment (also called the Age of Reason). It challenged the dogma of the Church and the power of the monarchy, and thereby paved the way for revolutionary movements in France and elsewhere. Rationalism and objectivity – together with a focus on equality, tolerance, and intellectual endeavour – were among the key principles of the Enlightenment, which presented a major threat to the established order.

LIBERTY LEADING THE PEOPLE, EUGENE DELACROIX, 1830; A DEPICTION OF THE JULY REVOLUTION IN FRANCE, 1830

▷ **SCHILLER BY GRAFF**
This image of Schiller was made by the renowned Swiss portraitist Anton Graff. The artist began the painting in 1786 but completed it only in 1791, reporting that Schiller could "not sit still".

Friedrich Schiller

1759–1805, GERMAN

Although most famous as a dramatist and poet, Schiller was also a noted philosophical thinker. His reflections on aesthetics, ethics, and politics constitute a profound meditation on human freedom and moral idealism.

◁ **SCHILLER'S GARDEN**
This sketch of Schiller's garden, seen from the bank of the River Leutra in Thuringia, central Germany, was made by Goethe. The building in which Schiller wrote many of his works stands in the middle distance.

Friedrich Schiller was born in 1759 in Württemberg. In 1773 he was sent to an elite military school in Stuttgart. During seven unhappy years at this institution he discovered the works of Jean-Jacques Rousseau and J.W. von Goethe and began to write poetry and drama. His first play, *The Robbers*, caused a sensation when staged in Mannheim in 1780. Its violent action, emotional extremism, and criticism of social injustice enthused the public and outraged the authorities.

Meeting with Goethe

Schiller abandoned a career as an army doctor and for a while led an itinerant life. His writings from this period include the historical drama *Don Carlos*, notable for its impassioned appeal for freedom of conscience, and the "Ode to Joy", a hymn to human brotherhood that was later set to music by Beethoven. In 1787 Schiller arrived in Weimar, where Goethe presided over court life. Goethe did not initially find the unkempt, impetuous young author much to his taste, but he nevertheless put him forward for the post of professor of history and philosophy at the University of Jena.

Philosophical writings

Schiller married Charlotte von Lengefeld in 1790, fathering four children. Occupying the chair at Jena, he produced his major texts on philosophy, including *On Grace and Dignity* (1793) and *On the Aesthetic Education of Man* (1794). Developed through a critique of the works of Emmanuel Kant, his philosophical ideas were also influenced by the descent of the 1789 French Revolution into a reign of terror. This led him to focus his hopes for freedom and the perfectibility of man on moral and spiritual progress rather than on political revolt. Only through the influence of artistic beauty, he argued, could people acquire the necessary

spiritual elevation to build a better world. Whereas Kant had seen the sensuous instincts as being opposed to a rational sense of morality, Schiller proposed the idea of the "beautiful soul", a higher state of moral being in which duty and desire would no longer be in opposition but in harmony. He saw an ideal society whose basic principle would be play – a ludic utopia.

In 1799 Schiller returned to Weimar, where he resumed his career as a dramatist, working closely with Goethe. Together, they became recognized as the hub of "Weimar Classicism" – a fusion of Romantic emotionalism with a classical sense of harmonious form.

In dramatic works such as the *Wallenstein* trilogy (1799), *Mary Stuart* (1800), *The Maid of Orleans* (1801), and *William Tell* (1804) Schiller explored themes of freedom, fate, and the "sublime" – self-sacrifice for an ideal. His life was tragically cut short when he succumbed to tuberculosis in 1805, dying at the age of 45.

△ **THE ROBBERS, TITLE PAGE**
Schiller's play uses the rivalry between two brothers, Karl and Franz, to examine human responses to injustice. It was widely seen as a protest against institutional corruption.

IN PROFILE
Caroline von Lengefeld

Schiller's sister-in-law Caroline von Lengefeld (1763–1847) made a significant contribution to Weimar Classicism. Schiller met Caroline and her sister Charlotte in 1785 and courted them both, but Caroline was already married (unhappily), so it was Charlotte that he wed. In the 1790s Caroline took up writing. Her novel *Agnes von Lilien*, written in 1793 but first published in book form in 1798, won her considerable renown. After her second marriage, to Wilhelm von Wolzogen, she wrote the first biography of Schiller, published as *Schillers Leben* in 1830, and then another novel, *Cordelia*, in 1840.

**SCHILLER WITH HIS FIANCEE
CHARLOTTE AND HER SISTER, CAROLINE**

Georg Hegel

1770–1831, GERMAN

With his belief in the centrality of *Geist* – "mind" or "spirit" – and his view of history as driven by a dialectical process of conflict and change, Hegel is arguably the most influential thinker of the past two centuries.

Georg Wilhelm Friedrich Hegel's life was largely uneventful. He was born in Stuttgart, where his father was a tax official. At the age of 18, he entered a Protestant seminary attached to Tübingen University, with a view to becoming a clergyman. There, his roommates were the poet Friedrich Hölderlin and the budding philosopher Friedrich Schelling. Finding that his own true calling was for philosophy, he decided not to enter the Church

on graduation – instead, he became a private tutor, first in Berne and then in Frankfurt-am-Main. At this time his thinking was influenced by Immanuel Kant, but he also immersed himself in historical studies.

An inheritance

On his father's death in 1799, Hegel inherited enough money to take up a position as an unpaid lecturer in philosophy at the University of Jena,

where his seminary friend Schelling was currently employed. Though not a popular teacher at that time, Hegel persevered and was rewarded with an appointment as honorary professor in 1805. One year later, Napoleon triumphed over the Prussian army at the Battle of Jena, which was fought on the outskirts of the city. Hegel, who viewed the existing Prussian state as incompetent and corrupt, welcomed this victory, but the disruption that was

▷ **GEORG HEGEL, 1825**
Jakob Schlesinger's somewhat stern portrait of Hegel depicts the great philosopher in his mid-50s, at the height of his career, but just six years before his tragic death from cholera.

IN CONTEXT
The University of Jena

The University of Jena, where Hegel taught from 1801 to 1806, was enjoying a golden era of intellectual excellence at the time. Johann Gottlieb Fichte had taught there in the 1790s, as had the poet Friedrich Schiller, who held the chair in history. Hegel's seminary friend Schelling was still in residence when he arrived, while the two Schlegel brothers, August and Friedrich, were laying the theoretical foundations for the Romantic movement in German literature, winning for it the title of Jena Romanticism. Napoleon's invasion of Prussia in 1806 disrupted life at the university and brought Hegel's stay to an abrupt end.

THE ARRIVAL OF FRESHMEN AT JENA UNIVERSITY, c.1770

> " Whatever is **reasonable** is **true**, and whatever is **true** is **reasonable**. "

GEORG HEGEL, *THE PHILOSOPHY OF RIGHT*

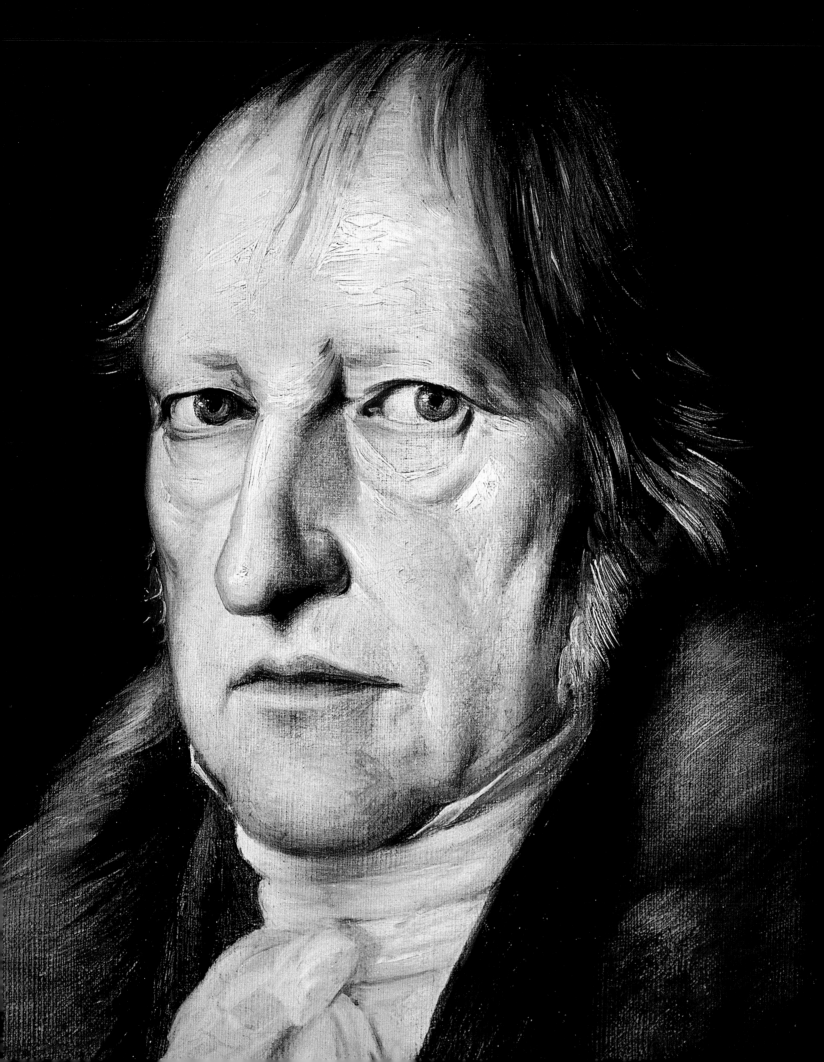

▷ **THE BATTLE OF JENA**
In October 1806 Hegel was forced to leave Jena when French troops occupied the town, having defeated the Prussians at the Battle of Jena, depicted here by the French painter Horace Vernet (1789–1863). Hegel is said to have sent the manuscript of his great work *The Phenomenology of Mind* to the printers virtually as the battle raged.

caused by the arrival of the French army in effect put a temporary end to his academic career.

In 1807 Hegel published his first major work, *The Phenomenology of Mind*, at a time when his fortunes were at a low ebb, thanks to the loss of his professorship. He was forced to take up new posts, first as the editor of a local newspaper and then as headmaster of a secondary school in Nuremberg. There, he produced the three parts of his *Science of Logic* (1812–16), a work that secured his academic reputation and earned him professorships at Heidelberg (1816) and then Berlin (1818).

The move to Berlin was significant for Hegel's career. His lectures there brought him a wide audience, which he also addressed via the publication of *The Philosophy of Right* (1821), in which he spelled out his thinking on political issues and the question of human rights and obligations.

Following its appearance he chose to concentrate his energies on lecturing, ranging in subject-matter from history and philosophy to psychology, aesthetics, and religion.

The concept of *Geist*

In his thinking, Hegel was very much a proponent of mind over matter. Central to all his ideas was *Geist*, meaning, alternatively, "mind" or "spirit". For him, how we experience the world is mediated through the mind. And what we experience is inevitably determined by the context in which we conceive it, which in itself is always changing. So reality is organic, and subject to a process of historical development.

Here Hegel introduced a novel and controversial element into his thinking, which some commentators have traced back to mystical notions imbibed in his religious youth; indeed, he remained a Christian all his life.

Unlike his friend Schelling, he did not identify his continually evolving reality with nature – that was too material for his taste. Rather, he considered it as mental or spiritual, the realm of *Geist*. Here too he saw a historical process, for in his view *Geist* was always evolving towards a goal – that goal was ultimate self-awareness. Once *Geist* gained full knowledge of itself, a state of Oneness would be attained, in which all conflict would be resolved. He called this condition "the Absolute", leading his philosophy, with its emphasis on the moral over the material, to be categorized as absolute idealism.

Constant transformation

Hegel applied the same principles to the study of history: reality was a historical process that could only be understood in terms of what had gone before. Change was central to his worldview, for in every situation there

> " Of **the Absolute** it must be said that it is essentially **a result**, that **only in the end is it what it truly is**. "
>
> GEORG HEGEL, *PHENOMENOLOGY OF SPIRIT*

KEY WORKS

1807
Publishes *The Phenomenology of Mind*.

1812
The Objective Logic, the first part of Hegel's *Science of Logic*, appears.

1816
Publishes *Subjective Logic*, the final part of *Science of Logic*, completing his massive project.

1817
The Encyclopedia of the Philosophical Sciences in Outline summarizes Hegel's thought for his students.

1821
The Philosophy of Right addresses political issues.

were destabilizing elements that had to be confronted or accommodated to create a new resolution, which itself would be liable to internal conflict and alteration. This process is known as the Hegelian dialectic (see box, right).

The end of history

For Hegel this transformation of reality was not necessarily endless. The one thing that could bring it to an end would be the end of conflict, for in a conflict-free world further change would be unnecessary: the dialectic process would come to a halt. This state of stasis would mark the end of history – a Hegelian concept that resonated with later thinkers, from Karl Marx to Francis Fukuyama.

Hegel saw this culmination taking the form of an organic state in which every individual could find fulfilment as a harmoniously adapted part of the whole; each of its members would accept their allotted role in a totality much greater than themselves.

In his conservative later years, Hegel regarded post-Napoleonic Prussia, with its constitutional monarchy, as an approximation of this ideal. Long after his death, though, both communists and fascists would, in their very different ways, look to the Hegelian endgame to justify the totalitarian societies each sought to impose.

In other respects too, Hegelian concepts have had an influence that only continued to grow for future generations. His view of history as a continuous process of development and, at least potentially, of progress fed into the Darwinian theory of evolution. Applied to individuals or groups, the notion of conflict and destabilization helped popularize the concept of social and psychological alienation, which again was to find its way into Marxist theory.

Finally, there was the almost theological vision of a metaphysical end-time: the Absolute, realizing itself as pure thought wrapped up in pure thought, or as he himself expressed it, as "the Idea that thinks itself". And what was the route to this ultimate state? For Hegel and the Hegelians, it obviously lay in Hegelian philosophy. With extraordinary self-assurance, Hegel not only foresaw the end of the entire historical process, but also firmly located its attainment in the correct understanding of his own works.

Final years

Hegel was an internationally known and highly respected figure when revolution struck his home city of Berlin in 1830. The prospect of civil disorder and mob rule profoundly affected him. In the following year, cholera broke out in the city. Returning from a summer retreat in the suburb of Kreuzberg for the beginning of the university's winter term, Hegel contracted the disease in a particularly virulent form. He died peacefully in his sleep the following day, aged 61.

IN CONTEXT

Hegelian dialectic

One of Hegel's most influential concepts was that of the dialectic. In his view, the natural state of the world and of people's minds was one of constant conflict and change. He saw the process in terms of three stages: the initial state, or "thesis"; the reaction caused by the conflicting elements within that state – the "antithesis"; and the "synthesis", the new state emerging from the reaction between thesis and antithesis. The synthesis will contain conflicting elements of its own, thereby causing the process to repeat itself endlessly. Later commentators would call this view "the law of change".

▽ **THE PHILOSOPHY OF HISTORY**
Hegel's *The Philosophy of History* is an introduction to a series of lectures he gave on this subject. The title page of the 1837 first edition is shown here.

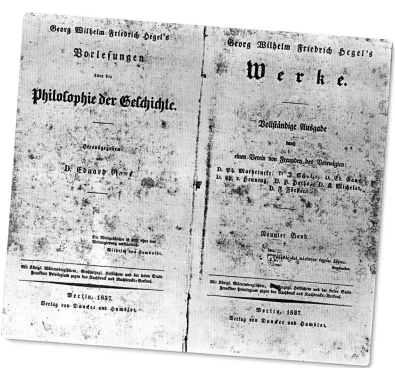

◁ **HEGEL'S HOUSE, BERLIN, 1921**
Hegel lived in this house in Kupfergraben, Berlin, from 1819 until his death in 1831. Several years before, he had apparently expressed his desire to die in the house in a letter to his wife.

Friedrich Schlegel

1772–1829, GERMAN

Schlegel was one of the inspirational forces behind the German Romantic movement. In a varied career he became a poet, philosopher, critic, philologist and – ultimately – a journalist and diplomat.

Born in Hanover, Friedrich Schlegel came from a literary background. His father – a Lutheran pastor – wrote poems and hymns for a weekly magazine, and his brother, August, was a distinguished poet and critic.

As a young man, Friedrich possessed the Romantic trait of taking on projects with a burst of enthusiasm, but not finishing them. He began his studies at Göttingen reading law, but his interest soon shifted to literature, and he avidly consumed the works of Shakespeare and Dante, and of the philosophers Immanuel Kant and Johann Herder. In 1791 he moved to Leipzig, this time to study ancient languages, but he began to run up gambling debts, prompting his brother to rescue him and remove him to Jena.

The Jena Romantics

In Jena, Schlegel came into contact with an influential circle of writers and thinkers. This circle included the poets Tieck and Novalis and the philosophers Fichte and Hölderlin, as well as Schelling, Schiller, and Hegel, who held posts at the city's university. The group, later known as the Jena Romantics, was philosophically associated with German Idealism (or post-Kantianism), the movement that had emerged in reaction to Kant's *Critique of Pure Reason* (1781).

Schlegel's main contributions to the movement came in the *Athenaeum*, the literary journal that he and his brother founded in 1798. In its brief, six-issue run, he experimented with his theory of "symphilosophy" (philosophizing together), writing a series of philosophical fragments, or aphorisms. These were both spontaneous and open-ended, designed to inspire and suggest, particularly when read in tandem with works by other authors. In true Romantic fashion, Schlegel described them as "continually becoming, never complete, and infinitely free". This experimental approach was never intended to replace more traditional philosophical systems, but rather to complement them.

Marriage and scandal

Having moved to Berlin, Schlegel embarked on an affair with a married woman, Dorothea Veit (see box, right), in 1797. This caused a furore, partly because he wrote a novel about their relationship, and also because the couple did not immediately marry after Dorothea's divorce, instead glorying in their unwed state.

The couple eventually married after moving to Paris, where Schlegel continued to write and lecture, and pursued his studies in Sanskrit and other Eastern languages. These resulted in the book now regarded as his most important work – *On the Language and Wisdom of India* – which contained his radical theories concerning the links between Indian and European languages.

Published in 1808, the book coincided with a dramatic shift in Schlegel's career path. The following year, when he moved with his wife to Vienna, he entered the service of the diplomat Prince Metternich. In his later years, the writer, who had started out as a youthful radical, turned into a conservative supporter of a reactionary politician.

IN PROFILE
Dorothea Schlegel

The daughter of the intellectual Moses Mendelssohn, Dorothea (1764–1839) seemed to attract controversy throughout her life. Born a Jew, she married and had children with a banker, Simon Veit, before meeting Schlegel in 1797 and becoming a Protestant (they both later converted to Catholicism). Their affair became a public scandal when he produced a thinly veiled account of it in his novel *Lucinde*, arguing that marriage is a bourgeois concept. Dorothea was a substantial literary figure in her own right, working as a novelist, translator, editor, and reviewer.

DOROTHEA SCHLEGEL

◁ **JENA, THURINGIA**
The city of Jena was at the centre of the first phase of German Romanticism, which began around 1798, led by Ludwig Tieck. Its second phase was focused on the city of Heidelberg.

▷ **SCHLEGEL, FRANZ GAREIS, 1801**
This portrait was painted in the same year that Schlegel left Jena. His departure from the city signalled the end of the intellectual collaborations that defined Jena Romanticism.

▷ **RAM MOHAN ROY, 1832**
Roy visited Bristol and met Dr Lant Carpenter, minister at the Lewin's Mead Unitarian Meeting House. During his stay, his portrait was painted by Henry Perronet Briggs, who exhibited it at the Royal Academy in 1832. Roy cuts an imposing figure at 1.8 metres (6 foot) tall and dressed strikingly in robes and turban.

Ram Mohan Roy

1772–1833, INDIAN

Roy was an Indian social reformer and philosopher who founded the movement now known as the Bengali Renaissance. His work brought together Western philosophy and ancient Hindu traditions.

Ram Mohan Roy was not only one of the most important thinkers of the 19th-century Bengali Renaissance (see box, right) but also a significant figure on the world stage. He was born into a wealthy Bengali family, the son of a landowner, or *zamindar*, which gave him the opportunity to travel widely at an early age. He became proficient in several languages, including Sanskrit, Persian, and Arabic, in addition to his native Bengali. In his twenties, Roy learned English and took up a position in the East India Company, which at that time was the major political and military power in the Indian subcontinent. Later he became a private money-lender, and also invested in shares and property, ventures that helped to make him a rich man by his forties. It was at this point that he turned his attention to study and to social reform.

Freedom and reform

Roy settled in Calcutta (Kolkata) and in 1815 established a philosophical salon called the Atmiya Sabha, or Friendly Society, which met at his garden-house in the north of the city and became the centre of a network of reformers and free thinkers. He published widely and became a champion of free speech and free expression, buying a newspaper, *Miratul-Akhbar* (*Mirror of News*), and a weekly journal, *Sambad Kaumudi* (*Moon of Intelligence*). As an activist, Roy opposed the excesses of colonial rule as well as certain traditional Indian customs, including child marriage, polygamy, and the caste system. He supported the rights of equal inheritance for women, and most notably, successfully lobbied for the banning of *sati* – the practice in which widows were expected to throw themselves onto the funeral pyres of their dead husbands.

Forging unity

Ram Mohan Roy synthesized Western philosophical traditions with Hindu concepts drawn from the ancient texts the Vedas, the Upanishads, and the Bhagavad Gita. His philosophy is

◁ **ADI SHANKARA**
The philosopher and theologian Adi Shankara consolidated the doctrine of Advaita Vedanta, unifying the principal streams of thought in Hinduism.

rooted in Advaita Vedanta, a tradition associated in particular with the 8th-century scholar Adi Shankara. One of its central claims is that the soul, or *atman*, is ultimately the same as *brahman*, the highest principle of reality (Advaita literally means 'not-two"); liberation is said to come from recognizing this fundamental identity. Roy attempted to reinstate Advaita Vedanta, claiming it was the philosophical underpinning of all Indian traditions. In 1828, he formed the organization that became Brahmo Samaj, a reformist movement that emphasized reason and monotheism.

In about 1830, Roy travelled to Britain as ambassador of the Mughal court in order to petition for an increase in the Mughal emperor's allowance. He used this opportunity to agitate in favour of retaining the *sati* ban, and to push his reform agenda. In Britain, he continued to work on reform with fellow freethinkers. He contracted meningitis while visiting Bristol, and died soon afterwards, in 1833.

IN CONTEXT
The Bengali Renaissance

The Bengali Renaissance is the name given to the flowering of intellectual and reformist activity in Bengal that was initiated by Ram Mohan Roy, and which continued up until the end of the British Empire. The Bengali Renaissance encompassed not only philosophy, but also jurisprudence, political theory, science, and the arts. Based in a commitment to reason, progressive social change, and intellectual inquiry, the movement aimed to recover and renew Indian traditions of thought. One of the most famous thinkers and writers who is associated with the Bengali Renaissance is Rabindranath Tagore, who won the Nobel prize in 1913.

POET, SCHOLAR, AND REFORMER RABINDRANATH TAGORE (1861–1941)

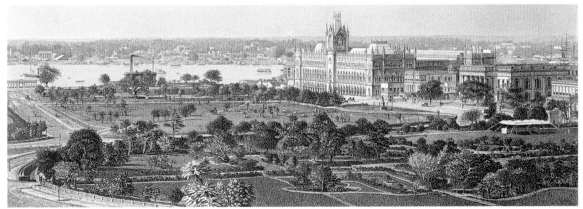

◁ **ROY'S CALCUTTA**
The colonial city of Calcutta was developed by the East India Company. On settling in there in 1797, Ram Mohan Roy made his living by lending money, principally to English employees of the company living beyond their means.

" Just **consider** how **terrible** the day of your **death** will be. Others will go on **speaking** and **you** will not be able to **argue** back. "

RAM MOHAN ROY, IN AMARTYA SEN, *THE ARGUMENTATIVE INDIAN*

Arthur Schopenhauer

1788–1860, GERMAN

Building on Kant's idealism, Schopenhauer proposed a more pessimistic metaphysics in *The World as Will and Representation*, which influenced generations of philosophers, writers, and scientists.

Arthur Schopenhauer is now regarded as one of the most important and influential 19th-century German Idealists; however, he achieved only modest recognition in his own lifetime. An irascible misanthrope, he did not endear himself to the philosophical establishment. Nevertheless, he made a name for his ideas, for the clarity of his arguments, and for his readable literary style, which – despite his gloom – is infused with dry wit.

He was born in the then independent port of Danzig (modern-day Gdansk), where his father was a successful merchant. It was always assumed that Arthur would follow into international trade – and even his name was

▷ **MOTHER, c.1800**
Schopenhauer had a tempestuous relationship with his mother, Johanna, pictured here. In later life, they communicated only via letters.

chosen because it was spelt the same in several languages. The Schopenhauers moved to Hamburg in 1793 after Danzig was annexed by Prussia; Arthur was sent to stay with a family in Le Havre, France, before returning to Hamburg to attend a private school in 1799.

A career in trade

He was a good student, becoming fluent in German, French, and English, and taking up the flute, which initiated a lifelong love of music. Despite his aptitude he decided, in deference to his father's wishes, to follow a career in trade, and in 1804 left school to take up an apprenticeship with a merchant in Danzig. This was cut short by news of the death of his father, allegedly by suicide. He went back to Hamburg to be with his mother, Johanna, and sister, Adele, and then resumed his apprenticeship

in trade. After his father's business closed down, Johanna and Adele moved to Weimar, but Schopenhauer persevered as a merchant in Hamburg. After two dull and frustrating years, he also left the city – to study at the Gotha Gymnasium for qualifications to enter university. At first, he adapted well to academic life, but his initial enthusiasm was short-lived: horrified by a satirical poem directed at one of his teachers, he left the school in complete disgust.

To gain the qualifications needed for university entrance, he took private lessons in Weimar. He did not share quarters with his mother in the city, because their relationship had always been uneasy. Schopenhauer resented the speed with which she had put her husband's death out of her mind in pursuit of her own ambitions as a novelist and hostess of a literary salon. He regarded his mother (with some justification) as a dilettante rather than a serious writer, and begrudged her her place in the literary limelight.

IN CONTEXT
Influence of Indian philosophy

Little was known in the West about Indian philosophy until 1802, when the Upanishads (Vedic texts that contain the key concepts of Hinduism) were translated from Sanskrit into Latin. A copy of the work was to hand in Schopenhauer's study and he acknowledged its influence on his *The World as Will and Representation*. It was not, however, until some years later, that he came across the teachings of the Buddha – specifically, the idea that all we can "know" of the world is illusion. Schopenhauer developed the argument that everything we experience is part of our own representation of reality, rather than how things actually are; nothing that is outside our own representations of reality can enter into this perception.

ANTIQUE BRONZE BUDDHA

◁ **BIRTHPLACE IN DANZIG**
Arthur Schopenhauer was born into a wealthy merchant family of Dutch heritage in this large and imposing Baroque house on Heiliggeistgasse in Danzig (Gdansk).

▷ **SCHOPENHAUER, c.1858**
Influenced by Eastern ideas, Schopenhauer held that people were motivated by their own desires rather than by social forces, and that desire was the root of all suffering.

IN PROFILE
German Idealism and Romanticism

Schopenhauer idolized Kant, regarding him not only as the inspiration for his own philosophy but as the pinnacle of all previous philosophical thought. He held a low opinion of the German post-Kantian thinkers (the "German Idealists"). He considered Hegel to be a charlatan, and dismissed Fichte and Schelling as naive Romantics with a shallow understanding of transcendental idealism (German Romanticism, as exemplified by Caspar Friedrich's figure of the wanderer, emphasized individual experience over reason). Neither did Schopenhauer have any regard for Ludwig Feuerbach and Karl Marx, whose materialist interpretations of Hegel drew them away from metaphysics into the examination of religion and political philosophy.

WANDERER ABOVE THE SEA OF FOG, CASPAR DAVID FRIEDRICH, c.1818

▷ **REWRITES AND REVISIONS**
Schopenhauer's repeated revisions to the text of *Die Welt als Wille und Vorstellung* (*The World as Will and Representation*) are evident in this manuscript from c.1844.

The inheritance that Schopenhauer received from his father's estate when he reached the age of 21 bought him some independence. He enrolled at Göttingen University and over the next two years of study became fascinated by the philosophies of Plato and Immanuel Kant. This prompted him to continue his studies at the University of Berlin, where he attended lectures on Kant by Johann Fichte, and on theology by Friedrich Schleiermacher.

In 1813, Schopenhauer relocated to Rudolstadt near Weimar to write his doctoral thesis. Its production further strained his relationship with his mother, who dismissed the work as incomprehensible; Schopenhauer was enraged both by her opinions and by her new relationship with a young lodger. Their rows grew ever more heated, leading to an irreversible breakdown in communications in 1814, after which the two never again met.

The importance of will

Schopenhauer left Weimar for Dresden, where he began work on his philosophical writings in earnest, taking as his starting point the transcendental idealism of his hero Kant. But where Kant had made the distinction between the phenomenal and noumenal worlds (the world as we experience it and the world as it is in itself), Schopenhauer described these two aspects of reality as worlds of representation (how the world appears to us) and "will", the impassive underlying universal force, of which our own individual wills are only a part.

Between 1814 and 1818, he finished the first draft of his major work, *The World as Will and Representation*, in which he meticulously presented his arguments for his understanding of the universe. The book also focused on the absolute futility of seeking personal satisfaction in a world driven by a dispassionate and unassailable universal will – an attitude similar to that of the Indian philosophical texts he was studying at that time.

Facing adversity

The book received little attention outside the world of philosophy and Schopenhauer is thought to have been disappointed by its tepid reception. In 1818, he also faced a series of personal problems: a young servant girl gave birth to his illegitimate daughter, who died after only a few months; and a banking crisis in Danzig triggered a collapse in the family fortune. No longer able to continue with his unsuccessful career as a writer, he applied for a teaching post at the University of Berlin, and thanks to a recommendation by Georg Hegel he was appointed as a lecturer.

Even though it was Hegel's influence that got him the job, Schopenhauer could not hide his contempt for the philosopher, who he thought had only a shallow understanding of Kant's idealism. Resentful of Hegel's success, Schopenhauer timetabled his lectures at Berlin to coincide with Hegel's in an attempt to lure his students away. The ploy backfired, as only a few students turned up, and Schopenhauer's academic career was constantly eclipsed by his rival's, prompting him to withdraw from teaching.

KEY WORKS

1813
Presents his doctoral thesis *On the Fourfold Root of the Principle of Sufficient Reason* to the University of Jena.

1818/19
Publishes the first edition of *The World as Will and Representation*; later two-volume editions are published in 1844 and 1859.

1820
Takes up a position as lecturer at the University of Berlin.

1841
Publishes *The Two Fundamental Problems of Ethics* made up of two essays: "On the Freedom of Human Will" and "On the Basis of Morality".

1851
Publishes *Parerga and Paralipomena* (Greek for Appendices and Omissions) to supplement his earlier philosophical writings.

Seeking consolation in music, Schopenhauer spent his evenings in Berlin at concerts, the ballet, and the opera. This brought him into contact with the young opera singer Caroline Medon in 1821, with whom he had an on–off affair lasting some 10 years. Quite apart from the misogyny for which he was famous, Schopenhauer was uncomfortable with intimate relationships of any kind; the couple never married, although they did have a son together.

Years of decline

After a period of travel, Schopenhauer returned to Berlin in 1825, to find that a long-forgotten incident had come back to haunt him. Four years earlier he had fallen into an argument with a neighbour, Caroline Luise Marguet, which ended in a scuffle in which she claimed to have been injured. The case went to court, but was dismissed. Now, Schopenhauer discovered that the verdict had been overturned, and

> " This world of what is **knowable**, in which we are and **which is in us**, remains both the material and the **limit** of our consideration. "
>
> ARTHUR SCHOPENHAUER, *THE WORLD AS WILL AND REPRESENTATION*

he was ordered to pay damages to Marguet for the rest of her life. She finally died in 1852, an event marked in Schopenhauer's account book with the comment "*obit anus, abit onus*" (the old woman dies, the debt goes away), an example of the wit and facility with language that is often eclipsed by his pessimism.

A cholera epidemic in Berlin prompted Schopenhauer to depart for Frankfurt am Main in 1831, leaving his partner, Caroline, and their son behind. Now aged 43, the philosopher decided to settle there alone, except for the company of a succession of

pet poodles (all called either Atman or Butz) and cats. He continued to write articles and books, and twice revised and expanded *The World as Will and Representation*, but continued to be virtually ignored by all but a few like-minded thinkers until the mid-1850s, after the publication of his essays under the title *Parerga and Paralipomena* (*Appendices and Omissions*). His health, which had been good all his life, finally started to deteriorate in 1860, and he died of heart failure peacefully on his couch, with his cat on his lap, in September that year, aged 72.

▽ **BERLIN UNIVERSITY**
Schopenhauer studied, and later taught, at Friedrich-Wilhelms-Universität in Berlin (it became Humboldt University in 1949). His lectures there were poorly attended, which helped to fuel his disdain for academic philosophy.

▷ **COMTE BY ETEX**
Comte was a precocious mathematician and an innovative thinker, who was hampered in life by his psychiatric problems and his abrasive personality, which is reflected in this portrait by French artist Louis-Jules Etex.

Auguste Comte

1798–1857, FRENCH

Although deeply eccentric and plagued by a tempestuous domestic life, mental illness, and megalomania, Comte was an influential anti-imperialist and the founder of positivism and sociology.

> "The **object** of all **true Philosophy** is to **frame** a **system** which shall comprehend **human life** under every aspect, **social** as well as **individual**."
>
> AUGUSTE COMTE, *A GENERAL VIEW OF POSITIVISM*

Hailed as the first philosopher of science, Auguste Comte was born in 1798 in Montpellier into a strict Catholic, monarchist family. He was later estranged from them owing to political and religious differences arising from his obsession with building a society based on republicanism and science.

Scientific method

In 1816, Comte was expelled from the Ecole Polytechnique in Paris for inciting a student rebellion. The next year, he became secretary to the philosopher Henri de Saint-Simon, whose ideas on the possibility of a science of society, based on stages and patterns of social progress, greatly influenced the young man. Comte came to think that scientific methodology could be applied to the study of society to bring about social order and reform, and in 1830 he described his approach as "sociology".

Following a bitter dispute, Saint-Simon and Comte went their separate ways in 1824. In the following year, Comte married Caroline Massin, a seamstress, but the union was an unhappy one and he was haunted by jealousy. (Some years later, Comte accused Caroline, incorrectly it seems, of being a sex worker.) Overworked and with financial worries, he suffered a mental breakdown while conducting a series of lectures. He discharged himself from hospital, but staff claimed that he was "not cured", and in 1827, he jumped off the Pont des Arts in Paris in an attempt to die by suicide.

Positive philosophy

Nursed back to health by Caroline, Comte resumed his lecture series in 1829, and between 1830 and 1842 published his most important work: the six-volume *The Positive Philosophy of Auguste Comte*. Here, he identified three stages in human evolution:

a religious stage, a metaphysical stage, and finally, a scientific or "positive" stage – the age in which he was writing. He termed his system "positivism". Based on a belief that the only authentic knowledge is that based on actual sense experience and the application of the scientific method, his system attracted many disciples, including the British economist and philosopher John Stuart Mill.

In 1842, Comte separated from his wife and was sacked from his long-standing teaching post at the Ecole Polytechnic. Following the death of the object of his obsessive love – Clotilde de Vaux – he again reached the edge of sanity. His four-volume *System of Positive Polity* appeared between 1851 and 1854, but he died from stomach cancer in 1857, isolated and impoverished.

Comte's scientific approach to the study of society established sociology as a distinct discipline and had a lasting impact on social and political thought. He was also a notable and influential anti-imperialist and conducted a sustained critique of empire for many years.

◁ ECOLE POLYTECHNIQUE

Originally founded to train military engineers, the Ecole Polytechnique became a school for advanced sciences. Comte's education there convinced him that science held the key to improving the human condition.

IN CONTEXT
The Ideologues

Saint-Simon and, later, Comte were greatly influenced by a group of Parisian intellectuals known as the Ideologues. The group was founded in 1795, before Comte's time in Paris, by the philosopher Antoine Louis Destutt de Tracy (1754–1836), who drew on the work of Locke and coined the word *idéologie* to refer to his "science of ideas", which he saw as "a part of zoology". (His use of "ideology" was quite different from Marx's later use of the term.) The group's members, including philosophers such as Comte de Volney and Georges Cabanis, called for a reformulation of society according to this new science, which was consistent with the ideals of the French Enlightenment, based on reason and empiricism.

19TH-CENTURY MEDALLION SHOWING THE PROFILE OF DESTUTT DE TRACY

Ralph Waldo Emerson

1803–1882, AMERICAN

Poet, lecturer, essayist, scholar of Asian cultures, and a major figure in the Transcendentalist movement, Emerson urged a distinctively new American way of thinking that influenced an entire generation.

Ralph Waldo Emerson was born in Boston, Massachusetts, to devout parents. His father, a Unitarian minister, died when Ralph was eight; the five children were brought up by their mother and an aunt. Ralph – who was known as Waldo – attended Harvard College and then Harvard Divinity School. In 1829 he was ordained as a minister, but his sermons strayed far from traditional doctrine, focusing on the idea of a direct, unmediated experience of God.

Emerson married Ellen Tucker in 1829. Her death just two years later exacerbated his crisis of faith, and in 1832 he left the Church. He spent almost a year travelling in Europe, and met with such thinkers as John Stuart Mill and Thomas Carlyle.

◁ **EMERSON, c.1870**
In his last decade, Emerson continued to lecture and write, but as his memory began to fail he withdrew from public life. He died of pneumonia in 1882.

On Emerson's return to Massachusetts, he began speaking on the newly developing lecture circuit; he also bought a house in Concord and married Lydia Jackson, with whom he would go on to have four children.

Universal spirit

In his first published work, *Nature*, Emerson set out his ideas about the interconnectedness of humans and nature, envisaging a "universal soul" and extolling a personal experience of the divine through nature. Eastern philosophies, together with European Romanticism, influenced ideas such as the human capacity to transcend the material world and become one with an all-pervading spirit of the universe. An exploration of these various concepts formed the basis of most of the rest of Emerson's work.

NATURE.

"Nature is but an image or imitation of wisdom, the last thing of the soul; nature being a thing which doth only do, but not know."
Plotinus.

BOSTON;
JAMES MUNROE AND COMPANY.
M DCCC XXXVI.

◁ ***NATURE*, 1836**
Emerson's *Nature*, published in 1836, was considered the manifesto for the Transcendental movement (see box, right).

In 1837, Emerson gave the famous speech "The American Scholar" to Harvard's Phi Beta Kappa Society, in which he exhorted US scholars to forge a new, genuinely American cultural identity. The speech was a huge success, but less than a year later an address to Harvard Divinity School caused outrage as his views on the failures of "historical Christianity" were perceived as far too radical for the time.

In the 1840s, Emerson published two volumes of essays, which contained some of his most famous works, including "Self-Reliance", "The Over-Soul", and "Experience", a critique of utopianism. In 1847–48, he travelled around Britain, a tour that resulted in the book *English Traits* (1856). He also campaigned for the abolition of slavery; and in his 1860 collection of essays, *The Conduct of Life*, published on the eve of the Civil War, he contemplated civil war as a means of national rebirth.

IN CONTEXT
Transcendentalism

Transcendentalism grew out of Unitarianism, a rationalistic, intellectual Christian sect popular around Boston, Massachusetts. The Transcendentalists, led by Emerson, sought to balance Unitarian rationality with an intense, personal spirituality, based in nature, that transcended the material world. Their sources included German Romanticism and ancient Indian and Chinese texts. Important Transcendentalists included Henry David Thoreau, and the early feminist Margaret Fuller, who edited the movement's magazine, *The Dial* (1840–44), with Emerson. Believing that humans were innately good but easily corrupted by society, they recommended self-reliance and independence. The Transcendentalists were leaders in a number of reform movements, such as feminism and the anti-slavery campaign.

FEMINIST AND WRITER MARGARET FULLER

◁ **STUDY AT CONCORD**
Emerson, known as "the Sage of Concord", worked at this desk in his study, where he also entertained luminaries including John Brown, Oliver Wendell Holmes, Henry Thoreau, Bronson Alcott, Margaret Fuller, and Elizabeth Peabody.

▷ **FEUERBACH, c.1865**
Feuerbach's trajectory as a philosopher took him from being a devout Christian to viewing religious belief as an anthropological phenomenon.

Ludwig Feuerbach

1804–1872, GERMAN

Feuerbach played a pivotal role in German philosophy, influencing the shift from the idealism of Kant and Hegel to the materialism of later 19th-century philosophers.

◁ **HOME IN RECHENBERG**
Finding himself in reduced circumstances after the failure of his wife's business, Feuerbach moved his family to this house near Nuremberg. Here, he wrote the final volume of his collected works.

△ **FAITH ACCORDING TO LUTHER**
In 1844, three years after Feuerbach published his acclaimed text *The Essence of Christianity*, he brought out a short supplement to it entitled *The Essence of Faith According to Luther* (shown above). In it he addressed the criticism that his earlier publication had neglected discussion of the German theologian Martin Luther (1483–1546).

Born in Landshut, Bavaria, Ludwig Feuerbach was one of eight children. His father was a respected legal scholar, and ensured that Ludwig and his four brothers received a good education – all went on to distinguished academic careers. The family was Protestant, and as a youth Ludwig was a devout believer who even considered a career in the Church. Encouraged by his father, he went to the University of Heidelberg in 1823 to study theology, where he was influenced by Professor Karl Daub, an ardent follower of Georg Hegel. The following year, Ludwig persuaded his father to let him transfer to the University of Berlin, where Hegel was a star attraction.

His suspected involvement in a controversial nationalist movement, *Burschenschaft*, delayed his admission, but he eventually entered Berlin's faculty of philosophy in 1825, where he attended almost all of Hegel's lectures over the next two years. Feuerbach was not entirely satisfied with Hegel's ideas, and with other like-minded young philosophers formed a group known as the Young Hegelians (see box, below), whose interpretation of Hegelian philosophy was a radical critique of contemporary German society. He left Berlin and completed his studies at the University of Erlangen, where he graduated in 1828 with his thesis *The Infinity, Unity and Universality of Reason*.

Independent thought
Feuerbach remained in Erlangen, teaching the history of modern philosophy, and in the 1830s he published several books on the subject. His ambition was to lecture at the University of Berlin, but even with his growing reputation he was unable to secure an academic post there. In 1837, he married and left Erlangen to live a simple rural life in Bruckberg, near Nuremberg, where his wife had inherited a share in a porcelain factory. With the income from this, along with a small pension from his father and what he could earn from his writing, he was able to pursue his career as an independent philosopher. He kept in touch with his fellow Young Hegelians, contributing articles for their periodical the *Halle Annals for German*

Science and Art, and slowly forged his own distinctive philosophy, which included his theory (outlined in *The Essence of Christianity*, 1841) that religion is a human construct, and that God is a projection of human ideals, and so more a matter of anthropology than theology. Despite his iconoclastic ideas, Feuerbach was reluctant to become too involved in politics, even in the turbulent 1840s, preferring to focus on the philosophy of religion; however, his interpretation of Hegelianism became a major influence on Karl Marx and Friedrich Engels.

In 1859 the porcelain business in Bruckberg went bankrupt, severely reducing Feuerbach's income. With his wife and daughter, he moved to more modest accommodation, but the financial strain took its toll. He wrote less and less and died in 1872, after a period of ill health.

IN CONTEXT
The Young Hegelians

After Hegel's death in 1831, a group of philosophers known as the Young Hegelians, or Left Hegelians, came together to reinterpret Hegelian philosophy. Where Hegel (and his followers, sometimes referred to as the Old Hegelians) had argued that the progress of history had culminated in the world as it is today, the Young Hegelians maintained that contemporary institutions, such as Christianity and the political status quo, were themselves only a stage in the development of society. Among them were Feuerbach, David Strauss (author of the controversially influential *Life of Jesus Critically Examined*), and a young Karl Marx.

GEORG HEGEL LECTURING AT BERLIN UNIVERSITY

John Stuart Mill

1806–1873, BRITISH

A philosopher, social reformer, and political economist, Mill was the pre-eminent British liberal thinker of the 19th century. An advocate of Utilitarianism, he examined the relationship of society to the individual.

Born in London on 20 May 1806, John Stuart Mill was the eldest son of James Mill, himself an eminent philosopher, economist, and ally of the reformer Jeremy Bentham (see pp.166–69). The young Mill's education was rigorous: he was schooled at home by his father with the intention of creating a genius who could further the movement of "Philosophic Radicals", of which Mill and Bentham were active leaders. He was taught Greek from the age of three and Latin at eight; by his teens he was considered capable enough to tutor his younger siblings. A year in France in 1820 led to a lifelong interest in French politics. Raised so immersed in his father's philosophical and political world, Mill later wrote that he "grew up in the absence of love and in the presence of fear".

Beyond expectations

In the early 1820s, Mill wrote for a number of journals, including the *Westminster Review* founded by his father. He established the Utilitarian

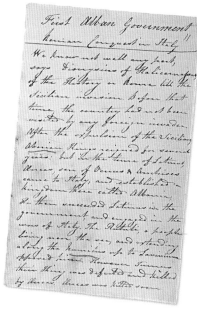

△ **A HISTORY OF ROME**
Mill was a child prodigy. By the age of six he had written a history of Rome. When he was eight, his father reported that "John is now an adept in the first six books of Euclid and in Algebra".

Society and took part in scholarly discussions and debates both with the distinguished thinkers who frequented his father's house and at the London Debating Society. Outwardly, he appeared to be living up to his father's ambition for him as the new leading light of the Utilitarian movement.

However, in the winter of 1826–27, Mill suffered what he later termed a "mental crisis", a long period of depression during which he came to realize that his pressurized education had focused too much on highly analytic forms of thought but had neglected "the culture of the feelings". Bentham's Utilitarianism aimed for the greatest happiness of the greatest number but, Mill now felt, failed to consider "the internal culture of the individual". He was aided in his recovery from depression by the reading of poetry – in particular that of Wordsworth, which opened him to the ideas of the Romantics and led him to explore thinkers from worlds beyond his father's circle, including Coleridge, Goethe, Thomas Carlyle, Alexis de

◁ **JOHN START MILL, 1873**
This portrait, made shortly before Mill's death, is by George Frederic Watts, who was considered the greatest English artist of his day. Watts reported that his sitter was "sensitive to all that was beautiful in form and poetic in thought".

IN CONTEXT
East India Company

By the 1820s, when Mill went to work there, the British East India Company was the de facto ruler of Britain's empire in India. The company was established in 1600 to import spices from the East Indies. However, as it expanded it turned its attentions to territory rather than trade. By the early 19th century, it had private armies of more than 250,000 men and governed most of India. The Indian Mutiny of 1857–58 led the British Crown to dissolve the company and take over the administration of the subcontinent, in what was the beginning of the British Raj.

EAST INDIAMEN IN THE CHINA SEAS,
WILLIAM JOHN HIGGINS, c.1820

" Over **himself**, over his own **body** and **mind**, the **individual** is **sovereign**. "

JOHN STUART MILL, *ON LIBERTY*

IN PROFILE
Harriet Taylor Mill

Harriet Taylor Mill (born Harriet Hardy, 1807–1858) was a British philosopher and early women's rights advocate who is now largely remembered for her influence on Mill. Their relationship lasted 32 years, with the tacit agreement of her much older husband. Mill's claim that she was joint author of most of his works is probably an exaggeration, but during the course of their "confidential friendship", she influenced his views on such issues as marriage, divorce, domestic violence, and women's rights, contributed a chapter to *Principles of Political Economy*, and collaborated on *On Liberty*.

HARRIET TAYLOR MILL BY AN UNKNOWN ARTIST, c.1834

Tocqueville, and Henri de Saint-Simon. This was a pivotal time for him, during which he threw himself back into his philosophical endeavours with a renewed vigour, in what would be a lifelong attempt to integrate his new ideas of "the cultivation of the feelings" into his ethical creed.

Professional life

In 1823 Mill had begun his career as a colonial administrator, going to work as a clerk at the East India Company (see box, p.195), where his father was an assistant examiner. He wrote that he "found office duties an actual rest from my other mental occupations". He would remain in the company's

employ until its dissolution in 1858, eventually becoming head of the department responsible for relations with India's princely states.

Mill met Harriet Taylor (see box, left) in 1830 and the two began an intense, intimate relationship that, although possibly platonic, was scandalous at the time owing to the fact that she was married. Along with his father, Taylor was one of the two most important figures in Mill's life and exerted an enormous influence on his thought.

Collaborative writing

Through the 1830s and 1840s Mill continued to meditate on morality, social reform, and political economy. He wrote prolifically, contributing essays to numerous periodicals, and also edited the *London Review* in 1835–40. In 1843 he published *A System of Logic*, a work concerned with scientific methodology in which he outlined his theory of inductive reasoning and attempted to apply the logic of causal explanation to social and moral phenomena.

Principles of Political Economy followed in 1848, in which an exploration of the moral impacts of industrialization led Mill to advocate a form of not-quite-socialism incorporating "industrial co-operatives". The work included analyses of economic theory and was a key text in British universities until the early 20th century.

Mill finally married Harriet Taylor in 1851, after the death of her husband. Tragically, the marriage was cut short, as Harriet died from lung congestion in 1858, shortly after Mill's retirement from the East India Company. She was buried in Avignon, France, and Mill bought a house near her burial place, where he lived for most of the rest of his life. During the course of their marriage, Mill and Harriet had together worked on what would be published – in 1859 – as *On Liberty*. In this, he defended the principle of freedom of speech, argued against "the tyranny of the majority", and considered "the nature and limits of the power which can be legitimately exercised by society over the

▷ **FRANCHISE FOR FEMALES**
In this 1867 work by John Tenniel, published in *Punch* magazine, Mill asks an indignant John Bull (a cartoon personification of England) to make way for women to cast their vote. Second from left at the front is Lydia Ernestine Becker, a prominent advocate of female suffrage.

MILL'S LOGIC; OR, FRANCHISE FOR FEMALES.
"PRAY CLEAR THE WAY, THERE, FOR THESE—A—PERSONS."

" **...actions** are **right** in **proportion** as they tend to **promote happiness**, **wrong** as they tend to produce **the reverse** of **happiness**. "

JOHN STUART MILL, *UTILITARIANISM*

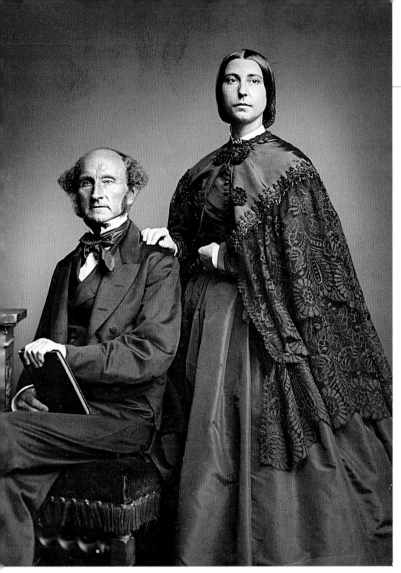

◁ **HELEN TAYLOR AND MILL**
Harriet Taylor Mill's daughter, Helen, worked closely with her stepfather, John Stuart Mill, after her mother's death in the advocacy of women's suffrage. She was a radical thinker and activist, especially in the areas of school reform and child welfare.

Two years later, Mill published a closely argued explanation of his ethics in *Utilitarianism* (initially in *Fraser's Magazine*, 1861). He followed in the tradition of Bentham's "greatest happiness principle" and in accepting pleasures and pains as the tests of right and wrong (see p.169), but departed from Bentham in positing a clear distinction between different qualities of pleasure. He categorized pleasures as "higher" (intellectual, aesthetic, or moral) and "lower" (physical or temporary), of which the higher forms were preferable.

Political life

Mill entered politics, standing as a Member of Parliament (MP) for Westminster for the Liberals in 1865. During his time as an MP he spoke on a range of more or less radical issues, including birth control, land rights in Ireland, the abolition of slavery in the United States, and various reforms of government. He was the first person to speak in Parliament in support of women's suffrage, and in 1869 he published *The Subjection of Women*, arguing for perfect equality between men and women.

On his defeat at the 1868 general election, Mill retired to his French home and lived quietly with his stepdaughter, Helen Taylor. He died in 1873 and was buried in Avignon next to his beloved Harriet.

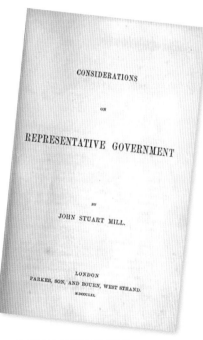

△ **IDEAL GOVERNMENT**
Considerations on Representative Government, first published in 1861, sets out Mill's views on forms of government, which he argues should be both democratic and representative.

individual". In the latter theme, his argument centred on the principle of harm: he asserted that the only occasion in which anyone – whether government or an individual – was justified in interfering with someone else's behaviour was to avoid harm to others or to the wider society.

Mill's philosophy was always tied to practical politics; in *Considerations on Representative Government* (1859) he asserted that the proper object of government was to promote "the virtue and intelligence of the human beings composing the community", and concluded the ideal type of government to be representative

democracy. He believed that participation in the democratic process would have an educational effect on citizens, and to this end he advocated the extension of the franchise not only to all men but to women as well – a radical argument for the time, and one that had been encouraged by Harriet.

However, Mill was also a defender of British imperialism, arguing in works such as *A Few Words on Non-Intervention* (1859) that there was a clear distinction between civilized and barbarous peoples, and that the latter benefited from a benevolent despotism.

KEY WORKS

1824
Begins to contribute to the *Westminster Review*, the journal of the philosophical radicals.

1843
Publishes *A System of Logic*, focusing on scientific methodology and the theory of inductive reasoning.

1848
Publishes *Principles of Political Economy* and attempts to reassess the system of property ownership.

1859
Publishes *On Liberty*, with a dedication to his late wife, in which he acknowledges her contribution to the text.

1861
Outlines his political and ethical stance in *Considerations on Representative Government* and *Utilitarianism*.

1869
Publishes *The Subjection of Women* and becomes one of the founders of the first women's suffrage societies.

1873
His autobiography is published posthumously.

▷ **SØREN KIERKEGAARD, c.1840**
Kierkegaard was never photographed, despite the emergence of photographic studios in Copenhagen a decade before his death. This unfinished sketch of the philosopher was made by his second cousin, Niels Christian Kierkegaard.

Søren Kierkegaard

1813–1855, DANISH

Kierkegaard is often described as the founder of modern existentialism. Grounded in his personal spiritual quest, his complex works express a belief in subjective truth and the value of the individual.

"The **crucial thing** is to find a **truth** which is **truth** for **me**, to find **the idea** for which **I am** willing to **live** and **die**. "

SØREN KIERKEGAARD, *DIARIES AND NOTEBOOKS*

Søren Aabye Kierkegaard was born in Copenhagen, Denmark, in 1813. His father, a strict Protestant, had been raised in poverty in rural Denmark but had risen to considerable wealth as a textile dealer with the benevolent assistance of a rich uncle. After his first wife's death he impregnated and then married his illiterate housemaid, Ane Sørensdatter Lund. Søren was the seventh, and last, of their children.

Possibly due to his perceived sin of fornication, Kierkegaard's father was burdened with guilt and felt earmarked for God's punishment. A melancholy sense of doom weighed on the household, and Søren later claimed convincingly to have never known the joy of childhood".

An individual philosophy

Sent to an elite private school, Kierkegaard was a physically weak, ungainly loner who defended himself against bullying by cultivating an acid wit. At 17, he enrolled at the University of Copenhagen to study for a degree in theology. His staid elder brother Peter had followed this course (and later became a bishop), but Søren proved rebellious and discontented. He soon lost interest in lectures that repeated accepted ideas and arguments, and in revolt against his family's puritanism, he explored the pleasures of drink, theatres, and parties, while also embarking upon intensive personal reading and reflection in pursuit of

what he called "a truth that is truth for me". Rejecting the lofty abstractions of the dominant Hegelian philosophy of his time, he sought to ground thought in the subjective reality of an individual spiritual life. By 1835 he was already arguing that the search for truth should be both a passionate and a personal quest, writing: "What good would it do me if truth stood before me, cold and naked, not caring whether I recognized her or not?"

Broken engagement

The death of Kierkegaard's father in 1838 marked a decisive turning point. Financially, inheritance made Kierkegaard comfortable for the rest of his life; psychologically he was infused with new energy and purpose. By the end of 1840 he had taken his degree in theology, published his first

book – a critique of Danish writer Hans Christian Andersen – and become engaged to Regine Olsen. Kierkegaard's relationship with her is one of the unresolved mysteries of his life. All that is known for certain is that he broke off the engagement after a year, causing both his fiancée and himself acute emotional suffering. His later writings suggest that he felt temperamentally unsuited to being a good husband. "There is something spectral about me," he wrote, "something that makes it impossible for anyone to have to endure seeing me every day." However, Kierkegaard's explanations of his erratic behaviour remain vague. Instead of making Olsen his wife, he adopted her as his muse and she became a constant reference point in his work, appearing in a variety of guises.

△ **REGINE OLSEN, 1840**
This portrait of Kierkegaard's fiancée is by Danish painter Emil Bærentzen. Regine Olsen was the daughter of a high-ranking bureaucrat. She first met Kierkegaard when she was 15 years old.

IN CONTEXT
Kierkegaard's Copenhagen

In Kierkegaard's day the Danish capital was a small but densely packed town with a population of around 100,000 living within its centuries-old ramparts. A resident of the city from birth, Kierkegaard was a well-known figure there, and regarded it "as one great social gathering." He liked to walk Copenhagen's narrow streets, stopping to chat to passers-by of all classes and to listen to gossip. He deliberately chose to write in Danish, preferring to address his fellow citizens rather than a wider European audience. He travelled away from his native city only four times in his life, for quite brief periods.

ENGRAVING OF THE HARBOUR IN COPENHAGEN, DENMARK

> " **Life** can only be **understood backwards**,
> but it must be **lived forwards**. "

SØREN KIERKEGAARD, *DIARIES AND NOTEBOOKS*

IN CONTEXT

The Danish Golden Age

The early 19th century was disastrous for Denmark. The capital, Copenhagen, was bombarded by the British during the Napoleonic Wars (1803–15); the Danes had to give up control of Norway; and the state went bankrupt in 1813. Yet these disasters heralded a period of intellectual and artistic flowering, whose products included Kierkegaard's writing in philosophy, the fairy tales of Hans Christian Andersen, the sculpture of Bertel

Thorvaldsen, the painting of Christopher Eckersberg (who established a "Danish School of Art"), the architecture of Christian Frederik Hansen, and, in science, the work of Hans Christian Orsted on electricity and magnetism. The period from about 1820 to 1860 is known as the Danish Golden Age; drawing for inspiration on Danish history, landscape, and mythology, it marked birth of a new national identity.

NUDE FROM BEHIND (MORNING TOILET), CHRISTOPHER ECKERSBERG, 1841

In the footsteps of Socrates

In the early 1840s Kierkegaard wrote a series of major works of outstanding originality. The prelude to this burst of creativity was the dissertation he presented for his master's degree, entitled *On the Concept of Irony with Constant Reference to Socrates* (1841).

In Kierkegaard's view, Socrates was a supreme ironist who subverted all certain knowledge. Instead of propounding a dogma, he provoked his audience into thinking for themselves: it was an approach that Kierkegaard intended to adopt for himself. Decrying the mass of clichéd information and ready-made ideas circulating in 19th-century Europe, he advocated "less knowledge, not more knowledge". The aim of his writings would be to lead his readers into an authentic personal engagement with the truth.

Aesthetics and ethics

In the winter of 1841–42, Kierkegaard travelled from Copenhagen to Berlin to attend a series of lectures by the German philosopher Friedrich Schelling. It was a highly frustrating experience that only confirmed Kierkegaard's low opinion of formal philosophical systems, which he felt

▷ **EITHER/OR, 1843**
The title page of the first edition of Kierkegaard's *Either/Or* (*Enten-Eller* in its original Danish) gives its editor's name as Victor Eremita – a Latin phrase meaning "victorious hermit".

failed to connect with the reality of individual life. While in Berlin he began writing a work built around his own experiences, expressing his radically different approach to thought.

Published as *Either/Or* in 1843, Kierkegaard's book consisted of anecdotes, aphorisms, musical and literary criticism, a fictional diary, and essays, all allegedly collected by a pseudonymous editor. Its first part related to Kierkegaard's experiences as a young man engaged in the pursuit of pleasure while suffering secret despair. This "aesthetic" approach to life was contrasted with "ethical" ponderings on marriage and moral duty in the book's second part. A section entitled "The Seducer's Diary", describing the cynical manoeuvres of a cold-hearted man, attracted most attention from the public and critics, with Hans Christian Andersen writing that, "One feels disgust for the author, but one profoundly recognizes his intelligence and his talent."

Either/Or made Kierkegaard an intellectual celebrity in Denmark, but fame in the wider world would

Enten — Eller.

Et Livs-Fragment

udgivet

af

Victor Eremita.

Første Deel.

◁ **HANS CHRISTIAN ANDERSEN**
Kierkegaard and Andersen were the most gifted writers of the Danish Golden Age, but often wrote scathing reviews of one another's work.

vicious caricatures of Kierkegaard made him a laughing stock in Copenhagen. He wrote: "Even the butcher's boy almost thinks himself justified in being offensive to me." The paradoxical result of this ridicule was to push Kierkegaard into a polemical engagement with public life. He mounted his own satirical campaign directed against the official Lutheran Church in Denmark, accusing its establishment of hypocrisy and materialism. He called on believers to quit the Church and take personal responsibility for their relationship with God. The venom of his attacks was bitterly resented by the Church hierarchy, including his bishop brother.

Later life

Kierkegaard enjoyed good food and lived amid elegant furnishings. His discomforts were all spiritual and emotional. He died in 1855, aged 42, after collapsing in the street. The cause of death is unknown. Despite his attacks on the Church, his funeral service was held in Copenhagen Cathedral, his brother addressing the large congregation.

Kierkegaard's works were first translated into German in the 1860s. His international reputation then continued to grow into the 20th century, when he was recognized as a major figure in European thought.

▽ **SATIRICAL ATTACKS**
This drawing by Peter Klaestrup appeared in the March 1846 issue of the satirical weekly *The Corsair*. It pokes fun at Kierkegaard's self-importance, depicting him as the sun around which all Copenhagen revolves.

have to wait until after his death. Over the following two years he wrote with furious energy, once publishing three books on the same day. In works such as *Fear and Trembling* (1843) and *The Concept of Anxiety* (1844) he expanded his thought from consideration of the aesthetic and ethical ways of life to the religious sphere. Kierkegaard never used the exact phrase "a leap of faith", which is often attributed to him, but he did describe true religious belief

as the product of an anguished choice that could not be based on convention, reason, or doctrine. Only a person who achieved faith through an authentic inner movement of the spirit could be happy in the world.

Critics and criticism

In 1846 a new phase of Kierkegaard's life began in an absurd way. He attracted the hostile attention of a satirical magazine, *The Corsair*. Its

KEY WORKS

1843
In *Either/Or* Kierkegaard contrasts the aesthetic and the moral approaches to life.

1843
Argues for the superiority of religious faith over ethics in *Fear and Trembling*.

1844
Publishes *The Concept of Anxiety*, a meditation on sin, guilt, and the anxiety that comes from the freedom to choose.

1844
Introduces the concept of the "leap of faith" in his *Philosophical Fragments*.

1845
Writes *Stages on Life's Way*, which includes reflections on marriage and allusions to his own engagement.

1849
Discusses religious despair and faith in *The Sickness Unto Death*.

▷ **THOREAU, 1856**
This daguerreotype by Benjamin D. Maxham shows Thoreau later in his life, when he became increasingly fascinated with natural history. Thoreau was an acute observer and kept detailed notes on ecological phenomena.

Henry David Thoreau

1817–1862, AMERICAN

Practical philosopher, essayist, poet, and naturalist, Thoreau influenced many civil rights campaigners with his call to nonviolent action, and his nature writings foreshadowed environmentalism and ecology.

David Henry Thoreau (he later inverted his forenames) was born in 1817 in Concord, Massachusetts, where he was raised with his three siblings. His father was a pencil manufacturer. After graduating from Harvard College in 1837, he set up a school with his elder brother, John, which closed after three years when John became fatally ill with tetanus.

Thoreau and Emerson

While at Harvard, Thoreau met Ralph Waldo Emerson (see p.191), who was 14 years his senior and had just published his seminal essay *Nature*. Emerson introduced him to his circle of writers and encouraged him to keep a journal. Thoreau found that Emerson's Transcendentalism echoed his own interest in nature and individualism, and he published his first essays and poems in the Transcendentalist magazine *The Dial*.

From 1841 to 1844, Thoreau lived as part of Emerson's household, serving as a tutor and general handyman, as well as working in his father's factory, but in 1845 he set out on his great experiment in solitary living. On a plot owned by Emerson in the woods around Walden Pond, he built a cabin, where he lived for the next two years.

Although the popular image is that of a man grappling with solitude in the wilderness, in fact Thoreau's cabin was a short walk from Concord and he often strolled home to have supper

> "The **mass** of **men** lead **lives** of **quiet desperation.** "
>
> HENRY DAVID THOREAU, *WALDEN*

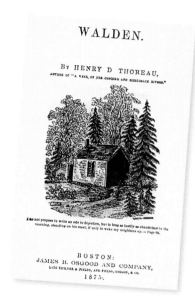

WALDEN.

BY HENRY D THOREAU,
AUTHOR OF "A WEEK ON THE CONCORD AND MERRIMACK RIVERS."

I do not propose to write an ode to dejection, but to brag as lustily as chanticleer in the morning, standing on his roost, if only to wake my neighbors up. — Page 92.

BOSTON:
JAMES R. OSGOOD AND COMPANY,
LATE TICKNOR & FIELDS, AND FIELDS, OSGOOD, & CO.
1875.

◁ **WALDEN**, 1875 EDITION
Thoreau's *Walden* is an account of his journey of self-discovery and a hymn to nature, written "because I wished to live deliberately, to front only the essential facts of life".

Activism and slavery

In 1846, Thoreau spent a night in jail for refusing to pay a poll tax, because of his opposition to the Mexican-American war and slavery. This led to the essay "Civil Disobedience" (first published as "Resistance to Civil Government"), which advocates nonviolent resistance to unjust government, and served as a model to later activists, notably Mohandas Gandhi and Martin Luther King Jr.

In 1849, Thoreau published *A Week on the Concord and Merrimack Rivers*, a memoir of a trip he had taken with his brother. Poor sales plunged him into debt and to supplement his income he worked as a land surveyor, which allowed him to continue his observations of the natural world. A fervent abolitionist, he helped escaped enslaved people flee north and spoke out against slavery, famously in "A Plea for Captain John Brown" (see box, right). Thoreau lived modestly for the rest of his life and continued to write essays on the natural world and accounts of trips that he made. He died from tuberculosis aged 44.

with his mother, who would also do his washing. Nonetheless, the work that came out of his stay in the woods was a paean to simple living, self-sufficiency, and nature. Thoreau's *Walden; Or, Life in the Woods* (1854) was a mix of practical description, personal reflection, and acute, lyrically detailed nature observations, and although it initially made little impact, the book became an enduring classic.

IN CONTEXT
John Brown's raid

John Brown was a radical abolitionist who believed that armed revolt was the only way to end slavery. In 1859, he led 21 men in a raid on the US Armory at Harpers Ferry, Virginia, in an attempt to initiate an armed insurrection. The planned uprising never materialized, and Brown was hanged for treason. Initial reaction to Brown's actions from abolitionists was disapproval, but after Thoreau vigorously defended him in a heartfelt speech, "A Plea for Captain John Brown" (later published in essay form), Brown was acclaimed as a hero and martyr.

JOHN BROWN PHOTOGRAPHED BY AUGUSTUS WASHINGTON, c.1846

◁ **NATURAL RETREAT**
This postcard shows the site of Thoreau's hut on the shore of Walden Pond in Concord, Massachusetts. A replica of the hut stands on the shore today.

11779   SITE OF THOREAU'S HUT, LAKE WALDEN, CONCORD, MASS.   COPR. DETROIT PUBLISHING CO.

Karl Marx

1818–1883, GERMAN PRUSSIAN

A leading thinker of the modern age, Marx was a philosopher, journalist, economist, and activist. He dedicated his life to the overthrow of the existing social order and the capitalist economic system.

◁ **MARX'S BIRTHPLACE**
The philosopher was born in this house in Trier, which now serves as a museum of his life and work, and of the early history of the communist movement.

IN PROFILE
Friedrich Engels

Friedrich Engels (1820–95) was the son of a German industrialist. He was a hedonist with expensive tastes but was moved by the poverty he witnessed working at his father's factory in Manchester, described in his 1845 book *The Condition of the Working Class in England*. During the 1848 revolutions, he fought on the barricades in Germany. In his close association with Marx he accepted the role of second fiddle, providing moral and financial support. After Marx's death Engels edited and published the last two volumes of *Capital*. He also wrote on the historical origins of the family and the subjugation of women.

Hegel (see pp.176–79), a new generation of German thinkers, including Ludwig Feuerbach, began reworking Hegel's thoughts to create a radical critique of state and religion. In Berlin, Marx became associated with these "Young Hegelians", who were looked on with suspicion by the authorities.

Marx was awarded a doctorate in philosophy in 1841, but found himself barred from an academic career because of his views on religion. Needing to make a living, he turned to journalism.

Radical journalism

Marx proved to be an excellent writer, with a tremendous talent for provocative rhetoric and biting satirical invective. He made his name as editor of a Cologne-based radical newspaper, *Rheinische Zeitung*, which combined articles on the poverty of German workers with veiled attacks on the Prussian monarchy.

Constantly harassed by the censors, the paper was banned in 1843, after which Marx moved to Paris, where

Karl Marx was born in 1818 in the Rhineland city of Trier, which was then ruled by Prussia. His father, Heinrich, was a prosperous lawyer who subscribed to the liberal ideas of the Enlightenment. Heinrich was Jewish and his ancestors included a succession of rabbis, but he pragmatically adopted the Protestant faith to avoid antisemitism.

Among Heinrich's friends in Trier was a liberal-minded Prussian official, the Baron von Westphalen. Karl Marx knew the baron's daughter, Jenny, from childhood and then fell in love with her in adolescence. They were secretly engaged when Karl was 18.

The young Hegelians
Unexceptional at school, Marx was sent to study law, first in Bonn and then at the University of Berlin. Initially a dissolute Romantic student given to poetry and drink, at university he developed the dedicated interest in philosophy and politics that was to last a lifetime. In the 1830s, after the death of the great philosopher Georg

RUSSIAN STAMP FROM THE 1970s BEARING AN IMAGE OF ENGELS

> " The **philosophers** have **only interpreted** the **world** in **various ways**. The **point**, however, is to **change it**. "

KARL MARX, *THESES ON FEUERBACH*

▷ **KARL MARX**
Marx, pictured here late in life, was one of the most important thinkers of the 19th century, but spent many years in poverty. His mother famously quipped: "If only Karl had made capital instead of writing about it!"

Das merkwürdige Jahr 1848. ____ Eine neue Bilderzeitung.

Europäische Freiheitskämpfe zweites Bild.
Kampf zwischen Bürger u. Soldaten in der Straße Frankfurter Linden in Berlin, am 18ten und 19ten März 1848.

IN CONTEXT
The 1848 revolutions

In 1848, popular uprisings took place in many European countries, including France, Germany, Austria, and Italy. In France, the monarchy was overthrown and a republic established. In Germany, which was then divided into several different states, a national parliament met. There were, however, fatal divides between middle-class radicals seeking individual freedoms, the working classes pursuing economic goals, and a conservative peasantry. Exploiting these divisions, kings and emperors were able to reimpose their authority. In France, the republic finally gave way to the authoritarian Second Empire under Louis-Napoleon. The failed revolutions were followed by an era of economic growth and declining radicalism.

LITHOGRAPH SHOWING FIGHTING IN THE GERMAN REVOLUTION, 1848

German émigrés were publishing subversive newspapers beyond the reach of the Prussian police. In 1845 the French government cracked down and Marx was forced to find a new refuge in the Belgian capital, Brussels.

Despite his precarious, insecure existence, Marx married the long-suffering Jenny von Westphalen and had fathered his first three children by 1848. He also met Friedrich Engels, who was to become his close ally and collaborator for the rest of his life. Temperamentally disobedient, Marx would at some time break off relations violently with every other colleague, but never with Engels.

◁ **THE COMMUNIST MANIFESTO**
The *Manifesto of the Communist Party*, written almost entirely by Marx, was published anonymously in the German language in London in 1848.

Class war

By the mid-1840s, Marx had fashioned most of the intellectual system later known as "Marxism". Expounded in largely unpublished manuscripts, Marx's thought developed through an extensive critical study of German philosophy, French Utopian socialism, and the work of British economists. It linked an analysis of the economic injustices of society in the age of industrial capitalism with the world historical perspectives of Hegelianism. Marx took Hegel's vision of the dialectical progress of history by logical stages – thesis, antithesis, and synthesis – and turned it into "historical materialism", a dynamic theory of class conflict leading to an eventual socialist paradise.

▷ **JENNY MARX, c.1840**
Like her husband, Jenny was a committed activist. She gave up a life of privilege to work for the emancipation of the working classes.

Marx maintained that the motor of change was economic development, which drove the transformation of society, politics, ideas, and culture. Each historical era was dominated by a social class. The rise of capitalism had placed the bourgeoisie firmly in the driving seat, but the capitalist economy itself created the industrial working class that was destined to overthrow the bourgeoisie and seize control. This upheaval would, in effect, end history, creating a harmonious communist society without private property in which work would no longer be "alienated" – a burden imposed on the worker – but a free creative activity.

Eliciting change

Marx's most original contribution to philosophy was perhaps his attack on the traditional role of the philosopher as a detached observer in search of absolute truth. He argued that the philosopher's role was not to contemplate the world but to engage with it – because only by engagement could it be understood. In 1847, his desire to change the world brought him into contact with the League of the Just, a clandestine international network of working-class would-be revolutionaries based in London. Forming an offshoot of the organization

> "**Religion** is **the sigh** of the **oppressed creature**, **the heart** of **a heartless world**... It is **the opium** of the **people**."

KARL MARX, *CRITIQUE OF HEGEL'S PHILOSOPHY OF RIGHT*

in Brussels, Marx and Engels quickly took over its leadership and relaunched it as the Communist League.

In February 1848, Marx wrote a pamphlet setting out the beliefs and programme of the League. Known as *The Communist Manifesto*, it became one of the most widely read texts ever written. Opening with the claim that "A spectre is haunting Europe; the spectre of communism", the *Manifesto*

provided a clear and vivid description of the progressive transformation of the world by industrial capitalism and the negative effect of this progress on the condition of the working class. The pamphlet ended with a call for the revolutionary overthrow of existing society: "The proletarians have nothing to lose but their chains. They have a world to win. Working men of all countries, unite!"

Revolution and exile

The immediate impact of Marx's pamphlet was negligible, but its prophecy of international revolution was soon fulfilled. Recession and failed harvests in the 1840s created poverty and distress that turned Europe into a powder keg ready to explode. An uprising in Paris led to much of the continent erupting in popular violence. Marx returned

▽ **RADICAL PUBLISHING**
A 19th-century watercolour painting imagines Karl Marx and Friedrich Engels examining the page proofs of the newspaper *Neue Rheinische Zeitung* at the printing house.

IN PROFILE
Eleanor Marx

Karl Marx's youngest daughter, Eleanor, born in 1855, aided her father in his work and became a prominent political activist after his death. She sat on the executive committee of the Social Democratic Federation, Britain's first socialist political party, and in 1885 joined a breakaway group that founded the more radical Socialist League. She was a prominent supporter of strike action by women workers, including the London matchgirls' strike in 1888. She died by suicide in 1898 after discovering that her long-term partner, Edward Aveling, had secretly married a young actress.

ACTIVIST ELEANOR MARX, DAUGHTER OF KARL MARX, c.1875

to Germany to advance the revolutionary cause, reviving his old radical newspaper as the *Neue Rheinische Zeitung*. A year of furious propagandist activity and vitriolic polemic followed. In 1849, as the revolutionary dream faded and reaction set in across Europe, Marx and Engels were arrested by the Prussian authorities. They avoided imprisonment but were forced to seek refuge in Britain, the only remaining haven for European revolutionaries.

Personal strife

In the 1850s Marx's life entered a dark phase. Poorly housed in London's Soho district, he and his family survived only through subsidies from Engels. Two children born in 1849 and 1851 died in infancy. Marx appears to have found solace in relations with the family's housekeeper, Helene Demuth, who gave birth to a boy in 1851.

Presumably to save Marx's marriage, Engels took responsibility for the illegitimate child, who was found a foster home. Jenny Marx's only surviving son, the much-loved Edgar, died in 1855, leaving a family of four daughters for Marx to support. He eventually found a source of income through freelance employment as a correspondent for a US newspaper, the *New York Daily Tribune*, but still struggled to bring up his daughters in the middle-class conditions to which, despite his revolutionary views, he consistently aspired.

Critique of capitalism

The failure of the 1848 revolutions posed an intellectual challenge that dominated the next two decades of Marx's life. As the immediate prospect of a workers' uprising receded, he sought to prove that the revolutionary transition to communism would still

△ **THE BRITISH LIBRARY**
London became Marx's home after he was exiled for his role in the German revolution of 1848. He wrote his works in the circular Reading Room of the British Museum, which had recently been completed to a design by the British architect Sydney Smirke.

inevitably happen. Spending his days in the Reading Room of the British Museum, he embarked upon a prolonged study of economic and social data, along with a theoretical reassessment of capitalist production. In particular, through the concept of surplus value, he attempted to show how the workers were being robbed of the product of their labour. His monumental work *Capital* aimed to provide a scientific basis for belief in the inevitability of the fall of capitalism, through the internal logic of the capitalist system itself.

KEY WORKS

1843
Critique of Hegel's Philosophy of Right is Marx's revision of Hegel, in which he describes religion as "the opium of the people".

1845
Writes *Theses on Feuerbach*, linking a materialist theory of history to political action.

1848
With Friedrich Engels, writes *The Communist Manifesto*, a pamphlet setting out the beliefs of the Communist League.

1852
Marx's essay "The Eighteenth Brumaire of Louis Napoleon" analyses the failure of France's 1848 revolution.

1859
In *A Contribution to the Critique of Political Economy*, Marx discusses the source of value and the nature of commodities.

1867
Marx's analysis *Capital* predicts the inevitable downfall of the capitalist system. Two volumes are published posthumously.

1871
In the pamphlet *The Civil War in France*, Marx analyses the successes and failures of the Commune uprising in Paris.

1875
Critique of the Gotha Programme criticizes the social democratic approach to the transition to communism.

The First International

Marx re-entered politics in 1864 as a dominant figure in the International Working Men's Association, commonly known as the First International. He guided this mild collection of trade unionists and humanistic socialists towards a commitment to the seizure of power by the working class. Despite gaining many adherents across Europe, the International played no part in the genesis of the continent's next violent upheaval. In 1871, as a reaction to French capitulation in the Franco-Prussian War, Paris was taken over by the revolutionary Commune. Marx remained a passive observer of this uprising, which was suppressed with heavy loss of life. *The Civil War in France*, his pamphlet analysing the events, gained a large readership and it became an accepted fact that Marx's International had been responsible for the uprising. For the first time, Marx was famous and had a wide public.

The First International collapsed in the early 1870s as a result of irresolvable conflict between Marx and the Russian anarchist Mikhail Bakunin. Marx's influence, however, continued to spread. As new socialist parties developed in Germany and Russia in the 1870s and 1880s, the question to what degree they should accept Marx's ideas became a crucial subject of debate. Marx intervened to criticize the programme of the nascent German Social Democratic Party in 1876, arguing against the possibility of a peaceful transition to socialism and emphasizing the need for a "dictatorship of the proletariat" after the revolution.

Final years

In the last decade of his life, Marx was plagued by ill health; he died of bronchitis in March 1883, 13 months after the death of his wife and two months after the death of his eldest daughter. He was buried in Highgate Cemetery, London, in the section reserved for atheists. Only his family and a few close friends, including Engels, attended the funeral.

△ **CAPITAL, VOLUME 1**
The opening volume of Marx's *Capital* (*Das Kapital*) was first published in German in 1867. The second and third volumes were published posthumously.

▽ **FROM MARX TO STALIN**
Communism was adopted in Russia in the early 20th century under Vladimir Lenin, who was succeeded by Joseph Stalin. This 1933 propaganda poster shows the supposed continuity in thought from Marx and Engels (left) to Lenin and Stalin (right).

ВЫШЕ ЗНАМЯ МАРКСА ЭНГЕЛЬСА ЛЕНИНА и СТАЛИНА!

" The **tradition** of **all dead generations weighs** like a **nightmare** upon **the brains** of **the living**. "

KARL MARX, "THE EIGHTEENTH BRUMAIRE OF LOUIS BONAPARTE"

Frederick Douglass

c.1818–1895, AMERICAN

One of the most famous and influential American voices of the 19th century, Frederick Douglass advanced the cause of abolition in the years leading up to the American Civil War.

△ **LINCOLN-DOUGLASS BADGE**

△ **LINCOLN-DOUGLASS BADGE**
Douglass encouraged Black Americans to fight in the Civil War (two of his sons enlisted) and met with President Lincoln to advocate for the rights of Black American soldiers.

◁ **PERSUASIVE ORATOR**
A "gentlemen's mob" and the police break up an antislavery meeting at Tremont Temple Baptist Church, Boston, in 1860. A powerful speaker, Douglass often addressed abolitionist meetings.

Frederick Douglass, an American Slave, catapulted Douglass to great fame. In 1846, English supporters purchased his legal freedom for around $700.

Natural law

In 1847, Douglass settled in Rochester, New York, and founded *The North Star* newspaper. It provided a vehicle for his unflinching rhetoric. Mocking the hypocrisy of Americans who lauded liberty but defended enslavement, he rooted his arguments in "natural law" – the idea that basic rights are derived from nature, not societal rules.

After Emancipation and the end of the Civil War (1861–65), Douglass advocated for the rights of freed slaves and accepted a series of government appointments, including Marshal of DC and Minister Resident and Consul General to Haiti.

In 1882, two years after the death of his first wife, Douglass married Helen Pitts, a white woman 20 years his junior. The union was controversial in Black and white communities. He died in 1895, likely of a heart attack.

Frederick Augusta Washington Bailey, the man later known as Frederick Douglass, was born into slavery in Talbot County, Maryland, in 1817 or possibly 1818. He was cared for by his maternal grandmother, Betty Bailey. Douglass barely knew his mother, Harriet Bailey, who was enslaved nearby, and never knew the identity of his biological father.

Douglass learned to read as a child, his initial lessons provided by Sophia Auld, the wife of his enslaver, until her husband forbade her. Douglass would later teach other slaves to read.

Rented out in his teens to Edward Covey, a particularly cruel farmer, Douglass was "broken in body, soul and spirit," but eventually stood up to him and beat him in a fight. Douglass cited this as a turning point. It may have led to his defence of violence as a means to end enslavement.

A new life

In 1838, Douglass boarded a train north armed with borrowed papers that identified him as free Black sailor. He married a woman named Anna Murray and settled in New Bedford, Massachusetts, using the name Douglass to hide his identity.

Abolitionist organizations asked him to share his story at their meetings. The 1845 publication of his first autobiography, *Narrative of the Life of*

◁ **FREDERICK DOUGLASS, c.1845**
Douglass had an impressive bearing. He sat for many portraits, including this one by an unidentified artist. He was also widely photographed and is sometimes cited as the most photographed American of the 19th century.

> " **Power** concedes **nothing** without a **demand**. "
>
> FREDERICK DOUGLASS

IN CONTEXT
Universal rights

Abolition was Douglass's primary aim, but he championed women's rights, in keeping with his belief in natural law. His newspaper, *The North Star*, proclaimed "Right is of no sex – Truth is of no color."

In 1848, Douglass took part in the Seneca Falls women's rights convention, where his endorsement of women's suffrage helped ensure that voting rights were included in its influential "Declaration of Sentiments". But while Douglass believed in universal suffrage and proudly called himself "a women's rights man", he pragmatically concluded that securing the vote for Back Americans was a more urgent issue than doing so for women.

DOUGLASS AT THE FUGITIVE SLAVE LAW CONVENTION, NEW YORK, 1850

William James

1842–1910, AMERICAN

James was a pioneer in the scientific study of psychology and one of the founders of the Pragmatic school of philosophy. His readiness to tackle big topics in clear, robust language made him an influential figure.

William James was born in New York in 1842. Of Irish Protestant descent, his wealthy family belonged to 19th-century US's small, cultured elite. His father, Henry James Sr, was an idiosyncratic thinker and writer who failed to achieve the recognition he felt he deserved. A man who never worked for money, he saw the purpose of existence as the cultivation of the spiritual life and despised all careers and mercenary effort. William would rebel against his father's lack of engagement with the material world but never shook off traces of his belief in a higher spiritual reality.

Early hardships

William James was the oldest of five children among whom was the future novelist Henry (see box, right). In their lifetime William was the dominant figure, winning far greater renown. Whether through genetic factors or the psychological pressures of their highly strung household, William, Henry, and their sister Alice suffered mental and physical problems that plagued them in adulthood. Until the age of 30, William experienced bouts of irrational fear and depression, even contemplating suicide, and he suffered chronic back pains that may have been psychosomatic. Alice, a woman of brilliant mind

△ **MEMORIAL HALL, HARVARD**
James helped establish the department of psychology at Harvard University, despite saying of the discipline: "This is no science; it is only the hope of a science."

who was closely attached to William, was crippled by mental illness, which was diagnosed as "hysteria".

Ambitious for the kind of success that his father despised, William tried to become an artist, studying under the US painter William Morris Hunt. In 1861, fearing he would never succeed, he transferred to science. Studying at Harvard, he took a degree in medicine, though he never practised as a doctor; instead, he became an academic and specialized in psychology. The study of the mind and its relation to the brain was a young discipline at that time, and the psychology course taught by James at Harvard in 1875 was the first of its kind in the US.

James's interest in psychology was partly stimulated by his own mental struggles. By his own account, these were resolved in the early 1870s as a result of a philosophical revelation. He became convinced that it was within anyone's power to change their life by acts of will. "My first act of free will", he wrote, "shall be to believe in free will." Armed with faith in his "individual reality and creative power", he took on the future with a fresh determination.

IN PROFILE
Henry James

A year younger than William, the novelist Henry James (1843–1916) was always somewhat in awe of his brother. Living for much of his life in Britain, Henry experienced literary success in the 1870s and 80s with works such as *Daisy Miller* and *The Portrait of a Lady*, contrasting US innocence with European corruption. By 1900, however, when William's reputation was at its height, Henry had failed as a writer for the theatre and his novels – considered far too obscure – had fallen from favour. William tended to patronize Henry, advising him to write in a simpler style with more straightforward plots.

HENRY JAMES, JACQUES-EMILE BLANCHE, 1908

> " **Be not afraid** of **life. Believe** that **life** is **worth living**, and **your belief** will help create **the fact.** "

WILLIAM JAMES, "IS LIFE WORTH LIVING?"

▷ **WILLIAM JAMES**
At Harvard, James was greatly respected for his empathy, charm, and modesty. His students reported his constant curiosity and open-mindedness, and his genius for clear expression.

KEY WORKS

1890
Publishes his 12,000-page textbook *The Principles of Psychology*, which includes his theory of the "stream of consciousness".

1897
Sets out his pragmatic approach to religion, immortality, and psychical research in *Will to Believe*, a collection of essays and lectures.

1902
In *The Varieties of Religious Experience*, James considers the evidence for religious belief presented by the lives of believers, saints, and mystics.

1907
The publication of *Pragmatism: A New Name for Some Old Ways of Thinking* confirms James as a leading thinker of his time.

1908
Presents his views on the nature of the universe in *A Pluralistic Universe*.

IN PROFILE
Leonora Piper

Leonora Piper (1857–1950) was a Bostonian trance medium who could apparently transmit messages from the spirits of the dead. William James became convinced that – unlike most mediums he had met – she was not a fraud. He wrote: "If you wish to upset the law that all crows are black, it is enough if you prove that one crow is white. Mrs Piper is my white crow." James made Piper famous, enabling her to reap a fortune from her work. Piper later denied that she was in touch with spirits, and suggested that her powers could in fact be explained by telepathy.

LEONORA PIPER

James's relations with women were often fraught with failure, but in 1878 he found happiness in marrying Alice Gibbens, with whom he had five children. His doubting and tortured earlier self receded and he developed into a benign, supremely confident figure. The philosopher Bertrand Russell, who knew James in the later phase of his life, wrote: "His warmheartedness and his delightful humour caused him to be almost universally beloved."

Psychical explorations

In his academic life, James focused on the study of brain function, but like other psychologists of his period he was also interested in exploring the stranger areas of the mind, including phenomena such as hypnotism and altered states of consciousness. Determined to base his ideas in direct experience, he experimented with consciousness-changing drugs, such as nitrous oxide, and in 1884 became a founder member of the American Society for Psychical Research, which examined phenomena such as telepathy and the activities of spiritualist mediums. The death of his infant son Herman gave a personal edge to investigation of the spiritual world, since James and his wife found difficulty in accepting that the child had simply disappeared forever.

James took part in seances with the noted medium Leonora Piper (see box, left), who exhibited an uncanny knowledge of his family's private affairs. He adopted a subtle attitude of suspended disbelief, arguing that it was right at least to behave as if one believed, even in defiance of one's logical intellect, in order to be able to explore psychical phenomena.

Pragmatism

In 1890, James published a massive textbook, *The Principles of Psychology*, which summed up his knowledge of the field. Its most fruitful innovation was the idea of the "stream of consciousness" as a way of describing our moment-by-moment experience: a concept that was to be widely adopted by Modernist writers in the 20th century. After this work he felt free to devote himself to the philosophical questions that had long fascinated him. As early as 1872 he

had participated in a philosophical discussion group in Boston called the Metaphysical Club, whose members included scientist Charles Sanders Peirce. It is Peirce who is credited with developing the approach to philosophy known as "Pragmatism", although James was the first to use the term in print and it became primarily associated with his name.

Pragmatists argued that concepts and beliefs were developed to solve problems or advance knowledge. If ideas made no difference to the world then they were meaningless. Thought was constantly on the move, not establishing eternal truths but tackling ever-changing dilemmas. James did not hold the simplistic view that a belief was true if it worked, but he often sounded as if that was what he was saying. This position resonated with the can-do US mentality, and James's essays and lectures in the 1890s became popular because they addressed questions people felt urgently needed an answer – is life worth living? Does immortality exist?

Faith and science

James wrote on the issue of religion in works such as *The Will to Believe* and *The Varieties of Religious Experience*. He took a modern scientific approach to the subject, but reassuringly for many, left the door open to belief

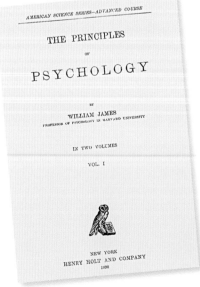

AMERICAN SCIENCE SERIES—ADVANCED COURSE

THE PRINCIPLES

OF

PSYCHOLOGY

BY

WILLIAM JAMES
PROFESSOR OF PSYCHOLOGY IN HARVARD UNIVERSITY

IN TWO VOLUMES

VOL. I

NEW YORK
HENRY HOLT AND COMPANY
1890

▷ **THE PRINCIPLES OF PSYCHOLOGY**
This original edition of James's seminal textbook dates from 1890. Its publication was instrumental in establishing psychology's credibility as a science.

Created by the Italian sculptor Gian Lorenzo Bernini in 1647–52, this work portrays a vision of the Carmelite nun Teresa of Avila in which her body is pierced by an angel's spear. William James studied the life of St Teresa and other mystics, and became fascinated by the transformative power of their ecstatic experiences.

△ **SELF-PORTRAIT, c.1866**
James's early artistic nature carried through into his love of the arts and literature, and his own refined prose style. His exposure to diverse cultural influences no doubt helped to shape his inclusive philosophy.

in some spiritual reality to which humans might have access. Even though he rejected religious dogma, James argued that people should not allow the sceptical fear of error to shut their minds off completely from the possibility of religious experiences, which as experiences were undoubtedly real and might change people's lives for the better.

In the last decade of his life, James became critical of the US's drift towards militarism and what he called "the exclusive worship of the bitch-goddess Success". But despite his ill health his works remained optimistic, focusing on his notion of "pluralism", a view that the universe was neither fully determined nor fully unified, but diverse and open-ended. This concept

reflected his strong preference for freedom and fluidity over certainty. James believed it was an appropriate philosophy for "the superabounding, growing, ever-varying and novelty producing" world of the new century. He was at work on an introduction to philosophy when he died of heart disease at his home at Chocorua, New Hampshire, in August 1910.

" **I myself believe** that the **evidence for God** lies **primarily** in **inner personal experience.** "

WILLIAM JAMES, *PRAGMATISM: A NEW NAME FOR SOME OLD WAYS OF THINKING*

Friedrich Nietzsche

1844–1900, GERMAN

Born into a Lutheran family, Nietzsche turned his back on faith and challenged the morality associated with it. He advocated living life in search of our full potential and according to our own individual standards.

Named after Friedrich Wilhelm IV of Prussia, whose birthday he shared, Friedrich Wilhelm Nietzsche was born on 15 October 1844 in the small village of Röcken bei Lützen in the Prussian province of Saxony. His father, Carl Ludwig, was the minister of the local Lutheran church, and both his parents came from families of Protestant clergymen. Friedrich was their first child, and was followed by a sister, Elisabeth, in 1846, and a brother, Ludwig Josef, in 1848.

Education and influences

Nietzsche's childhood was marred by tragedy. His father suffered from a painfully debilitating brain disease, and died shortly before Friedrich's fifth birthday in 1849. Six months later, two-year-old Ludwig also died, after which Friedrich and Elisabeth moved with their mother to Naumberg, where Nietzsche was educated at the local boys' school. In 1858 he was offered a scholarship at a prestigious boarding school, Schulpforta, thanks to being an orphan of a state employee. Here he received a solid, if conservative, education in classical and modern languages and the sciences. However, Nietzsche also showed an interest in poetry, especially the philosophical poems of Friedrich Hölderlin, and organized a literary and musical club

in Naumberg, through which he was introduced to the music of Richard Wagner. More significantly, his curiosity for ideas beyond the school's curriculum also led him to seek out and absorb iconoclastic works, such as *The Life of Jesus, Critically Examined* (1835–36) in which the German author David Strauss reinterpreted the gospels as historical myths, or a form of societal wish-fulfilment.

Studies in philology

After graduating from Schulpforta in 1864, Nietzsche went to the University of Bonn to study theology and philology, and under the tutorship of Friedrich Wilhelm Ritschl decided to concentrate on the study of classical texts. When Ritschl moved to the University of Leipzig the following year, Nietzsche followed in order to continue his studies. He established

△ **FRANZISKA NIETZSCHE**
Nietzsche had a complex relationship with his mother, Franziska. In his youth, she had called him "little pastor", but to her great dismay he rejected her values and faith as he grew up.

IN CONTEXT
Secularization in Germany

Industrialization and urbanization came later to Germany than they had to Britain and France. As the country sought to catch up with its neighbours (it had become the largest economy in Europe by 1900) profound changes occurred very rapidly in German society, and particularly in its institutions. For centuries, the Church had been at the heart of every rural German community, but during the 19th century, it became increasingly marginalized. Religious observance began to change from a community obligation or convention to a question of individual choice.

BEFORE 1800, COMMUNAL LIFE IN GERMAN VILLAGES CENTRED AROUND CHURCH SERVICES AND HOLY DAYS

" **God** is **dead! God** remains **dead!** And **we** have **killed him**. "

FRIEDRICH NIETZSCHE, *THE GAY SCIENCE*

▷ **NIETZSCHE BY MUNCH, 1906**
Norwegian Symbolist painter Edvard Munch was a great admirer of Nietzsche's work, although the two never met. This likeness – called an "idea portrait" – was commissioned by Swiss banker and art collector Ernest Thiel.

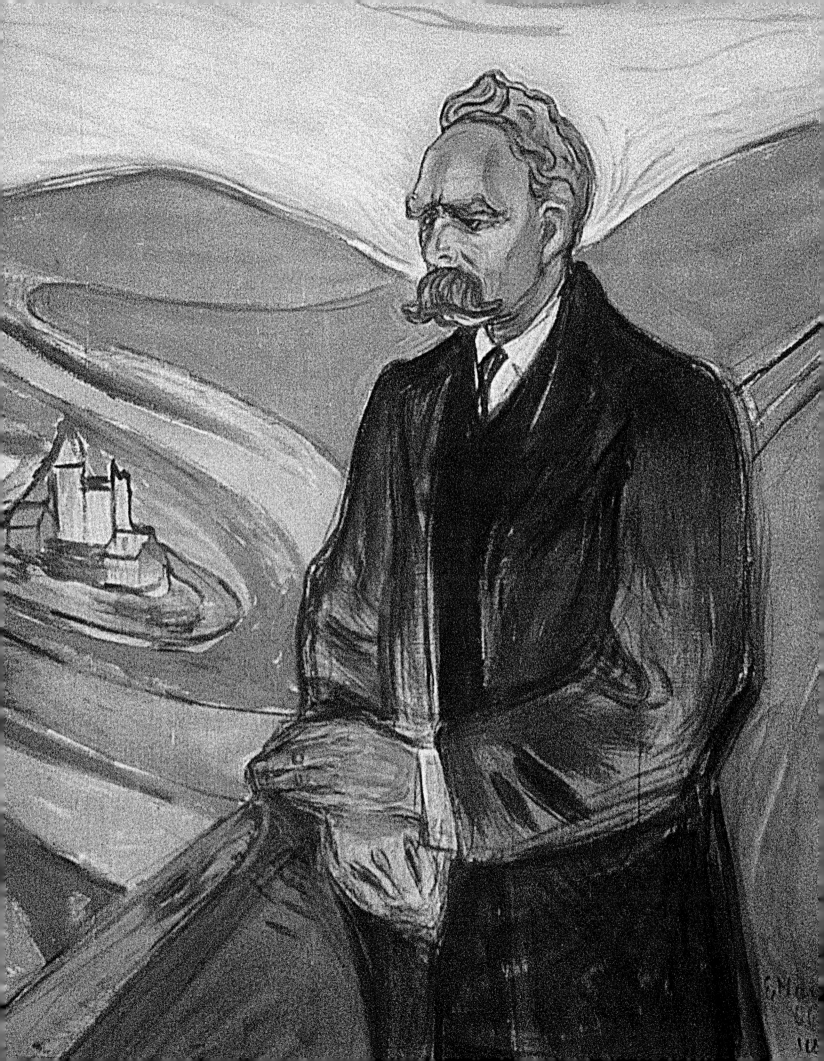

a reputation as a brilliant student, and soon began publishing articles on philology, but it was the chance discovery of a book that set him on the path to becoming a philosopher. That book was Schopenhauer's *The World as Will and Representation* (1819), which set out a concept of a godless and indifferent universe. To Nietzsche, Schopenhauer was more than an accomplished thinker: he was the "ideal philosopher" whose ideas could be personally transformatory; he wrote later that Schopenhauer was one of the few thinkers that he respected.

Military service
Nietzsche interrupted his studies in 1867 to undertake military service, joining an artillery unit near Naumberg so that he could live at home with his family. While mounting a horse, he suffered a serious chest injury and was invalided out of the service. The injury was to trigger health problems that plagued him for the rest of his life.

Nietzsche returned to his studies in Leipzig shortly afterwards, and completed his degree in 1868. At about this time, he befriended Hermann Brockhaus, a scholar of Asian cultures whose special interest was Sanskrit and Persian writings, including the texts of Zoroastrianism.

Friendship with Wagner
It was Hermann Brockhaus who introduced Nietzsche to his brother-in-law, Richard Wagner (see box, below), and through a mutual interest in music and the philosophy of Schopenhauer, the two struck up a firm friendship. Wagner's music-dramas, it seemed to Nietzsche, provided a much-needed antidote to the music of the early part of the century, and fitted with his own ideas of a full-blooded Dionysian culture replacing the rationalist Apollonian culture of the Enlightenment.

Move to Basel
Nietzsche was still only 24, and had not yet completed his doctorate when Ritschl recommended him as a teacher to the University of Basel in Switzerland. He was appointed a full professor there and began teaching philology in 1869. However, he was already totally disenchanted with his chosen field of study, and distanced himself from his colleagues at the university, preferring instead to associate with the theologian Franz Overbeck, who lived in the same building as Nietzsche and would remain a lifelong friend.

Nietzsche had renounced his Prussian citizenship when he moved to Switzerland, but at the outbreak of the Franco-Prussian War in 1870, he served as a hospital orderly. His health, which was already fragile, suffered a further knock when he contracted dysentery and diphtheria during his service. He returned to Basel after the war, but did not apply for Swiss citizenship, and remained stateless for the rest of his life.

During the 1870s, Nietzsche often visited Wagner and his wife Cosima, and they developed a relationship of mutual admiration. His first book, *The Birth of Tragedy* (1872), was praised by Wagner, but received a cool reception from his fellow academics, including his mentor Ritschl, who felt that it was not sufficiently rigorous in its approach to the classics. Disappointed by the response – and by now less interested in philology – Nietzsche applied for a post in the department of philosophy at Basel, but was rejected.

IN PROFILE
Richard Wagner

One of the most influential composers of the 19th century, Richard Wagner (1813–83) stretched the bounds of Romantic artistic expression in his "music-dramas" through his concept of opera as a *Gesamtkunstwerk* – a comprehensive work encompassing the poetic, visual, musical, and dramatic arts. He made his name in the 1840s with the operas *Rienzi* and *The Flying Dutchman*, and introduced many innovations in *Tristan and Isolde*, but his vision of a *Gesamtkunstwerk* was realized most completely in the four-opera cycle *The Ring of the Nibelung*. He organized the building of an opera house in Bayreuth, Bavaria, for the performance of his work, which opened in 1876 with the premiere of the complete Ring Cycle.

RICHARD WAGNER WITH HIS WIFE COSIMA
AND FRANZ LISZT, c.1880

> " **Thoughts** are the **shadows** of our **feelings** –
> always **darker, emptier, simpler.** "

FRIEDRICH NIETZSCHE, *THE GAY SCIENCE*

△ THE FRANCO-PRUSSIAN WAR
The heavy loss of lives at the Battle of Weissenburg in August 1870 prompted Nietzsche to enlist in the army to fulfil his duty to the Prussian fatherland.

Encouraged by Wagner, he spent the next few years working on a series of essays critiquing German culture and promoting the ideas of Schopenhauer. They were published in 1876 as *Untimely Meditations*. However, in that same year, after Nietzsche attended the performance of Wagner's Ring Cycle at the newly opened Bayreuth opera house, he became disillusioned by his friend's apparent love of fame, and by his enthusiasm for xenophobic German nationalism. He increasingly distanced himself from Wagner's circle, and in later years became critical of the man and his music.

A new direction
Thanks to his friendship with the philosopher Paul Rée, Nietzsche was persuaded to embark on a new, less pessimistic course in his next book. *Human, All Too Human* was published in 1878, and as well as adopting a more positive approach, it was marked by a change of style, to the staccato, aphoristic writing that eventually became a characteristic of much of his mature work.

This significant change may have been made for more than merely aesthetic reasons: Nietzsche's health was deteriorating dramatically, and he suffered from digestive problems and blinding headaches, as well as failing eyesight,

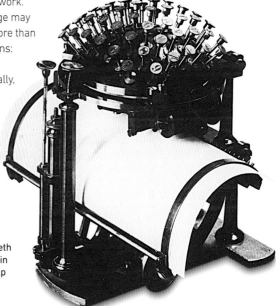

▷ WRITING BALL
Nietzsche's sister Elisabeth gave him this typewriter in 1882, hoping it would help him work through his failing eyesight.

"Man is something to be surpassed."

FRIEDRICH NIETZSCHE, *THUS SPOKE ZARATHUSTRA*

IN PROFILE
Elisabeth Förster-Nietzsche

Nietzsche's sister Elisabeth (1846–1935) is widely blamed for the misinterpretation of his philosophy as advocating totalitarian dictatorship, especially by Adolf Hitler and the Nazi regime. She and her brother became estranged after her marriage to Bernhard Förster, whose antisemitic nationalism was anathema to Friedrich. The couple attempted to found an Aryan colony, Nueva Germania, in Paraguay in 1887, but when it failed two years later, Bernhard died by suicide. In 1893 Elisabeth returned to Germany, where she later became Nietzsche's carer, editing, and possibly rewriting, her brother's unpublished work to reflect her own prejudices, and after his death promoting them as curator of the Nietzsche Archive. She was a Nazi sympathizer and her funeral in 1935 was attended by Hitler.

all of which made it difficult for him to write for protracted periods and badly degraded the legibility of his manuscripts. From this time, his writing became imbued with a sense of urgency that suggests he adopted the style in order to get his thoughts down on paper as quickly as possible.

Travels and writing

Nietzsche's poor health began to affect his work at the university, and in 1879 he resigned from his post. His pension was adequate for him to live comfortably, and to devote his time to writing. In the following decade, he travelled extensively in Italy and southern France, hoping to benefit from the warmer climate, and returned to Switzerland in the summer. This was the most productive period of his career, in which he affirmed his rejection of Christianity, and indeed all religion, and developed his idea of morality in a godless world.

In *The Gay Science* (1882), which Nietzsche himself described as "perhaps my most personal book," he famously asserted that "God is dead", and suggested that as a consequence conventional ideas of morality were no longer relevant, and should be replaced with an ethos that is life-affirming rather than prohibitive.

He elaborated this theme in his later works: in *Thus Spoke Zarathustra* (1883–85), he introduced the idea of the *Übermensch* ("Superman") – the man who could create his own morality and purpose to become dedicated to the betterment of humanity; and in *Beyond Good and Evil* (1886) and *The Genealogy of Morality* (1887) he expounded upon the concept of "will to power" – a drive

▽ **SUMMER RETREAT**
The Swiss village of Sils Maria in the Engadine valley is where Nietzsche spent his summers from 1881 to 1888. His house there is maintained as an archive.

to exert an influence over other things (including the self) that he considered fundamental to human existence.

Breaking apart

While travelling around Italy, Nietzsche met up with his friend Paul Rée, who introduced him to his companion Lou Salomé. Rée had proposed marriage to Salomé and had been turned down, but the pair nevertheless remained travelling companions and planned to set up a literary commune together. Nietzsche fell for Salomé, and asked her to marry him, but was also refused. The trio travelled to Switzerland and Germany together, but jealousies led to an inevitable falling out.

By the mid-1880s, after a rift with his sister over her marriage to Bernhard Förster (see box, left), Nietzsche felt increasingly isolated, and became reliant on opium and other drugs. Although in 1888 he had a burst of creativity, writing five books in less than 12 months, his mental health finally let him down.

Final years

While visiting Turin in 1889, Nietzsche collapsed while – it is said – trying to protect a horse from being beaten in the Piazza Carlo Alberto. Shortly afterwards, he started sending bizarre letters to his few remaining friends. Overbeck travelled to Turin and brought Nietzsche back to a clinic in Basel, where his breakdown was attributed to tertiary syphilis, although this has since been disputed.

He was released from the clinic into his mother's care in 1890, and lived with her until her death in 1897, when Nietzsche's sister Elisabeth took over responsibility, renting a house in

◁ **TRAVEL COMPANIONS**
Nietzsche (right) poses for a photograph with his travelling companions Paul Rée (centre) and Lou Salomé. The rift that developed between the friends contributed to a marked decline in Nietzsche's mental health.

Weimar to house the philosopher and his papers in what was to become the Nietzsche Archive.

Nietzsche suffered a number of strokes over the next years, becoming totally reliant on his sister. Because of his illness, he was unaware that his work had at last been recognized, and never had the chance to enjoy his celebrity. He died of pneumonia on 25 August 1900, and in a cruel twist for such an avowed atheist, was given a Christian funeral and buried next to his father in the graveyard in Röcken.

▷ **THUS SPOKE ZARATHUSTRA**
Nietzsche's most famous work (here in a 1908 German edition) describes how the Persian prophet Zarathustra descends to tell humanity that God is dead.

ALSO SPRACH ZARATHUSTRA

FRIEDRICH NIETZSCHE

KEY WORKS

1878
Presents his ideas in the form of a collection of aphorisms in *Human, All Too Human*.

1882
The Gay Science examines the concept of power, and introduces ideas that recur in Nietzsche's later work.

1883
Begins *Thus Spoke Zarathustra*, developing the ideas of eternal recurrence, the *Übermensch*, and the death of God.

1886
Takes a critical view of moral philosophers and their dogmatic approach in *Beyond Good and Evil*.

1887
On the Genealogy of Morality examines the history of moral systems, and the emergence of "slave-morality".

1888
Completes both *The Antichrist* and *Ecce Homo*, but because of their controversial content, publication is delayed until 1895 and 1908 respectively.

1906
A collection of Nietzsche's notes, controversially edited by his sister Elisabeth, is published posthumously as *The Will to Power*.

Directory

Etienne Bonnot de Condillac

1714–1780, FRENCH

A prominent figure in the French Enlightenment, Condillac was born in Grenoble, the son of a member of France's legal and administrative aristocracy. He was a sickly child who could not read until the age of 12. Educated at the seminary of Saint-Sulpice in Paris, he was ordained as a priest in 1740 but adopted the life of a secular Parisian intellectual, numbering Jean-Jacques Rousseau and Denis Diderot among his friends. In his most admired work, the *Treatise on Sensations*, he followed John Locke in arguing that all knowledge came from the senses. From 1758 to 1768 he was tutor to the prince of Parma, grandson of French king Louis XV.

In his later work *Commerce and Government*, written after returning to Paris, he argued for free trade, denying any contradiction between human rights and property rights. Elected to the French Academy in 1768, he died at Beaugency on the Loire in 1780.

KEY WORKS: *Essay on the Origin of Human Knowledge*, 1746; *Treatise on Sensations*, 1754; *Treatise on Animals*, 1755; *Commerce and Government*, 1776

△ GOTTHOLD LESSING, JOHANN HEINRICH TISCHBEIN THE ELDER, c.1755

Dai Zhen

1724–1777, CHINESE

A critic of the neo-Confucian tradition, Dai Zhen was born in Anhui province. A member of a poor family, he was largely self-taught and failed to pass the exam required for higher state administrative posts. His first works concerned mathematics and philology.

Around 1756 he was the victim of an injustice in a lawsuit concerning ancestral tombs, an event that alerted him to the misuse of Confucian thinking. Inspired to undertake a critical reading of classic texts, he developed an empirical position that favoured observation of the world as the path to truth. His *Inquiry into Goodness* insisted on the importance of empathy as a guide to value judgements. His scholarship won recognition when he was appointed to the Imperial Academy in 1775, but he did not become influential until the 20th century. He is hailed by some as the greatest thinker of the Qing era.

KEY WORKS: *Inquiry into Goodness* (*Yuan Shan*), c.1765; *Prefatory Words*, c.1766; *Evidential Study of the Meaning and Terms of the Mencius*, c.1768

◁ Gotthold Lessing

1729–1781, GERMAN

Dramatist, critic, and philosopher, Gotthold Lessing was born in Kamenz, Saxony, the son of a Lutheran pastor. Although destined, it seemed, for the study of theology, he instead became a playwright. His dramas and critical essays rejected Greek and French classicism in favour of naturalness and sincerity. In Berlin in the 1750s he met Jewish philosopher Moses Mendelssohn, who became a close friend and ally in the advocacy of religious tolerance. *Laocoön*, Lessing's major work of critical theory, was written in Breslau fortress during the Seven Years War (1756–63). After involvement with a short-lived national theatre in Hamburg, from 1770 he worked as librarian to the duke of Brunswick at Wolfenbüttel. There his public defence of deism against pastor Melchior Goeze led to conflict with the censors.

Lessing's final years were darkened by the deaths of his wife and infant son in 1778, but his late masterpiece *The Education of the Human Race* optimistically represented history as a progress towards moral and spiritual perfection.

KEY WORKS: *Laocoön: or, On the Limits of Painting and Poetry*, 1766; *Anti-Goeze*, 1768; *The Education of the Human Race*, 1780

Moses Mendelssohn

1729–1786, GERMAN

German Jewish philosopher Moses Mendelssohn was born in a ghetto in Dessau. He suffered from curvature of the spine and endured years of illness. In addition to his rabbinical education, he taught himself philosophy, mathematics, and languages.

While living in Berlin he befriended dramatist Gotthold Lessing, who had his *Philosophical Conversations* published in 1755. In 1763 he won a prize from the Berlin Academy for his essay "On Evidence in the Metaphysical Sciences", and Prussian king Frederick II gave him the status of a Protected Jew. Publication of *Phaedo*, a rational argument for the immortality of the soul, won Mendelssohn Europe-wide fame. He advocated the integration of Jews into European society, urging them to adopt the customs and language of the countries in which they lived. Rebutting accusations of atheism, he argued for religious tolerance and a rational faith. Mendelssohn had six children; the composers Fanny and Felix Mendelssohn were two of his descendants.

KEY WORKS: *Phaedo or On the Immortality of Souls*, 1767; *Jerusalem*, 1783; *Morning Hours*, 1785; *To Lessing's Friends*, 1786

▷ Motoori Norinaga

1730–1801, JAPANESE

Motoori Norinaga was the key figure in the *Kokugaku* (National Learning) revival of traditional Japanese culture. He was born into the merchant class at Matsusaka, and at the age of 22 went to study medicine in Kyoto. Under the influence of Kamo no Mabuchi (1697–1769) he was drawn to the study of ancient texts, such as *Nihon Shoki* (*Chronicles of Japan*) and *Kojiki* (*Records of Ancient Matters*), which offered a Japanese alternative to the Chinese Confucian and Buddhist thought that was dominant in Japan.

Returning to Matsusaka aged 30, he worked as a doctor for the rest of his life while continuing his studies and writing. He revived interest in the classic *The Tale of Genji* (c.1000–1012), defining a Japanese aesthetic of "sensitivity to the transience of things", and proposed a purified version of traditional Shinto beliefs and rites. His masterwork, a commentary on the *Kojiki*, took 34 years to complete.

KEY WORKS: *Commentary on the Kojiki*, 1798

Joseph de Maistre

1753–1820, SAVOYARD

De Maistre was the leading philosopher of the royalist Catholic reaction against the 1789 French Revolution. Born into a prominent family in Savoy, an area of the Kingdom of Piedmont-Sardinia, he studied law in Turin and entered the senate in 1787. After French Revolutionary armies occupied Savoy in 1792 he fled to Switzerland, becoming a member of Madame de Staël's circle and writing his first counter-revolutionary polemics.

In 1803, he was made ambassador to St Petersburg, where he remained for 14 years, writing his most famous works, the *Essay on Political Constitutions* and the unfinished *St Petersburg Dialogues*. He rejected Enlightenment rationalism, which he

△ **MOTOORI NORINAGA**

deemed responsible for the Terror of the Revolution, advocating the rule of an absolute monarch. He believed the right to power came from God and that the pope's authority was absolute.

KEY WORKS: *Considerations on France*, 1797; *Essay on the Generative Principle of Political Constitutions*, 1814; *On the Pope*, 1819; *The Saint Petersburg Dialogues*, 1821

Johann Gottlieb Fichte

1762–1814, GERMAN

The founder of German idealist philosophy, Fichte was the child of a peasant family in Rammenau, Saxony. A local landowner paid for him to

attend an elite school, and he later studied at the universities of Jena and Leipzig. He worked as a tutor until publication of his *Critique of All Revelation* in 1792. It made his reputation and earned him the post of professor of philosophy at Jena.

Fichte proposed a radical rejection of materialism, viewing the universe as spiritual and empirical reality as a projection of mind and will. In 1808, after Prussia had suffered a crushing defeat by Napoleon's French Empire, he published *Addresses to the German Nation*, one of the founding texts of German nationalism.

KEY WORKS: *Critique of All Revelation*, 1792; *Foundations of Natural Right*, 1797; *The Vocation of Man*, 1800; *Addresses to the German Nation*, 1808

Germaine de Staël

1766–1817, SWISS FRENCH

A prominent thinker on literature, politics, and society, as well as a gifted novelist, de Staël was born Anne-Louise Germaine Necker, daughter of the Swiss banker who was France's finance minister before the French Revolution. A marriage to the Swedish ambassador, Baron de Staël-Holstein, left her free to live an independent life. During the French Revolution and subsequent rule of Napoleon Bonaparte, she lived chiefly at Coppet in Switzerland, where her salon became a focus of liberal thought.

In her political writings de Staël analysed the problems of securing freedom in the light of the aberrations of the Revolutionary Terror. Her cultural essays examined the influence of social conditions on writing and contrasted German Romanticism favourably with French classicism and rationalism. Her novels *Delphine* (1802) and *Corinne* (1807), focused on the conflict between love and duty in a patriarchal society.

KEY WORKS: *On the Influence of the Passions*, 1797; *On Literature in its Relationship to Social Institutions*, 1800; *Of Germany*, 1813

Friedrich Schleiermacher

1768–1834, GERMAN

A liberal theologian and the founder of modern Protestant theology, Schleiermacher rejected the conservative orthodox Christianity of his time and sought an interpretation of the Bible he felt to be more relevant for the Enlightened age.

Schleiermacher studied at the University of Halle in Germany, where his philosophical studies formed his core belief that religion was the feeling of being part of the infinite in the midst of finiteness. He believed that to be human was to have the experience of the divine. He studied the history of language and lectured on the art of hermeneutics – the theory of interpretation – reading translations and interpretations of the New Testament to better understand the minds and intent of its writers.

A co-founder of the University of Berlin, Schleiermacher lectured there on all areas of philosophy and religious thought up to his death.

His works continued to influence theologians throughout the 19th and early 20th centuries. Today he is considered to be the father of liberalism, hermeneutics, and modern theology.

KEY WORKS: *On Religion: Speeches to Its Cultured Despisers*, 1799; *The Soliloquies*, 1800; *Christian Faith*, 1821; *Hermeneutics and Criticism*, 1838

▷ Novalis

1772–1801, GERMAN

Early Romantic philosopher and poet Friedrich von Hardenberg, more often known by his pen name Novalis, was born at Oberwiederstedt. His family were impoverished nobility and devout Protestants. Educated at a Lutheran school, he studied law at Jena University and geology at a mining academy.

As a member of the Jena Romantics circle, to which Friedrich Schelling also belonged, Novalis published his writings in the movement's journal *Das Athaeneum*. Influenced by the idealist philosophy of Johann Gottlieb Fichte, he rejected the mechanistic view of the universe, adopting instead a mystical form of pantheism. He believed that only the rediscovery of spiritual community could heal the rifts that existed in fragmented European societies.

Fiercely opposed to the ideas of the rationalist Enlightenment, Novalis planned to produce a Romantic encyclopedia, but only a few fragments were written.

KEY WORKS: *Pollen*, 1798; *Faith and Love or The King and Queen*, 1798; *Christianity or Europa*, 1799

△ **NOVALIS, FRANZ GAREIS, c.1799**

Wilhelm Dilthey

1833–1911, GERMAN

The polymath philosopher Dilthey studied at the University of Berlin under Friedrich Adolf Trendelenburg and August Böckh, pupils of the theologian Friedrich Schleiermacher. He wrote his doctoral thesis on Schleiermacher's ethics, later editing his letters, and was influenced by his work on hermeneutics.

Dilthey developed a system to classify and distinguish between the natural and human sciences. He believed that while the former could be studied with the aim of seeking mechanical law-based explanations, the human world required more complex analysis. He thought historical context and culture could both free and restrict human behaviour and creativity of spirit, and only a study of all human history, and the patterns revealed by that study, could reveal a common thread of humanity and a better understanding of modern humans.

KEY WORKS: *Introduction to Human Science*, 1883; *Ideas Concerning a Descriptive and Analytical Psychology*, 1894; *The Formation of the Historical World in the Human Sciences*, 1910

Friedrich Schelling

1775–1854, GERMAN

Idealist Schelling was the son of a school chaplain and born near Stuttgart. He studied at the Lutheran seminary in Tübingen, where fellow pupils included the future philosopher Georg Hegel.

Schelling's first books were a Romantic reaction to the ideas of Johann Gottlieb Fichte. He envisioned nature as infused with a "universal spirit" fulfilling itself in a creative process with human consciousness at its apex. His "nature philosophy" earned him a post as professor at the University of Jena when he was 23.

His influence declined considerably with the rise of Hegel to prominence, and *Of Human Freedom* (1809) was his last published work. Interest in his work was revived in the 20th century.

KEY WORKS: *Ideas Toward a Philosophy of Nature*, 1797; *On the World Soul*, 1798; *System of Transcendental Idealism*, 1800; *Of Human Freedom*, 1809

Mary Shepherd

1777–1847, SCOTTISH

A philosopher much admired by her British contemporaries, Lady Mary Shepherd was born Mary Primrose, the second daughter of the 3rd Earl of Rosebery. She was brought up on the family estate near Edinburgh. While her brothers were sent to university, Mary and her sisters were educated at home by tutors.

In 1808, Mary married an English barrister, Henry Shepherd, and settled in London. Her acquaintances included some of the foremost thinkers of the time, such as mathematician Charles Babbage, scientist and polymath Mary Somerville, and the Cambridge academic William Whewell.

Shepherd's philosophical views, expressed in two lengthy essays published in the 1820s, were based on a critique of the scepticism of 18th-century Scottish thinker David Hume, and especially his dismissive account of causality. She sought a firm basis for the pursuit of scientific enquiry that would also confirm the existence of God. Admired by Whewell, one of her books was used as set text at Cambridge University.

KEY WORKS: *An Essay upon the Relation of Cause and Effect*, 1824; *Essays on the Perception of an External Universe*, 1827

Bronson Alcott

1799–1888, AMERICAN

An important figure in the New England Transcendentalist movement, Alcott was born into a poor farming family in Wolcott, Connecticut. He was self-educated and worked as a salesman before becoming a teacher. His radical approach to education was based on developing a child's inner nature and intuitive knowledge, which encountered considerable opposition from parents. His most successful educational experiment, the Temple School in Boston, ran for six years from 1834.

Befriended by poet and essayist Ralph Waldo Emerson, he gravitated to Concord, Massachusetts, the hub of Transcendentalism, where he served as superintendent of schools from 1859 to 1864. His philosophical essays, the "Orphic Sayings", were influenced by German idealism.

An impractical man, Alcott failed to provide for his wife and four children. The success of his daughter, Louisa May Alcott, as a novelist rescued the family from poverty.

KEY WORKS: *Records of a School*, 1835; *Conversations with Children on the Gospels*, 1836–37

Franz Brentano

1838–1917, GERMAN

An influential thinker in philosophy and psychology, Brentano was born into an intellectual Catholic family. He obtained a doctorate in philosophy with a thesis on Aristotle in 1862, and two years later was ordained.

Unable to reconcile himself to the concept of papal infallibility, he left the priesthood in 1873 and became a professor at the University of Vienna. As an ex-priest, his marriage in 1880 was deemed unacceptable by the church authorities, who took away his professorship. Nevertheless, he continued to teach as an unpaid lecturer for 14 years.

△ **GOTTLOB FREGE, c.1879**

Brentano's teachings influenced a number of major figures, including phenomenologist Edmund Husserl and psychoanalyst Sigmund Freud. Rejecting German idealism, he believed that philosophy should be conducted with the same rigour as the sciences.

KEY WORKS: *On the Several Senses of Being in Aristotle*, 1862; *Psychology from an Empirical Standpoint*, 1874; *The Origin of the Knowledge of Right and Wrong*, 1889

Charles Sanders Peirce

1839–1914, AMERICAN

The son of a Harvard professor, Peirce was an early proponent of pragmatism. He spent most of his working life as a scientist, while publishing essays on logic and

the philosophy of science in various publications. He was a founding member of the Metaphysical Club, a philosophical discussion society, with William James (see pp.214–15) and others in 1872, and taught logic at Johns Hopkins University from 1879.

His aim was to clarify the bases of science and mathematics – hence the "pragmatic" approach to philosophical ideas, regarded as "true" or "false" insofar as they were useful or otherwise to the progress of science.

In 1886, as a result of official outrage at his living openly with a lover, he was effectively banned from academic work. Despite the support of William James, his thought was largely ignored during his lifetime and he died in poverty.

KEY WORKS: "How to Make our Ideas Clear", 1878; *Studies in Logic* (editor), 1883; *Chance, Love, and Logic: Philosophical Essays*, 1923

◁ Gottlob Frege

1848–1925, GERMAN

One of the founders of modern logic and analytical philosophy, Frege was born at Wismar, where his parents ran a girls' school. He studied at Jena and Göttingen universities, and in 1874 began teaching mathematics at Jena.

His *Concept Script* (1879) proposed a formal language for philosophy modelled on arithmetic. In subsequent works he argued that mathematics was a form of logic and revolutionized the understanding of logic itself. He also ventured into the analysis of language, offering a new account of the relationship between words and their meanings.

KEY WORKS: *Concept Script*, 1879; *The Foundations of Arithmetic*, 1884; "On Sense and Reference", 1892; *Basic Laws of Arithmetic*, 1893, 1903

Josiah Royce

1855–1916, AMERICAN

Philosopher and historian Royce was born in Grass Valley, California. His family were immigrants from Britain, pioneers in opening up the American West. The sense of community among the settlers, rooted in the Church and Bible, was a formative influence on him. He was one of the first graduates from the University of California and studied in Germany for a year, where he encountered idealist philosophy.

In 1882 Royce began teaching at Harvard, where he remained for the rest of his life. He argued for the existence of an absolute unifying consciousness that made the human mind comprehensible. His writing on ethics stressed the priority of society over the individual.

KEY WORKS: *The Religious Aspect of Philosophy*, 1885; *The Spirit of Modern Philosophy*, 1892; *The World and the Individual*, 1899, 1901; *The Philosophy of Loyalty*, 1908

20th CENTURY

CHAPTER 5

Edmund Husserl

1859–1938, CZECH

Husserl was the founder of Phenomenology, one of the most important and influential movements in 20th-century philosophy, which set out to directly explore the structures of consciousness.

Leipzig. Universität mit Pauliner Kirche.

◁ **UNIVERSITY OF LEIPZIG**
When at Leipzig in 1876–78, Husserl attended lectures by Wilhelm Wundt, who helped distinguish the new "scientific" discipline of psychology from philosophy.

IN PROFILE
Franz Brentano

One of the major influences upon Husserl was the German philosopher, psychologist, and priest Franz Brentano. Husserl attended Brentano's lectures in Vienna in 1884 and was particularly impressed by his ideas on the "intentionality" of consciousness, an idea with its roots in medieval philosophy. Its fundamental premise is that consciousness must always be consciousness of something. This became a central idea for Husserl in how he developed his explorations of the structures of consciousness.

FRANZ BRENTANO (1838–1917)

Edmund Husserl was born into a Jewish family in Prossnitz, Moravia, then part of the Austrian Empire but now within the Czech Republic. As a young man, he was drawn to the study of astronomy and mathematics, but during his time at the University of Leipzig he also attended philosophy lectures, and quickly developed a taste for the subject. After gaining his PhD in mathematics in Vienna in 1883, Husserl taught briefly in Berlin but returned to Vienna to study with the philosopher and psychologist Franz Brentano (see box, right).

A convert to Christianity, Husserl was baptized as a Lutheran in 1886, and, the year after, married Malvine Steinschneider, with whom he had two sons and a daughter. Malvine was to be his constant companion and support throughout his life, most of which was dedicated to teaching.

Husserl taught at the University of Halle, Germany, from 1887 under the guidance of Carl Stumpf, professor of philosophy and psychology, who had also been a student of Brentano's. His inaugural lecture, "On the Goals and Problems of Metaphysics" showed the transition of his interests from mathematics to philosophy.

In 1901, Husserl left Halle to teach at Göttingen, where he stayed for the next 16 years, refining his philosophy slowly and with meticulous care. The outbreak of war in Europe in 1914 disrupted Husserl's life in Göttingen; many of his younger colleagues were killed in the conflict and both of his sons were wounded. Husserl wrote that he himself became hospitalized for nicotine poisoning – a sign of the stress that he was under. His younger son, Wolfgang, was sent back to the front when he recovered, only to die in action at Verdun in 1916.

Husserl and Heidegger

When he was appointed professor at the University of Frieburg in 1916, Husserl was able to fully develop his ideas on Phenomenology. It was around this time that he met Martin Heidegger, who was 30 years his junior. At first, Husserl supported Heidegger and took him as his assistant; in return, Heidegger dedicated his first major work, *Being and Time* (1927), to his mentor.

When Husserl retired as professor in 1928, Heidegger was his natural heir. Over the following years, however, Husserl became displeased with his protégé for his radical rethinking

> " To **begin** with, we put the **proposition**: **pure Phenomenology** is the **science** of **pure consciousness.** "
>
> EDMUND HUSSERL, IN DERMOT MORAN, *THE PHENOMENOLOGY READER*

▷ **EDMUND HUSSERL, c.1920**
Husserl is little known outside academic philosophical circles, where he is widely considered to be one of the most influential thinkers of the 20th century.

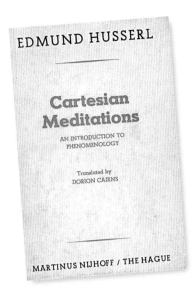

△ **CARTESIAN MEDITATIONS**
Husserl's great work on Phenomenology is divided into five "meditations". His belief was that Phenomenology could provide general concepts that were fundamental to all the sciences.

"Philosophy – wisdom – is the philosophizer's quite personal affair."

EDMUND HUSSERL, *CARTESIAN MEDITATIONS*

of Phenomenology. The rift between the two grew when the Nazis came to power in 1933; Husserl was barred from the University of Freiburg, where Heidegger became Rektor of the faculty and joined the Nazi party.

For the next five years, against a darkening political background in Germany, Husserl continued to write, research, travel, and lecture. Late in 1937, at the age of 78, he had a fall, and was confined to his bed. He died eight months later.

Following Descartes

In one of his most famous works, *Cartesian Meditations* (1931), Husserl writes that anybody who wants to do philosophy must once in their lives try to withdraw from all opinions, and begin again from scratch – in other words, if we want to do philosophy, it is necessary to put aside all of our assumptions about the world, so that we can build a system of knowledge that is free of biases. In this, Husserl followed the lead of 17th-century philosopher René Descartes (see pp.116–21).

Descartes argued that we could be wrong about almost everything that we think is true. He wanted to know just what we could know for certain and employed the method of doubt to help answer this question. We can doubt the knowledge we gain from books and even from our senses, he argued, but there is one thing we cannot doubt – the fact that we are doubting. This was the notion that

△ **UNIVERSITY OF FREIBURG**
Racial laws enacted by the Nazis in 1933 denied Husserl access to the university. He resigned from the German Academy in the same year.

he encapsulated in one of the most famous and enduring lines in Western philosophy: *dubito, ergo cogito, ergo sum* – "I doubt, therefore I think, therefore I am". In his *Cartesian Meditations* (its title derives from Descartes' name), Husserl maintains that Descartes has made a philosophical error. The problem, he says, lies in the move from "I think" to "therefore I am". Husserl, argues that, at this point, Descartes introduces all kinds of assumptions about what it means to exist, and about what it means to be a thing or a substance. These

IN CONTEXT
Europe In Crisis

In the final years of his life, Husserl became increasingly concerned with what he called a "crisis" in European philosophy and culture. For him, the rise of Nazism in Germany was rooted in a much deeper spiritual malaise: while Husserl regarded the roots of this crisis as philosophical, the effects were political. Husserl predicted two possible outcomes for this crisis – either a spiritual rebirth, or a decline into chaos. With the outbreak of World War II, after Husserl's death, it became clear just how deep this crisis had become.

ADOLF HITLER ADDRESSES SOLDIERS AT A NAZI RALLY IN DORTMUND

assumptions in turn entail a whole barrage of unexamined philosophical positions about what things are, and about what the world in general is. Rather disdainfully, Husserl accused Descartes, just at the point where he had claimed to doubt everything, of rescuing "a little tag-end of the world".

The structures of experience

Since its beginnings, philosophy in the West has drawn a distinction between what is the case (what Immanuel Kant calls things-in-themselves, noumena), and what appears to our experience (phenomena). Kant argues that we cannot know directly about things-in-themselves, only about appearances, although he believes we can make inferences about the noumenal world.

Husserl goes further than Kant. He argues that we should rigorously stick with phenomena – with things as they appear to consciousness – and study these phenomena more systematically, completely putting aside concerns with things-in-themselves. If we do this, we might be able to succeed where Descartes failed, and build absolutely certain knowledge free from previous assumptions.

Failure or success?

For Husserl, the task of philosophy is the systematic description and mapping of our conscious experience from the inside – without making any claims about the existence or non-existence of the world. If we can give a complete and systematic description of the world of experience, then we will have a complete system of philosophy that is free of any assumptions about the world in which this experience arises. Husserl's ultimate goal was for

his Phenomenology to become a completely rigorous science, but he was hugely frustrated in his ambitions. Three years before his death, Husserl wrote the following words: "Philosophy as a science... the dream is over."

There were several reasons for his failure. One was that Husserl never managed to fully set out a clear, replicable method (one of the hallmarks of science) for conducting his phenomenological studies. Another was that his many followers took Phenomenology in all kinds of different directions: they seemed incapable of agreeing even on the simplest of matters. And yet another

reason was that language itself seemed to be too imprecise to do justice to the strange, ephemeral phenomena of consciousness.

If the success of Phenomenology is judged not against Husserl's stated ambitions, but rather in the light of the sheer richness of ideas to which it gave rise in the 20th century, it must be considered as one of the most successful of recent philosophical movements. Thinkers as diverse as Martin Heidegger, Emmanuel Levinas, Jean-Paul Sartre, Simone de Beauvoir, and Maurice Merleau-Ponty all drew upon the tradition started by Husserl, developing it in rich and varied ways.

▽ **DESCARTES TO HUSSERL**
This engraving shows René Descartes writing his *Treatise on the Light* (1629–33; also called *The World*), an account of his mechanical philosophy. Husserl considered Descartes to be his spiritual mentor and believed his own work to be the culmination of Cartesian philosophy.

KEY WORKS

1900
Publishes the first volume of his *Logical Investigations*, which introduces phenomenological analysis.

1913
Publishes his major work, *Ideas I*, which argues for Phenomenology as the fundamental science of philosophy.

1929
Accepts an invitation to present a series of lectures in Paris; these form the basis of his *Cartesian Meditations*.

1931
Cartesian Meditations is published in French translation. It does not appear in Germany during Husserl's lifetime.

1935
Husserl presents his lecture "The Crisis of the European Sciences" in Prague.

Jane Addams

1860–1935, AMERICAN

Addams was a social reformer, activist, and feminist and is considered by some to be the founder of social work in the US. She was also a prolific thinker and writer in the philosophical tradition of US Pragmatism.

Jane Addams was born in Illinois in 1860, one of eight children. When she was two, her mother died in childbirth and Jane was brought up by her father, with whom she had a strong bond. She went on to study at Rockford Female Seminary, where she developed her taste for community activism. Graduating in 1881, she planned to study medicine but after the death of her father and recurrent bouts of poor health she embarked instead on years of travelling, reading, and writing. When she was 27, she travelled to Europe with her partner

◁ **ADDAMS IN HER STUDY**
In 1919, Addams founded the Women's International League for Peace and Freedom, which worked for world peace and disarmament.

Ellen Starr, and in London visited the "settlement house", Toynbee Hall – an institution established in 1884 as a hub for education and social reform. Deeply impressed, she and Starr established Hull House, a similar project in one of the most desperately underprivileged areas of Chicago.

A social centre

Hull House provided a wide range of social services focused strongly, but not exclusively, on women. These included medical and child care; a social club, gym, and swimming pool; opportunities for further education; a library; and art and music studios. Hull House became the base for Addams's increasing engagement with broader social issues. In 1910, Yale University awarded her an honorary degree, and

in 1931, she was awarded the Nobel Peace Prize for her work on peace activism. By this time, Addams was already in poor health, and unable to travel to Oslo to accept the prize. She died four years later, in 1935.

Philosophy and writing

Addams was not only an activist and reformer, but also a hugely prolific writer. As a philosopher, she was firmly in the US Pragmatist tradition and was a friend and correspondent of John Dewey (see pp.236–37) – an influence that flowed in both directions.

One of Addams's key ideas is that of "sympathetic knowledge". For Addams, this knowledge arises out of a social connection with others from different backgrounds. When we are brought into contact with people who have radically different experiences from ourselves, this has the power to positively disrupt our lives, opening up new possibilities for empathy. Once we can empathize, then we find ourselves acting for the sake of those we care about. And this – for Jane Addams – lies at the very foundation of democratic society.

Hull House, then, was not only the centre of a radical social programme, but also an experiment in living philosophy, a way of exploring sympathetic knowledge in action.

△ **ELLEN STARR**
The co-founder of Hull House, Ellen Starr, received less recognition than Addams, but was instrumental in imbuing the settlement house with a creative spirit and, later, in campaigning for reform of the US child-labour laws.

IN CONTEXT
The settlement house movement

The settlement house movement in the US began with Hull House in 1889, and continued into the 1920s. These houses were places where volunteer workers could "settle" in deprived communities, to provide services and to build hubs for social reform. By the early 20th century, there were almost 500 settlement houses throughout the US. These settlement houses were not just social projects, but also centres for a specific social vision and philosophy — one that saw social problems as rooted in social causes rather than in individual life choices.

TWENTY YEARS AT HULL-HOUSE

JANE ADDAMS

JANE ADDAMS'S MEMOIR OF HER INVOLVEMENT WITH HULL HOUSE

▷ **HENRI BERGSON, 1911**
The celebrated philosopher posed for
this portrait by Jacques-Emile Blanche
(1861–1942) while in his early sixties.
Bergson argued that it was an error to
imagine that we see the world as a series
of static snapshots of passing reality.

Henri Bergson

1859–1941, FRENCH

The most famous French philosopher of the early 20th century, Bergson
valued intuition over intellect and lived experience over logical analysis. His
works were admired for their literary quality as much as for their ideas.

"Our **body** is **co-extensive** with our **consciousness**... it **reaches** as far as the **stars**. "

HENRI BERGSON, *THE TWO SOURCES OF MORALITY AND RELIGION*

Henri-Louis Bergson was born in Paris in 1859, the son of a Polish Jewish pianist and an Anglo-Irish mother. After an elite education at the Lycée Condorcet and the Ecole Normale Supérieure, he published his first essay, *Time and Free Will*, while teaching at a provincial lycée in 1889. This introduced his idea of "duration": the notion of time as a continuum experienced through memory, which contrasted with the measurable series of discrete moments that constituted the scientific notion of time.

In his second major work, *Matter and Memory* (1896), Bergson rejected the scientific description of memory and other aspects of mind as functions of the brain, arguing for a fundamental division between mind and matter. He accepted that scientific knowledge, which saw reality as consisting of discrete material objects in space, was useful for human survival, but asserted that the true spiritual nature of reality was revealed by the human experience of durable time, directly accessible through memory and intuition

As a professor at the Collège de France from 1900, Bergson became a dominant influence in French culture. His 1907 work *Creative Evolution* challenged the Darwinian view of the development of life as determined by physical causation. Instead, he proposed the existence of an *élan vital* – a vital impetus – that propelled living beings into a multi-pathed evolution, neither predetermined nor pursuing any fixed goal. His theory applied to human lives, which he saw as having potential for open-ended creativity.

Time and mysticism

Although criticized by rationalists, Bergson's philosophy chimed with the innovative spirit of the early 20th century, providing inspiration for Modernists revolutionizing art and

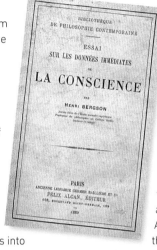

◁ **TIME AND FREE WILL**
Bergson's essay, first published in Paris in 1889, introduced his theories of time and consciousness.

political radicals bent on transforming society. Bergson's reputation waned after World War I, when he unwisely argued with physicist Albert Einstein over the nature of time, a debate that left him looking ill-informed about contemporary science. Nevertheless, he remained a pillar of official culture, working diligently for the League of Nations promoting international intellectual cooperation. In 1927 he was awarded the Nobel Prize in Literature and in 1930 the Grand-Croix de la Legion d'honneur.

His last major work, *The Two Sources of Morality and Religion* (1932), argued for a creative open society and for faith based on mystical experience. Bergson was attracted to Catholicism but refused to convert because he did not want to abandon his Jewish identity in the face of mounting antisemitism in Europe: "I wanted to remain among those who tomorrow were to be persecuted." He died of bronchitis in 1941, soon after the Nazi occupation of Paris.

IN PROFILE
Marcel Proust

The celebrated French novelist Marcel Proust (1871–1922) was a cousin of Bergson's wife, Louise Neuburger, and acted as best man at their wedding in 1891. Proust's masterpiece, *In Search of Lost Time*, in which he slows down and magnifies experience and consciously flouts clock time, was extensively influenced by Bergson's ideas. A seven-volume novel, it is structured around the phenomenon of involuntary memory, interpreted as offering access to a higher spiritual reality in which the passage of time does not exist – in effect, Bergson's "duration".

MARCEL PROUST

◁ **COFFEE GRINDER**, **JUAN GRIS**
Bergson's radical ideas on "duration" exerted their influence on Cubists such as Picasso, Braque, and Gris, who sought to explore the dimension of time by capturing an object from several perspectives at once.

John Dewey

1859–1952, AMERICAN

Philosophically a Pragmatist, Dewey also took an active stand in democratic politics and progressive education. Widely admired, he came to be seen as a standard-bearer of the US liberal tradition.

Columbia University, New York City.

Copyright 1915 by Irving Underhill, N. Y.

◁ **COLUMBIA UNIVERSITY**
Dewey taught at Columbia University for 25 years from 1904, subsequently serving as professor emeritus almost to the end of his long life.

IN CONTEXT
Dewey the educator

In the field of education, Dewey applied his ideas to oppose rote learning in schools in favour of the development of pupils' skills and abilities through problem-solving and interaction with their teachers. To put his views into practice, he helped to establish the University of Chicago Laboratory Schools, initially accepting children through nursery school up to 12th grade. The schools, which still operate to this day, became flagships of the progressive education movement, which always encouraged students to be active participants in the learning process.

Dewey had a modest upbringing in the small town of Burlington, Vermont. On graduating from the state university, he spent three years as a high-school teacher before studying for a PhD at Johns Hopkins University in Baltimore, and then taking a post as professor of philosophy at the University of Michigan. There he married Alice Chipman, one of his students, with whom he would have six children.

In 1894 he transferred to the University of Chicago, abandoning his Hegelianism in favour of an approach that he called "instrumentalist". This way of thinking adopted an empirical view of ideas as tools that could be used to address problems raised by the conditions of living. At this time, Dewey wrote extensively on psychology and built a reputation as a leading educational theorist with books such as *The School and Society* (1899) and *The Child and the Curriculum* (1902).

In 1904, disagreements with his employers over the school he helped to set up (see box, right) led him to move to Columbia University in New York City, where he wrote his most influential academic work, *Experience and Nature* (1925). Dewey also reached a much wider public audience through his articles on current events for magazines such as *New Republic* and *The Nation*. He travelled widely at the invitation of foreign governments, and embraced a number of liberal causes, holding office with the American Civil Liberties Union; he famously called for a new political party on the grounds that Republicans and Democrats had both failed to address the hardship caused by the Great Depression.

The US Pragmatists

Philosophically, Dewey was – along with C.S. Pierce and William James – one of the three leading US Pragmatists of the late 19th and early 20th centuries. The essence of their approach lay in seeing knowledge not as a grasp of established facts but rather as an adaptive response to the environment shaped by the need to solve problems. Truth, then, was always provisional, and ideas were tools with practical uses – hence his concern with the outside world, putting theory into practice by seeking new pathways and solutions in such fields as education. Dewey's was an empirical, outward-looking worldview, well in keeping with the dynamic optimism of the US at the turn of the 20th century.

DEWEY'S *THE SCHOOL AND SOCIETY*, FIRST EDITION, 1899

◁ **DEWEY AT HIS DESK, 1946**
In later life Dewey became an international celebrity, publishing books and articles on topics ranging from philosophy and psychology to art, the social sciences, and religion.

" **The self** is not something **ready-made**, but something in **continuous formation** through **choice** of **action**. "

JOHN DEWEY

▷ **SANTAYANA, 1944**
Santayana – despite his progressive deafness and partial loss of sight – wrote well into old age, publishing his last major work, *Dominations and Powers*, in 1951.

George Santayana
1863–1952, SPANISH

Despite his Spanish birth and his many years in Europe, Santayana saw himself as American. A poet and novelist as well as metaphysician, he was a key figure in the golden age of Harvard University's philosophy faculty.

⊲ **HARVARD YEARS**
Santayana was an influential teacher at Harvard, where his students included T.S. Eliot, Gertrude Stein, Robert Frost, and W.E.B. Du Bois.

IN CONTEXT
Santayana the novelist

In 1935, Santayana brought out *The Last Puritan*, his only novel, and had the satisfaction of seeing it become an instant bestseller; only Margaret Mitchell's *Gone with the Wind* sold more copies that year. Set in 19th-century Massachusetts and, later, Oxford, it tells the story of the son of a well-to-do New England family trying to come to terms with his Puritan heritage. Santayana subtitled the book *A Memoir in the Form of a Novel*, and elements of his own life are reflected in his protagonist's progress. This allowed him to reflect on the cultural inheritance of his adopted US homeland.

George Santayana had a complicated childhood. His father was a Spanish colonial civil servant, his mother a widow who already had three children from a previous marriage to a New England merchant. When George was six years old, his mother decamped to Boston, leaving him with his father in Madrid. Three years later they followed her, but the father soon returned to Spain without George, who continued his education in the US.

Santayana won a place at Harvard, where he was taught by the eminent psychologist and philosopher William James (see pp.212–15). He continued his studies in Berlin for a couple of years before returning to Harvard to teach, and apart from a brief sojourn at Kings College, Cambridge, he remained there for the next 24 years. Then, in 1912, he left the US to spend the rest of his life in Europe, moving between Spain, Paris, Oxford, and Italy.

By this time, Santayana already had an international reputation. His first major publication, *The Sense of Beauty* (1896), addressed aesthetics, defining the pleasure we experience from contemplating beautiful objects as a quality of the objects in themselves. Even though he spoke disparagingly of the book in later life, it proved highly influential and established his reputation as a thinker.

The "Catholic atheist"
Santayana's great work, *The Life of Reason*, praised as much for its poetic expression as for its message, came out in four volumes in 1905–06. In it, he sought a rational basis for morality, regretfully rejecting religion on intellectual grounds; nonetheless, he continued to feel affection for the faith in which he grew up, leading him to be described as a "Catholic atheist". Politically, he was suspicious of the demagogic aspects of democracy, but argued strongly for equality of opportunity for all.

European years
Santayana continued to write copiously after his return to Europe, publishing essays and poems as well as purely philosophical works. The most important of these was *Realms of Being*, his chief contribution to metaphysics. In it he identified four different realms – essence, matter, truth, and spirit – each irreducibly different from the others. Through these concepts he sought to harmonize his lifelong materialism with the Platonist tradition of essences and spirit, adding the concept of truth as an objective reality that can only be grasped in fragmentary, often symbolic form.

Having settled in Rome in 1925, Santayana spent the last years of his life in a clinic attached to the Convent of the Blue Nuns. He continued to write into old age, bringing out his autobiography, *Persons and Places*, in 1944 at the age of 80.

⊲ **WALLACE STEVENS**
At Harvard, Santayana befriended the young Wallace Stevens (who would later win the Pulitzer Prize for Poetry). The two debated matters of belief, exchanging sonnets on the subject.

> "Those who **do not remember** the **past** are **condemned** to **repeat** it."
>
> GEORGE SANTAYANA, *THE LIFE OF REASON*

W.E.B. Du Bois

1868–1963, AMERICAN

An intellectual, activist, socialist, and editor, W.E.B. Du Bois spent his long career battling prejudice and inequality and looking for ways to advance the interests of the Black race.

◁ **MAN OF LETTERS**
A scholar as well as an activist, Du Bois wrote 17 books, including five novels, and countless papers. He founded several journals, and developed the sociology department at Atlanta University.

William Edward Burghardt Du Bois was born in Great Barrington, Massachusetts in 1868, the son of Alfred Du Bois, a Haitian-born barber, and Mary Silvina Burghardt, a domestic worker whose family had lived in New England for generations. His father left before he turned two, but Du Bois would write that he had a happy childhood in his largely white home town. A gifted student, he was the first Black graduate of the town's high school and began writing articles for newspapers at the age of 15.

Philosophy evolves

Du Bois studied philosophy at Harvard, where his professors included William James, Josiah Royce, and George Santayana. James was particularly influential. Du Bois would later credit him with helping him to see past the "lovely but sterile land of philosophic speculation" in favour of gathering and interpreting data.

After graduating from Harvard in 1890, Du Bois studied in Germany, at Berlin's Friedrich Wilhelm University. He was forced to return to the US when his grant money ran out, but completed his PhD in history at Harvard, thus becoming the first Black American to receive a Harvard PhD. His doctoral dissertation, *The Suppression of the African Slave Trade to the United States of America, 1638–1871*, reflected his interest in socio-economic analysis. DuBois' still-influential 1897 address "The Conservation of Races" argued that humanity is divided into multiple groups separated by history and culture, not merely physical factors.

Several academic positions followed. His 1903 book *The Souls of Black Folk*, presented the concept of "double consciousness" – how being American and Black formed "two unreconciled strivings; two warring ideals." He later played a role in the Pan-Africanism movement, which sought to unite people of African descent globally. He urged Black Americans to embrace their African heritage rather than seek to integrate with white America.

Later life

In 1951, Du Bois was indicted as an unregistered Soviet agent but acquitted. He had come to view communism as the path to economic equality. Increasingly alienated from the US, he moved to Ghana in 1961 and died as a citizen of that nation two years later – one day before the March on Washington, a pivotal event in US history that paved the way for the end of state-sanctioned discrimination.

IN CONTEXT
The Crisis

Co-founded by W.E.B. Du Bois in 1910, and edited by him until 1934, *The Crisis* was the official publication of the NAACP (National Association for the Advancement of Colored People). At the end of its first decade, it had a circulation of about 100,000 and was arguably the country's most influential periodical on the topic of race.

The Crisis regularly reported on discrimination and violence against Black Americans. But it also profiled prominent Black Americans, offered a platform for the opinions of Black intellectuals, including Du Bois himself, and helped foster the Harlem Renaissance by featuring the work of Black poets and authors. In 1921, for example, it published a poem titled "The Negro Speaks of Rivers" by a never-before-published poet named Langston Hughes.

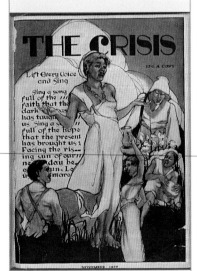

THE CRISIS, NOVEMBER 1927

" The **problem** of the **twentieth century** is the problem of **the color line**. "

W.E.B. DU BOIS

▷ **W.E.B. DU BOIS, 1949**
Du Bois addresses the World Peace Conference in Paris in 1949. He believed that decolonization, Black liberation, and nuclear disarmament were crucial to world peace.

Bertrand Russell

1872–1970, WELSH

Admired by philosophers for his work on logic and the foundations of mathematics, Russell was famous among a wider public for his radical stance on social issues, from free love to nuclear disarmament.

IN PROFILE
G.E. Moore

English philosopher George Edward Moore was a friend of Russell's at Cambridge and a considerable influence on his early philosophical thought. Moore's *Principia Ethica* (1903) argued for intuitive knowledge of the good and the beautiful as the basis for ethics, rather than fixed rules or a calculation of the consequences of actions. His ethical views were adopted by the Bloomsbury group of artists and intellectuals, with which both Moore and Russell became associated. Moore also proposed the common-sense analysis of everyday language as a philosophic method, an approach that was adopted in the "ordinary language" philosophy of the Austrian thinker Ludwig Wittgenstein.

◁ **PEMBROKE LODGE**
Russell grew up in this Georgian mansion in Richmond Park on the outskirts of London "accustomed to wide horizons and to an unimpeded view of the sunset".

Admitted to Trinity College, Cambridge, to read mathematics in 1890, he soon extended his studies to philosophy. Russell became a member of the intellectually elite Cambridge Apostles society and was elected a fellow of Trinity College in 1895.

Mathematics and logic

In the face of fierce opposition from his grandmother, in 1894 Russell married an American-born Quaker five years his elder, Alys Pearsall Smith. This high-minded liaison did not bring happiness to either party. By 1901, Russell had decided he no longer wished to share a bed with his wife, although they remained together for another 10 years.

This was the period of Russell's greatest philosophical achievement. Finding refuge from unhappiness in intellectual work, he set out to prove that mathematics was an expression of logic rather than a deduction from empirical observation. The many and complex ramifications of this approach were worked out in detail with Alfred North Whitehead, formerly

Born in 1872, Bertrand Russell was by birth a member of the British liberal aristocracy. His father, Lord Amberley, was the son of Lord John Russell, a political reformer and twice British prime minister. Amberley held radical views on religion, women's rights, and sexual morality, happy to let his wife sleep with the tutor who was engaged to teach his children. When Bertrand was aged two, his mother and sister

◁ **BERTRAND RUSSELL**
Russell was a habitual pipe smoker. He claimed that the habit saved his life when he insisted upon choosing a smoking seat on a passenger flight that later crashed.

died of diphtheria; his father died two years later. The grandparents took custody of the children, who were then raised by Lady Russell at Pembroke Lodge in Richmond.

Although liberal in politics, Lady Russell was strictly conservative in religion and morals. Bertrand grew up as a stifled inner rebel, lonely, sexually repressed, and hiding a private loss of religious faith. At the age of 11, Bertrand's elder brother Frank introduced him to the works of Euclid. He immediately fell in love with mathematics, which became, he wrote, "my chief interest, and my chief source of happiness".

**GEORGE EDWARD MOORE
(1873–1958)**

"The **man** who has **no tincture** of **philosophy** goes through life **imprisoned** in the **prejudices** derived from **common sense.** "

BERTRAND RUSSELL, *THE PROBLEMS OF PHILOSOPHY*

△ **TRINITY COLLEGE, CAMBRIDGE**
Russell became a fellow of Trinity College in 1895; his most famous student there, from 1911, was Austrian philosopher Ludwig Wittgenstein.

▽ **BEACON HILL**
Russell is pictured here with pupils at his school in Hampshire. The school was a coeducational establishment run on progressive principles, offering sex education but no religious instruction and an almost complete absence of discipline.

Russell's maths tutor at Trinity, in *Principia Mathematica*, a work considered to be of foremost importance in the development of both logic and mathematics.

Russell applied the same form of logical analysis to some of the most stubborn problems in philosophy, especially the nature and reliability of our knowledge of the external world. Some of his thinking revolved around issues such as the truth or falsehood of the sentence "The current king of France is bald", when no such king existed. These considerations could seem trivial to non-philosophers, but Russell's logical analysis of such propositions proved immensely fertile and the approach was established as a central feature of Anglo-American philosophy in the 20th century.

Writing and activism

Alongside his philosophical work, Russell engaged in political issues and movements for social reform. He was a member of the mildly socialist Fabian Society from 1897 and stood as a Women's Suffrage candidate in a parliamentary by–election in 1907. The outbreak of war in 1914 brought his activism to the fore. Adopting a pacifist stance, he campaigned vigorously against the war, in defiance of the law and most popular opinion. He was dismissed from his fellowship at Trinity College and, in 1918, jailed for six months in Brixton prison. Russell continued his philosophical investigation of the basis of knowledge and the nature of the world in works such as *The Philosophy of Logical Atomism* (1918) and *An Enquiry into Meaning and Truth* (1940), but from the 1920s onward much of his writing was journalistic, and he was more involved in social and political issues.

Unlike many other activists, Russell was not an admirer of the communist state in Russia. A visit there in 1920, during which he which he met Lenin, convinced him that communism would become a form of oppression, rather than a liberation. Russell's projects for social reform thus focused on sexual morality and education rather than on political revolution.

▽ **THE PRINCIPLES OF MATHEMATICS, 1903**
Russell's book was labelled "Volume I"; the second volume was effectively Russell and Whitehead's *Principia*.

THE PRINCIPLES
OF
MATHEMATICS

BY
BERTRAND [RUSSELL M.A.,
LATE FELLOW OF TRINITY COLLEGE, CAMBRIDGE

VOL I.
[No more published]

CAMBRIDGE:
at the University Press
1903

> " **Mathematics**, rightly viewed, possesses not only **truth**, but **supreme beauty**. "
>
> BERTRAND RUSSELL, *THE STUDY OF MATHEMATICS*

Separating from his wife, Alys, in 1911, Russell embarked on a series of affairs, and mixed with the Bloomsbury group of artists and intellectuals in exploring unconventional relationships. Having escaped his own repressive Christian upbringing, he became a campaigner for sexual freedom and a liberal approach to child-rearing.

In 1921, he married Dora Black, a young socialist and feminist who shared his views on "open marriage" and birth control – then a highly controversial issue. The couple had two children, who were raised in accordance with Russell's theoretical views, which perhaps surprisingly involved paying as little attention to infants as possible, on the grounds that this would lessen their egotism. Together with Dora, Russell founded the highly progressive Beacon Hill school in Hampshire.

Liberal education

Russell's ideas about society found expression in popular works such as *On Education* (1926) and *Marriage and Morals* (1929), but in reality, some of the practices that he promoted proved problematic. He admitted that children at his school would have benefited from more order and structure; and his marriage to Dora was scarred by extramarital affairs, ending in divorce in 1935, after Russell began an affair with the children's governess Patricia Spence, who became his third wife.

Russell's views on sexual matters and his atheism made him a highly controversial figure. In the US in 1940 he was refused a post at City College, New York, after public protests and a court judgement that he was "morally unfit" to teach.

IN CONTEXT
The Campaign for Nuclear Disarmament

CND was founded in 1958 with Bertrand Russell as its president. It attracted significant public attention with an annual protest march that went from the Aldermaston Atomic Weapons Establishment in Berkshire to London. In 1960, Russell resigned the CND presidency to head the Committee of 100, a radical offshoot committed to civil disobedience and acts of nonviolent resistance. The following year he was imprisoned for incitement to illegal action. The civil disobedience campaign soon lost momentum and from 1963 CND's support went into decline. It revived in the 1980s in response to the emplacement of US Cruise missiles in Britain.

ALDERMASTON MARCH AGAINST NUCLEAR WEAPONRY, 1961

During the 1930s, Russell was prominent in the pacifist movement, refusing to accept that Britain needed to defend itself against the rising power of Nazi Germany. Within a year of the outbreak of World War II, however, he had decided that war was a lesser evil than the triumph of Nazism. He spent the war years in the US, producing his *History of Western Philosophy*, one of the bestselling philosophy books ever written. He was awarded the Nobel Prize for Literature in 1950.

Final years

Russell lived into old age after surviving an air crash off the coast of Norway when he was 76. He married his fourth wife, Edith Finch, in 1952,

forming a happy and durable union. Russell's main concern in the postwar period was the threat of nuclear war. He considered that the only true answer lay in world government, but he pressed for nuclear disarmament via the Russell–Einstein Manifesto, which was drawn up with physicist Albert Einstein and others in 1955. He was one of the founders of the British Campaign for Nuclear Disarmament (CND) and in 1961 was imprisoned for a week – at the age of 89 – for his part in anti-nuclear protests in London. The Bertrand Russell Peace Foundation, which he established in 1963, became chiefly a vehicle for investigating and condemning the US war in Vietnam. Russell died in February 1970, aged 97.

△ **COMMITTEE OF 100 HANDBILL**
The Committee of 100 radically opposed nuclear weapons, not only in the West but also in Russia, organizing meetings in Moscow as well as in London.

KEY WORKS

1903
Presents his thesis that mathematics is a form of symbolic logic in *The Principles of Mathematics*.

1905
Publishes an article in the journal *Mind* that is considered a key contribution to understanding how propositions work.

1910–13
Produces *Principia Mathematica* with A.N. Whitehead; it is a monumental work on the logical foundations of mathematical truth.

1912
Publishes *The Problems of Philosophy*, a general introduction to his views.

1929
In *Marriage and Morals*, Russell denies the value of chastity before marriage and fidelity in marriage.

1938
Describes society in terms of power relations in *Power: A New Social Analysis*, rejecting Marx's focus on economic power.

José Ortega y Gasset

1883–1955, SPANISH

Ortega was Spain's most prominent liberal intellectual of the 20th century. A champion of elitism and creative individualism, he decried the rise of mass culture and the political populism that led to dictatorship.

José Ortega y Gasset was born in Madrid in 1883. His family were wealthy members of the urban elite and publishers of a prominent liberal newspaper. He was brought up to regard Spain as lamentably backward in its culture and society, and after graduating from the University of Madrid in 1904 he left to study in Germany, "fleeing the vulgarity of my country", as he later wrote. At the universities of Leipzig, Berlin, and Marburg he absorbed the German philosophical tradition, with Friedrich Nietzsche and Edmund Husserl in particular becoming major influences.

Ortega returned home fired with the purpose of regenerating Spain through contact with advanced European ideas. Installed in the chair of metaphysics at the University of Madrid at the age of 27, he co-founded the newspaper *El Sol* in 1917, and went on to establish the prestigious intellectual journal *Revista de Occidente* in 1923.

European ideals

Ortega's first major book, *Meditations on Quixote*, appeared in 1914. A series of broad reflections on philosophy and the arts, it included his most famous philosophical statement: "I am I, and my circumstances." This phrase encapsulated his subjective and relativistic approach to life and

◁ **FIRST ISSUE**
Ortega's highbrow journal *Revista de Occidente* (*Magazine of the West*) was first published in July 1923. It championed avant-garde artistic and literary work in 1920s Spain.

culture, regarding each self-creating individual as embedded in his or her specific historical situation and offering a unique take on reality.

His works of the 1920s, *Invertebrate Spain* (1921) and *The Revolt of the Masses* (1929), focused on politics and society and made Ortega internationally famous. *The Revolt of the Masses* was principally a reflection on the rise of fascism and communism. It argued that modern society's empowerment of the common man had undermined the cultured elite who upheld European liberal civilization. Incapable of sustaining the complex principles that allowed such a civilization to

flourish, the rule of the masses resulted in cultural decline and populist dictatorships.

In 1923, Spain itself – although officially a monarchy – came under the rule of a military dictator, Miguel Primo de Rivera. Ortega's *Revista de Occidente* was highly critical of Primo de Rivera and in 1929 Ortega resigned from his university post in protest at encroachments on academic freedom. As a leading figure in the intellectual opposition, Ortega played a significant role in the downfall of the dictatorship and the creation of Spain's Second Republic in 1931. He was elected to the Republic's constituent assembly but became disillusioned with politics as extremism flourished. At the start of the Spanish Civil War in 1936, he fled into exile with his family, living in Argentina and Portugal. An opponent of the Francoist dictatorship that resulted from the Civil War, Ortega did not return to Madrid until 1948, when he founded the Institute of Humanities to continue the struggle for a liberal Spain. He died in Madrid aged 72.

IN CONTEXT
The Generation of '27

Ortega's thinking on art and culture, especially in his essay *The Dehumanization of Art* (1925), was an influence on the gifted young writers and artists who emerged in Spain in the 1920s. Often loosely referred to as the Generation of '27, these included the poet Federico García Lorca and the artist Salvador Dalí. Ortega was supportive of their iconoclastic work, which he saw as aiming at a Modernist transformation of society and culture. Lorca was murdered in the early days of the Civil War because of his association with left-wing and liberal ideas.

FEDERICO GARCIA LORCA (LEFT) AND SALVADOR DALI IN CADAQUES, SPAIN

▷ **ORTEGA Y GASSET BY ZULOAGA**
This portrait was made by Ignacio Zuloaga, an artist who became famous for his depictions of traditional Spanish figures, such as bullfighters and dancers.

" The mass **crushes** beneath it **everything** that is **excellent**, **individual**, **qualified** and **select**. "

JOSE ORTEGA Y GASSET, *THE REVOLT OF THE MASSES*

Karl Jaspers

1883–1969, GERMAN

Jaspers was a psychiatrist and philosopher, and a major figure in Phenomenology and existentialism. He also had a keen interest in philosophical traditions beyond Europe and the West.

Karl Jaspers was born in 1883 in Oldenburg, Germany. A sickly child, he developed chronic bronchitis, which severely affected his health. In 1901, he began his degree in law and medicine at the University of Heidelberg, and qualified as a doctor seven years later. His first job was in Heidelberg psychiatric hospital.

Jaspers developed a keen interest in Phenomenology, which led to the publication of his book *General Psychopathology* (1910), as well as to a teaching post in philosophy at Heidelberg University. He accepted a chair in philosophy in 1922 and the following year published his three-volume book, *Philosophy*.

Dark days

Jaspers married a Jewish woman, Gertrud Mayer. After the Nazis seized power in 1933, his life at the university became increasingly restricted and in 1937 he was dismissed and banned from publishing. Following the

◁ **THE IDEAL NAZI STUDENT, c.1935**
The Nazis founded the National Socialist German Students' League to promote ideological training in universities. The rise of Nazism led to Jaspers' removal from his university post. A poster from the Students' League is shown here.

◁ **KARL JASPERS, AGED 73**
Two years before his death, Jaspers took Swiss citizenship in protest against criticism of his text *The Future of Germany* (1967), which attacked the failure of democracy in his country of birth.

outbreak of World War II in 1939, Jaspers was given permission to leave Germany in 1942, on condition that his wife remained. He refused, and the couple stayed in the country. In April 1945, they heard of plans to send them to a concentration camp: they were spared only by the ending of the war. Jaspers was then reinstated in his job at the university.

Jaspers' work explores the limits and possibilities of human experience. Human existence is both finite and open; limited and full of possibility. According to Jaspers, this means

that there are many situations in which we experience transcendence: we become increasingly aware not only of the limitations of our current ways of thinking, feeling, acting, and knowing, but also of the possibilities that exist for new ways of thinking, feeling, acting, and knowing.

Mysticism and politics

Jaspers says that human experience takes place within *das Umgreifende*, "the encompassing", or "that which always makes its presence known, which does not appear itself, but from which everything comes to us". In his work, he explores experiences of mystery, faith, and transcendence – experiences that are most often associated with religion (see box, right).

For the remainder of his life after World War II and the fall of Nazism, Jaspers committed himself to political engagement and reform, as well as to the rebuilding of the university system and philosophical writing. He died of a stroke in Basel, Switzerland, aged 86.

IN CONTEXT
The Axial Age

One contemporary idea that is particularly associated with Karl Jaspers is that of the Axial Age (in German, *Achsenzeit*), or "pivotal age". This is a term that he coined to describe the period of ancient history between the 8th and the 3rd centuries BCE. This was a time of tremendous cultural and philosophical change from China to the West. The Axial Age witnessed the establishment of many important religious and philosophical systems, including Buddhism, that continue to shape our lives in the modern world. Jaspers referred to the Axial Age as "a deep breath bringing the most lucid consciousness".

BUDDHISM FLOURISHED DURING THE AXIAL AGE; SEATED BUDDHA, WOOD

> " If **religion** were not the **life** of **mankind**, there would be **no philosophy** either. "

KARL JASPERS, "ON MY PHILOSOPHY"

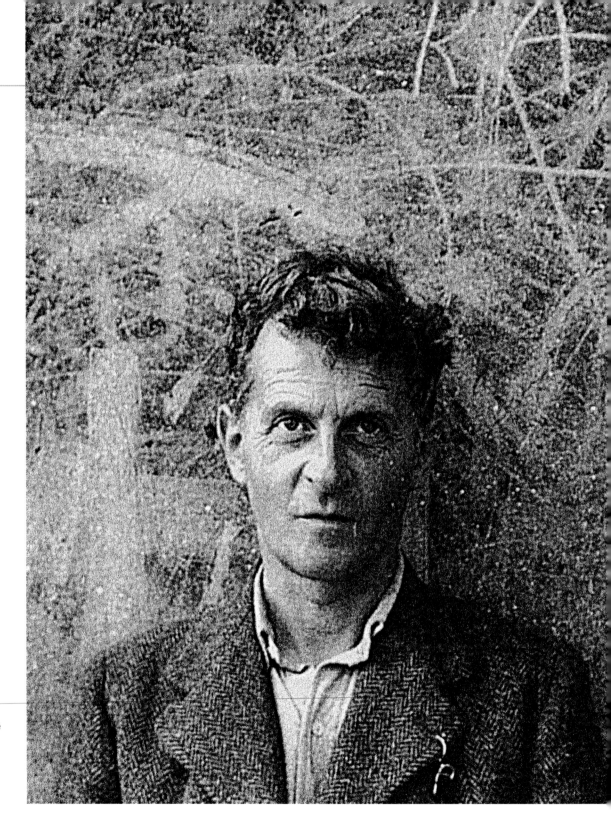

▷ **WITTGENSTEIN, 1947**
This portrait of Wittgenstein was taken
by his lover Ben Richards, a Cambridge
medical student who was 40 years the
philosopher's junior. Wittgenstein had
four significant loves in his life: three
were men and one a Swiss woman,
Marguerite Respinger, whom at one
point he planned to marry.

Ludwig Wittgenstein

1889–1951, AUSTRIAN

Wittgenstein was an enigmatic thinker who became hugely influential
in the mid-20th century. His gnomic aphorisms and striking personality
made him an iconic figure, much referenced in modern culture.

"Whereof **one cannot speak,** thereof **one must be silent.**"

LUDWIG WITTGENSTEIN, *TRACTATUS LOGICO-PHILOSOPHICUS*

Ludwig Wittgenstein was born in Vienna to a very wealthy family that was largely of Jewish descent. The family played a prominent role in the city's cultural life, patronizing famous artists and musicians. The youngest of eight children, Ludwig was considered by his parents the least gifted of their offspring. His siblings excelled at music and the arts, but Ludwig's talents seemed to be practical, though he shared the family's characteristic refined sensibility and neuroses.

Studies in England

In 1908, after studying engineering in Berlin, Wittgenstein moved to the UK, pursuing research in aeronautics at Manchester University. He later described this as a time of "loneliness and suffering". It was while working on the mathematics associated with propeller design that he discovered an obsessive interest in the logical foundations of mathematics. Torn between intellectual excitement and self-doubt, he took his thoughts on the subject to the leaders in the field, Gottlob Frege in Jena and Bertrand Russell in Cambridge.

IN PROFILE
Paul Wittgenstein

Ludwig Wittgenstein's older brother Paul (1887–1961) was a promising concert pianist when World War I broke out. Conscripted into the Austrian army, he was wounded fighting the Russians and had his right arm amputated. After the war, he commissioned composers to write piano pieces for him to perform one-handed, the most famous being Maurice Ravel's *Piano Concerto for the Left Hand*. After Nazi Germany took over Austria in 1938 he found refuge in the US. Of Ludwig Wittgenstein's four brothers, Paul was the only one not to die by suicide.

PAUL WITTGENSTEIN AT THE PIANO ON A CONCERT TOUR OF THE US

Russell initially found this unknown 22-year-old engineer irritatingly odd, describing him as "argumentative and tiresome" because he would not agree "it was certain that there was not a rhinoceros in the room". After Russell agreed to tutor him, Wittgenstein soon became his favourite pupil and Russell later referred to him as, "the perfect example... of genius as traditionally conceived, passionate, profound, intense and domineering".

However, Wittgenstein never completed his university studies. He disliked the company of academic philosophers and read little of the work of the great philosophers of the past, dismissing most of their thinking as "stupid and dishonest".

In 1913, against Russell's advice, Wittgenstein left Cambridge to live in a village on a Norwegian fjord where he could pursue his own thoughts in isolation. He had fallen in love with an undergraduate, David Pinsent, who was his frequent companion at this time.

◁ **PORTRAIT OF FORM 1B**
Initially tutored at home, Wittgenstein was later sent to the Realschule in Linz, a state technical school. This portrait is notable for showing not only the young philosopher (second row from top, third from the right), but also his classmate Adolf Hitler (top right).

▷ **AT HOME IN VIENNA**
This portrait of the Wittgenstein family
in summer 1917 shows, from left,
the siblings Kurt, Paul, and Hermine
Wittgenstein; their brother-in-law,
Max Salzer; their mother, Leopoldine
Wittgenstein; Helene Wittgenstein
Salzer; and Ludwig Wittgenstein.

▽ **THE *TRACTATUS***
Wittgenstein's *Tractatus Logico-
Philosophicus* – shown here in a
1955 edition published in London –
expressed his early views on logic,
language, and the world.

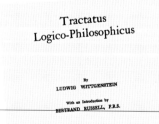

War writings

Wittgenstein was not liable for
conscription when World War I
broke out, but volunteered to join
the Austrian artillery. He saw military
service as a form of self-sacrifice,
writing that the war gave him "a
chance to be a decent human being,
standing eye to eye with death". He
served throughout the four years of
war, surviving fighting in the trenches
and winning several decorations for
exceptional bravery. David Pinsent
did not survive the conflict, a loss
Wittgenstein felt bitterly. The war did
not stop him working at philosophy,
jotting thoughts in a notebook during
quiet periods in the trenches and while
a prisoner of war at the end of the
conflict. By 1921 he had finished the
book that made him famous: *Tractatus
Logico-Philosophicus*.

Presented as a series of numbered
points, the *Tractatus* mixed formal
logic with aphorism. Wittgenstein
wrote in the preface: "Perhaps this
book will be understood only by
someone who has himself already
had the thoughts expressed in it."
Although only some 70 pages long,
it was broad in its ambition, covering
issues ranging from epistemology and
logic to death and ethics. It attempted
to define the limits of language,
distinguishing the facts of the world
appropriate to language from that
which could be shown but not
meaningfully spoken of. Wittgenstein
describes his own logical arguments
as an elucidation rather than a system
of thought, to be discarded once
understanding has been attained –
"He must, as it were, throw away the
ladder after he has climbed up it."

A simpler life

By the time the *Tractatus* was
published in 1922, Wittgenstein felt
he had finished with philosophy. The
experience of shared suffering in war
had encouraged his bent towards a
saintly asceticism. He had inherited
an immense fortune from his father
but had given most of the money
away, determining instead to live
a more useful life in poverty.

He worked for a time as a gardener
at Klosterneuburg monastery just
outside Vienna and enrolled in a
teacher training course so that he
could earn a living as a primary school
teacher in rural Austria. This proved
a difficult experience – Wittgenstein
did not fit easily into village life and
there were complaints from parents
about his unconventional methods.
In 1926, tired of rural isolation and

> "If **a lion** could **talk**, we would **not**
> **understand** him."
>
> LUDWIG WITTGENSTEIN, *PHILOSOPHICAL INVESTIGATIONS*

◁ **ARCHITECTURAL EXPERIMENTS**
Wittgenstein, in collaboration with the architect Paul Engelmann, designed this Vienna house for his sister Margarethe.

peasant hostility, Wittgenstein returned to Vienna. Here, he flirted with architecture, designing a Modernist house in Vienna for one of his sisters, but by then philosophy was regaining its hold on his life.

Return to Cambridge
In 1927, meetings with members of the Vienna Circle of logical positivists revealed that they had misunderstood the *Tractatus*, interpreting it as support for their exclusively scientific view of the world. Wittgenstein began himself to see flaws in the book's arguments and sense new directions in which his thought might develop. In 1929 he returned to Cambridge, where Bertrand Russell's backing ensured him a fellowship at Trinity College. He was elected to a chair in philosophy in 1939. Wittgenstein came to regard himself as a therapist, curing people of false philosophical problems that arose through misuse of language.

His teaching was fluid and exploratory rather than dogmatic. Instead of seeking to purify language into a form of logic, he explored how words were actually used, analysing the rules that applied to different "language games". He rejected his earlier belief in a logical foundation for mathematics, asserting that "the mathematician is an inventor, not a discoverer". Seeking to break up fixed patterns of thought, he proffered questions rather than answers, examining thought, perception, communication, and ethics from new angles. His thinking from this period survives only as notes from lectures and seminars.

Wartime and beyond
When Nazi Germany took over Austria in the Anschluss of 1938, Wittgenstein took British nationality. After the outbreak of World War II, he came increasingly to regard the practice of philosophy as useless, and in 1941 found a manual job as a porter at Guy's Hospital in blitzed London. After the war he resigned from the University of Cambridge and moved to a village in Ireland. Intermittently in love with young men throughout his life, in his final years he experienced both the pleasures and the pains of love with an undergraduate, Ben Richards.

Ideas continued to flow despite declining health: he began work on only his second book of philosophy, the *Philosophical Investigations*, and on a refutation of scepticism, *On Certainty*. Both were unfinished when he died of cancer in Cambridge in 1951. He was given a Catholic burial, although he could probably be properly described as an agnostic. Posthumous publication of the *Philosophical Investigations* and material from his notebooks and lectures continued to enhance his reputation long after his death.

◁ **ANSCHLUSS POSTER**
A German propaganda poster celebrates the announcement of the Anschluss (union) of Germany with Austria. At this time, Wittgenstein helped arrange for his relatives in Vienna to escape persecution by paying a huge bribe to the Nazis.

13·MÄRZ 1938
EIN VOLK EIN REICH
EIN FÜHRER

IN PROFILE
Alan Turing

A contemporary of Wittgenstein at Cambridge in the 1930s, Alan Turing (1912–54) was one of the fathers of modern computing. Turing and Wittgenstein debated the foundations of mathematics at Wittgenstein's seminars in 1939. Turing went on to work as a cryptologist, decoding output from the Enigma machine in World War II. After the war he was highly successful in the development of computers and the theory of artificial intelligence. In 1952 he was arrested for an alleged homosexual act and subjected to chemical castration. He died by suicide two years later.

ALAN TURING

KEY WORKS

1922	**1953**	**1956**	**1958**	**1969**
Tractatus Logico-Philosophicus is the only book of Wittgenstein's published in his lifetime.	Addresses a range of philosophical problems through linguistic analysis in *Philosophical Investigations*.	*Remarks on the Foundations of Mathematics* is published posthumously.	*The Blue Book* – a series of lecture notes first circulated privately in 1935 – is published.	A set of Wittgenstein's notes, written in around 1949, is published as *On Certainty*.

▷ **MARTIN HEIDEGGER, 1965**
Fritz Eschen's portrait of Heidegger
shows the eminent philosopher
in his mid-seventies, wearing his
much-photographed Loden jacket with
oak leaves on the lapels. By the time this
photograph was taken, he had largely
withdrawn from teaching, writing, and
university life, and was still affected by
the controversy surrounding his earlier
alleged alignment with fascist ideology.

Martin Heidegger

1889–1976, GERMAN

Heidegger was a major figure in the fields of Phenomenology and
existentialism, but his outstanding contribution to philosophy has been
overshadowed by controversy over his membership of the Nazi Party.

"The most **thought-provoking thing** in our **thought-provoking time** is that we are **still not thinking**."

MARTIN HEIDEGGER, *WHAT IS CALLED THINKING?*

◁ **VIEWS OF MESSKIRCH**
Heidegger was born and grew up in this southwest German country town and returned there to die in old age. A museum dedicated to the philosopher is situated in the Messkirch castle.

Martin Heidegger was born in 1889 in Messkirch, a small rural town in Saxony, southwest Germany. It was a quiet, conservative town and, like much of southern Germany, it was mainly Catholic; Heidegger's family were devout believers; his father was sexton at the local Catholic church. This had a profound influence on Martin's thinking, and it was initially assumed he would become a priest.

Early years
Martin did well at school, and was awarded a scholarship by the church to study at the high school in nearby Konstanz. In 1906 he moved to Freiburg to complete his schooling. It was there that his interest in

philosophy was sparked when he read Franz Brentano's *On the Manifold Meaning of Being According to Aristotle* (1862), a book that inspired the focus of his own philosophical enquiry – the meaning of Being. After graduating from high school in 1909, he joined a Jesuit order but was soon discharged because of poor health. He enrolled at Freiburg University to study theology, but two years later abandoned his course, ostensibly through ill health, and transferred to study philosophy, mathematics, and science.

Heidegger completed his doctorate in philosophy at Freiburg and went on to study for the *habilitation* (certificate for university teaching). It was then that he met another teacher at

Freiburg, Edmund Husserl, whose *Logical Investigations* (1901–02) was to prove a formative influence. In 1915 Heidegger completed his thesis, *Duns Scotus' Doctrine of Categories and Meaning,* and was appointed as an unsalaried lecturer. The next year he worked alongside Husserl when he became a professor at Freiburg.

A time of change
Heidegger had not only changed the course of his career from theology to philosophy, but had also begun to question his allegiance to Catholicism. This was further confirmed in 1917, when he married a Protestant, Thea Elfride Petri.

IN PROFILE
Friedrich Hölderlin

A poet and philosopher, Friedrich Hölderlin (1770–1843) played an key role in the development of both the Romantic movement and German Idealism. His poetry, and the novel *Hyperion,* influenced his philosopher contemporaries Hegel, Schelling, and Fichte – whom he counted among his friends – and much later, were picked up by Martin Heidegger. Hölderlin had a troubled life, always struggling for recognition, and was plagued by mental illness. After a period in a institution, he was taken in by an admirer of his work, Ernst Zimmer, and spent the last 36 years of his life in his house in Tübingen.

FRIEDRICH HOLDERLIN, FRANZ KARL HIEMER, 1792

△ **VANITAS**

This 17th-century painting, *Vanitas: Still Life with a Tulip, Skull, and Hour-Glass*, by French artist Philippe de Champaigne, with its symbols of transience and degeneration, encourages reflection on mortality and the inevitability of death. According to Heidegger in *Being and Time*, all of life is defined by the concept of time and also therefore by the certainty of death, which acts as an ever-present horizon in human existence.

Heidegger had been excused military service at the beginning of World War I because of bad health, but he was called up again in 1918 and served for the last few months of the war in a meteorological unit. On his return, he announced his break from "the system of Catholicism".

Freed from the constraints of Catholic interpretation, his research became ever more insightful and he gained a reputation as a brilliant and inspiring lecturer. He was appointed as Husserl's assistant, and for the next few years set about a reinterpretation of his mentor's Phenomenology.

Bold new perspectives

In 1923, Heidegger was offered an associate professorship at Marburg University, where he spent the next five years. His teaching attracted some gifted students, among them the budding philosophers Hannah Arendt (pp.276–79) and Elisabeth Blochmann, who were among the young women he had affairs with.

It was an exhilarating period in his life, and he spent much of his time working on a systematic organization of his ideas on the meaning of Being. As he had not published anything since his arrival at Marburg, the

university pressed him to publish earlier than he had anticipated, and only the first part of a two-part work was ready. Nonetheless, when *Being and Time* was published in 1927 it secured his reputation as one of the foremost thinkers of the 20th century.

The groundbreaking work showed Heidegger's debt to Husserl but also demonstrated that he was not simply following in his mentor's footsteps. At its core is the idea that philosophy has hitherto examined all manner of things that have Being, but has not addressed the question of Being itself. And that, he argued, can be

KEY WORKS

1927

Heidegger's magnum opus, *Being and Time*, is published, despite being only part of the much longer project he had planned.

1935

In his *Introduction to Metaphysics*, Heidegger gives a controversial view of Greek thought from what is regarded as a Nazi perspective.

1936–38

A shift in focus, known as "the turn" becomes evident in Heidegger's work, as in *Contributions to Philosophy (From Enowning)*.

1954

A collection of his lectures from 1951–52, *What Is Called Thinking?*, offers an overview of Heidegger's later philosophy.

1959

A collection of essays from his lectures of the 1950s, *On the Way To Language*, presents the famous phrase "language speaks".

"**Why** are there **beings** at all, and **why not** rather **nothing**? **That** is the **question**."

MARTIN HEIDEGGER, *WHAT IS METAPHYSICS?*

done by an examination of the being for whom the question is important, what he called the *Dasein* – the experience of Being that we, as humans, have. This experience of Being is defined by birth, the moment a being is thrust into the world, and by death, the moment that being comes to an end. So, according to Heidegger, Being is not only characterized by time – Being actually is time.

The innovative concepts described in *Being and Time* earned Heidegger a full professorship at Marburg, and one year later the chair of philosophy at Freiburg when Husserl retired. Nevertheless, *Being and Time* remained an unfinished project in Heidegger's mind, and he never completed the second half as planned. However, he continued to develop its ideas in further books.

Controversy and discredit

Heidegger's fortunes soon changed. Since the end of World War I, support for the National Socialist German Workers' Party (NSDAP), or the Nazi Party, had grown, and in 1933 Adolf Hitler became chancellor. That same year, Heidegger was elected rector of the University of Freiburg, having been persuaded to stand by his colleagues to avoid the possibility of a Nazi Party appointment to the post. But once in the post, Heidegger joined the NSDAP; his acceptance speech as rector was a

thinly veiled endorsement of the Nazis, which he followed up with further speeches in support of the party.

He resigned from the rectorship after just one year, but did not give up his party membership. His relationship with the Nazis was ambiguous: he remained a party member, but was critical of the regime; his philosophy was discredited by the party, and he had to give up teaching at Freiburg to join the war effort, digging trenches along the Rhine in 1944.

After Hitler's defeat, the French authorities accused Heidegger of being a Nazi sympathizer, and he was removed from the faculty at Freiburg and banned from teaching. In 1949, he was cleared of the most serious charges and he returned to the university the following year, lecturing there until 1958.

Heidegger's reputation was in tatters, but he did not deny his Nazi membership or his support for the

regime. Some scholars claim there is evidence of his Nazi sympathies in his philosophical approach from around 1930. While this is highly debatable, there was what is known as *die Kehre* ("the turn") at around this time, with a subtle shift of emphasis in his thinking from the style of *Being and Time*.

Final years

More damning was the discovery of Heidegger's notebooks from 1931 to 1941, which make antisemitic references, and raise the issue of how much his enthusiasm for Nazism is reflected in his philosophy. After World War II, he continued writing, but other than his commentaries on modern life and technology, did little more than simply reiterate his earlier ideas. Marginalized by all but a few of his friends and former students, including Hannah Arendt, Heidegger gradually disappeared from the limelight, and died in his home town of Messkirch.

△ **BEING AND TIME**
The title page of the first, 1927, edition of Martin Heidegger's groundbreaking masterpiece *Being and Time* is shown here. It was published by Max Niemeyer.

IN CONTEXT
The Third Reich

In the 14 years following World War I, Germany was plagued by political unrest and financial instability. The Weimar Republic faced an existential crisis in the 1930s, with resentment over the terms of the Treaty of Versailles, exacerbated by hyperinflation, a sense of loss of German identity, and cultural decadence. As a result, Adolf Hitler and his Nazi Party came to power in 1933, establishing the so-called Third Reich. This rapidly became a totalitarian dictatorship, with a programme of restoring Germany's status as a great nation of pure-bred German people.

GERMAN TROOPS ARE WELCOMED WITH NAZI SALUTES, 1938

Herbert Marcuse

1898–1979, GERMAN-AMERICAN

Marcuse was an activist and philosopher who reinterpreted the works of Marx and Freud, made major contributions to "critical theory", and produced radical critiques of capitalist society.

Born in Berlin to a prosperous Jewish family, Herbert Marcuse was drafted into the German army in World War I, although poor eyesight spared him from combat. He returned to academia, completing a PhD in German literature in 1922 at the University of Freiburg. He became interested in politics and was keen to make rigid Marxist orthodoxy more relevant to the individual.

Following a stint as a bookseller in Berlin, Marcuse returned to Freiburg to study philosophy under Martin Heidegger. In 1933, after the rise of Nazism and Heidegger's alignment with the fascists, he fled to Switzerland to work at the Frankfurt School (see box, right). The following year, he moved to the US, where he stayed for the rest of his life. Also in the 1930s – after a series of essays in the previous decade attempting to unify the work of Heidegger, Karl Marx, and Georg Hegel – Marcuse became preoccupied with the concept of truth.

His first book, *Reason and Revolution* (1941), is a major study refuting Hegel's claim that what is actual is rational; it stresses the importance of Marx's early works, which Marcuse revisits to develop his own theories on alienation and reification (fetishizing objects or commodities).

Academic appointments

Marcuse became a US citizen in 1940 and married Sophie Wertman, a mathematician – the first of his three wives. In World War II, he worked in military intelligence and produced a report on how the Allies could make use of the mass media to present images of German fascism.

After the war, he turned to the works of Sigmund Freud. In *Eros and Civilization* (1955), he claims that Freud's theory of repressive society in *Civilization and its Discontents* (1930) is overly pessimistic and fails to account for humanity's immense potential for happiness. The book brought widespread acclaim. He was appointed professor of philosophy at Brandeis University, Massachusetts, in the mid-1950s. However, the university later refused to renew his contract because of his Marxist views. He transferred to the University of California at the age of 67.

Media and society

Marcuse's most influential work was *One-Dimensional Man* (1964). Here, he argues that mass culture reinforces political oppression, pointing to the "democratic un-freedom" that persists in "totally administered" advanced industrial capitalist societies. The culture industry insinuates individuals into networks of production and consumption, creating "false needs" through advertising and the mass media that obscure the real needs for social change. By the mid-1960s, Marcuse – to his horror – had been branded father of the New Left and soared to superstardom as a voguish social theorist and political activist. His popularity declined from the late 1970s, when his work was eclipsed by postmodernism, but has re-emerged in recent times as issues surrounding consumerism, technology, and new media become increasingly pertinent.

◁ **HERBERT MARCUSE, 1968**
In the late 1960s, Marcuse became a hero of the student anti-war movement. Throughout his life, he remained fascinated by the revolutionary potential of the arts for social transformation.

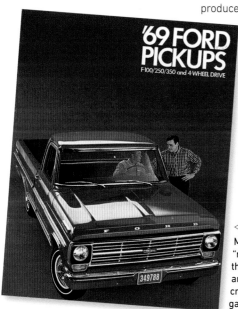

◁ **CONSUMER SOCIETY**
Marcuse argued that people "recognize themselves... their soul" in their commodities, and that advertising helps to create an insatiable desire for gadgets and inessential goods.

IN PROFILE
Angela Davis

Philosophers influenced by Marcuse include feminist and social activist Angela Davis. Born in Birmingham, Alabama, in 1944, Davis studied with Marcuse at Brandeis University in Boston, and at the University of California, San Diego. On his advice, she also spent time at the Frankfurt School in Germany – the seat of "critical theory", the use of philosophical theories to critique political and cultural institutions.

Determined to translate academic theories into real-world practice, Davis became both a distinguished academic and a tireless activist, the latter role leading at one point to her wrongful imprisonment and inclusion on the FBI's most wanted list. She has been an important voice in Black feminism and campaigns for the abolition of prisons. She is currently professor emeritus at the University of California, Santa Cruz.

ANGELA DAVIS SPEAKING AT A RALLY IN SAN FRANCISCO IN 1973

Gilbert Ryle

1900–1976, ENGLISH

Ryle spent most of his life at the University of Oxford, and achieved wider fame for his book *The Concept of Mind*, a refutation of mind–body dualism, which he called "the dogma of the ghost in the machine".

Born in Brighton, Sussex, Gilbert Ryle was a classic product of the liberal English middle class. His father was a family doctor with intellectual interests and several of Ryle's nine siblings also had distinguished careers. Educated at Brighton College private school, Ryle went to Queen's College, Oxford, to read classics, but was soon drawn to the study of philosophy. After graduating in 1924, he taught at Christ Church College.

Approaching the subject without veneration for the "great thinkers" of the past, Ryle sought a place for philosophy in a world dominated by the sciences. Like his contemporary Ludwig Wittgenstein, he was interested in how ordinary people used language and understood the world. He sought to give a higher-level account of everyday experience, providing "the theory of our daily practice, the geography of our daily walks". But he also believed that philosophy could prevent specialists such as scientists from making mistakes through unclear thinking.

After World War II, during which Ryle worked in military intelligence, he was elected to a professorship at Oxford University, and appointed editor of the influential journal *Mind*.

Clear thought

The book that made his name, *The Concept of Mind*, was published in 1949. Lucid and witty, it did not use jargon or opaque logical notation, yet its analyses of perception, thought, choice, and meaning were profoundly subtle and complex.

Most attention focused on Ryle's catchy phrase "the ghost in the machine", referring to the Cartesian model of a disembodied mind existing inside the physical body. Ryle called this a "category mistake" – the assumption that because the body was a material object, the word "mind" must also correspond to an object, this time an immaterial one.

◁ *THE THINKER*, RODIN
Ryle used Rodin's sculpture as a departure point for the question "What does thinking consist of?" He failed to find a satisfactory answer.

Because of this scepticism about mind, the book was misinterpreted as supporting the Behaviourist school of psychology (see box, right). But Ryle objected to the idea of the "machine" as well as the "ghost". He did not believe science required us to think of humans as robots explicable by physical causality. He wrote: "Man need not be degraded to being a machine by being denied to be a ghost in a machine."

Late years

Ryle never married, living with his twin sister in an Oxfordshire village. He was much liked as a tolerant and encouraging tutor. One of his last lectures was titled "What is Le Penseur Doing?", a reflection on Rodin's famous sculpture of a thinking man. It is typical of Ryle that he found the idea of thinking – something that had consumed his whole life – to be puzzling. He retired in 1968 and died eight years later.

IN CONTEXT
Behaviourism

The Behaviourist school of psychology was established primarily in the US in the first half of the 20th century. Its leading protagonists, John B. Watson and B.F. Skinner, claimed that human behaviour could be analysed as the product of patterns of stimulus and response, without a need to postulate any inner mental life, which might exist in some form but had no role in explaining or predicting behaviour. Ryle's philosophy has often been described as "Behaviourist", but he himself expressly rejected this label.

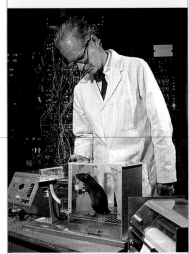

PSYCHOLOGIST B.F. SKINNER CONDUCTING EXPERIMENTS ON RATS

◁ MAGDALEN COLLEGE, OXFORD
Ryle was a fellow of Magdalen College, where he was known as a sociable conversationalist and a fierce debater, who had no time for pomposity or pretentiousness.

▷ RYLE BY WHISTLER
This portrait of Ryle was made by the celebrated artist and designer Rex Whistler, a contemporary of Ryle's. Whistler was killed in action in Normandy in World War II.

▷ **HANS-GEORG GADAMER**
Gadamer gained widespread international recognition only after his retirement from academia. He continued to write, give lectures, and deliver courses in Europe and the US, working until well after his hundredth birthday.

Hans-Georg Gadamer

1900–2002, GERMAN

Despite his association with the controversial philosopher Heidegger, Gadamer emerged as a pivotal figure in re-establishing the reputation of German philosophy in the wake of World War II.

Hans-Georg Gadamer was born in Marburg, Germany in 1900, but the family moved to Breslau two years later when his father became a professor of chemistry at the university there. After his mother died when he was just four, Hans-Georg found refuge from his father's strict manner in literature and the arts, rebelling by studying classics and philosophy rather than sciences.

Early influences

Gadamer enrolled at the University of Breslau but, dissatisfied with the curriculum, moved to Marburg to study under Paul Natorp and Nicolai Hartmann, whose work on neo-Kantian philosophy was a key influence on his thinking. During his doctoral research, he came across the writings of the young Martin Heidegger, and after gaining his doctorate in 1922, moved to Freiburg University to study with Edmund Husserl and Heidegger himself – a rising star of the time. His studies were interrupted when he contracted polio in 1922; while convalescing, he married a friend of Hartmann's, Frida Katz.

When Heidegger was made a professor at Marburg, Gadamer followed soon after. The two became close friends, and while Heidegger was undoubtedly a formative influence, they did not always see eye to eye; Heidegger was unsure of Gadamer's competence, and suggested he concentrate on philology rather than philosophy, though he later revised his opinion and invited him to become his assistant.

With Heidegger's backing, Gadamer was offered a post teaching ethics and aesthetics at Marburg in 1929; he was working there when Hitler's National Socialists came to power. Unlike his mentor Heidegger, he resisted the pressure to join the party, but agreed to sign a declaration supporting them, and for a short time in 1934 taught at the Nazi-supporting University of Kiel. It is now generally accepted that he had little sympathy for the Nazi regime, and complied reluctantly because this allowed him to take on a professorship at Marburg in 1937, and then at Leipzig in 1939.

Excused military service because of his polio, he continued with his academic career at Leipzig during

World War II, and remained there when it became part of Soviet-controlled East Germany after the war. However, the communist authorities were critical of his work and in 1948 he left for the West, taking up posts first at Frankfurt and then Heidelberg, where he remained until his official retirement in 1968.

Philosophical hermeneutics

In the 1950s, while teaching at Heidelberg, he married again, and worked on his magnum opus, *Truth and Method* (1960), which established his academic reputation, especially after the translation into English appeared in 1975. In it, he set out his theory of philosophical hermeneutics, arguing that Being and consciousness should be interpreted in terms not of history and culture, but of language. language is essential to human understanding, in that if people do not have the language to express something, it does not exist.

△ **UNIVERSITY OF HEIDELBERG**
In 1949, Gadamer succeeded German existentialist philosopher Karl Jaspers as professor at Heidelberg. He retired and became professor emeritus in 1968, a position he held until his death in 2002 at the age of 102.

◁ **GADAMER AND HEIDEGGER**
Hans-Georg Gadamer (left) saws wood with his friend and mentor Martin Heidegger at Heidegger's mountain hut in Todtnauberg in the Black Forest.

IN CONTEXT
The Gadamer–Derrida debate

In the latter part of the 20th century, divisions between different branches of continental philosophy became more marked, especially between the French and German traditions. Gadamer, however, was keen to engage in debate with his French counterparts to identify common ground. This first came about in 1981, at a conference at the Sorbonne, with a famous debate between Gadamer and Jacques Derrida. Unfortunately, it was more confrontation than dialogue, and a subsequent meeting in Heidelberg in 2001 was equally unproductive. Despite their differences, there was a mutual respect, and Derrida expressed regret that Gadamer died before they had achieved a real dialogue.

"In truth **history** does **not belong** to **us** but rather **we** to **it.**"

HANS-GEORG GADAMER, *TRUTH AND METHOD*

Karl Popper

1902–1994, AUSTRIAN

In the 1930s, Popper made a major contribution to the understanding of scientific method. In his later political philosophy he argued against utopian ideological projects and in favour of a freely evolving "open society".

IN CONTEXT
The Einstein experiment

Physicist Albert Einstein's general theory of relativity, proposed in 1915, challenged the theories of Isaac Newton, which had been considered scientific truth since the 17th century. Einstein's theory made a number of predictions: among them was that gravity was a warp in the geometry of space-time, and that massive objects could therefore bend light beams. On 29 May 1919, astronomical observations of a total eclipse of the Sun that were conducted in Brazil and on the island of Principe off West Africa confirmed this prediction. The Newtonian version of the universe had to be revised. Popper was impressed that such a venerable theory as Newton's, apparently confirmed by experiments and observations over centuries, could still be tested and found wanting.

◁ **COMMUNIST DEMONSTRATION**
Popper was witness to the death of six demonstrators in Vienna's Hörlgasse. This display of political violence helped to shape his view of the world.

Karl Raimund Popper was born in 1902 in Vienna, then the capital of the multi-ethnic Austrian Empire. His parents, prosperous members of the Viennese upper middle class, were Jews who had converted to Protestantism and adopted the empire's dominant German culture. They raised their children in a belief in

◁ **KARL POPPER, 1987**
Popper retired from university teaching in 1969. He remained active as a writer and broadcaster until his death in 1994 as his theories – especially those relating to falsification – gradually fell out favour.

social progress based upon rationalist principles, and regarded national and ethnic identities as outdated barriers to human development. From the age of six Karl was sent to a "free school" that provided a liberal education.

These progressive aspirations were shattered by the outbreak of World War I in 1914. After four years of slaughter and hardship, the defeated Austrian Empire collapsed in chaos and Popper's parents lost most of their money to hyperinflation.

The 16-year-old Karl Popper initially reacted to the disintegration of the stable world of his childhood by

embracing revolution. In 1919 he worked in a lowly capacity for the nascent Austrian communist movement. When the communists made a failed attempt to seize power in Vienna in June, police fired on a crowd of protesters. Popper's reaction was to blame the communists for having carelessly sacrificed workers' lives in their pursuit of violent revolution; for the rest of his life he would advocate nonviolent democratic methods of achieving social change.

Career moves
As Austrian life returned to a precarious normality in the 1920s, Popper struggled to find a sense of direction. He flirted with the idea of becoming a classical musician, then served an apprenticeship to qualify as a cabinet maker, and finally trained as a schoolteacher. An interest in progressive school reform led him to study cognitive psychology at the University of Vienna, and it was there that he began working out his distinctive views on scientific method.

ALBERT EINSTEIN, ERICH BÜTTNER, 1917

"...the **attempt** to make **heaven** on **earth** invariably produces **hell**."

KARL POPPER, *THE OPEN SOCIETY AND ITS ENEMIES*

KEY WORKS

1934
Publishes (in German) his seminal *The Logic of Scientific Discovery*; it appears in English in 1959.

1945
Defends liberal democracy and critical rationalism against utopian dogmatists in *The Open Society and Its Enemies*.

1957
Criticizes the pursuit of grandiose schemes aimed at fulfilling historical destiny in *The Poverty of Historicism*.

1976
Unended Quest, Popper's intellectual autobiography, locates the origins of his ideas in different life experiences.

1977
Writes *The Self and Its Brain* together with neurophysiologist John Eccles.

△ **FREUD'S THEORIES**
Popper came to think that the pioneers of psychoanalysis, such as Sigmund Freud and Alfred Adler, constructed their theories in such ways that they could never be falsified. For this reason, he argued that psychoanalysis could not be considered a science.

By his own account, Popper had been struck by the contrast between true science and pseudo-scientific dogma as early 1919. Enthused by the observational confirmation of Albert Einstein's theory of relativity (see box, p.265), he contrasted it with the unverifiable assertions of the Marxist communists, whom he mixed with in Vienna. In the 1920s, briefly attracted by Sigmund Freud's theory of psychoanalysis, then at the peak of its prestige, he had been disappointed to discover its arbitrary, dogmatic character. But both Marxism and psychoanalysis claimed to be "scientific". What exactly was it that distinguished them from true science?

It was in 1930, after leaving the university and while employed as a teacher, that Popper worked out his ideas on science in detail in his first book, *The Two Fundamental Problems of the Theory of Knowledge*. He argued that the mark of a true scientific proposition or theory was not that evidence could be accumulated to prove it, but that evidence could potentially be produced to falsify it – to prove it wrong.

Scientific method

The trouble with Marxism and psychoanalysis was not a lack of evidence supporting the theories, but that no possible evidence could show them to be untrue. For example, if one of Freud's patients killed themselves, or someone else, or no one, these outcomes would have no effect on the truth or falsehood of psychoanalytic theory. In true science, once a theory was advanced, scientists repeatedly mounted experiments to test it, trying to prove it wrong. If it was a robust theory it would survive – but always provisionally, always open to criticism and revision. Popper's book was not published but it attracted interest from the prestigious Vienna Circle of scientists and philosophers (see box, left). Their influence allowed him to publish a condensed version of the text as *The Logic of Scientific Discovery* in 1934.

At this time Popper was building a solid position in life. Married to Josefine Henninger, whom he met while training as a teacher, he was gaining an academic reputation as a philosopher of science. But political turmoil ruined any prospect of stability. The Austrian Republic, which had replaced the empire, had proved unstable and parliamentary government was replaced by a right-wing dictatorship in 1932. Two years later the socialist movement in Vienna was crushed by the army. Adolf Hitler had come to power in neighbouring Germany, the Nazi Party was increasingly strong in Austria, and antisemitism was on the rise.

In 1937 Popper found an escape from the gathering storm by taking a post as a lecturer at the University of Canterbury in New Zealand. The year after he emigrated, Hitler took over Austria in the Anschluss (literally meaning "the joining").

Dangerous utopias

The following years were grim for a man of Popper's liberal rationalist views. He and his wife decided not to have children, believing that the world at that time was too awful a place in which to raise them. Although he was protected from the effects of World War II and the Holocaust in remote New Zealand, the political debacle in Europe obsessed his thoughts. Working throughout the war on the book that became *The Open Society*

IN CONTEXT
The Vienna Circle

The Vienna Circle was a group of scientists and philosophers formed in the 1920s to discuss the theoretical bases of science and scientific method. The group was led by Moritz Schlick and its key members included Otto Neurath and Rudolf Carnap. Under Carnap's influence they largely embraced logical positivism, the belief that the only meaningful statements were those that could be confirmed by empirical evidence. Popper was associated with the Circle in the early 1930s, but was not a logical positivist. Schlick was murdered in 1936 and the Circle broke up as most of its members fled abroad to escape Nazism.

MORITZ SCHLICK, 1930

◁ **VIENNA DURING THE ASCHLUSS**
Nazi soldiers parade through the streets of Vienna during the Anschluss. The annexation of Austria in 1938 forced Popper into permanent exile and prompted him to focus his work more on social and political philosophy.

he attacked the idea of historical inevitability (the notion that there exist "laws" of change that dictate history) which he saw as being used by ideologists to justify oppressive projects of social transformation.

Popper's political views gained prominence in the context of the Cold War confrontation between the US-led "Free World" and Soviet communism, which reached its height in the 1950s. As a philosopher supportive of liberal democracy and critical of Marxism, his work was often cited in support of the Western democracies. This brought him under attack from left-wing intellectuals who denounced him as an apologist for capitalism and imperialism.

Popper showed no interest in the rise of identity politics from the 1960s. True to his parents' principles of universal humanitarianism, he did not commit on specifically Jewish issues. *The Poverty of Historicism* was typically dedicated to "the countless men and women of all creeds or nations or races who fell victim to the fascist and communist belief in inexorable Laws of Historical Destiny".

Popper retired from academic life in 1969 but continued to work at philosophy. His final book, *The Self and Its Brain*, was a bold attempt to resolve the age-old problems of free will and of the relation between the mind and the body in a scientific evolutionary perspective. Popper died in Surrey in 1994, aged 92. He was buried alongside his wife in Vienna.

△ **CRITIQUE OF HISTORICISM**
According to Popper's ideas, a knowledge of natural laws allows scientists to predict events such as eclipses, but it does not follow that social scientists can formulate historical laws to predict events such as political change.

and Its Enemies, Popper set out to connect his thinking on scientific method to the lessons he had learned from observing the rise of fascism and communism between the wars. He argued that liberal democracy was the equivalent in political terms of correct scientific method, because it allowed progress through rational criticism and the constant testing of ideas against outcomes. He contrasted this with the utopian tradition that

he traced from Plato to Marx, in which an ideal society is dogmatically posited as a goal and any deviation from that ideal is suppressed.

Political philosophy

After the war Popper was offered, and accepted, a post at the London School of Economics and settled in Britain for the rest of his life. Revisiting political philosophy in his 1957 book *The Poverty of Historicism*,

"You cannot have a **rational discussion** with a man who **prefers shooting you** to being **convinced by you**. "

KARL POPPER, *UTOPIA AND VIOLENCE*

Theodor Adorno

1903–1969, GERMAN

Adorno is associated with the theoretical approach known as "critical theory". As well as a cultural critic, he was also a composer and musician with a strong interest in aesthetics.

◁ **KAISERSTRASSE, FRANKFURT**
This bustling scene shows Frankfurt in 1903 – the year of Adorno's birth. The city had been home to a thriving Jewish community since the 12th century. Hitler's ascendency forced many Jews, including Adorno, to flee the city.

Adorno's interests were broad. He was deeply concerned with questions of aesthetics, and was also interested in the application of Marxist thought to cultural criticism. His thesis for his *habilitation* certificate (a requirement for university teaching), which he presented in 1931, focused on the aesthetics of Søren Kierkegaard.

Frankfurt, Oxford, the US

After returning to Frankfurt, Adorno became involved in the Institute for Social Research, which was under the directorship of Max Horkheimer (see box, right). The institute was a semi-independent research centre affiliated with the university and it became the hub for what was later known as the Frankfurt School (see p.259). Initially Marxist in focus, the institute saw the task of philosophy as that of critiquing the society and culture in which it found itself.

In 1934, following Hitler's rise to power, Adorno left Germany for the UK, where he took up a post

Theodor Adorno was born Theodor Ludwig Wiesengrund in Frankfurt am Main in 1903. He later adopted the surname "Adorno". His mother, an excellent singer, was a Catholic from Corsica, and his father made a living as a wine exporter, and was a Jewish convert to Protestantism. Adorno's family background was comfortable

◁ **THEODOR ADORNO, 1958**
Adorno is shown here in his mid-fifties, a few years after returning to his home town of Frankfurt, having lived overseas for some 15 years. He then remained in Frankfurt until his death in 1969.

and relatively affluent. Influenced by his mother, he grew up playing the piano and had a tremendous talent for the instrument. He wanted to become a composer; but he also had a passion for philosophy, and it was this discipline that finally took up most of his attention.

Adorno was awarded his doctorate in philosophy from Goethe University, Frankfurt, in 1924. He then moved to Vienna to study music composition with the composer Alban Berg. After a period of travelling, he returned to Frankfurt, where his intention was to teach and write philosophy.

IN PROFILE
Max Horkheimer

The German Jewish philosopher and sociologist Max Horkheimer (1895–1975) collaborated with Adorno on several major projects, including the development of "critical theory", which he outlined in his 1937 paper "Traditional and Critical Theory". With Adorno, Habermas, Marcuse, and Benjamin, he shared a fundamental concern with Marxist critiques of capitalist societies. He was most famous for his work at the Frankfurt School (see p.259) and for *Dialectic of Enlightenment* (1944, with Adorno).

MAX HORKHEIMER, NEW YORK, 1960

> "The **paradise** offered by the **culture industry** is the **same old drudgery**."
>
> THEODOR ADORNO, *DIALECTIC OF ENLIGHTENMENT*

▷ **FAMILY VIEWING, 1957**
According to Adorno, when we sit in our living rooms mesmerized by our favourite television programmes, we not only become passive consumers, subject to the erosion of intelligence and meaningful thought, but we also run the risk of collaborating in our own oppression.

△ *LYRIC SUITE*
This is a handwritten score of the *Lyric Suite* by the composer Alban Maria Johannes Berg (1885–1935), who was Adorno's music tutor in Vienna.

at Oxford University. In the late 1930s he moved again, this time to the US, where he taught – first in New York and then in California.

He was heavily influenced by World War II and also by his own personal experiences of fascism. He focused extensively on authoritarianism, the role of art, music, mass culture, and the necessity of criticism within contemporary society. During this period of his life, he wrote a number of works that were eventually to secure his academic reputation, including *Dialectic of Enlightenment* (1944, with Max Horkheimer), *Philosophy of New Music* (1949), *The Authoritarian Personality* (1950, with others), and *Minima Moralia* (1951).

Adorno did not return to Germany again until 1949, when he began working with Horkheimer in re-establishing the Institute for Social Research, which reopened its doors two years later, in 1951.

Marx and the Enlightenment

Adorno is famous as a spokesman of "critical theory", a mode of thought that takes society as its object of study and draws on a range of disciplines (including art, philosophy, history, and literature) in its critique of social, political, and cultural institutions. This approach was inspired by Karl Marx's social and economic theories of capitalist production. Adorno is largely aligned with Marx in his critique of capitalism, but sees this as part of a larger problem with Enlightenment thinking in general.

It is often claimed that the thinkers of the Enlightenment (the 17th- and 18th-century European philosophical movement that prized logic and reason, and was associated with the Scientific Revolution) helped liberate us from the chains of religion and superstition. In the *Dialectic of Enlightenment*, however, Adorno and Horkheimer argue that although the Enlightenment claims to free us from fear, in fact "the wholly enlightened earth is radiant with triumphant calamity". Knowledge becomes a matter of mastery over the world by means of technology; and the knowledge-based societies in which we live are not concerned ultimately with liberation but with domination. In this way, Adorno and Horkheimer draw a direct line from Enlightenment ideas to the horrors of Nazi rule; mass culture becomes not a matter of what human beings collectively do to make meaning and give richness to their

" The **world** is not **just mad**. It is **mad** and **rational** as well. "

THEODOR ADORNO, *TOWARDS A NEW MANIFESTO?*

lives, nor an expression of the diversity of possibilities of human life, but an industrial complex that serves to make everything the same, and that renders us docile and passive.

Art and aesthetics

Adorno is arguably best known for his attack on the culture industry. Television, radio, and popular music have a narcotic effect upon us, he says; they annihilate intelligence, feeling, and active engagement in the world. In fact, we are so thoroughly immersed in our own oppression that not only can we not do anything about it, we are also unable even to see it.

This does not mean that Adorno opposes all forms of art. But he says that the role of art should not be to provide entertainment, enjoyment, or pleasure; instead it should be to disrupt, criticize, and unsettle. According to Adorno, art has the power to break with our desire for things to be easy, and to provoke reflection both on ourselves and on the world. When we engage with this kind of art, we go from being passive consumers to active subjects.

For Adorno, the composer who best exemplifies this is Arnold Schoenberg (see box, right), the teacher of Adorno's mentor, Alban Berg. Schoenberg wrote awkward, unsettling, difficult music with the

KEY WORKS

1936
Adorno's "On Jazz" considers jazz as a mass commodity and part of mass culture.

1944
In the *Dialectic of Enlightenment* Horkheimer and Adorno launch a ferocious attack on what they call "the culture industry".

1951
Adorno's *Minima Moralia* presents new perspectives on intelligence and morality.

1970
Aesthetic Theory is published posthumously. The dense work offers a definitive account of Adorno's thoughts.

capacity to make us re-evaluate the world around us. Adorno maintains that Schoenberg's music allows us to identify with "the terror of men in the agonies of death under total domination". In this way great art, Adorno says, can provoke in us the subjective response of "concern", a kind of tremor, whereby we lose our footing and can see new truths and possibilities, giving rise to the potential for a new kind of politics.

In the summer of 1969, in an attempt to restore his strength after a stressful few months working and travelling, Adorno left Frankfurt for the foothills of the Matterhorn in Zermatt, Switzerland. He died there of a heart attack on 6 August 1969.

Adorno's legacy

Adorno has had an immense influence on the development of 20th-century philosophy and cultural theory. His

arguments about the darker side of the Enlightenment remain important. However, he was also a controversial figure and his writing has often been criticized for being overly complex.

For Adorno, this complexity is not accidental: in writing, as in music, he insists that difficulty has an important role to play because it requires us to actively engage with thinking rather than to be passive consumers, a claim that has laid him open to charges of elitism and intellectualism. He was, for example, famously disapproving of jazz, which he saw as a part of the mass culture that he critiqued so fiercely. However, it has often been argued that far from being conformist, jazz is frequently "tremor-inducing" and disruptive: not necessarily the disruption of Adorno's high seriousness, but of generating irrepressible energy and joy in the face of forces that seek to repress joy.

IN PROFILE
Arnold Schoenberg

The composer Arnold Schoenberg (1874–1951) was a major figure for Adorno. He is associated with what is known as "12-tone music", which aims to give equal weight to all 12 tones of the chromatic music scale. Schoenberg was also a teacher, a writer, and a painter who exhibited alongside artists such as Kandinsky. As a result of this breadth of interests, he stands at the meeting-place of music, the arts, and Modernist theory.

PORTRAIT OF ARNOLD SCHOENBERG, EGON SCHIELE, 1917

◁ **JAZZ MUSICIANS, 1943**
Duke Ellington (piano), Dizzy Gillespie (trumpet, front row, centre), behind him Mezz Mezzrow (clarinet), and other jazz musicians playing in the studio of the photographer Gjon Mili. Adorno considered jazz to be popular music and therefore part of the culture industry that helps sustain capitalism and oppress the people.

Jean-Paul Sartre

1905–1980, FRENCH

Existentialist philosopher, novelist, playwright, and political activist, Sartre believed that humans were "condemned to be free". He spent his life and work grappling with the ideas of freedom and action.

Jean-Paul Sartre was born into a middle-class Parisian family. His father, a naval officer, died of yellow fever before Jean-Paul's second birthday; his mother then moved to her parents' house. His grandfather, Charles Schweitzer, a respected intellectual, tutored him at home and introduced him to classical literature.

When Sartre was 12, his mother remarried and the family moved to La Rochelle on France's Atlantic coast. He was bullied at the city's lycée, and so transferred to a school in Paris. He excelled in his studies and in 1924 was accepted into the Ecole Normale Supérieure, one of France's most prestigious universities, where he gained a reputation as much for his practical jokes as for his prodigious intellectual abilities.

It was in Paris, while preparing to qualify as a philosophy teacher, that he met Simone de Beauvoir. She would become his life companion – his "necessary love", the woman he was committed to beyond all others, despite the famous open relationship that the couple cultivated in a challenge to "bourgeois" convention.

After carrying out his military service from 1929 to 1931, Sartre spent the next 14 years teaching philosophy at various high schools. During a year's study at the French

IN PROFILE
Albert Camus

Algerian-born French writer and thinker Albert Camus (1913–1960) met Sartre in Paris in 1943 and the two forged a close friendship, which lasted until they fell out in 1951 over their opposing views on communism. Although he rejected the label of existentialism, Camus explored many of the same themes, such as individual freedom and the futile, or "absurd", attempt to find meaning in a meaningless world. His 1946 novel *The Stranger* **(or** *The Outsider***) is a brilliant study of 20th-century alienation, while in the essay** *The Myth of Sisyphus* **(1956) he analyses the nihilism prevalent in postwar thought.**

ALBERT CAMUS OUTSIDE HIS PUBLISHER'S OFFICE IN PARIS, 1955

Academy in Berlin (1933–34) he was introduced to the phenomenological philosophy of Edmund Husserl (see p.228), which would have a huge impact on his own thought.

Existentialist writing

In 1938, Sartre published his first novel, *Nausea*, a philosophical and partially autobiographical work influenced by Phenomenology (the study of objects as we consciously experience them). The book's protagonist, Roquentin, is filled with despair, overcome with nausea as the meaninglessness of existence reveals itself. This is the human condition of freedom to which, in his existentialist philosophy, Sartre believes we are condemned and that can be relieved only by taking responsibility for our own existence. Often seen as a manifesto for existentialism, *Nausea* is the first substantial work in which Sartre expressed many of the ideas that would recur in his later writing.

▷ **SARTRE AT THE DOME**
The Dome café in Montparnasse, Paris, was a favourite haunt of Sartre's, who would spend many hours at a time writing there. When he moved from Montparnasse to St Germain-des-Prés, he decamped to another now-famous venue, Café de Flore.

"**Hell** is *other* people."
JEAN-PAUL SARTRE, *NO EXIT*

KEY WORKS

1938
Sartre publishes his first novel, *Nausea*, which presents his existentialist philosophy in fictional form.

1943
The monumental *Being and Nothingness* is published, his most important philosophical work.

1944
Stages *No Exit*, a play depicting an existentialist version of hell, which ends with the famous words "Hell is other people".

1945
The Age of Reason and *The Reprieve* are the first two volumes in what was to have been a four-volume work communicating his ethical message.

1948
In the play *Dirty Hands*, Sartre investigates the motives for a crime that could be personal or political.

1960
Publishes *Critique of Dialectical Reason*, in which he attempts to reconcile Marxist and existentialist views.

1968
Arrested for civil disobedience during the May uprisings in Paris, and immediately pardoned by President Charles de Gaulle.

Sartre was drafted into the French army shortly after the onset of World War II, and in 1940 was captured by the Germans. His experience in a prison camp affected him profoundly, leading to his political awakening; while his early writing had concentrated on ideas of individual freedom, his later works gave more emphasis to social responsibility and political commitment.

In 1941 Sartre was released on health grounds and was given a teaching position in Paris, which he held until the end of the war. He became involved in the Resistance, but after the failure of his underground group, he decided that his pen was his best tool. In 1943, he wrote *The Flies*, a drama based on the myth of Electra. The play escaped the German censors by using the symbolism of Greek mythology to cloak its message of resistance against oppression – as well as incorporating the existentialist themes of freedom and responsibility. On the opening night, Sartre met Albert Camus, who recruited him to a Resistance group, Combat. Sartre began contributing articles to the clandestine journal of the same name.

Taking responsibility

In the same year, Sartre published his great work, *Being and Nothingness*. In this monumental treatise, he turned the traditional philosophical idea that "essence precedes existence" on its head, espousing the concept that "existence precedes essence". He extolled the importance of free choice, which makes its own burden because it brings responsibility, condemning man to create his own meaning in a meaningless existence.

Central to Sartre's thought in this work are two contrasting modes of being: "for-itself" (*pour-soi*), essentially understood as consciousness; and "in-itself" (*en-soi*), or the world of ordinary things. Another key idea is the concept of "the Other", through which an individual's consciousness of self is made concrete. He further explored the idea of the Other in the one-act play *No Exit* (*Huis Clos*), staged in Paris in May 1944.

Political engagement

Following the liberation of Paris in 1944, Sartre wrote *Anti-Semite and Jew*, an attempt to analyse the origins of hate. After the war, he gave up teaching and concentrated on activism and writing. He believed that writers should be engaged with the world and that they should not evade political, social, and moral responsibility.

In 1945, he founded *Modern Times*, a magazine that set out to provide a forum for existentialist literature – works that were socially useful as well as culturally valuable. The magazine was an outlet for Sartre's works, together with those by other prominent writers, such as Simone de Beauvoir, philosopher Raymond

IN CONTEXT
The Theatre of the Absurd

Existentialist views as expressed by Sartre and Camus (see box, p.272) lay at the basis of a new kind of theatre that rose to prominence in Paris in the 1950s. The works of such playwrights as Samuel Beckett, Jean Genet, and Eugène Ionesco abandoned traditional dramatic structure and logical stories in favour of anti-realistic situations, non-linear or entirely absent plots, and baffled-seeming, purposeless characters who are often confused about their own identity. Beckett's famous *Waiting for Godot* (1956) is the seminal Absurdist play, the plight of its two endlessly, hopelessly waiting characters Vladimir and Estragon exemplifying the essential precariousness and futility of existence.

PRODUCTION OF *WAITING FOR GODOT* IN PARIS, JUNE 1956

◁ **CHE GUEVARA**
In 1960 Sartre travelled with Simone de Beauvoir to Cuba, where he met Fidel Castro and Che Guevara, declaring the latter to be the "most complete human being of our age".

Aron, Jean Genet, and Samuel Beckett. Meanwhile, the lecture *Existentialism Is a Humanism*, published in 1946 in essay form, consolidated Sartre's standing as a public intellectual.

In 1945 Sartre published *The Age of Reason* and *The Reprieve*, the first two volumes of the trilogy *The Roads to Freedom*. The third volume, *Troubled Sleep* (also translated as *Iron in the Soul*) was published in 1948. Partly autobiographical, the trilogy uses fiction to explore philosophical themes of freedom, responsibility, authenticity, and self-deception, and demonstrates the shift of Sartre's focus on to the importance of action and engagement.

Stage work

Relinquishing the novel as a useful tool of expression, Sartre turned back to the medium of drama in an attempt to portray man as he is, exploring political commitment in the play *Dirty Hands* (1948). A Marxist himself, Sartre supported the Soviet Union, though he never joined the Communist Party. His commitment to Soviet communism was shaken by the

▷ **A VOICE OF PROTEST, 1971**
Sartre spoke out against US involvement in Vietnam and the Soviet suppression of the Prague Spring, and campaigned for the rights of Palestinians.

regime's invasion of Hungary in 1956 and by its human rights abuses and oppression of writers. Yet he came to regard Marxism as "the philosophy of our time", and in 1960 published *Critique of Dialectical Reason*, an attempt to reconcile Marxism and existentialism. The book has been viewed by some as his repudiation of his earlier views, while others see it as a continuation of his original thought.

Later years

Sartre remained politically active in his later years, opposing antisemitism and colonialism, and campaigning against French rule in Algeria – which led to a bomb attack against him in 1961. He remained an ardent supporter of often radical left-wing causes, including the May 1968 uprisings in France.

In 1964 Sartre was awarded the Nobel Prize in Literature, but he refused the honour, not wishing to be "turned into an institution", and telling the press that he feared the award would limit the impact of his writing. That same year, he published his brilliant, witty autobiography of his childhood, *The Words*.

With his eyesight failing, Sartre gave up his writing in the mid-1970s, leaving unfinished a biography of Flaubert that he had begun in the 1960s. After his death in 1980, more than 50,000 people turned out to accompany his funeral cortege through the streets of Paris.

△ **DIRTY HANDS, 1948**
In the play *Dirty Hands* (*Les Mains Sales*), Sartre explored political commitment, and in particular the use of political violence in revolutionary action.

> " In **life man commits himself** and **draws** his **own portrait, outside** of which there is **nothing**. "

JEAN-PAUL SARTRE, *EXISTENTIALISM IS A HUMANISM*

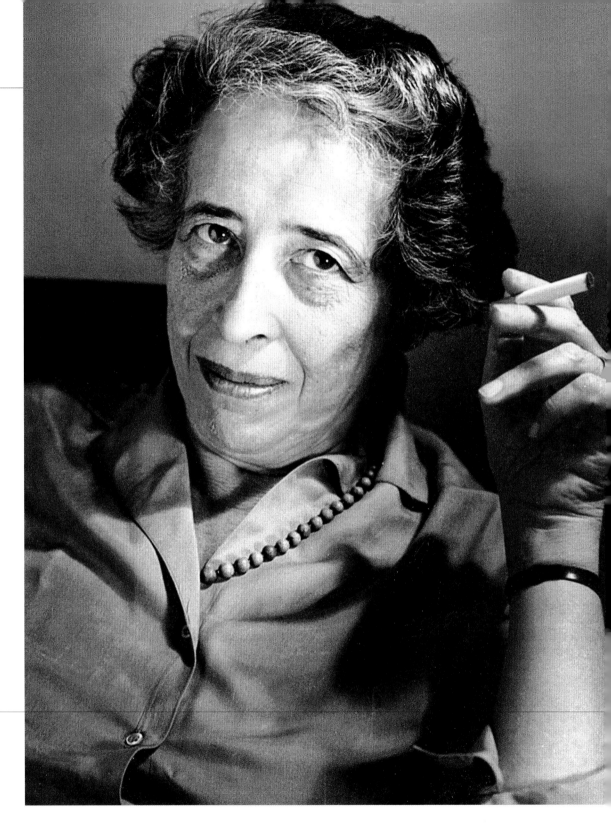

▷ **HANNAH ARENDT, 1963**
Arendt was a divisive figure in the
Jewish diaspora. Many of her friends
felt betrayed by what they saw as her
implication that Europe's Jews had
been partly to blame for the magnitude
of the Holocaust during World War II.

Hannah Arendt

1906–1975, GERMAN

With first-hand experience of Nazism and the antisemitism it espoused,
Arendt developed a unique perspective on the nature of political power
and moral judgement, the basis of her controversial philosophical writing.

"The **sad truth** of the matter is that **most evil** is done by **people** who **never** made up their **minds** to be or do **either evil** or **good**."

HANNAH ARENDT, *THE LIFE OF THE MIND*

Both of Hannah Arendt's parents' families had settled in the Prussian city of Königsberg (now Russian Kaliningrad) in the mid-19th century, after seeking a refuge from the antisemitism that was rife in Russia. Königsberg attracted many Jewish refugee families who established themselves as merchants, and as they prospered became assimilated into the city's middle class. As a result, Königsberg became a centre of the so-called Jewish Enlightenment, the *Haskalah*, led by mainly secular Jewish intellectuals who sought integration into European society.

This was very much the cultural atmosphere of the Arendt family when Hannah was born in 1906, in Linden, where her mother's family, the Cohns,

had a tea-importing business. At this time some Jews were advocating Zionism – the formation of a separate homeland for the Jewish people – as a solution to the "Jewish Problem" (a widespread debate about the appropriate status and treatment of Jews in society). However, the Arendts had become thoroughly "Germanized", and saw assimilation as the way to counter antisemitism.

Return to Königsberg

Owing to his failing health, Hannah's father moved the family back to his native Königsberg in 1909, and after a battle with syphilis he died in 1913. Now only seven, Hannah was brought up by her mother and grandparents, surrounded by the cultural and

intellectual society of Königsberg. This was the city where Kant had spent almost all of his life, and young Hannah soon became fascinated by philosophy. Her education in Königsberg was interrupted briefly at the outbreak of World War I, when she and her mother stayed with an aunt in Berlin. She resumed her studies at school, but was expelled for boycotting one of the teachers. In 1924 Arendt went to Marburg University, where she studied classical languages, Protestant theology, and philosophy.

Affair with Heidegger

It was at Marburg that Arendt met Martin Heidegger, one of her tutors, who had a lasting influence on her philosophy. She also became his lover.

IN CONTEXT

20th-century totalitarianism

Tyrants have existed throughout history, but the 20th century saw the rise of a number of specifically totalitarian regimes, characterized by extreme nationalism and the exercise of political power over every aspect of the state. Various authoritarian ideologies emerged at either end of the political spectrum: Hitler's Nazism and Mussolini's fascism grew from nationalist socialist movements, but became dictatorships. Similarly, Stalin and Mao rose to power on the back of communist revolutions, and more recently North Korea has been ruled by the totalitarian Kim dynasty.

◁ **KÖNIGSBERG, c.1900**
Arendt was raised largely in the culturally diverse city of Königsberg, East Prussia, which by the beginning of World War II had a population of 250,000, including a high percentage of Jews.

KEY WORKS

1929
Publishes her doctoral thesis, *Love and Saint Augustine*.

1933
Publishes part of her biography of Rahel Varnhagen in the daily paper *Kölnische Zeitung*, and later in the periodical *Jüdische Rundschau*.

1944
Begins work on what will become her first major book, *The Origins of Totalitarianism*.

1958
Publishes her most influential book, *The Human Condition*, and the completed biography *Rahel Varnhagen: The Life of a Jewess*.

1963
Her commentary on the 1961 Eichmann trial is published in the *New Yorker*, and later as a book.

△ **RAHEL VARNHAGEN**
The writer Rahel Varnhagen was one of the first Jewish women to make her presence felt in German intellectual society, running a salon in Berlin. Arendt identified closely with Varnhagen, even though the two never met, Varnhagen having died in 1833.

Because Heidegger was married, this was a secret affair, but Arendt later had another reason to prevent it from becoming public: when Hitler came to power in 1933, Heidegger declared his support for the Nazi Party – a shock for Arendt, but also potentially very damaging to her career. After a year at Marburg, she moved to Freiburg University to study with Edmund Husserl, and from there to Heidelberg, where she completed her degree under Karl Jaspers in 1929, and met and married the philosopher Gunther Stern, a German Jew. At this time, Arendt turned her attention to writing a biography of Rahel Varnhagen (a 19th-century Russian Jew), a work through which she could explore her ideas of Jewish assimilation.

Arrest and flight
Arendt's work was interrupted by the rise of Nazism, and in 1933 Stern, a communist activist, fled Germany. As a Jew, it was impossible for Arendt to get an academic appointment, and her research into antisemitism and assimilation for the German Zionist Association soon came to the attention of the authorities. She and her mother were arrested by the Gestapo, but released after eight days.

The time had come for Arendt to leave Germany too. She lived briefly in Czechoslovakia and Switzerland

before joining Stern in Paris. Her ideas of assimilation had been shaken by her experience of Nazi antisemitism, and while in Paris she worked for the Zionist organization Youth Aliyah, which helped to send Jewish orphans, especially those from Austria and Czechoslovakia, to Palestine, then under British control. As a prominent member of the Jewish community in Paris, she came into contact with Heinrich Blücher, a German émigré philosopher who had been a founding member of the German Communist Party, and in 1937 she began divorce proceedings in order to marry him.

Internment and escape
As war loomed in 1939, it became increasingly likely that Hitler would invade France, and in the following year, the French government began to round up "enemy aliens". Although she had been stripped of her German citizenship in 1937, Arendt fell into this category, and was sent to Camp Gurs, in the south-west of France, a camp originally set up to hold Republican refugees from Spain. Blücher was interned separately in a camp near Paris. Arendt did not miss the irony of the situation, as a Jew facing either a German concentration camp or a French internment camp. As expected, the Nazi invasion of France came soon after, and the movement of internees

around the country offered both her and Heinrich the chance to escape into Spain, and from there to make their way to the US.

New York had become a haven for European Jews, and Arendt and Blücher quickly became involved with the Jewish community there. Heinrich found teaching work at Bard College, while Hannah continued her research into antisemitism, earning a living writing for German-language journals for the émigré Jewish population. She was also an active campaigner for Jewish rights, and after the war worked as director of the Commission for European Jewish Cultural Reconstruction. At last having found a place where she could live and work, she became a US citizen in 1950.

Prolific writing
Through her work as an editor at Schocken Books, Arendt found a publisher for her books, and began her writing career in earnest in 1944. The first of her major works, *The Origins of Totalitarianism*, was published in 1951, and its study of this peculiarly modern phenomenon established her as one of the foremost political philosophers of her generation.

The 1950s were an extraordinarily productive time for Arendt. She took temporary teaching posts at several universities, but never compromised

> " It is **well known** that the most **radical revolutionary** will become **a conservative** the **day after** the **revolution.** "

HANNAH ARENDT, *NEW YORKER* INTERVIEW

"The **concentration camps**, by making **death** itself **anonymous**... **robbed death** of its **meaning** as the end of a fulfilled life."

HANNAH ARENDT, *THE ORIGINS OF TOTALITARIANISM*

her writing career for the life of an academic. Her most influential book, *The Human Condition*, appeared in 1958, and in the same year she published the finished version of her biography, entitled *Rahel Varnhagen: The Life of a Jewess*.

During this time, Arendt developed her own philosophical ideas, but these were much influenced by her earlier teachers, Jaspers and Heidegger.

Despite her painful affair, and the disillusionment with his involvement with the Nazis, she made contact with Heidegger again, and it is rumoured that they resumed their relationship. Arendt also publicly dismissed criticism of Heidegger's Nazi connections, describing him as weak and naive, but not evil – which did not help her reputation in the Jewish community.

The banality of evil

Arendt's standing as a philosopher was already in question (among Jews at least) when in 1961 she was commissioned by the *New Yorker* to report on the trial in Jerusalem of Adolf Eichmann (see box, right). Her reports were published in book form in 1963, as *Eichmann in Jerusalem: A Report on the Banality of Evil*. The work provoked a storm of protest. Her portrayal of Eichmann as dull-witted, unimaginative, and almost automaton-like, rather than the monster he had been presumed to be, was widely interpreted as a betrayal of the suffering of the Jews in the Holocaust, as her defence of Heidegger had been.

Anatomy of atrocity

Arendt's concept of the "banality of evil" gave a philosophical insight into what makes apparently ordinary people capable of acts of appalling atrocity. It influenced psychological research into the phenomenon, such as Stanley Milgram's experiment in which subjects were asked to deliver electric shock punishments to others in a test of their obedience to authority versus their personal conscience.

The 1960s saw the publication of Arendt's last major work, *On Revolution* (1963), and she soon began to concentrate more on her teaching and campaigning activities. A heavy smoker all her life, she died of a heart attack in 1975 in New York.

IN PROFILE
Adolf Eichmann

Adolf Eichmann joined the Nazi Party and the Schutzstaffel (SS) in 1933, the year Hitler came to power. He was given a job in the Security Service, and became head of the department for Jewish affairs, responsible for the isolation of Jews into ghettoes in the major cities. After the outbreak of World War II, his department's brief changed from segregation and deportation to transportation to extermination camps, and Eichmann became a leading architect of the Holocaust. After the war, he fled to Argentina, but was captured by Mossad agents in 1960 and taken to Jerusalem to stand trial. He was hanged on 1 June 1962.

ARENDT'S *EICHMANN IN JERUSALEM, A REPORT ON THE BANALITY OF EVIL*

◁ **NAZI TRIAL**
A leading architect of the Holocaust, Eichmann stands in a protective glass booth flanked by Israeli police during his trial on 21 April 1961, in Jerusalem.

Simone de Beauvoir

1908–1986, FRENCH

Novelist, essayist, and existential philosopher, de Beauvoir was revered for her groundbreaking analyses of patriarchy and gender and had a major influence on feminist theory, ethics, and politics in the 20th century.

Simone de Beauvoir's most famous and controversial work, *The Second Sex*, was published in 1949 to a largely hostile audience. The radical text sparked outrage for its challenging and unflinching engagement with patriarchy, gender, subordination, and female sexuality – all of which seemed to act as indicators of the author's monstrosity: "I was everything, even an unmarried mother," said de Beauvoir in her memoirs. "Unsatisfied, cold, priapic, nymphomaniac, lesbian, a hundred times aborted."

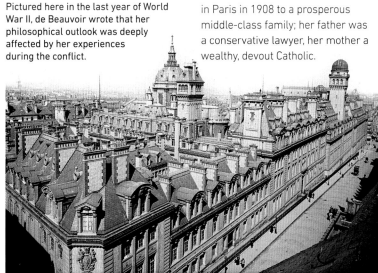

◁ **SIMONE DE BEAUVOIR, 1945**
Pictured here in the last year of World War II, de Beauvoir wrote that her philosophical outlook was deeply affected by her experiences during the conflict.

The threats posed by the text were reflected by those (including Albert Camus) who railed against its contempt for the French male and by its addition to the Vatican's list of forbidden books. Nonetheless, the text sold 22,000 copies in its first week of publication. It was later recognized as a key work of feminist theory that formed the basis of the "second wave" feminism of the 1960s to 1980s, placing its author as one of France's most admired thinkers.

Early influences
Simone Lucie Ernestine Marie Bertrand de Beauvoir was born in Paris in 1908 to a prosperous middle-class family; her father was a conservative lawyer, her mother a wealthy, devout Catholic.

De Beauvoir jettisoned her bourgeois upbringing early in life, announcing her atheism at the age of 14 and, soon after, her interest in philosophy and in books deemed unsuitable for girls. At school she formed a deep friendship with Elizabeth Mabille, or Zaza, who died in 1929, apparently from meningitis – de Beauvoir claimed it was from a broken heart, following her family's attempt to impose an arranged marriage on her.

The memory of Zaza had a lifelong impact on de Beauvoir, in particular shaping her ideas surrounding the bourgeois attitudes to women. At the age of 19, she wrote in her diary "I don't want my life to obey any other will but my own" – and this was to remain her clarion call.

Teaching and scandal
Following World War I, by the 1920s the family faced financial ruin and it became clear that de Beauvoir would need to secure her own future. Wanting to become a teacher and writer, in 1926 she began studying at the Sorbonne in Paris, where she

◁ **THE SORBONNE, PARIS**
De Beauvoir was one of the first women to graduate from the Sorbonne. There, she mixed with a clique of students that included Sartre and Paul Nizan.

IN CONTEXT
Les Temps Modernes

In 1945 de Beauvoir and Sartre, along with philosophers such as Maurice Merleau-Ponty and Raymond Aron, launched the left-wing journal *Les Temps Modernes*, which became a forum for cultural and political debate. Its initial stated aim was to publish "engaged literature": de Beauvoir's *The Second Sex* appeared in the journal, as did contributions from other notable writers, including Jean Genet and Samuel Beckett. De Beauvoir acted as the journal's editor and also contributed articles on a wide range of themes. The magazine continues to inform on cultural and political issues throughout the world.

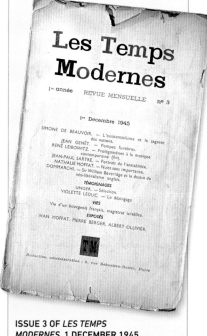

ISSUE 3 OF *LES TEMPS MODERNES*, 1 DECEMBER 1945

> "I don't want **my life** to **obey any other will** but **my own.**"
>
> SIMONE DE BEAUVOIR, DIARY

Novels and essays

De Beauvoir's first novel, which she had started in 1937 and described as a metaphysical novel, appeared at the end of the same year as the sex scandal. *She Came to Stay* tells the story of an ultimately disastrous love triangle between a man and two young women, and is often interpreted as a fictional reworking of the sexual trios that de Beauvoir and Sartre indulged in. Like so many of her fictional works, the text engages with philosophical themes – in this case, desire, otherness, and bad faith.

The book brought public recognition and was followed by a string of notable publications, including *Pyrrhus and Cineas* (1944), her first full-blown philosophical essay, and *The Blood of Others* (1945), which was hailed as a leading existential novel of the French Resistance. In 1945, de Beauvoir cofounded the journal *Les Temps Modernes* (see box, p. 281); two years later, when she had begun lecturing in the US, she recorded some of her observations and experiences in her travel diary, *America Day by Day* – and also published *The Ethics of Ambiguity*, her most detailed exploration of the issues surrounding freedom, ethics, and responsibility.

Gender and sexuality

These and other existentialist themes reappeared, combined with feminist theory, in *The Second Sex*, which affirms that woman "is the incidental, the inessential, as opposed to the essential," whereas man "is the Subject... the Absolute – she is the Other". Crucially, it perceives gender not as innate and determined by nature, but as socially and culturally

IN PROFILE
Sartre and de Beauvoir

De Beauvoir's lifelong relationship with the existentialist philosopher Jean-Paul Sartre is legendary. The couple met in their early 20s and became immersed in one another's lives and work. Although many of de Beauvoir's insights were themselves groundbreaking, for decades she was often unfairly relegated as Sartre's disciple – a label that, bizarrely enough, she seemed to fully endorse. The high-profile, glamorous couple attracted immense public scrutiny. Their relationship, according to de Beauvoir herself, was particularly notable for its "freedom, intimacy, and frankness": they had numerous affairs and never lived together or married (she viewed marriage as a desperately oppressive institution, for men and women), but were nevertheless devoted to one another. They are buried together at Montparnasse Cemetery in Paris.

SARTRE AND DE BEAUVOIR IN 1980, THE YEAR OF SARTRE'S DEATH

met her lifelong partner, Jean-Paul Sartre (see box, above). Three years later, having finished her thesis on Leibniz, she became the youngest student ever to pass the *agrégation*, France's prestigious exams to recruit secondary-school teachers. The qualification gave her tenure to teach philosophy – and from 1931, in Marseilles, Rouen, and Paris, this is what she did. However, her certificate was revoked in 1943 after she, with Sartre, seduced a female student (the couple often shared female lovers).

De Beauvoir showed no interest in having children, material possessions, or the trappings of bourgeois decency; for many years, she lived mostly in cheap hotels or lodging houses and,

like other Parisian intellectuals, frequented the capital's vibrant cafés, where she and Sartre could be found – often at separate tables – engrossed in work.

After the scandal in 1943, she did not return to teaching, but focused instead on her writing. Her major influences included Heidegger, Husserl, Marx, Engels, Kant, and Hegel, along with the leading French social and philosophical thinkers, from Rousseau, Descartes, and Bergson up to Camus and Sartre, the latter being immensely influential in the development of her oeuvre. In fiction, she admired, among many others, Kafka, Proust, Joyce, Hemingway, the Brontës, George Eliot, and Woolf.

△ **THE SECOND SEX**
In her 1949 work, de Beauvoir dissected the established sexual order at a time when French women had no legal access to birth control and had only just won the right to vote.

KEY WORKS

1926	1943	1947	1949	1954	1981
Begins her studies at the Sorbonne in Paris, where she meets Jean-Paul Sartre.	Publishes her first novel, *She Came to Stay*, an exploration of an ill-fated ménage à trois.	*The Ethics of Ambiguity* is published, drawing on Sartrean existentialism.	*The Second Sex* is initially vilified as a violation of human decency but later acclaimed as a major contribution to philosophy.	Receives the Prix Goncourt, France's most prestigious literary honour, for *Les Mandarins*.	*Adieux: A Farewell to Sartre*, published the year after Sartre's death, is a mournful narrative of the philosopher's final years.

" **One** is **not born**, but rather **becomes, a woman**. "

SIMONE DE BEAUVOIR, *THE SECOND SEX*

△ **LES MANDARINS**
De Beauvoir's book claimed France's prestigious literary award, the Prix Goncourt, in 1954. Previous recipients of the prize include Marcel Proust and André Malraux.

▽ **ABORTION RIGHTS MARCH**
De Beauvoir campaigned for abortion rights in France in the 1970s. She signed the "Manifesto of the 343", a document in which she admitted to having had an abortion – an act that could have led to her prosecution.

constructed – a proposition that gave rise to a massive reappraisal of the role of gender and sexuality in society by theorists such as Judith Butler and Michel Foucault. But it was the publication of her novel *Les Mandarins* in 1954 that brought de Beauvoir international acclaim and the prestigious Prix Goncourt for her vivid depiction of a group of French intellectuals, often thought to be Sartre, Camus, and the author herself.

Later works

In 1960 de Beauvoir met 17-year-old Sylvie Le Bon, a woman 35 years her junior, whom she adopted in 1980 and who remained a lifelong companion and, eventually, her literary executor. The author's later life also saw the publication of several autobiographies, more fictional works, and her much-lauded exploration of the plight of the elderly, *Old Age* (1970), in many ways a companion text to *The Second Sex*.

Always a campaigner for equality and justice – as in her outspoken opposition to the Algerian War (1954–62) – her political activism increased as she got older. She was, for example, president of the League for the Rights of Women – which focused on discrimination against women – and of *Choisir*, a pressure group for abortion reform.

The death of Sartre in 1980 left de Beauvoir grief-stricken; she published *Adieux: A Farewell to Sartre* – an account of the last decade of his life – in the following year. She herself died of pneumonia five years later, at the age of 78.

The author is not without her critics, on the left as well as the right: poststructural feminists, for example, have criticized her as a "universal humanist" who endorses phallocentric discourse and the assimilation of male notions of authority. Nonetheless, de Beauvoir is remembered as a major philosopher who has had a profound impact on transforming the ideas of the modern world.

▷ **SIMONE WEIL**
Weil empathized deeply with the struggling and the dispossessed. She brought about her own death by starvation by refusing to eat more than her compatriots, who had little food under the German occupation of France.

Simone Weil

1909–1943, FRENCH

A political activist, mystic, and philosopher, Weil lived a short life of exceptional intensity. Her reflections on state power and social injustice, and her idiosyncratic religious vision, attracted interest only after her death.

◁ **WORKERS UNITED**
From her late teens, Weil became passionately involved in trade unionism and the workers' movement, marching in numerous demonstrations. She was a Marxist and a pacifist.

Born into an affluent secular Jewish family in Paris in 1909, Simone Weil showed great intellectual aptitude from an early age. After having received an elite education at the Lycée Henri IV and the Ecole Normale Supérieure, she graduated in 1931 and began a career as a philosophy teacher at a school in the provinces.

From her youth, Weil was noted for her radical political attitudes and her identification with the suffering of the poor and oppressed. In 1934 she took a year-long sabbatical from teaching in order to work in factories, attracted by the wish to understand the working class and to share their affliction.

SIMONE WEIL
ATTENTE DE DIEU
INTRODUCTION PAR
LE R. P. PERRIN O. P.

LA COLOMBE

Although she was initially drawn to Marxism, she criticized the Soviet Union for establishing an oppressive bureaucratic state. In historical essays that focused on the Roman Empire, she denounced all forms of state power as "the great beast". When the Spanish Civil War broke out in 1936 (see box, right), Weil volunteered to fight with the anti-fascist cause, joining the anarchist group Durruti Column. Short-sighted and in poor health, she proved useless as a soldier and was repatriated after accidentally injuring herself.

Spiritual experience
In the late 1930s, Weil's thinking evolved towards mysticism and spirituality. Although brought up without religious belief, a series

◁ **WAITING FOR GOD, 1950**
Weil's essays and letters (to the Reverend J.M. Perrin), published posthumously as *Waiting for God*, explore the author's personal faith in God.

of visionary experiences – notably an ecstatic rapture in a church at Assisi, Italy, in 1937 – led her to place a belief in God at the centre of her worldview.

Weil was attracted to Catholicism but remained outside any formal belief system, developing her own mystical theology. For her, God was necessarily absent from his creation – his absence explained the predominance of evil and suffering in the world. The spiritual reality outside the world – the only true reality – could never be directly experienced but only intuited through encounters with beauty and suffering.

A commitment to others
In 1942, after the defeat of France by Nazi Germany, Weil escaped with her parents to the US. She then joined the Free French movement in the UK and wrote her only completed book, *The Need for Roots* (1949). This was an analysis of the malaise of European civilization and hopes for renewal in the future, based on a reconciliation between science and spirituality, and a patriotism grounded in compassion rather than conquest.

Weil asked to be sent into Nazi-occupied France as a secret agent, but her health was deteriorating, exacerbated by her decision to limit her food intake in sympathy with the undernourished in occupied Europe. She died in Ashford, Kent, in 1943, of tuberculosis and malnutrition. After the war, publication of her essays and excerpts from her notebooks won her an international reputation as a provocative thinker.

IN CONTEXT
The Spanish Civil War

The Spanish Civil War began in July 1936 with a military revolt against a left-wing Republican government. Weil was one among many idealistic writers and intellectuals from other countries drawn to participate in the conflict. For most of them, the experience ended in disillusionment; Weil was no exception, and later expressed revulsion at the cruelty and casual killing on both sides that devalued human life. After intervention by German and Italian troops in support of the rebels and the Soviet Union on behalf of the Republicans, the government was defeated in 1939, bringing General Francisco Franco to power.

SIMONE WEIL IN THE DURRUTI COLUMN DURING THE SPANISH CIVIL WAR, 1936

"There is a **reality outside** the **world,** that is to say, **outside space** and **time.**"

SIMONE WEIL, *A STATEMENT OF HUMAN OBLIGATION*

Arne **Næss**

1912–2009, NORWEGIAN

Næss was a Norwegian philosopher and environmentalist who is associated in particular with the concept of deep ecology. He was also known as an activist and an accomplished mountaineer.

Arne Dekke Eide Næss was born in Oslo in 1912. His father died when he was a year old, and he was raised by his mother. He developed a passion for mountaineering, and from his early teens would go on long expeditions into the mountains.

Næss also had an enthusiasm for philosophy. He initially studied and wrote on the subject within the empiricist tradition of the Vienna Circle (see box, p.266), which aimed to make the discipline scientific. Næss was appointed to Norway's only chair in philosophy – at the University of Oslo – at the age of just 27. However, he never abandoned his love of the mountains. Although his philosophical output was broad, his love of the natural world and of philosophy came together in his most famous concept – that of "deep ecology".

Shallow and deep ecology

For Næss, there is an important distinction between shallow and deep ecology. According to him, the environmental issues that we

⊲ **ARNE NÆSS**
Pictured here in middle age with his climbing gear, Næss is famous for, among other things, introducing the technique of using bolts in mountain climbing in Norway after World War II.

⊲ **MARDALSFOSSEN WATERFALL**
In 1970, Næss chained himself to rocks at this Norwegian waterfall in protest against plans to build a dam there. The plans were later dropped.

face are a symptom of philosophical problems with how we relate to the world around us. Næss sees human attempts to deal with pollution and resource depletion as examples of shallow ecology. The end-goal of these attempts, he claims, is simply to maintain the affluence and well-being of the developed world.

The aim of deep ecology, however, is to completely realign our relationship with the rest of the natural world. In place of a hierarchical image that positions human beings at the very top of an environmental ladder, in deep ecology the natural world is seen as a highly complex and tangled network of interdependent relations

and beings (for example, plants, animals, mountains, and rivers), of which humans are only one part.

Interdependence

Næss argues for recognizing this interdependence, and of turning our backs on hierarchy. Once we accept interdependence, we retreat from anthropocentric perspectives that put human beings at the centre of things. This, Næss argues, opens the door to new ways of coexisting in the world and makes us more sensitive to the complexity of the systems of which we are a small part. It also supports a politics based on decentralization and local autonomy.

Deep ecology continues to influence environmental philosophy. However, the deep ecology movement has also given rise to political and activist initiatives around the world. Næss himself – an activist and advocate of nonviolent resistance – was involved in public protests against dam-building and also campaigned for the Norwegian Green Party. He died in 2009, at the age of 96.

IN CONTEXT
Origins of deep ecology

Arne Næss arrived at the concept of deep ecology through his readings of the works of Spinoza, Gandhi, and the Buddha. He collaborated closely with George Sessions, a philosophy professor at Sierra College in Rocklin, California. It was on a camping trip to Death Valley in 1984 that the pair drew up the eight basic principles of deep ecology, which were later elaborated in Sessions's work.

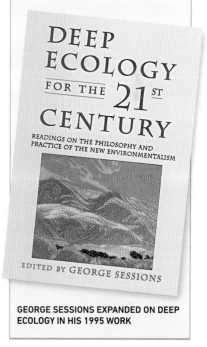

DEEP ECOLOGY FOR THE 21ST CENTURY
READINGS ON THE PHILOSOPHY AND PRACTICE OF THE NEW ENVIRONMENTALISM
EDITED BY GEORGE SESSIONS

GEORGE SESSIONS EXPANDED ON DEEP ECOLOGY IN HIS 1995 WORK

"The **smaller** we come to **feel ourselves** compared with **the mountain**, the **nearer** we come to **participating** in its **greatness**."

ARNE NÆSS, *ECOLOGY OF WISDOM: WRITINGS BY ARNE NÆSS*

Roland Barthes

1915–1980, FRENCH

Barthes' work was central to the development of Structuralism and Poststructuralism, and he was famed above all for his brilliant semiotic analyses of the myths of bourgeois culture.

△ **RED WINE AND FRENCHNESS**
Red wine, argues Barthes, is a signifier of French culture. It presents a number of often contradictory myths: it is blood-like and life-affirming; it is a social equalizer; it is at once warm and cool. These myths build a shared idea, but it is one that ignores notions of capitalism and expropriation, which are also associated with the production of wine.

In February 1980, after lunching with François Mitterand, Roland Gérard Barthes was run over by a laundry van on a Paris street. He died a few weeks later. Commentators noted the strangely premonitory tone of his final book, *Camera Lucida*, published the same year, in which the semiotician contemplated the nature of chance, trauma, and mortality.

Barthes was born 64 years earlier, in Cherbourg, just months before his father's death in World War I. He was brought up – and indulged – by the women in his family and formed an unusually deep bond with his mother (*Camera Lucida* was, in part, a eulogy to her). At the age of 19, he was struck down with tuberculosis, and after this was plagued by illness, in spite of

which he graduated with a degree in French literature and classics from the University of Paris.

From 1948, Barthes taught part-time in Romania and Egypt and also developed an interest in linguistics. Four years later, he began studying lexicography and sociology at the Centre National de la Recherche Scientifique in Paris.

Myth and society

Barthes' theories on language and literature reached maturity in his first major text, *Writing Degree Zero* (1953). Influenced by the work of Karl Marx and Jean-Paul Sartre, this book challenges the idea that writing is the expression of a writer's subjectivity: for Barthes, it is steeped in ideology, a product of social and cultural values.

Barthes developed these ideas in *Mythologies* (1957) – which drew on the Structuralist theories of the Swiss linguist Ferdinand de Saussure. Here, in a series of brilliant, playful essays, Barthes decodes various bourgeois "myths" that underlie French popular culture, showing how the signs society

◁ **FERDINAND DE SAUSSURE**
The work of the pioneering Swiss philosopher (1857–1913) formed the basis of modern linguistics, semiotics (or semiology), and Structuralism.

uses to express itself – a glass of red wine or a plate of steak-frites, for example – reflect discourses of power, such as colonialism and sexism. Myth, says Barthes, is depoliticized speech that makes things appear natural when they are not: it "abolishes the complexity of human acts, it gives them the simplicity of essences".

Barthes travelled to the US and Japan in the late 1960s. A series of groundbreaking texts followed, signalling his rise to international fame, a shift to Poststructuralism, and the influence of the heavyweights of French philosophy, including Derrida, Foucault, Julia Kristeva, and Jacques Lacan. In books such as *The Death of the Author* (1967), *S/Z* (1970), and *The Pleasure of the Text* (1973), Barthes questions the status of the author and claims that literary texts are open to multiple interpretations and have shifting connotations.

Barthes' life and work were inextricably linked: his inner circle included intellectual giants such as Foucault and Susan Sontag; and he once claimed that Kristeva, whom he adored, was "the only woman who could make me change my sexuality". However, his real love was his mother, with whom he lived for 60 years and whose death – just three years before his own – left him grief-stricken.

IN CONTEXT
Working methods

Barthes was an obsessive note-taker and described this act of "notatio" as a kind of drug, "a refuge, a security". He devised words to indicate different types of notes: "notula" referred to a couple of key words jotted in a notebook and "nota" to the development of that initial idea, recorded on an index card. He also admitted to an addiction to pens: "I have far too many... And yet, as soon as I see a new one I start craving it." Barthes used a range of ballpoint pens for spontaneous note-taking and wore clothes with pockets in which to carry them so that he could record his thoughts at any time or place.

> " **myth... abolishes** the **complexity** of **human acts**, it gives them the **simplicity of essences.** "

ROLAND BARTHES, *MYTHOLOGIES*

▷ **ROLAND BARTHES, 1979**
By all accounts, Barthes was a kind, charismatic man with a deep sense of irony. He is said to have frequented the gay bars of Paris, but never publicly declared his homosexuality.

▷ **LOUIS ALTHUSSER, 1978**
Althusser's life was blighted by
schizophrenia and bipolar disorder.
From the 1950s onwards he endured
aggressive treatments for his conditions,
and by the late 1970s had spent around
15 years in clinics and hospitals.

Louis Althusser

1918–1990, FRENCH–ALGERIAN

One of the towering left-wing thinkers of the 1960s and 70s, Althusser
is best known for his rigorous reinterpretation of the work of Marx, and
also for murdering his wife at their university home in November 1980.

Louis Pierre Althusser was born to French parents in Algeria in 1918; his father was a banker, his mother a schoolteacher. After moving to France in 1930, Althusser was captured during World War II and spent five years in a German prison camp, which led to the terrible psychological problems that he battled for the rest of his life. After the war he returned to France, and in 1948 graduated with a degree in philosophy from the prestigious Ecole Normale Supérieure in Paris, where he worked as a professor for more than 30 years.

As a young student, Althusser had been influenced by two Catholic scholars: Jean Guitton, a philosopher, and John Hours, a professor of history. In 1948, Althusser joined the French Communist Party because, he claimed, he was a devout Catholic, or what he termed "an internationalist universalist". The Church, he said, had great respect for social problems, and he believed that social change in the West was dependent on an alliance between Catholics and communists – "I thought that inside the Communist Party there were more adequate means to realize universal fraternity".

Marxist analysis

In the late 1940s, Althusser met and became deeply influenced by the communist activist and sociologist Hélène Rytmann, a woman eight years his senior who had fought in the French Resistance. The couple had an alarmingly tempestuous relationship (during which Althusser had several affairs) but were nevertheless inseparable; they married in 1975.

In 1965 Althusser received acclaim for his works of Marxist analysis *For Marx* and *Reading Capital*, the latter co-authored with the philosopher Etienne Balibar. He identified a

clear divide between Marx's early works – with their Hegelian emphasis on humanism and such concepts as alienation – and his later, more "objective" writings, which, according to Althusser, regard Marxism itself as a "science". In his reinterpretation of Marx's later work, Althusser sees historical development as being determined not by individuals, but by the structural conditions of society at any given time.

Key concepts

Althusser's reinterpretation of Marx identified the role of "ideological state apparatuses" (ISAs) – for example the family, the police, education, the law, and the media – which underpin ideologies that are central to the domination of one class by another. He introduced the influential concept of "interpellation", a process whereby individuals are constituted by ISAs as subjects and become products of the dominant ideology: just as we instinctively turn around when someone calls our name, so too does ideology "interpellate", or hail us.

Importantly, Althusser also adapted Sigmund Freud's psychoanalytic theory of "overdetermination" for use in a quite different context: for Marxists such as Althusser, any

contradiction in the social structure (for example, popular support for a fascist regime), can never have just a single explanation (determination), but is always "overdetermined" (has multiple determinations). According to Althusser, any social analysis must therefore identify how many determinations there are and then analyse each one separately – only then will it become clear how these factors operate in conjunction to produce the contradiction in question.

Althusser's ideas influenced the work of intellectual giants such as Foucault, Derrida, Bourdieu, Macherey, Poulantzas, Balibar, and Butler, and he remains influential in political philosophy, literary and cultural theory, history, economics, and sociology.

Late decline

Althusser's mental and physical health rapidly deteriorated in later life: "I wanted not only to destroy myself physically but to wipe out all trace of my time on earth." In 1980 he strangled his wife to death (see box, below) and then withdrew from public life. Heavily medicated and alienated, he spent his last decade in and out of psychiatric wards. He died of a heart attack in a psychiatric hospital near Paris in 1990, aged 72.

△ **MARXISM AND PHILOSOPHY**
Althusser argued that philosophy and Marxism needed one another to become fully realized. His works explored the nature of, and connections between, politics, science, and philosophy.

IN CONTEXT
The murder of Hélène Rytmann

As dawn broke on 16 November 1980, Althusser ran across a courtyard at the Ecole Normale Supérieure, where he lived and worked, screaming in terror that he had killed his wife. Doctors confirmed the philosopher had crushed her larynx while massaging her. Althusser's mental state was so severe that he was sent directly to a psychiatric hospital; he was never tried or charged. Five years later, while confined in hospital, he wrote *The Future Lasts Forever: A Memoir*, an account of the murder, and of what he identified as the roots of a mental illness that led to him to be medicated and hospitalized for decades.

COURTYARD AT THE ECOLE NORMALE SUPERIEURE, PARIS

Iris Murdoch

1919–1999, ANGLO-IRISH

Murdoch was an acclaimed novelist as well as a philosopher. Her specific brand of moral philosophy influenced contemporary as well as later thinkers and her ideas have assumed increasing importance.

Jean Iris Murdoch was an only child, born to Irish parents in a suburb of Dublin in 1919. Her father, a civil servant, moved the family to London early in her life, and Iris would later identify as "Anglo-Irish". After graduating from Oxford in 1942 with a first-class degree in classics, she worked at the Treasury in London for two years, then for two years with the United Nations Relief and Rehabilitation Administration. While working with refugees in Belgium, she met Jean-Paul Sartre and took inspiration from his blending of philosophy and fiction.

Following a year of postgraduate study at Cambridge, Murdoch moved back to Oxford to take up a fellowship at St Anne's College, where she taught philosophy until 1963. Passionate and unconventional, she had affairs with men and women, giving free rein to her (at times almost overwhelming) sense of the importance in life of love and sexual relationships.

Her first published philosophical work was a critique of existentialism: *Sartre: Romantic Rationalist* (1953).

◁ **IRIS MURDOCH**
Murdoch's novels often featured animals, which she endowed with rich personalities. She wrote 27 novels in total, reportedly forbidding her publisher from changing a single word in her manuscripts.

With its focus on free will and individual choice, existentialism appealed to her, but she felt it ignored the role of love and goodness. The next year, she published her first novel, *Under the Net*. A prolific writer, she published a book approximately every two years for the next four decades.

Works of fiction

Murdoch's novels embraced plots that veered from the comic to the melodramatic and from the erotic to the grotesque. They examined themes such as love, altruism, sin, and what it means to be good. As a philosopher, she was interested in the way such

◁ **A SEVERED HEAD**
Murdoch's fifth novel, published in 1961, deals with themes of adultery, morality, abortion, and suicide, yet is acclaimed for its wry wit.

elements derive from the inner life of a person, and the solidity and specificity of narrative was a way of exploring her ideas. She married John Bayley (see box, right) in 1956. They had a long marriage, during which she enjoyed the freedom to indulge her passions with other partners.

Philosophical tract

Seven years after she had stopped teaching, Murdoch published *The Sovereignty of Good* (1970), containing three essays that argued against the prevailing schools of thought – analytic philosophy and existentialism. Influenced by Simone Weil and Plato, she investigated what she called the "fat, relentless ego" as the source of moral blindness. She considered how people can become morally better, and referred to Plato's concept of the Form of the Good, or the idea of the good, as an effective way of approaching a "progressive education in the virtues".

Murdoch continued writing until a couple of years before her death from Alzheimer's disease in Oxford in February 1999 at the age of 79.

IN PROFILE
John Bayley

Bayley (1925–2015) was a literary critic, novelist, and academic: he was Warton Professor of English at Oxford University from 1974–92. He and Murdoch had a remarkable, loving, and enduring marriage during which he tolerated her frequent affairs, while he himself believed that sex was "inescapably ridiculous". After Murdoch's death he wrote three memoirs about his life with her, sharing the daily struggles he had in caring for her in her final years as she went, in her own words, "sailing into the darkness" of her disease.

IRIS MURDOCH WITH HER HUSBAND, JOHN BAYLEY

"**Love** is the extremely difficult **realisation** that **something other** than **oneself** is **real**."

IRIS MURDOCH, "THE SUBLIME AND THE GOOD"

Philippa Foot

1920–2010, BRITISH

Foot is associated with the ideas of moral naturalism and the revival of virtue ethics. She is best known for introducing the "trolley problem" into contemporary philosophical debate.

Philippa Foot was born in 1920 into a privileged family in North Yorkshire. Her father ran a steelworks, and her maternal grandfather was Grover Cleveland – twice president of the US (1885–89; 1893–97). Despite a patchy early education, and being tutored by a governess, Foot was accepted at Somerville College at the University of Oxford to study philosophy, politics, and economics.

The gender balance at Oxford had shifted greatly during World War II: many of Britain's leading 20th-century philosophers were women who had studied there in wartime, including Iris Murdoch, Elizabeth Anscombe, and Mary Midgley – all of whom became part of Foot's inner circle.

Academic career

Foot graduated in 1942 with a first-class degree. After the war, she took up a teaching post at Oxford, and in 1949 was appointed to a fellowship. In two essays from 1958, "Moral Arguments" and "Moral Beliefs", she entered the debate as to whether moral values can be considered to be cultivated (chosen) or based in nature.

In 1969, Foot resigned her fellowship and took up short-term teaching posts in the US, eventually accepting a permanent position at the University of California, Los Angeles (UCLA).

Ethical naturalism

In *Natural Goodness* (2001), Foot argues against a long tradition in philosophy that claims that ethics is what sets humans apart from nature. According to this tradition, the realms of nature (what "is" the case) and ethics (what "ought" to be the case) are distinct. Foot, however, argues that ethics should be seen naturalistically. If we say a one-eyed cat is defective, we are saying its eye does not allow it to do the things fully functioning cats do (hunt, judge distances, and so on).

Virtue ethics

Foot argues that virtues and vices should be seen in the same way: as defects and excellences when it comes to our functions as living things. If we say someone is just, courageous, or compassionate, what we are saying is that they are fully expressing what it means to be a functioning human being. When we say they are cowardly, or cruel, we are saying they have defects that mean they are not fully capable of doing the things humans should do.

This concern with excellence and defect position Foot at the forefront of the revival of "virtue ethics", an approach to ethics that comes ultimately from Aristotle, for whom the practice of the virtues allows us to flourish fully as human beings. Virtue ethics is now an important area of contemporary philosophy.

From the time of her appointment at UCLA in the mid-1970s until her retirement, Foot was migratory, splitting her time between the US and Oxford. She died in Oxford in October 2010, on her 90th birthday.

△ **NATURAL GOODNESS**
Foot's 2001 book, which challenged traditional philosophy, secured her reputation as one of Britain's most notable postwar thinkers.

▷ **PHILIPPA FOOT**
Foot's parents seemed more keen to secure their daughter's marriage than her education. She was, however, later recognized for her work on ethics and as a prominent figure in the charity Oxfam.

IN CONTEXT
The trolley problem

In 1967, Philippa Foot formulated, and later became famous for a thought experiment known as the "trolley problem", as follows: you are standing by a track and a runaway trolley is heading towards five people who are tied to the tracks. A nearby lever would enable you to change the direction of the trolley immediately, diverting it to a side-track, where just one person is tied up. Should you or should you not pull the lever? In the mid-1970s, Foot's moral dilemma was taken up and developed by the US philosopher Judith Thomson. It is now an area of philosophy known as "trolleyology".

FOOT'S TROLLEY PROBLEM URGES US TO EXPLORE MORAL INTUITION

▷ **JOHN RAWLS, 1987**
Despite the considerable fame Rawls achieved following the publication of *A Theory of Justice*, he remained a modest, unassuming man who shunned publicity and had, according to one commentator, a "bat-like horror of the limelight".

John Rawls

1921–2002, AMERICAN

Rawls was one of the most important political philosophers of the 20th century. His book *A Theory of Justice* explores his concept of "justice as fairness" and has been widely influential.

◁ **US FORCES IN THE PHILIPPINES**
US soldiers attack Japanese forces during World War II. Rawls served in the Philippines – his experience of war led to the erosion of his religious faith.

John Rawls was born in Baltimore in 1921 to a large and prosperous family. Two of his brothers died in childhood, having caught diphtheria from him – this trauma is said to have triggered the stutter that afflicted his life. He studied at Princeton University, where he became preoccupied with theology and considered entering the priesthood. After graduating, he joined the US Army and was sent to fight in New Guinea and the Philippines, where he was involved in the horrors of battle at the frontline. Although he was awarded a medal for bravery, Rawls disliked military discipline and was demoted for refusing to reprimand a soldier.

In 1946 he left the army for good and returned to Princeton to pursue a PhD in philosophy. He married in 1949 and had four children. He taught throughout his life, at Oxford, Harvard, Massachusetts Institute of Technology, and Cornell. His major works include *Political Liberalism* (1993) and *The Law of the Peoples* (1999). However, the book that secured his academic reputation was *A Theory of Justice* (1971).

Justice as fairness

Rawls argues that justice is fundamental to all well-functioning societies. "Justice," he says, must be understood "as fairness". Here he draws on a philosophical tradition associated with Jean-Jacques Rousseau – that of social contract theory (see p.154): the idea that all societies are underpinned by an agreement about duty and obligation. If we have a clear view on what this contract is, or should be, we can make our institutions more just.

The original position

Rawls formulated what he calls the "original position" experiment, asking what kind of social contract would we agree on if we could choose the principles upon which a society was based, but did not know what position we would have in it: we would not know our individual race, gender, sexuality, health, abilities, and so on.

A Theory of Justice argues that under these conditions, there are two things upon which all people would agree: these are "equal basic liberties" and "fair equality of opportunity" – that every citizen of this society should have an identical right to liberty, as long as that liberty does not infringe the liberty of others. We would also agree that society be arranged so that the greatest advantages should be awarded to those who are least advantaged, ensuring an equality of opportunity.

Following the publication of his masterpiece, *A Theory of Justice*, Rawls's contribution to political philosophy was acknowledged globally, and thereafter his work influenced generations of students and scholars. He died of heart failure at his home in Lexington at the age of 81.

IN CONTEXT
Isaiah Berlin

While he was studying at the University of Oxford in the early 1950s, Rawls became influenced by the British philosopher and historian of ideas Isaiah Berlin (1909–97). Berlin was preoccupied by what is called "value pluralism", the idea that we may hold different, equally valid, but wholly incompatible values. This means that the collision of different values is an inevitable part of human life. The echo of this can be seen in Rawls's concern with justice, and with how one can agree on common standards when society is made up of competing sets of concerns, values, and conceptions of the good life.

" We **strive** for **the best** we can **attain** within **the scope** the **world allows.** "

JOHN RAWLS, *POLITICAL LIBERALISM*

◁ **LADY JUSTICE, LONDON**
A statue of Lady Justice – with the scales of justice in one hand and a sword in the other – stands above Britain's central criminal court, the Old Bailey. Rawls's *A Theory of Justice* was written during the Vietnam War (1955–75), when issues surrounding justice and liberty were uppermost in many people's minds.

Thomas Kuhn

1922–1996, AMERICAN

Kuhn was a physicist, historian, and an immensely influential philosopher of science. He was responsible for the concept of the "paradigm shift", in which one scientific worldview is replaced by another.

◁ **THE LIBERATION OF PARIS, 1944**
Kuhn witnessed the liberation of Paris from occupying German forces in August 1944. Here, military tanks are flanked by jubilant crowds on the Champs-Elysées.

Thomas Samuel Kuhn was born in Cincinnati, Ohio, in 1922. He was brought up in a liberal, non-practising Jewish family. Kuhn's father was an engineer and a veteran of World War I, while his mother worked freelance as an editor, as well as a writer of texts for politically and socially progressive organizations.

The intellectual, socially engaged environment of Kuhn's early years helped to foster his tremendous independence of thought. He was schooled privately at institutions that placed emphasis on questioning rather than on learning facts.

It soon became clear that he had an aptitude for physics and mathematics. He studied for his bachelor's degree in physics at Harvard University and was also editor of the student newspaper.

Kuhn graduated from Harvard in 1943, at the peak of the World War II, and joined researchers at Harvard working on radar technology. This research took him to Europe where, in 1944, he saw the surrender of the occupying German army in Paris.

He returned to Harvard after the war, where he took a master's degree in physics and enrolled for a PhD. However, he became interested in

philosophy. While studying for his PhD, he was appointed a teaching fellow and ran a course on the growth of the experimental sciences.

Early career

The idea of the course was to explore how scientists went about their work, by means of case histories in the history of science. As part of this course, Kuhn went back to read original texts, and was struck by the disjunction between the image of scientific progress represented in science textbooks, and the erratic, strange and irregular ways in which science actually worked in practice.

In 1948 Kuhn was appointed a junior fellow of Harvard, submitted his PhD dissertation, and also got married. His interests then turned towards the philosophy of science and he started work on *The Structure of Scientific Revolutions*, which was not published until 1962, by which time he was a full professor at the University of California. Kuhn's book was enormously influential – its significance eclipses all his later work.

IN PROFILE
Michael Polanyi

One of Kuhn's influences was the philosopher of science Michael Polanyi (1891–1976), who questions the objectivity of scientific truth, insisting that our thinking is always shaped by "tacit knowledge" – that is, knowledge that is not fully conscious but that nevertheless informs how we see, explore, question, and interact with the world of which we are a part. When applied to scientific research, this means that although such research may appear to be "objective", it is always partially subjective – influenced, informed, and shaped by the deeply personal commitments of the people who are undertaking the research.

▷ **THOMAS KUHN**
This multiple-exposure portrait of Kuhn shows the eminent philosopher during his time at Princeton University. Kuhn married twice in his life: the first time, in 1948, to Kathryn Muhs, with whom he had two daughters and a son; and the second time, in 1981, to Jehane Barton Burns.

> "**Normal science...** is **predicated** on the assumption that the **scientific community knows** what the **world is like**."

THOMAS KUHN, *THE STRUCTURE OF SCIENTIFIC REVOLUTIONS*

> " Only when they **must choose** between **competing theories** do **scientists** behave like **philosophers**. "
>
> THOMAS KUHN, "LOGIC OF DISCOVERY OR PSYCHOLOGY OF RESEARCH?"

The Structure of Scientific Revolutions is long and meticulously detailed, and yet it has been translated multiple times and sold well over a million copies worldwide. The reason for the book's wide influence is, in part, the manner in which it raises questions about how science happens.

Science as a social practice
Kuhn's starting point for *The Structure of Scientific Revolutions* was a puzzle. He had read, and taught, Aristotle's *Physics*, a book that is not only enormously sophisticated, but also misguided in many ways. Kuhn

regarded Aristotle as one of the greatest minds in history. And yet, Kuhn wrote later, he seemed "not only ignorant of mechanics, but a dreadfully bad physical scientist"; his work was "full of egregious errors, both of logic and of observation". The puzzle, then, is this: how is it possible that someone of Aristotle's immense intelligence could be so mistaken about the world?

At the core of Kuhn's response to this question is the simple idea that science is, at root, a human social practice, rather than an abstract set of truths about the world. The history

of science is often represented as an incremental, progressive revelation of truths about how things are, with each generation building upon the last. But Kuhn argues that this gradualist view does not seem to reflect the reality of how science works.

Disruption and change
The idea of "paradigm shift", explored and developed by Kuhn, has become so widespread that it has entered everyday language and popular culture. Modern politicians, business executives, artists, economists, and so on, frequently express the need

▽ **SCIENTISTS AT WORK, 1900**
Scientists are shown here carrying out research in a chemistry laboratory at the Sorbonne in Paris at the start of the 20th century – an example of what Kuhn refers to as "normal" science in progress.

for paradigm shifts. However, what Kuhn is referring to is something far more specific. For him, most science is practised within a particular paradigm, a specific set of underlying assumptions about the world – a basic pattern or model that is taken for granted by the community as a whole. A paradigm may consist of worldviews, sets of precise methods, ways of experimenting or proceeding, or formal theories.

Paradigm shifts

What Kuhn calls "normal science" takes place within a particular paradigm. If results turn up that do not fit with the paradigm, then the paradigm may be extended, tweaked or adjusted – or, alternatively, the results may be ignored or overlooked as anomalies. Most of the time, science proceeds in this "normal" phase, with scientists solving individual puzzles and problems within a particular paradigm. The paradigm does not just define how we go about solving these puzzles and problems, it also defines the kinds of puzzles and problems that seem worthy of attention.

Scientific revolutions

These periods of normal science are disrupted by periods of revolution: here, Kuhn gives the examples of the Copernican Revolution, which put the sun at the centre of the planetary system of which Earth is a part (see box, above), and the revolution prompted by general relativity and quantum physics, which overthrew classical Newtonian mechanics.

For Kuhn, different paradigms are incommensurable, meaning that they do not correspond with each other.

IN CONTEXT
The Copernican Revolution

In around 1514, the astronomer Nicolaus Copernicus (1473–1543) wrote a treatise arguing that the Earth rotated around the sun. This proposition overturned the widely accepted view at that time that the Earth was the unmoving centre of the universe. The "Copernican Revolution" was one of the examples given by Kuhn of a "paradigm shift" in the history of science. The idea of a Copernican Revolution was used metaphorically by the philosopher Immanuel Kant to describe the revolutionary shift in perspective of his own philosophy.

PLATE FROM THE COSMOGRAPHICAL *ATLAS HARMONIA MACROCOSMICA*, **ANDREAS CELLARIUS, 1660**

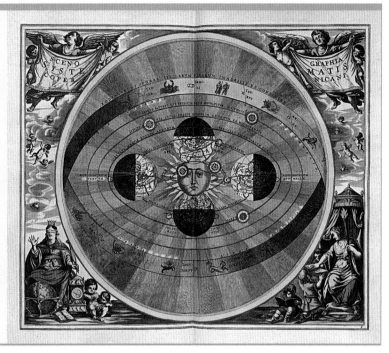

Once a new paradigm is in place, it generates a new set of puzzles, problems, ways of experimenting, theories, and worldviews. Things settle down into another period of normal science, and the community of scientists work within this new paradigm. However – and this is one of the intriguing things about Kuhn's idea – the new paradigm may be less good at explaining certain things that were considered to have satisfactory explanations within the old paradigm.

Kuhn's influence

Following the success of *The Structure of Scientific Revolutions* from the 1960s onwards, Kuhn continued to teach and write, working at Princeton and then, in 1983, at Massachusetts Institute of Technology (MIT). In 1994 he was diagnosed with lung cancer and died two years later.

Thomas Kuhn is one of the most influential of all philosophers of science; *The Structure of Scientific Revolutions* has sold a remarkable 1.5 million copies. His reminder that science is a social activity has been hugely fruitful for later philosophers and historians. However, some scholars have questioned whether the history of science really fits so neatly into this division of "revolutionary" and "normal" phases, arguing that the reality of science as it is practised lies somewhere in the middle, and that different paradigms are not as incommensurable as Kuhn claims.

▷ **ARISTOTLE'S *PHYSICS*, PAGE 1**
Physics was compiled from a collection of Aristotle's manuscripts. Kuhn's initial bewilderment with the text led eventually to his formulation of the idea of the paradigm shift in science.

KEY WORKS

1957
Publishes *The Copernican Revolution: Planetary Astronomy in the Development of Western Thought.*

1962
Publishes *The Structure of Scientific Revolutions* to considerable worldwide acclaim.

1977
The Essential Tension: Selected Studies in Scientific Tradition and Change appears.

1978
Black-Body Theory and the Quantum Discontinuity, 1894–1912 analyses quantum mechanics.

2000
The Road since Structure – compiled in collaboration with Kuhn before his death – charts the philosopher's ideas in later life.

Jean-François Lyotard
1924–1998, FRENCH

Active in the second half of the 20th century, Lyotard examined a range of philosophical, political, and aesthetic issues, but is best known for his influential analysis of the human condition in the postmodern world.

Born in the Paris suburb of Vincennes, Jean-François Lyotard had a middle-class upbringing and was educated in old-established Paris lycées. He held early ambitions of becoming an artist, a writer, a historian, and even a Dominican monk, but later admitted that these were unrealistic dreams; his attempts at writing and painting showed up his "unfortunate lack of talent", and he realized he had no aptitude for memorizing history. The idea of taking religious orders was also abandoned in favour of marrying and starting a family.

Towards the end of World War II he worked as a first-aid volunteer supporting the resistance in Paris, a profound experience that impressed on him the importance of social responsibility rather than personal

⊲ **JEAN-FRANÇOIS LYOTARD**
After his retirement in 1987, Lyotard remained active, lecturing throughout the 1980s and 1990s at universities in the US, Canada, Germany, and Brazil.

aspirations. After the war, he studied philosophy and literature at the Sorbonne, graduating with an MA in 1947. The following year, he married, started a family and decided upon a career in teaching. After gaining his *agrégation* (teaching certificate) he accepted a job teaching philosophy at a boy's school in Constantine, Algeria, where he witnessed the run-up to the Algerian War (1954–62), a formative influence on his political thinking. Lyotard's sympathy with the Algerian struggle against French colonialism instilled in him a firm belief in the desirability of socialist revolution, but also highlighted an urgent need to re-examine Marxist theory in the light of current events – not only in Algeria but also in the Soviet Bloc.

He returned to France in 1952, taking up a post at Collège Henri-IV de La Flèche, a school for sons of the military. While there, he published *Phenomenology* (1954), influenced by his interest in Heidegger, but his work then became increasingly political,

especially after he joined the left-wing Socialisme ou Barbarie ("Socialism or Barbarism") organization led by Cornelius Castoriadis (see box, right).

La Flèche was perhaps not the ideal place for his radical politics, and in 1959 he took up a post as a lecturer at the Sorbonne. Uncomfortable with the direction Castoriadis was taking, he left Socialisme ou Barbarie to join the socialist group Pouvoir Ouvrier ("Worker Power"), but resigned from this too, becoming involved in the student uprisings in Paris in 1968.

Retreat to philosophy
Towards the end of the 1960s, Lyotard, became increasingly disillusioned with revolutionary politics and returned to his philosophical work. He moved to the philosophy department at the newly founded University of Paris VIII in Vincennes in 1970 with his friend and colleague from his student days Gilles Deleuze, and gained his doctorate with the thesis *Discourse, Figure* (1971), which established his reputation among the emerging poststructuralist movement.

He remained at Vincennes until his retirement in 1987, and there wrote many of his most influential works, including *The Postmodern Condition* (1979) and *The Differend* (1983). He died of leukaemia in Paris in 1998.

IN CONTEXT
Socialisme ou Barbarie

The radial socialist organization Socialisme ou Barbarie ("Socialism or Barbarism") was founded in 1948 by Cornelius Castoriadis and Claude Lefort as a breakaway group from the French Internationalist Communist Party, disenchanted with its Trotskyist and Leninist tendencies. The group attracted both intellectuals and workers wishing to establish an alternative to revolutionary communism, and a counter to bureaucratic capitalism. Castoriadis was, from the beginning, the leading light, but his autocratic leadership and control over the organization's journal, coupled with his increasing criticism of Marxism, drove many members away to form splinter groups. The journal finally folded in 1965, and the organization was declared finished in 1967.

PHILOSOPHER AND PSYCHOANALYST CORNELIUS CASTORIADIS, 1990

⊲ **ALGERIAN INDEPENDENCE**
A contemporary postcard shows troops of Algeria's National Liberation Front (FLN) parading through Algiers in 1962. The FLN launched their war of independence from France in 1954.

▷ **FRANTZ FANON**
Frantz Fanon's short life was rich and eventful. In addition to his activism, journalism, and medical career, he wrote three plays and served for a time as ambassador to Ghana for the Provisional Algerian Government.

Frantz Fanon

1925–1961, MARTINICAN

Fanon was a psychiatrist, philosopher, and militant Marxist who called for a radical rejection of colonialism. His passionate, emblematic texts have influenced some of the world's leading politicians, thinkers, and activists.

Born into a middle-class family in July 1925 in the French colony of Martinique, Frantz Fanon was the fifth of eight children. His father – a descendant of an enslaved African – was a customs agent, his mother a shopkeeper of mixed race.

At school, Frantz was discouraged from speaking the local Martinican Creole in favour of French. A brilliant student, he later attended a prestigious lycée, where he was taught by Aimé Césaire (see box, below). His dream at that time was to be a playwright.

At the age of 18, during World War II, he left to fight in the French army; in 1944, he was wounded in battle and later decorated for bravery. His awareness that he and his fellow Black servicemen remained colonial subjects, along with the racism he endured in France, shaped his political and philosophical development.

Alienation and liberty

Fanon graduated from the University of Lyon, France, where he studied medicine and psychiatry but also attended lectures by the philosopher Maurice Merleau-Ponty. It was also in Lyon that he met his future wife, Josie Dublé, a white Frenchwoman, with whom he later had a son, Olivier.

In 1952, Fanon published his first book, *Black Skin, White Masks*, an important study of the psychology of racism and of the alienation suffered by the colonized under colonial rule; it drew on diverse sources, including Jean-Paul Sartre and the psychoanalyst Jacques Lacan. Soon after, during the French–Algerian war (1954–62), he became head of a psychiatric hospital in Algeria (then a French colony) and heard the harrowing stories of those who had been tortured and brutalized in the war. The experience prompted his

active involvement in the armed struggle for Algerian independence. However, in 1957, the French government expelled him from the country; he moved to neighbouring Tunisia and worked for the Algerian National Liberation Front.

The dispossessed

In 1959 Fanon was injured by a mine near the Moroccan border, escaped an assassination attempt in Rome, and published *The Fifth Year of the Algerian Revolution* and *A Dying Colonialism*, both about the Algerian war. The next year, he was diagnosed with leukaemia and wrote his most famous book, *The Wretched of the Earth* – allegedly in 10 weeks – while battling the disease. In this powerful and brilliant analysis of the dehumanizing effects of colonialism he famously advocates armed resistance in the struggle for decolonization. The text appeared in 1961, the year of his death, with a preface by his friend Sartre, who noted that "the Third World finds

itself and speaks to itself through [Fanon's] voice". The book became an international bestseller and positioned Fanon, albeit posthumously, as a leading thinker on decolonization.

An adopted country

Although treated for his illness in Russia and the US, Fanon died in a Washington hospital in December 1961. He was 36 years old. On hearing the news, French authorities removed copies of his recently published text from bookshops, claiming it was a threat to national security.

Fanon's wish had been to be buried in his adopted country, Algeria. Following sensitive negotiations with, among others, the US State department and the CIA, the request was granted. Algeria won independence from France the year after Fanon died. Since then, his work has influenced liberation movements and inspired major thinkers and revolutionaries, including Malcolm X, Steve Biko, and Che Guevara.

> "**To speak** means... to assume a culture, **to support** the weight of a **civilization**."
>
> FRANTZ FANON, *BLACK SKIN, WHITE MASKS*

△ **ALGERIAN STRUGGLE**
Fanon wrote for and edited the newspaper *El Moudjahid*. This was the voice of the National Liberation Front, which was formed to resist the French colonial presence in Algeria.

IN PROFILE
Aimé Césaire

A prominent poet and politician, Césaire (1913–2008) was a key figure in Fanon's intellectual development. Although less radical than his former student, Césaire was a fierce and tireless critic of European colonialism and a co-founder of the influential Négritude, or Black consciousness, movement of the 1930s–50s, which primarily argued for a reclamation of African identity. His major texts include the groundbreaking *Return to my Native Land* (1939). Césaire was mayor of Fort-de-France, the capital of Martinique, for almost 56 years.

THE FORMER TOWN HALL IN FORT-DE-FRANCE, NOW THE CESAIRE THEATRE

Michel Foucault

1926–1984, FRENCH

A major influence on Structuralism and Poststructuralism, Foucault developed his own distinctive blend of philosophy, psychology, and history to analyse the way in which power is exercised in society.

Both of Michel Foucault's parents came from families of doctors: his father, Paul-André, was a surgeon in Poitiers, western France; his mother, Anne, the daughter of a surgeon, would have liked to have been a doctor, but this was out of the question for women at the time. It was expected that their children would continue the family tradition.

However, this was not to be. Their first child was a girl, Francine, and medicine was not an option for her. The second child, born in 1926, Paul-Michel, rebelled against the idea, and it was only the youngest child, Denys, who took up a career in medicine. Paul-Michel felt repressed by the atmosphere of his conservative, conventional, and Catholic family. It was a family tradition for the first son to be named Paul, a name he disliked, and once he left school he insisted on being known as Michel.

Rebellious youth

Michel was a rebellious youth, rejecting the middle-class values of his parents, and especially what he regarded as his father's bullying. He was sent to the local lycée in 1930, two years earlier than most children, where he stayed until the German invasion of France in 1940. His mother then moved him to a Catholic school in Poitiers, where he showed an aptitude for philosophy, and decided to defy his parents' wishes and follow an academic career, rather than to become a surgeon.

In 1945, once the war was over, Foucault left Poitiers for Paris, where he studied for the entrance exams for the Ecole Normale Supérieure (ENS). His tutor Jean Hyppolite (see box, right) instilled in Foucault the Hegelian idea of the importance of history to the study of philosophy. Competition for places at the ENS was fierce, but Foucault was among the highest ranked of the applicants, and began his course in the autumn of 1946. He studied philosophy under the existentialist Maurice Merleau-Ponty, but was also later mentored by Louis Althusser, who encouraged Foucault to examine philosophy from a Marxist perspective, and even to join the Communist Party. Foucault also attended lectures in psychology at the University of Paris, and graduated in psychology in the same year, 1949, as he received his *diplôme d'études supérieures* in philosophy.

◁ **ECOLE NORMALE SUPERIEURE**
Foucault attended the Ecole Normale Supérieure (ENS), one of France's prestigious Grandes Ecoles. He studied at the ENS from 1945 and started teaching there six years later.

IN PROFILE
Jean Hyppolite

French philosopher Jean Hyppolite (1907–68) was a contemporary of Jean-Paul Sartre's at the Ecole Normale Supérieure in Paris, and went on to follow an academic career with a special interest in Hegelian philosophy. His major contribution was not, however, in his original research, but as a teacher. A professor at the University of Strasbourg, the Sorbonne, and later at the Ecole Normale Supérieure and the Collège de France, he had a strong formative influence on the next generation of French Structuralist and Poststructuralist philosophers, including Foucault, Gilles Deleuze, and Jacques Derrida.

"I'm **no prophet**. My **job** is **making windows** where there were once **walls**."

MICHEL FOUCAULT, *DISCIPLINE AND PUNISH*

▷ **MICHEL FOUCAULT**
One of the most influential and original thinkers of the modern age, Foucault transformed a wide range of intellectual disciplines with his compelling analyses of power, knowledge, and systems of thought in the Western world.

▷ **A RAKE'S PROGRESS,** 1735
This illustration of the Bethlem Royal Hospital in London (popularly known as Bedlam Insane Asylum) is from an 18th-century engraving from *A Rake's Progress* by William Hogarth. In *Madness and Civilization*, Foucault suggests that as late as 1815, inmates at this psychiatric hospital were exhibited on Sundays – visitors paid one penny for viewing privileges.

Although Foucault was doing well academically, he was not always happy at the ENS. He was something of a loner, and spent much of his time reading and researching.

A period of self-discovery

There were periods of depression, including incidents of self-harm and even an alleged suicide attempt, and his fellow students remarked on what they regarded as an unhealthy obsession with the macabre. From Foucault's perspective, however, he was going through a period of self-discovery – coming to terms with his homosexuality, his interest in sado-masochism, and the excitement of recreational drug use and casual sex.

Foucault's teaching career began at the ENS as a lecturer in psychology, but he also took up other teaching posts in Paris in the early 1950s. He immersed himself in psychology but also read literary works that focused on sex, violence, and madness. He began a relationship with the avant-garde composer Jean Barraqué, who initially shared his taste for violent sexual practices and drug abuse, but later came to regard Foucault's intensity as a kind of mental illness and separated from him in 1956.

In 1955, Foucault left the ENS and taught in Uppsala, Sweden, then spent a year as a cultural attaché in Poland, and a further year in Hamburg at the Institut Français.

Foucault returned to France in 1960, having completed his doctoral thesis, *Madness and Insanity* (which was published in 1964 as *Madness and Civilization: A History of Insanity in the Age of Reason*). This text heralds the start of Foucault's massive project to dismantle post-Renaissance Western culture, exposing its contradictions, instabilities, and fissures. In *Madness and Insanity* he focuses his attention on the discourse of psychiatry; in later works he turns to the human sciences, medicine, the penal system, and sexology. In all of these texts his aim is to show how power is exerted by the state at all levels of society: "Power," he says, "is everywhere and comes from everywhere."

"**The soul** is the **prison** of the **body.**"

MICHEL FOUCAULT, *DISCIPLINE AND PUNISH*

KEY WORKS

1961
Publishes his doctoral thesis *Madness and Insanity: History of Madness in the Classical Age.*

1963
The Birth of the Clinic: An Archaeology of Medical Perception, details the history of attitudes in medical institutions.

1966
The Order of Things: An Archaeology of the Human Sciences extends his idea of "archaeology" to scientific discourse.

1969
The Archaeology of Knowledge discusses his idea of discourse: systems of thought that underlie ideas and beliefs.

1975
Modern concepts of punishment and control are examined in *Discipline and Punish: The Birth of the Prison.*

1976–84
The first three volumes of *The History of Sexuality* are published; against Foucault's wishes Volume IV is also published.

In the autumn of 1960 Foucault began teaching psychology at the University of Clermont-Ferrand, where he met the student Daniel Defert, a Marxist activist – the two became lifelong lovers. This led to awkwardness when Foucault became head of the philosophy department and used his position to get a job for Defert.

In 1964 Defert undertook military service in Tunisia and, two years later, Foucault became head of philosophy at the university there. He and Defert were left-wing activists, but Foucault was in Tunisia at the beginning of the period of civil unrest in Paris in May 1968 (see box, p.311), and therefore did not become involved until things had quietened down somewhat.

International recognition

In 1966, the publication of *The Order of Things* – Foucault's "archaeology" of the human sciences – had secured his reputation, and he was invited to help set up a philosophy department at the

Centre Expérimental de Vincennes. From its opening in 1969, it continued the student protests of the previous year, and there were frequent clashes with the police. Encouraged by Defert, Foucault appointed a mainly militant left-wing staff in his department, and the Marxist bias of the curriculum resulted in the authorities not recognizing its degrees.

Lectures and travels

Foucault was then elected a fellow of the Collège de France, and gave the first of the 12 annual lectures expected of him in December 1970. These became a popular fixture in the Paris intellectual calendar, and he continued to give these talks for the rest of his life. He travelled widely, giving lectures and taking on visiting professorships. He also took the opportunity to concentrate more on his writing, and to campaign on various issues – especially of human rights and the abuse of power.

Through his activism on behalf of political prisoners, he became involved with a prison reform movement, which resulted in his book *Discipline and Punish* (1975). Here, he examines the penal system using the same method of historical analysis he had developed in his examination of mental and medical institutions.

The History of Sexuality

From then on, Foucault became less politically active, and for a time worked as a newspaper journalist covering the revolution in Iran (1978–79), but settled back into a life of lecturing and writing. His next major project was the massive *The History of Sexuality* (1976–84), which was to occupy the rest of his life. He spent a lot of time in the US; it was probably there that he contracted HIV, which developed into AIDS in 1984. Foucault was one of the first Europeans to have the virus, which had been identified only three years earlier in New York, and at first his symptoms went undiagnosed. He was taken into hospital in June 1984, but within two weeks he died. It is sadly ironic that he should die of a disease that reinforced many stereotypically repressive ideas of homosexuality and conventionally "deviant" behaviour because he was completing a comprehensive study of precisely those attitudes.

IN CONTEXT
HIV/AIDS

Although initially identified in the early 1980s in the US, the human immunodeficiency virus (HIV) probably had its origins in the Belgian Congo in the 1960s or even earlier, and had spread to the US by the 1970s. It rapidly spread from isolated cases among gay communities and intravenous drug users to become a global pandemic, affecting millions worldwide. The term AIDS (which stands for "acquired immune deficiency syndrome") is used to describe a range of conditions that are due to HIV infection, generally appearing in the later stages of the disease.

AIDS AWARENESS RIBBON

◁ **UNIVERSITY OF UPPSALA**
Foucault was offered a job at the Maison de France at the University of Uppsala, Sweden, in 1955, and taught there for three years.

Jean Baudrillard

1929–2007, FRENCH

A guru of postmodernity, famous for his analyses of reality and simulation, Baudrillard attracted media attention for his activism and provocative commentaries on global events and consumer society.

Jean Baudrillard was born in Reims in 1929. He was accepted into the Sorbonne in Paris to read German, and was the first member of his family to attend university. His doctoral thesis was later published as his first major book, *The System of Objects* (1968).

By 1966, Baudrillard was teaching sociology at the University of Paris X Nanterre, where he stayed for 20 years, becoming radicalized in the process (see box, below). His interests were wide-ranging, straddling politics, Marxism, photography, philosophy, psychoanalysis, semiology, literary theory, and cultural studies.

In *Symbolic Exchange and Death* (1976), he made a radical break from his earlier Marxist-inspired economic analyses of consumer culture to focus more firmly on semiotics, signs, and society. But it was the publication of *Simulacra and Simulation* in 1981 that really launched his career.

Cautionary tales

In this dense work, Baudrillard questions the status of "the real". Prefiguring issues such as virtual reality and fake news, he argues that there is now such a proliferation of signs and media messages that our understanding of the world has been derailed: it is impossible to know what is and isn't real; all that exists are

versions or "simulacra" – a concept that refers to postmodern society's simulation of reality, producing copies of original experiences or objects. The real, says Baudrillard, is "that which can be reproduced". The more accurate the copy, the greater the risk that it will become more real than the original on which it was based. His famous example is Disneyland – an idealized version of the US.

After leaving the University of Paris X in 1987, Baudrillard taught at the University of Paris IX Dauphine and at the European Graduate School in Switzerland. He also travelled widely, indulging his passion for photography and commenting on global events, including the Gulf War (1990–91) and 9/11 (2001).

Intellectual celebrity

The 1999 film *The Matrix*, in which humans are simulated by machines, catapulted Baudrillard to cult status. The film makes various references to *Simulacra and Simulation*, though the philosopher claimed that these were based on misreadings of his text.

Baudrillard's critics have accused him of obscurity and dilettantism. Nonetheless, his compelling and, for some, prophetic analyses continue to reach a large audience, and he is seen by many as an important commentator on the dangers of the modern age and of Western culture and politics in particular.

Baudrillard married twice and had two children from his first marriage. He died, after a long illness, in 2007.

△ **THE TRUMAN SHOW**
In this 1999 film starring Jim Carrey, life is depicted as nothing more than a stage set, a simulation of reality – much like the replicated, "hyperreal" worlds described by Jean Baudrillard.

◁ **BAUDRILLARD, 1994**
Baudrillard was by all accounts a modest, unassuming man. He did, however, once wear a gold lamé jacket to one of his lectures in Las Vegas, possibly in ironic acknowledgement of his celebrity status.

IN CONTEXT
Events of 1968

Baudrillard broke with Marxism in the 1970s but was politically active all his life. His activism became apparent in the 1960s, during his early years at Paris X Nanterre. Members of the university's sociology department, in which Baudrillard was based, began the "March 22 Movement" – a student protest movement, founded on 22 March 1968, that occupied the university's administration buildings, ending in clashes with the police. This was one of the events throughout France that sparked the widespread and notorious student and worker civil unrest two months later – now known simply as "May 68" – in which Baudrillard himself participated. The movement was responsible for the largest general strike in European history and almost succeeded in bringing down the conservative Gaullist government in France.

PROTESTERS ATTACK A POLICE VAN IN PARIS DURING THE UNREST IN MAY 1968

Jacques Derrida

1930–2004, FRENCH–ALGERIAN

Derrida is most often associated with the form of textual analysis known as "deconstruction". A central concern of his was, by means of rigorous analysis, to unravel tensions and contradictions in different discourses.

△ **ALGERIAN FLAG**
Derrida fully embraced his life in Paris, but always retained something of his status as an outsider, an Algerian and a Jew – a thinker from the margins.

Jacques Derrida was born in 1930 in El-Biar, a suburb of Algiers in French-governed Algeria. His parents were Sephardic Jews, and he experienced discrimination from an early age. Derrida's education was affected by the climate of increasing antisemitism, particularly after the outbreak of the World War II.

In 1942 he was expelled from his high school because of the imposition of quotas on the number of Jewish students. His broken education meant that he frequently skipped school, and when he was young he dreamed of being a professional footballer. But while a teenager, he also read works by Jean-Paul Sartre, Albert Camus (a philosopher who shared his love of football), and Friedrich Nietzsche.

France, the US, and Algeria

Derrida moved to Paris at the age of 19 and sat his exam for the Ecole Normale Supérieure. He failed, but was successful on his second attempt. He flourished in Paris, but as an Algerian was always conscious of being an outsider.

In 1956, having written his master's thesis on the philosopher Edmund Husserl, he travelled on a scholarship to Harvard University, US. After leaving Harvard, he returned to Algeria, which at that time was engaged in the

Algerian War of Independence, and avoided being drafted into military service by taking up a post teaching French and English to the children of military officers.

By the 1960s, Derrida was back in France, teaching philosophy at the Sorbonne in Paris – he plunged himself into the city's vibrant literary, artistic, and philosophical life.

Derrida returned to the Ecole Normale Supérieure in 1964 to teach. During the 1960s, his work became increasingly well known outside the French-speaking world, and in 1967 he published three of his most influential and important philosophical works: *Writing and Difference*, *Of Grammatology*, and *Speech and Phenomena*.

IN CONTEXT
The Cambridge controversy

When the University of Cambridge announced in 1992 that Derrida was to be awarded an honorary degree, a group of leading philosophers wrote an open letter to *The Times* newspaper in protest. They claimed that Derrida's work "defies comprehension", being full of "tricks and gimmicks".

This correspondence exposed deep divisions among philosophers about the very purpose of philosophy: is it about developing clarity, or is it concerned with bringing to light hidden, and perhaps insoluble, contradictions? When it came to a final vote, however, it was decided that the university should proceed with Derrida's honorary doctorate.

THE WESTERN COLLEGES OF THE UNIVERSITY OF CAMBRIDGE

> "**Language** is a structure – a **system** of oppositions."
>
> JACQUES DERRIDA, *OF GRAMMATOLOGY*

▷ **JACQUES DERRIDA, 1997**
One of the most influential thinkers and literary theorists of the modern age, Derrida is pictured here at home in Paris, with his trademark pipe in hand, at the age of 67.

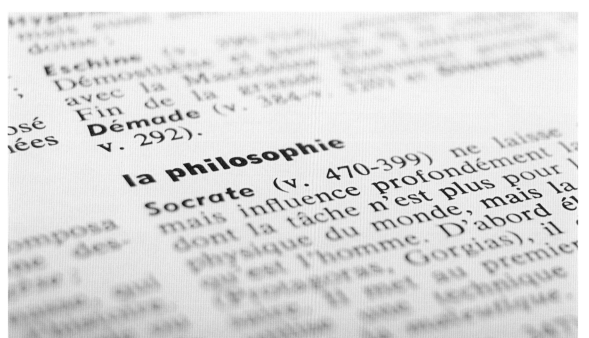

△ **SOCRATES AND DERRIDA**
The Ancient Greek philosopher Socrates never wrote anything, arguing that speech was superior to writing. Centuries later, in works such as *Of Grammatology* and *Speech and Phenomena*, Derrida launched a ferocious attack on the Western philosophical tradition's reverence for the spoken over the written word.

On deconstruction

Derrida is often closely associated with the concept of "deconstruction". As the name suggests, deconstruction is a philosophical strategy that aims to take apart the philosophical tradition, to dismantle common philosophical assumptions and prejudices to see some of the puzzling buried tensions that lie behind them.

The Western philosophical tradition is based, as Derrida indicates, on unspoken hierarchies: for example, speech is privileged over writing, mind over body, literalness over metaphor, men over women, and so on. When the threads of these oppositions are systematically unravelled, their contradictions and tensions become glaringly apparent.

On the primacy of speech

In *Of Grammatology*, Derrida explores how the philosophical tradition has consistently argued that the sincerity and directness of face-to-face speech is primary, and that writing is secondary – that the written word is a pale, and often deceptive, reflection of the spoken word. Derrida uses the term "logocentrism" to describe this privileging of speech over written language. In the logocentric view, there is a clear hierarchy: thought gives rise to speech; speech gives rise to written language.

Challenging hierarchies

In the first part of *Of Grammatology* Derrida deconstructs the hierarchies that underpin Western thought, asking how we might begin to think about written texts without regarding them simply as a reflection of speech. In the second part of the book, he goes on to apply these insights to texts that were written by other thinkers, including the philosopher Jean-Jacques Rousseau, the anthropologist Claude Lévi-Strauss, and Ferdinand de Saussure, the founder of modern linguistics.

Derrida is fascinated by the fact that meaning is never fully present in a text. In *Speech and Phenomena* he coined the term *différance* (with an "a"), which he used in opposition to logocentrism. Its anomalous spelling combines "differing" and "deferring", to describe how meaning is always slipping away from being fully present to us.

The deferring that takes place in language happens because words always depend for their meaning on other words, which, in turn, depend on other words (whether within or outside the text), and so meaning is never fully present in the text – it is endlessly deferred. Nothing appears in language as a straightforward reflection of "reality".

There is a twist in the tale here. In French, the term *différer* means both "to differ" and "to defer". In speech, Derrida's new term *différance* is indistinguishable from the usual French noun *différence*: it is only in written language that the two can be distinguished. This lends considerable weight to Derrida's claim that the traditional hierarchy between spoken and written language is something that is not to be fully trusted.

▽ **OF GRAMMATOLOGY, COVER**
The translation into English of Derrida's *De la grammatologie* by the literary theorist and feminist critic Gayatri Spivak helped to extend his readership to diverse fields such as postcolonial theory.

" What **cannot be said** above all must **not be silenced** but **written.** "

JACQUES DERRIDA, *THE POST CARD: FROM SOCRATES TO FREUD AND BEYOND*

"An **act of forgiveness** worthy of its name, if there ever is such a thing, **must forgive** the **unforgivable**. "

JACQUES DERRIDA, *ON COSMOPOLITANISM AND FORGIVENESS*

◁ **TRUTH AND RECONCILIATION**
Archbishop Desmond Tutu and fellow commissioners listen here to testimony from witnesses on acts of violence under apartheid in South Africa at the Truth and Reconciliation Commission in London in 1996. Derrida discusses proceedings of the Commission in his analysis of the concept of forgiveness.

Derrida goes on to ask who has the right to forgive, and here he tells a moving story of a woman at the Truth and Reconciliation Commission in South Africa whose husband has been tortured and killed by police officers under apartheid. "A commission or a government cannot forgive," the woman says. "Only I, eventually, could do it. (And I am not ready to forgive.)"

The more Derrida picks at the idea of forgiveness (Is it conditional or unconditional? Is it possible or impossible? Is it within the power of the law or beyond the power of the law?), the more he reveals the hidden contradictions in the concept. And yet, even while deconstructing the notion of forgiveness, he maintains that it is urgently necessary.

Derrida died in a Paris hospital in 2004 of pancreatic cancer, which had been diagnosed the previous year. His work continues to provoke, to annoy, and to inspire scholars – not only in philosophy and literature, but in many other fields.

The decades following the publication of Derrida's major titles saw his global fame increase substantially. He held visiting positions at many universities in Europe and the US, and was awarded an honorary degree at the University of Cambridge in 1992 – a move that provoked protests from many philosophers working in the analytic tradition (see box, p.312).

Ethical thinking

Also later in his career, Derrida focused more explicitly on questions of ethics, and was influenced by the philosopher Emmanuel Levinas (see box, right). Derrida's way of thinking through ethical questions reveals something of his deconstructive impulses. For example, in his essay on the concept of forgiveness, he argues that what really demands forgiveness is the unforgivable.

If you commit a minor offence against someone (such as stealing their biscuit), this is not really a situation that calls for forgiveness. Forgiveness, Derrida argues, is required precisely in situations in which we encounter the unforgivable. And in this sense, forgiveness is impossible – because it is most urgent, and most necessary, just at the point where it encounters acts that cannot be forgiven. And yet, it nevertheless happens.

IN PROFILE
Emmanuel Levinas

One of Derrida's major influences was the philosopher Emmanuel Levinas (1906–95). Born in Lithuania, he was naturalized as a French citizen, and was one of the leading philosophers in the phenomenological tradition. His philosophy explores the ethics of face-to-face encounters, arguing that in encountering another human being, we are subject to an infinite responsibility. In *Writing and Difference*, Derrida wrote a long, detailed analysis of Levinas's work. Derrida's later work on ethics also owes an enormous debt to Levinas.

LEVINAS IN HIS STUDY IN PARIS, 1988

KEY WORKS

1964
Writes "Violence and Metaphysics", a lengthy essay on the work of Levinas.

1967
Publishes his major works: *Of Grammatology*, *Writing and Difference*, and *Speech and Phenomena*.

1972
Dissemination discusses language and the differences between philosophy and literature.

1974
Glas includes readings of the philosopher Hegel and the playwright Genet.

1978
Publishes *Edmund Husserl's "Origin of Geometry"*, an examination of Husserl's privileging of speech over writing.

▷ **RICHARD RORTY, 1995**
Rorty was deeply committed to the idea of social justice and argued passionately for a hopeful, creative democracy, where policy would be driven by social utility.

Richard Rorty

1931–2007, AMERICAN

Rorty was a philosopher in the American Pragmatist tradition. He argued ferociously against the claim that knowledge and language can simply and effectively "mirror" the way that the world is.

"**Philosophy** makes **progress** not by becoming more **rigorous** but by becoming more **imaginative**."

RICHARD RORTY, *TRUTH AND PROGRESS: PHILOSOPHICAL PAPERS, VOLUME 3*

IN CONTEXT
Socrates, irony, and philosophy

Irony as a philosophical tool goes back to Socrates in Ancient Greece, who became infamous for his "Socratic irony" – his insistence that he had no knowledge when it came to ethical questions. When Socrates discussed these issues with others, he did so in a way that undermined their own beliefs and convictions, rather than proposing any of his own. Rorty's "ironism" – a term he coined himself – is rooted in the tradition of recognizing that our deepest ethical and philosophical convictions are never fully grounded, and that we do not have a privileged access to reality.

Richard Rorty was born in New York in 1931, the child of activist parents. He grew up in a progressive, left-leaning environment, steeped in the traditions of American Pragmatism, which holds that the usefulness of an idea is the measure of its merit. He was a strange child with a number of unusual obsessions, including orchids and Leon Trotsky. Later in life, he said that from the age of 12, he knew "that the point of being human was to spend one's life fighting social injustice". However, the path he took to do this was not the activist path of his parents, but the path of philosophy.

Rorty studied at the University of Chicago and at Yale University, Connecticut, graduating with a PhD in 1956. After spending two years in the army, he took up a teaching position at Wellesley College, Massachusetts. In 1961 he moved to Princeton, New Jersey, where he stayed for the next two decades. Rorty never felt at home within philosophy departments, so in 1997 he moved to Stanford University, California, where he became professor of comparative literature. He died in 2007 of pancreatic cancer.

The mirror of nature

Initially, Rorty worked firmly within the traditions of analytic philosophy. However, by the time of his first book, *Philosophy and the Mirror of Nature* (1979), he had turned his back squarely on this tradition, criticizing the idea of philosophy as a means of elucidating objective truths. The publication was an immediate success, projecting Rorty to fame, but it also caused major controversy. In it, Rorty argues that the idea that knowledge can accurately "mirror" nature is fundamentally misguided. Instead of seeing knowledge as a way of representing the world, he proposes that its role is to help individuals to cope with the world: it has evolved to enable people to deal with the environment in which they find themselves. Rorty maintains, therefore, that the question that should be asked is not "is this claim true?" in an absolute sense, but instead "what can this claim do for us?" This put Rorty within the tradition of Pragmatism that is associated with philosophers such as John Dewey.

The concept of "ironism"

The implications of Rorty's rejection of the idea that knowledge mirrors nature are far-reaching. If language and knowledge do not mirror the world – if they are simply a particular society's attempts to deal with the problems that life throws at the members of that society – then there can be no absolute basis for deciding between different knowledge claims. People are able to hold the positions that they hold, but must do so with a dose of irony, recognizing that they are not seeing the world from an informed perspective, but from within a specific historical context, and that for those in another context the world would look very different. Rorty referred to this approach as "ironism" (see box, right).

BUST OF SOCRATES

◁ **THE MIND AS MIRROR**
Rorty argued against the view held by philosophers since the 17th century that the mind could be considered a mirror that gave a true reflection of reality,

Directory

Nishida Kitarō

1870–1945, JAPANESE

Nishida was born near Kanazawa and studied Daoism and Confucianism at school. In 1884, he graduated from the University of Tokyo with a degree in Western philosophy. In 1910, he began teaching at Kyoto Imperial University, and four years later became professor of philosophy there.

Nishida is renowned for striving to synthesize Eastern and Western philosophy. He is famous for his theory of *basho*, or place, which aims to overcome the subject–object dualism of Western philosophy via Zen.

KEY WORKS: *An Inquiry into the Good*, 1910; *Intuition and Reflection in Self-Awareness*, 1917; *From That Which Acts to That Which Sees*, 1927; *The Self-Awareness and Determination of the Nothingness*, 1930–32

Max Scheler

1874–1928, GERMAN

Scheler pioneered phenomenology, a movement that began with the philosopher Edmund Husserl as an attempt to understand consciousness from the standpoint of ourselves as conscious beings.

In *Man's Place in Nature* (1928), and other works, he addresses what he considers to be the most important philosophical issues: What does it mean to be human? What is the place of humans in the nature of things? His view – that we share our vital nature with other animals, but our spiritual being makes us unique – echoes the division that runs deep in the Western tradition. He believed that through love, our spiritual being can be detached from the "bondage and pressure of life".

KEY WORKS: *On the Phenomenology and Theory of Sympathy*, 1913; *Formalism in Ethics and Non-Formal Ethics of Values*, 1913–16; *On the Eternal in Man*, 1921; *Man's Place in Nature*, 1928; *Philosophical Perspectives*, 1929

▽ Martin Buber

1878–1965, AUSTRIAN

Religious thinker, educator, translator, and political activist, Buber helped to redefine religious existentialism through his "philosophy of dialogue".

△ MARTIN BUBER, c.1961

He was born into a Jewish family in Vienna and studied at the universities of Vienna, Leipzig, Zürich, and Berlin.

Buber's most important work, *I and Thou* (1923), urges a shift from an obsession with things towards deeper, more meaningful encounters with other human beings: only in this way, he says, can meaning emerge.

KEY WORKS: *I and Thou*, 1923; *Between Man and Man*, 1936; *Good and Evil*, 1952; *The Knowledge of Man*, 1958

Gaston Bachelard

1884–1962, FRENCH

Bachelard was born in the town of Bar-sur-Aube. As a young man he was a post office employee, and studied chemistry and physics. In 1919, aged 35, he became a professor of natural sciences. In the 1930s he switched to philosophy, teaching at the University of Dijon and then the Collège de France in Paris.

His initial focus was the philosophy of science – in particular, a critique of scientific knowledge – securing his reputation in books such as *The Experience of Space in Contemporary Physics*. His most influential concept – the "epistemological break" (a major historical or scientific break) – was developed in around 1938.

Bachelard later turned his attention to aesthetics and to the role of the imagination, as in *Water and Dreams: an Essay on the Imagination of Matter*. In *The Poetics of Space*, which brought him global recognition, he examines the interplay between the mind, our sense of self, and our surroundings.

KEY WORKS: *The Experience of Space in Contemporary Physics*, 1937; *Water and Dreams: an Essay on the Imagination of Matter*, 1942; *The Poetics of Space*, 1958; *The Poetics of Reverie*, 1960

Tanabe Hajime

1885–1962, JAPANESE

Tanabe was born into a family of educators in Tokyo and studied at the University of Tokyo and then at Kyoto Imperial University, where he was later appointed as a lecturer in philosophy. With Nishida Kitarō and others, he was an influential member of the Kyoto School of philosophy, which sought to merge Eastern and Western philosophical traditions. However, Tanabe became increasingly critical of Nishida's philosophy.

In 1925, Tanabe published *A Study of the Philosophy of Mathematics,* which established him as Japan's foremost philosopher of science. His *Philosophy as Metanoetics*, influenced by the work of Martin Heidegger and published just after World War II, takes the form of a confession, a lamentation of the "blind militarism" of the war and of racial and militaristic ideology, which he had previously espoused. The shame of Japan's actions in the war haunted Tanabe for the rest of his life.

KEY WORKS: *A Study of the Philosophy of Mathematics*, 1925; *Philosophy as Metanoetics*, 1946

Gabriel Marcel

1889–1973, FRENCH

Christian philosopher Marcel was a musician and composer, and made a living as a playwright, drama critic, author, and editor, while lecturing and developing his philosophy. He was born into an agnostic family and his mother died when he was four. The sense of her spiritual presence led him toward religion and to explore the concept of life after death – the first philosopher to do so since Plato. At the age of 40, he converted to Catholicism.

Marcel argued that the horrors of World War I, and the rise of empirical science, had led to disenchantment and a loss of mystery in human life. He wrote of the powerful longing for mystery and the feelings humans have that allow them to glimpse it.

KEY WORKS: *Metaphysical Journal*, 1927; *Being and Having*, 1933; *Homo Viator*, 1945; *The Mystery of Being*, 1951; *Man Against Mass Society*, 1955

▷ Edith Stein

1891–1942, GERMAN

Philosopher, writer, and nun, Stein was born in Breslau. Her father died when she was young and she was brought up by her mother, a devout Jew. Edith renounced Judaism in her teens and later converted to Roman Catholicism.

In 1916, she received her doctorate, from the University of Göttingen. In 1932–33 she was a lecturer at the German Institute for Pedagogy in Münster. Stein challenged aspects of

Husserl's phenomenology and issues centring on human existence, metaphysics, and science, and the nature of God. During World War II, while training as a Carmelite nun in Holland, she was arrested by the Nazis and gassed to death.

KEY WORKS: *The Problem of Empathy*, 1917; *The Science of the Cross*, 1938

Susanne Langer

1895–1985, AMERICAN

Born in New York, Langer (née Kauth) was the daughter of German emigrants. As a child, severe illness meant she was schooled at home,

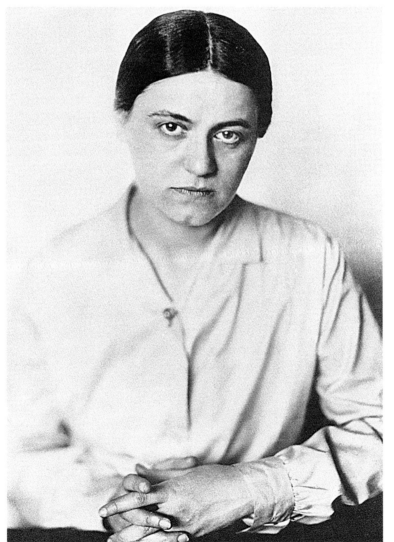

△ **EDITH STEIN, c.1930**

becoming an accomplished musician. Langer studied philosophy at Radcliffe College, Massachusetts, and in 1926 gained her doctorate from the University of Harvard. She then taught philosophy at Radcliffe from 1927 to 1942, and thereafter at a number of US universities.

Many believe that her theories on the importance of art, the influence of the arts and music on the mind, and her belief that these are essential human activities, changed the course of aesthetics.

KEY WORKS: *Philosophy in a New Key: A Study in the Symbolism of Reason, Rite, and Art*, 1942; *Feeling and Form*, 1953; *Mind: an Essay on Human Feeling* 1967, 1972, 1982 (three vols)

Feng Youlan

1895–1990, CHINESE

Born in Henan province, Feng graduated from Peking (Beijing) University in 1918, and five years later was awarded his PhD from Columbia University, US; his thesis compared Chinese and Western traditions.

Feng returned to China, where he held a succession of university posts, including, from 1927, as chair of philosophy at Tsinghua (Qinghua) University, Beijing. He is best known for his *History of Chinese Philosophy* (1934), which reworks traditional Chinese thought from a contemporary perspective, but incorporating Western ideas. It was the standard history of Chinese philosophy until the early 21st century. Following the communist takeover of China in 1949, Feng was preoccupied with rethinking his earlier work from a Marxist perspective.

KEY WORKS: *History of Chinese Philosophy*, 1934; *Xin Li-xue* (*New Rational Philosophy*), 1939; *A Short History of Chinese Philosophy*, 1946

Keiji Nishitani

1900–1990, JAPANESE

A prominent philosopher of the Kyoto School, and a disciple of Nishida Kitarō, Nishitani was born in Udetsu, near Noto. He combined his interest in Western philosophy – Nietzschean nihilism in particular – with detailed study of Zen and Mahayana Buddhism, eventually combining his pursuits in the development of his own distinctive brand of comparative philosophy.

Nishitani was awarded a PhD in philosophy from Kyoto University in 1924, and later studied at the University of Freiburg, Germany. The problem of *sunyata* ("emptiness" or "nothingness") became central to his philosophical thinking.

KEY WORKS: *History of Mysticism*, 1932; *Self-Overcoming of Nihilism*, 1952; *Religion and Nothingness*, 1961

María Zambrano

1904–1991, SPANISH

Born in Vélez-Málaga, Andalusia, Zambrano studied philosophy at the University of Madrid. She was a republican and opponent of dictator Francisco Franco (ruled 1939–75). She taught at the University of Madrid and the Cervantes Institute, Madrid.

Zambrano was exiled in the year that Franco seized power and did not return until 1984. This underpins her writing, which looks at politics, ethics, poetic reason, and metaphysics.

KEY WORKS: *Philosophy and Poetry*, 1940; *Delirium and Destiny: A Spaniard in her Twenties*, 1953, pub. 1989; *Man and the Divine*, 1955

▽ Emmanuel Lévinas

1906–1995, FRENCH

The work of Lithuanian-born thinker Lévinas focuses on existentialism, ethics, ontology, phenomenology, and Jewish philosophy. He relocated from Lithuania to France in 1923, to study philosophy at the University of Strasbourg. Five years later he moved to the University of Freiburg to study under Edmund Husserl. His early work focused on Heidegger and Husserl, and his 1930 doctoral thesis, *The Theory of Intuition in Husserl's Phenomenology*, helped to establish phenomenology as a key branch of philosophy in France.

During World War II Lévinas spent five years in a prison camp, after which he taught mainly in Jewish institutions until 1961, when he took up a post at the University of Poitiers; he later taught at the University of Paris X and the Sorbonne. His major work, *Totality and Infinity*, argues that Western "reason" is repressive and serves to eradicate otherness.

KEY WORKS: *Existence and Existents*, 1943; *Time and the Other*, 1947; *Totality and Infinity: An Essay on Exteriority*, 1961; *Difficult Freedom*, 1963

△ EMMANUEL LEVINAS, 1993

Maurice Merleau-Ponty

1908–1961, FRENCH

Along with Jean-Paul Sartre, Merleau-Ponty was a leading figure of French phenomenology. He was born in Rochefort, and studied philosophy at the prestigious Ecole Normale Supérieure in Paris, where he met other major thinkers, including Sartre, de Beauvoir, and Weil. He was particularly influenced by the work of Husserl and Heidegger.

In one of his leading texts, *The Phenomenology of Perception*, Merleau-Ponty rejects Descartes' mind–body dualism (the separation of mind and matter) in favour of his own concept of the "body-subject", which sees mind, body, and consciousness as being interconnected. Merleau-Ponty contributed to, and was on the editorial board of, the leftist journal *Les Temps Modernes*, and taught at the Collège de France in Paris from 1952.

KEY WORKS: *The Structure of Behaviour*, 1942; *The Phenomenology of Perception*, 1945; *The Visible and the Invisible*, 1964

Willard van Orman Quine

1908–2000, AMERICAN

Quine was born into a middle-class family in Ohio. In 1930, he graduated with a degree in mathematics from Oberlin College, Ohio, and in 1932 received his doctorate in philosophy from the University of Harvard. He then travelled to Europe, where he met various leading philosophers, including members of the influential Vienna Circle.

During World War II, Quine served in military intelligence, decoding German submarine messages for the US Navy. After the war he emerged as a notable philosopher of language, ontology, and epistemology, and became a professor of philosophy at Harvard in 1956. Among his major concepts is that of "indeterminacy of translation". He suggests that far from having fixed meanings, words become meaningful not because there is a link between words and things, but from the context in which they are used and the fact that we have learned what to say and when to say it: language is a social art.

KEY WORKS: *Methods of Logic*, 1952; *From a Logical Point of View*, 1953; *Word and Object*, 1960; *The Pursuit of Truth*, 1990

Mou Zongsan

1909–1995, CHINESE

One of the foremost disciples of the modern Chinese philosopher Xiong Shili, Mou was born into a peasant family in Shandong province. Aged 24, he graduated in philosophy from Peking (Beijing) University, and then taught at various universities in mainland China. He taught in Taiwan from 1949 until 1960, when he took up a post at Hong Kong University.

His interests included abstract metaphysical thinking and China's cultural reconstruction. He was one of the leading proponents, with Xiong, of the New Confucianism movement, and sought to modernize traditional Chinese philosophy by means of a dialogue with Western thought.

KEY WORKS: *Substance of Mind and Substance of Human Nature*, 1968–69 (three vols); *Phenomenon and Thing-in-Itself*, 1975; *The Buddha-Nature and Prajna*, 1977; *Nineteen Lectures on Chinese Philosophy*, 1983

Paul Ricoeur

1913–2005, FRENCH

One of the most prolific and influential French philosophers of his age, Ricoeur embraced literature, history, historiography, theology, ethics and politics. He taught in France and the US and published widely; his works focused on the meaning of life, how to live, and the nature of the individual.

He fused phenomenology with hermeneutics, taking analysis beyond that of texts and on to the self, which he saw as a construction. In his narrative theory, the stories of past, present, and projected futures, together with the ideas that flow through and around us in our lives, are part of that selves' construction.

KEY WORKS: *Freud and Philosophy: Essays on Interpretation*, 1965; *The Rule of Metaphor*, 1975; *Time and Narrative*, 3 Vols 1984–88; *Oneself as Another*, 1990

▷ Gilles Deleuze

1925–1995, FRENCH

Deleuze was born in Paris, studied philosophy at the Sorbonne and passed his *agrégation* (teaching certificate) in 1948. He taught in high schools for the next eight years, then became an assistant professor at the Sorbonne in 1957, and later taught at the universities of Lyon and Paris VIII at Vincennes.

In 1987, Deleuze was introduced to the radical psychoanalyst Félix Guattari, with whom he collaborated on four key, politically engaged texts, including *Capitalism and Schizophrenia* and his most influential work, *Anti-Oedipus*. Deleuze is also famous for his controversial work on the history of philosophy.

KEY WORKS: *Nietzsche and Philosophy*, 1962; *Difference and Repetition*, 1968; *Anti-Oedipus* (with Félix Guattari), 1972; *What is Philosophy?* (with Guattari), 1991

John Searle

BORN 1932, AMERICAN

Famous for his work in the philosophy of language, especially speech-act theory, and the philosophy of mind and consciousness, Searle was born in Denver, Colorado. He was educated at the universities of Wisconsin and Oxford, where he was awarded his doctorate in 1959.

Searle's reputation was established with his early work *Speech Acts: An Essay in the Philosophy of Language*, in which he develops J.L. Austin's theories by emphasizing aspects of communication and intentionality. Searle is the Slusser Professor Emeritus of the Philosophy of Mind and Language and Professor of the Graduate School at the University of California, Berkeley, where he began his teaching career in 1959.

KEY WORKS: *Speech Acts: An Essay in the Philosophy of Language*, 1969; *The Construction of Social Reality*, 1995; *Mind, Language, and Society*, 1999;

Derek Parfit

1942–2017, BRITISH

The son of British missionary doctors, Parfit was born in China during World War II, although the family moved to Oxford when he was a year old. He was educated at Balliol College, Oxford, where he read history, switching to philosophy while in the US on a fellowship at Columbia and Harvard universities. Soon after, aged 29, he won international acclaim for his article "Personal Identity" (1971). He was a research fellow at All Souls, Oxford, from 1974 to 2010.

Parfit was an influential moral philosopher from the 1980s, but wrote just two books, both notable for their originality and their inspirational nature: *Reasons and Persons*, which presents radical new perspectives on personal identity; and *On What Matters*, which analyses three different, ostensibly incompatible, approaches to ethics. In 2014, he was awarded the highly prestigious Rolf Schock Prize in logic and philosophy.

KEY WORKS: *Reasons and Persons*, 1984; *On What Matters*, 2011, 2017

△ **GILLES DELEUZE, c.1965**

TODAY

CHAPTER 6

> **NOAM CHOMSKY, 1969**
By the age of 10, Chomsky – a child
prodigy, already deeply immersed in
political discourse – had published
his first article. Just a few years later
he taught Hebrew to fund his education.
Today, with numerous bestselling political
and academic works to his name, he
has been described by *The New York
Times* as "arguably the most important
intellectual alive".

Noam Chomsky

BORN 1928, AMERICAN

Chomsky is a towering intellectual, famous for his pioneering work in
linguistics. A rigorous scholar and resolute campaigner, his influence
extends from philosophy and cognitive science to international affairs.

> "The **more** you can **increase fear** of drugs, crime, **welfare mothers**, immigrants, and **aliens**, the **more** you **control all** of the **people**."
>
> NOAM CHOMSKY

Avram Noam Chomsky was born into a multilingual, working-class Jewish family in Philadelphia in 1928. His father was a distinguished Hebrew scholar. From the age of two, Noam attended an experimental, progressive primary school. By the time he was 10 years old he had published his first article: an attack on the terrifying spread of fascism and Nazi power in Europe. He has remained an activist and an anarchist all his life.

Father of modern linguistics

In 1945 Chomsky began his studies at the University of Pennsylvania and six years later was admitted to the Society of Fellows at Harvard University. He was awarded a PhD from Pennsylvania University in 1955. His first child, Aviva, was born in 1957, which was also the year in which he published one of his most famous and influential works, *Syntactic Structures*. Over the next 20 or so years, Chomsky secured his reputation as "the father of modern linguistics" in major works such as *Aspects of The Theory of Language* (1965) and *The Logical Structure of Linguistic Theory* (1975), the latter a complex technical book

that examines the underlying structures governing language use. However, Chomsky's most significant contribution to the history of thought, developed from the late 1950s onwards, relates to his theories on the human ability to master the complex rules of language.

In a radical departure from the prevailing view in the first half of the 20th century that language is learned, Chomsky put forward his groundbreaking theory of "universal grammar", arguing that in fact language is an innate human capacity that has developed out of the evolutionary process. He has further argued that certain rules of language structure are common

◁ **UNIVERSITY OF PENNSYLVANIA**
Chomsky's academic career began in 1945 when he was admitted to the University of Pennsylvania to study linguistics, philosophy, and mathematics.

to all languages. His ideas have redirected the course of modern linguistics and, according to fellow linguist John Lyons, "revolutionized the scientific study of language".

A resolute campaigner

Despite his towering academic status, and the fact that he is a notoriously private person, it is Chomsky's tireless political activism that keeps him in the global spotlight. The war in Vietnam (1955–75) prompted his book *The Responsibility of Intellectuals* (1967), which is a damning indictment of US intellectual culture. Since then he has remained a resolute political and human-rights campaigner (highlighting atrocities in East Timor, Cambodia, and Turkey, for example). His focus has turned increasingly on the distortions and hypocrisy of Western ideology.

Chomsky continues to teach and write, on linguistics, philosophy, and international affairs, and to unmask the machinations of power and propaganda. He is professor emeritus in the department of linguistics and philosophy at the Massachusetts Institute of Technology, where he has taught for more than 60 years.

IN CONTEXT
A New York newsstand

According to Chomsky, by far the biggest influence in his life from the late 1930s onwards was his uncle, who owned a newspaper stand at 72nd Street and Broadway in New York, and was immersed in Marxist sectarian politics. From his early teens, Chomsky would often take a train from his home town in Philadelphia to New York to visit his uncle, who was also from a Jewish, working-class background. The kiosk was a vibrant meeting place not only for his extended family – some of whom were communists – but for European émigrés and radical, left-leaning thinkers of all types. It was "a rich and lively intellectual culture", according to Chomsky. "We'd hang out all night and have discussions and arguments, there or in his small apartment nearby. The great moments of my life in those years were when I could work at the newsstand at night and listen to all this."

◁ **DONALD TRUMP**
A ferocious opponent of profit-first Neoliberalism, Chomsky has been highly critical of former US president Donald Trump.

Jürgen Habermas

BORN 1929, GERMAN

One of the leading philosophers of the modern age, Jürgen Habermas has devoted his life to understanding the roots of the world's bleakest episodes and upholding reason as the solution to its most pressing problems.

◁ **RENOWNED TEACHER**
Habermas conducts a seminar in the Institute of Social Research at the University of Frankfurt in 1969. He became the institute's chair in philosophy and sociology in 1964.

Born in Düsseldorf, Germany, in 1929, Jürgen Habermas came of intellectual age in the aftermath of the Allied destruction of Nazi Germany. The radio broadcasts of the Nuremberg trials made clear to many of his generation that the Nazis had reduced German civilization to lawlessness and caused "a return to barbarity".

By 1945, the aspirations of German Idealism espoused by Immanuel Kant (see pp.160–63), and the idea that Enlightenment rationality would lead to the positive evolution of moral and political norms, had been derailed.

Two types of reason

After completing his PhD on Schelling at Bonn University in 1954, Habermas studied under Max Horkheimer and Theodor Adorno (see p.268–71) at the Frankfurt School, absorbing their theories on how "instrumental rationality" (an overriding concern for efficiency) was intertwined with fascism and state capitalism.

By the 1970s, however, he was drawing a distinction between instrumental and communicative rationality. He asserted that instrumental rationality and the systems that drive it – capitalism and national struggles for technological and military domination – rests on reasoning that is functional. Communicative rationality, on the other hand, is the attempt to achieve consensus through dialogue and communication. It is open to revision when the facts that inform it change.

While Adorno and Horkheimer veered toward abandoning the reason defended by Enlightenment thinkers, Habermas argued that the heirs of the Enlightenment had inherited two forms of rationality, one instrumental and the other communicative. He attributed the rise of fascism and the advance of global capitalism to the eclipse of communicative rationality by instrumental reason.

The illusion of democracy

Habermas went on to argue that democracy in the post-war world has been systematically undermined by capitalism. Markets, Habermas claims, depend on state regulations and the establishment of a social safety net to maintain an impression of equality. These, he argues, together with the global inequalities generated by colonial and post-colonial histories, and the subjugation of women, produce economic crises, welfare inadequacies, and dangerous and unfairly distributed environmental consequences for the planet.

IN CONTEXT
Belief in the EU

The collapse of the Soviet Union in 1989 refuelled discussions about the nation state and the potential of supra-national entities to represent, govern, and negotiate peace on an international level. Habermas's rousing support for the creation of the European Union was based on his commitments to global human rights, democratically negotiated peace, and economic justice. He also saw the EU as a counterweight to US supremacy.

In the 21st century, however, Habermas began to voice reservations about the EU, expressing worries regarding the limits of democratic engagement in the organization and its tendency to become a vehicle not for democratic politics, but for control by elites.

THE EUROPEAN PARLIAMENT OPENS IN BRUSSELS IN 1993

> " Habermas has long been **recognized** as the most **persistent** and **influential defender** of an **Enlightenment rationality**. "

STANLEY FISH, *THE NEW YORK TIMES*

▷ **JURGEN HABERMAS**
A prolific public speaker, committed to a just and equitable society, Habermas argues that Enlightenment values should not be abandoned but re-conceived.

Luce Irigaray

BORN 1932, FRENCH

Challenging prevailing cultural and philosophical traditions, Luce Irigaray promotes women's liberation and, more generally, human liberation through a philosophy of sexual difference.

Educated in Belgium and France, Irigaray earned her first graduate degree in philosophy and literature at the University of Louvain in 1955. Her involvement with the international women's movement, and her training in psychoanalysis, further shaped her philosophical path as she went on to complete doctorates in linguistics (1968) and philosophy (1974).

Key theories

The first of her groundbreaking books, *Speculum of the Other Woman* (1974), critiqued the absence of women

in the history of philosophy and the role assigned to them as the "other". Fearless in its approach, its denunciation of male-focused philosophy and psychoanalysis led to Irigaray's exile from French intellectual circles and her dismissal from her post at the University of Vincennes. She would later recount how she coped with this difficult period by finding refuge in nature.

This landmark publication, coupled with Irigaray's other works, spurred a shift in feminist theory and philosophy and inspired generations of work on sexual difference. Her books (more than 30) persist in critiquing patriarchal culture, focusing not merely on the liberation of women but also on the construction of a culture that recognizes women's unique subjectivity instead of considering it secondary to that of men.

Irigaray's central philosophical project first critiques patriarchal culture. She then explores feminine subjectivity, and promotes recognizing

◁ **ANTIGONE AND ISMENE**
For Irigaray, Antigone in Greek mythology embodies a commitment to life and living through her resistance to masculine law. In *Antigone and Ismene* (1896) by Emil Teschendorff, Ismene (left) attempts to influence the resolute Antigone.

all humans as "sexuate" – embodying not only the physical qualities of their sexed bodies, but also the psychological, political, linguistic, and relational aspects of their sex. Her thought aims at building an intersubjective (masculine and feminine) culture based on difference.

Political and cultural work

Beyond academia, Irigaray expanded her influence into politics, especially in France and Italy. Her linguistic research in schools and elsewhere highlighted gendered uses of language, illuminating relations of sexual difference and offering guidance on building a new politics.

In recent years, Irigaray's focus has moved towards explaining what an intersubjective culture might be like, emphasizing the act of touch and its role in human interactions, as she articulates in *The Mediation of Touch* (2023). This development in her work underscores her lifelong commitment to enriching philosophical discourse and human relations through a living rather than a theoretical understanding of human subjectivity.

Now in her nineties, Irigaray continues to contribute to the intellectual discourse on feminism, philosophy, and the exploration of human existence.

IN CONTEXT

Eastern inspiration

Irigaray began practising yoga and studying Patanjali's Yoga Sutras (2nd century BC) while recovering from a car accident in the late 1970s. In *Building a New World* (2015), she said that yoga brought her back to the innocence of her natural perception "towards a personal development but also towards communication and sharing with the other."

Irigaray's interest in yoga is not just personal. Throughout her career, she has drawn on both Eastern and Western philosophies, cultivating a rich dialogue that crosses beyond geographic and cultural boundaries. Her book *A New Culture of Energy* (2021) relates – controversially according to some critics – yogic principles to Western philosophical ideas, developing an inclusive conception of human belonging.

INDIAN BUDDHIST MANUSCRIPT

> "**Sexual difference** is one of the **major philosophical issues**, if not the issue, **of our age**."
>
> LUCE IRIGARAY

▷ **LUCE IRIGARAY, 2008**
Shown here at the Turin International Book Fair, Irigaray organizes annual seminars on her work for emerging scholars. In *Building a New World* (2015), she wrote, "No one can appropriate the thought of a thinker because it takes root in his or her own life."

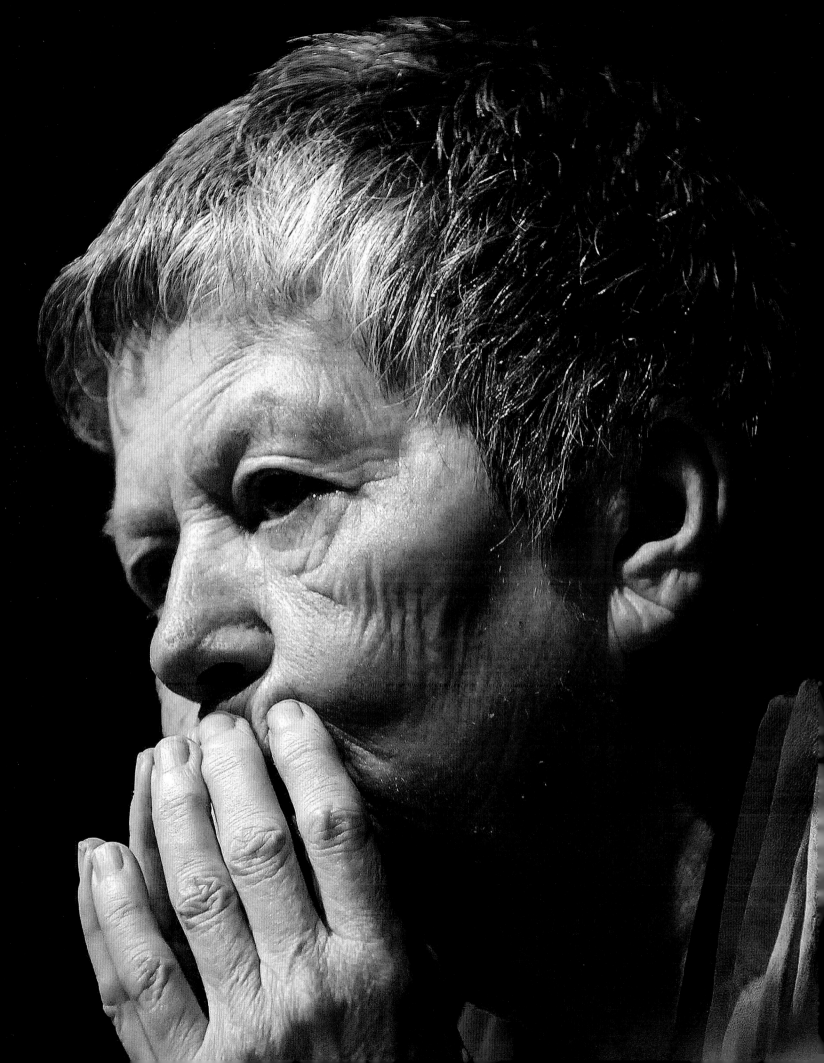

Stuart Hall

1932–2014, JAMAICAN–BRITISH

A leading British intellectual, teacher, and cultural theorist, Stuart Hall wrote on imperial decline, neoliberalism, racism, and diaspora. His work has influenced scholars, activists, and artists for more than six decades.

Stuart Hall was born into a middle-class family in Jamaica in 1932, during the waning decades of British colonial rule. A clever student, he attended the elite Jamaica College before winning a Rhodes Scholarship to study English at Oxford University. Arriving in Britain in 1951, he found an imperial power in decline, and would spend the rest of his life there "unlearning the norms" of the colonized society in which he was raised.

The New Left

Hall became increasingly disillusioned with Oxford's highly formal approach to literature and eventually gave up his doctorate to focus on political activism. In 1957, he joined the Campaign for Nuclear Disarmament (CND). He also started to write for publications on the British New Left, including the *Universities and Left Review* and its successor, the *New Left Review*.

Along with intellectuals such as Charles Taylor and E.P. Thompson, he responded to the Soviet Union's invasion of Hungary in 1956 and the Suez Crisis, when Egyptian leader Gamel Abdel Nasser nationalized the Suez Canal, then controlled by British interests, by advocating a more democratic and humanist Marxism.

In 1964, Hall joined Birmingham University's Centre for Contemporary Cultural Studies (CCCS). While there, he and his colleagues developed a radically contextualist approach to the study of popular culture. In 1978, he and his students published the seminal CCCS text, *Policing the Crisis*, which traced the authoritarian consensus emerging in 1970s Britain to the moral panic over muggings, whipped up by the police and the media to justify the criminalization of Black youth.

Over the next three decades, Hall refined his critique of the forces driving the neoliberal turn in British politics, coining the term Thatcherism (after Margaret Thatcher) in his 1979 essay "The Great Moving Right Show".

Diaspora and identity

In 1979, Hall became professor in sociology at the Open University. He began to write more explicitly about race, multiculturalism, and the diasporic perspective. He viewed identity as positional – as "a never-completed process of shifting identifications".

Hall stepped down from the Open University in 1997. That year, his feted lecture "Race, the Floating Signifier", clarified the idea of race as a social construction. When he died in London in February 2014, tributes poured in from around the world.

◁ **COMMITTED ANTI-NUCLEARIST**
Hall speaks at a CND rally in Trafalgar Square, London, in 1958. It was on a CND march that Hall met his wife Catherine, who went on to become an influential historian of the Caribbean.

▷ **STUART HALL, 2000**
Hall spent most of his adult life in Britain. He left the Caribbean at the age of 19 and would never again call it home, but it remained a shaping influence and source of diasporic identification.

IN CONTEXT
The British Black Arts Movement (BAM)

Drawing on Stuart Hall's theories of culture and representation, second generation Black and Asian artists established the British Black Arts Movement in 1982. Largely as a response to the rampant discrimination and exclusion they faced in the white-dominated art world, its members sought to carve out an oppositional space for Black art in Britain by creating their own infrastructure, including galleries and visual arts organizations.

British BAM members used their art to explore the impact of racism, gender subordination, and the effects of empire on Black people. Famous participants in the BAM include artists Rasheed Araeen, Claudette Johnson, Lubaina Himid, and Sonia Boyce; photographer David A. Bailey; and filmmakers John Akomfrah, Isaac Julien, and the Black Audio Film Collective. In 2022, the organization celebrated its 40th anniversary.

" The **colonial relationships** were... the **sugar** at the bottom of the **emblematically** English **cup of tea**. "

STUART HALL

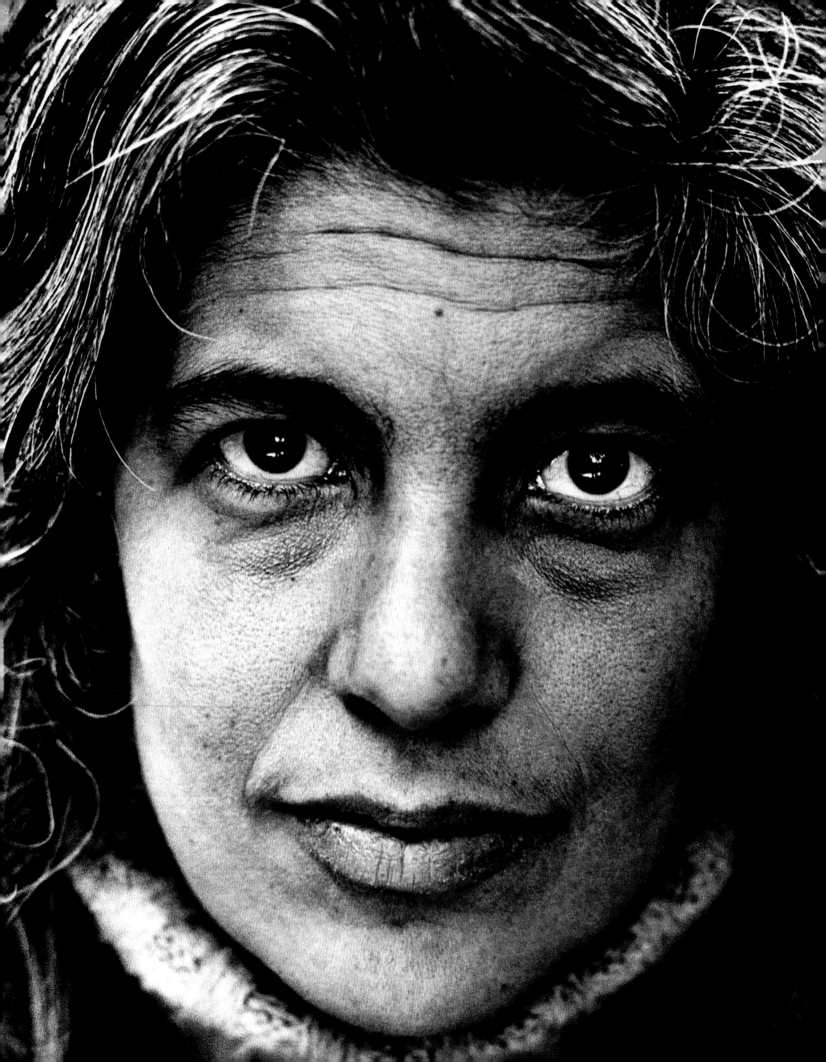

Susan Sontag

1933–2004, AMERICAN

One of the most famous intellectuals of the postwar period, Sontag was a polymath: a philosopher, writer, filmmaker, and activist. Brazen and adversarial, she frequently changed her opinions and perspectives.

Susan Sontag (formerly Rosenblatt) began writing around the age of six. "It was like enlisting in an army of saints... I felt that I was taking part in a noble activity," she said. The military metaphor clearly had resonance for her: years later she described herself as "a newly minted warrior in a very old battle: against philistinism, against ethical and aesthetic shallowness and indifference". The theme of war was to reappear throughout her life.

Growing up

Sontag was born into a wealthy family in New York, but after the death of her father – a fur trader – she was largely raised by her relatives and her nanny. When she was 12, her mother married Nathan Sontag, a war veteran, "full of medals and shrapnel"; Susan inherited his name.

At the age of 15, she had her first lesbian relationship and left home to study at the University of Chicago. At 17, she married the sociologist Philip Rieff and at 19 had a son, David. She undertook graduate studies, in literature and then philosophy, at the universities of Harvard and Oxford, and was divorced by the age of 27. She eventually settled in New York, where she indulged her passions, which included photography, film, literature, and philosophy.

Essays and criticism

Sontag is known best for her essays and reviews, which tackle a wide range of subjects, from modern culture and the media to illness, war, human rights, and politics. In 1966, she stepped into the limelight with *Against Interpretation*, a collection of essays that stages her assault on interpretative criticism: the role of criticism, according to her, should be "to show how it is what it is, even that it is what it is, rather than to show what it means".

The collection includes her first major work, "Notes on 'Camp'" (1964), which analyses "high" and "low" culture in the context of the gay community; it also includes reflections on the work of, among others, the writers and philosophers Albert Camus, Georg Lukács, and Jean-Paul Sartre, and the filmmaker Jean-Luc Godard. Later, in the 1980s, Sontag produced important commentaries on the philosophers Roland Barthes and Walter Benjamin.

Among Sontag's 17 published works are seven other works of non-fiction, as well as numerous short stories, plays, and four novels, including *The Volcano Lover* (1992) and *In America* (1999), which won the National Book Award in 2000.

Living with illness

Sontag was diagnosed with cancer in the mid-1970s and suffered with the disease for more than three decades. The struggle is reflected in her *Illness as Metaphor* (1978), an analysis of the language and metaphors invoked in the representation of cancer – an argument she extended in *Aids and its Metaphors* (1989). Her battle with cancer was captured by one of Sontag's lovers, the photographer Annie Leibovitz (see box, right).

Sontag's son, David, a writer, has said that his mother was terrified of death and fantasized that she was not dying. At the age of 70 (having visited some of the world's worst war zones) his mother noted, "When I turned 40 I was in China; when I turned 50 I was in France; when I turned 60 I was in Sarajevo and the bombs were falling. Being 70 sounds very awesome. Despite my two bouts of cancer I feel fine. I feel as if a lot of things are still ahead." Sontag died of leukaemia a year later.

◁ **SUSAN SONTAG, 1979**
Articulate, poised, and glamorous, Sontag was eminently marketable. Embraced by the press from the 1960s onwards, she undoubtedly colluded in the creation of her powerful media image.

◁ **AGAINST INTERPRETATION**
In her 1966 book, Sontag became one of the first writers to consider "high" and "low" culture on the same terms. The collection made her name as one of the most incisive thinkers of her generation.

IN CONTEXT
Leibovitz and Sontag

Sontag said she had been in love nine times in her life: "Five women, four men." The renowned US portrait photographer Annie Leibovitz (born 1949) was one of those women. The couple met in New York in 1988, while Leibovitz was doing publicity shots for Sontag's *Aids and its Metaphors*. They travelled the world together during their 15-year relationship. Leibovitz's retrospective *A Photographer's Life: 1990–2005*, which she says, "came out of grief", includes images of Sontag on her deathbed.

ANNIE LEIBOVITZ

▷ **HELENE CIXOUS, 1994**
Cixous has been a professor of English literature at the University of Paris VIII for more than 50 years. She remains head of the Centre de Recherches en Etudes Féminines, which she created in 1974.

Hélène Cixous

BORN 1937, FRENCH–ALGERIAN

A leading voice in Poststructuralist feminist theory, Cixous is a philosopher, novelist, poet, and playwright. She is best known for her *écriture féminine*, a theory of writing that focuses on sexual difference.

Born in Oran, Algeria, Hélène Cixous is the daughter of an Austro-German mother and a French father of Jewish faith. She recalls her early childhood as a "paradise", despite having experienced antisemitism in World War II, in which the family lost their French nationality, and the children were barred from public school and her father from practising medicine.

Her father died when she was just 11, and the themes of loss and of the father/daughter relationship were to appear frequently in her writing: for example, her semi-autobiographical text, *Inside* (1969), is in part a meditation on her father's death.

Philosophical influences

By the age of 27, Cixous had emigrated to Paris, passed her teaching exam, had two children (one of whom died as an infant), been married, divorced, and begun her doctoral research into the Modernist writer James Joyce. In 1962, she met the philosopher Jacques Derrida – who became a lifelong friend – while working as an assistant teacher at the University of Bordeaux. She was later appointed at the Sorbonne in Paris. With Derrida, who was also a French Jew raised in Algeria, she shared a sense of "belonging constituted of exclusion and nonbelonging". Both addressed questions of identity and nationality in their writings.

Cixous took a research trip to the US in 1963 and was introduced to the eminent psychoanalyst Jacques Lacan the same year. Psychoanalytic theory

was to have an immense impact on her work, much of which evolved out of her readings of Lacan and of Sigmund Freud. The Brazilian novelist Clarice Lispector was also a huge influence (see box, right).

In 1968, in the wake of the student riots in which she participated (see box, p.311), Cixous was one of the founders of the innovative Université de Paris VIII at Vincennes, which has since attracted major thinkers, including Genette, Foucault, Todorov, Deleuze, and Guattari. Six years later, at the same university, she set up the Centre de Recherches en Etudes Féminines, the first centre for women's studies in Europe.

Challenging power structures

In the mid-1970s, Cixous wrote *The Newly Born Woman* (with Catherine Clément), "Sorties", and the work for which she is best known, "The Laugh of the Medusa", texts in which she developed the concept of *écriture feminine* (feminine writing). Influenced by the work of Derrida, and by the

◁ **SIGMUND FREUD**
Cixous challenged Freud's theories on gender roles and sexual identity – including penis envy and the Oedipus and castration complexes.

belief that language can generate social change, this theory of writing focuses on sexual identity, difference, and bisexuality; it challenges the hierarchical oppositions on which Western epistemology is based (for example man/woman, self/other, speaking/writing, nature/culture).

History and theatre

In 1975 Cixous met Antoinette Fouque – psychoanalyst, luminary of the women's movement in France, and founder of the publishing house *des femmes*, where Cixous published many of her books. Two years later she suffered an agonizing break-up of a relationship (chronicled in *Angst*), followed by an intense period of feminist study and the start of her interest in Martin Heidegger's work on language. In the 1980s and 90s her focus turned to avant-garde theatre and political and historical writing; from the late 1990s it shifted again to explore autobiography, memoir, and genealogy (in *Osnabrück*, *Reveries of the Wild Woman*, *Portrait of Jacques Derrida As a Young Jewish Saint*, and *Benjamin à Montaigne*).

A hugely prolific writer, Cixous has produced dozens of works across diverse genres and disciplines, including philosophy, literary theory, poetry, and fiction. In France she is especially revered as a playwright; her first play, written in 1975, was a reworking of Freud's fascinating "Dora" case. She has received several honorary doctorates and numerous prizes and awards, including, in 1994, the prestigious Légion d'Honneur.

IN CONTEXT
Clarice Lispector

From the late 1970s, the work of Brazil's celebrated novelist and short-story writer Clarice Lispector (1920–77) is said to have inspired the mythical quality that runs through Cixous's fiction. Cixous also engages directly with the Brazilian author's work in several texts (*To Live the Orange*, "Extreme Fidelity", *Reading with Clarice Lispector*, and *Three Steps on the Ladder of Writing*) and in 1989 received Brazil's Southern Cross award for her work on Lispector. She says that the Brazilian's writing holds an "exceptional place" for her and that both Lispector and Derrida, take "sexual difference into account, he occupying the space of a certain masculinity capable of femininity, and she occupying the space of a femininity capable of masculinity."

STATUE OF CLARICE LISPECTOR, LEME BEACH, RIO DE JANEIRO, BRAZIL

◁ **ORAN, ALGERIA**
One of Cixous's fictional works, *Reveries of the Wild Woman* (2000), focuses on the sense of displacement and alienation she suffered growing up in colonial Algeria.

Julia Kristeva

BORN 1941, BULGARIAN–FRENCH

Challenging and provocative, Kristeva has been a prominent voice in philosophy, linguistics, literature, art, politics, feminism, and psychoanalysis since the 1980s, and has received widespread acclaim for her work.

Julia Kristeva was born in 1941 into a middle-class family in Bulgaria. She later graduated with a degree in linguistics from the University of Sofia and then won a scholarship to pursue doctoral research in France on the application of psychoanalytic theory to language and literature.

Settled in Paris, she became heavily influenced by the major voices in Structuralism and Poststructuralism, including Jacques Lacan, Michel Foucault, and Roland Barthes, and wrote for the left-wing publication *Tel Quel*, which had been co-founded by the novelist Philippe Sollers, whom Kristeva married in 1967.

In 1974 Kristeva began teaching linguistics at the University of Paris VI, developing her interest in the

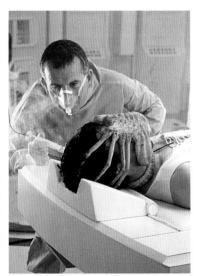

◁ **JULIA KRISTEVA**
Kristeva is currently an emeritus professor at Paris Diderot University and a visiting professor at Columbia University, New York.

relationship between language and the human body, and between the semiotic and symbolic aspects of language. Her rise to prominence began in 1980 with *Desire in Language: A Semiotic Approach to Literature and Art*, in which she elaborates on the concept of "intertextuality" (see box, right).

Horror and identity

In 1980, Kristeva published *Powers of Horror: An Essay on Abjection*, in which she explores what gives rise to feelings of horror and disgust in humans. From this analysis she developed the psychoanalytic concept of "abjection" (literally, of being "thrown out"). This process describes the traumatic separation of the child from the mother that is central to the development of identity and establishing boundaries between inner and outer, self and other, ego and non-ego. Abjection may refer to aspects of the self, or the social body, which have been rejected but have not disappeared: much like Sigmund Freud's concept of the uncanny, the rejected/present of the abject will often return to haunt the self.

◁ **ABJECTION**
Kristeva qualified in psychoanalysis in 1979. She drew on the theories of Lacan and Freud in her 1980 *Powers of Horror.*

Kristeva has since built up an extensive body of work across a wide range of themes and disciplines, including psychoanalysis, linguistics, feminism, literary theory, semiotics, art, and love; in recent years she has also turned to writing novels and biographies of exceptional women. However, her relationship with feminism has sometimes been uneasy – one of her claims is that feminism has an inherent tendency to reproduce the power structures and discourses that it seeks to subvert.

In 2018 Kristeva was accused by Bulgarian authorities of having acted as a communist secret agent in the 1970s, under the name "Sabrina" – an accusation that she denies. She remains, nonetheless, one of the Western world's most respected intellectuals. As well as numerous honorary degrees, she has received the Vaclav Havel Prize, the Hannah Arendt Prize, and France's Commander of the Légion d'honneur for her work.

◁ **ABJECTION AND *ALIEN***
Kristeva's idea of abjection has been used in the analysis of texts and movies, such as Ridley Scott's *Alien* (1979). In it, the characters are made to confront the abject – the entity they have ejected and tried to suppress.

IN CONTEXT
Intertextuality

Kristeva is perhaps best known for the concept of intertextuality, an idea built upon the work of the theorists Ferdinand de Saussure and, especially, Mikhail Bakhtin. "The literary word," she writes, "is an intersection of textual surfaces", emphasizing not only the social, cultural, and ideological contexts from which literary texts are produced but also their essential interdependence. Far from being the products of an author's creative originality, Kristeva sees all literary works as constructed from pre-existing discourses whose meanings intersect or are overlaid with meanings from other discourses. All texts, then, are linked in some way, great or small, with others, sometimes through parody or allusion, and sometimes through the connections that readers perceive between seemingly very different texts.

RUSSIAN THINKER MIKHAIL BAKHTIN

Martha Nussbaum

BORN 1947, AMERICAN

Nussbaum's philosophy focuses in particular on human emotions. She is also a passionate advocate of the positive role that philosophy can play within public life in the modern world.

Martha Nussbaum (née Craven) was born in 1947 to a prosperous family in New York City. She went to a private school, studying drama and classics, and thereafter attended Wellesley College, Massachusetts. Having left the college in her second year, she spent some time acting – she had an early love of Greek drama – and then went to New York University, where she took an undergraduate degree in theatre and classics.

It was there that she met her future husband – the renowned Jewish linguist Alan Nussbaum. Martha converted to Judaism and the couple were married in 1969. They later divorced, but her commitment to Judaism has remained steadfast.

In the 1970s, Nussbaum attended graduate school at the University of Harvard. She found it an inhospitable environment – rife with antisemitism, sexism, and homophobia. However, it was here that she researched her PhD on the Greek classics, with a focus on Aristotle's account of human and animal life. She was appointed a junior

◁ **MARTHA NUSSBAUM, 2005**
Nussbaum has written more than two dozen books. Her latest, *Monarchy of Fear* (2018), is critical of the philosophical tradition that minimizes the role of emotion in our response to the world.

fellow – the first woman at Harvard to receive such an appointment. She taught at the university into the 1980s, but was refused tenure and eventually moved to Brown University.

Development economics
From the mid-1980s (while at Brown), at the suggestion of the economist Amartya Sen, Nussbaum took up a post at the United Nations University World Institute for Development Economics Research in Finland, where she spent a month a year for the next seven years.

With Sen, she developed what they referred to as the "capabilities approach" to national development: an attempt to understand quality of life in an approach that is broader than the usual measures of Gross Domestic Product (GDP) and Gross National Product (GNP).

Nussbaum continues to explore the meeting places between philosophy, law, politics, economics, development, and public policy. In 1995, she began teaching at the University of Chicago Law School, where she is currently Ernst Freund Distinguished Service Professor of Law and Ethics.

Public engagement is central to Nussbaum's practice of philosophy. For her, philosophy is far from an ivory-tower pursuit. She sees the

role of the philosopher today, much as in the time of Ancient Greece, as being one of engagement with the social, political, and legal realities of contemporary society.

Accessible scholarship
Nussbaum's writing is both scholarly and accessible: she engages in philosophical debates, but resists the temptation to see these debates as a matter of relevance only among philosophers. In addition to her more formal philosophical work, she often

IN PROFILE
Bernard Williams

One of Nussbaum's significant philosophical influences was the British philosopher Bernard Williams (1929–2003). Williams worked within the analytic tradition of British philosophy, but as Nussbaum herself wrote, he was never entirely at home there, finding much of this tradition to be "narrow, dry, and in flight from some of the most important aspects of human existence". While he was highly respected for his philosophical skill, he was also sceptical about the extent to which moral philosophy could really account for the huge complexities of human life.

BERNARD WILLIAMS, KINGS COLLEGE, CAMBRIDGE UNIVERSITY, 1978

" What **I** am **calling for**, in effect, is… **a society** of **citizens** who **admit** that they are **needy** and **vulnerable**. "

MARTHA NUSSBAUM, *HIDING FROM HUMANITY: DISGUST, SHAME, AND THE LAW*

KEY WORKS

1986
Her first major work, *The Fragility of Goodness: Luck and Ethics in Greek Tragedy and Philosophy*, is published.

2000
Women and Human Development argues that public policy must address women in developing countries.

2006
In *Frontiers of Justice: Disability, Nationality, Species Membership* Nussbaum looks at theories of social justice.

2011
Creating Capabilities is published, offering new goals and models for human development.

2016
Anger and Forgiveness: Resentment Generosity, Justice is published.

2018
The Monarchy of Fear: A Philosopher Looks at Our Political Crisis examines the climate of fear in Trump's US.

△ **VINE LEAVES**
Nussbaum envisages human beings as "plant-like" – soft and vulnerable, but also capable of tremendous growth and able to survive considerable hardship.

writes articles for a broader, far more popular audience. She has made multiple appearances on television and in the mass media, and has been an expert witness in court, arguing on both philosophical and historical grounds for gay rights.

Life and the emotions

One of Nussbaum's recurrent preoccupations is with the role of the emotions in human life. For her, any reasonable theory of human action and existence must begin with a recognition of human vulnerability. To be able to grow and develop as human beings, it is essential that we recognize the fact of our own vulnerability, as well as the vulnerability of others. This idea is associated with a concept that is derived from Greek

philosophy (Aristotle in particular) – that of "eudaimonia", or flourishing, as the end of human life. A life of flourishing is a life in which individuals are able to realize their potential as human beings, and to develop their capacities and abilities. Nussbaum first explored the link between flourishing and vulnerability in her 1986 book, *The Fragility of Goodness*, in which she examines the idea of "moral luck" through an analysis not only of ancient philosophy, but also of ancient tragedy.

At the heart of *The Fragility of Goodness* is the following problem: although we may often aspire to lead a good life and to act ethically, we live in a world in which our ability to do so is constantly constrained by chance events. One image that Nussbaum uses in her later work to tie together

these two ideas of flourishing and vulnerability is that of human life as "plant-like" rather than "jewel-like". Human beings are soft, tender, and capable of being wounded; but it is because we are all of these things that we are capable of vigorous growth.

For Nussbaum, the idea of vulnerability has far-reaching implications. Many of our approaches to ethics, politics, law, and the good life completely disregard the fact of vulnerability. In doing so, they misconstrue what human beings are, and so fail to adequately address the urgent ethical questions that face us.

▽ **D'ANGELO LAW LIBRARY, CHICAGO**
In 1995, Nussbaum began teaching at the University of Chicago Law School, where she is currently a professor of law and ethics.

◁ **MAN SHOUTING, MICHELANGELO**
Nussbaum claims that anger – however justified it may seem to be – is almost always a wholly inadequate response to life's problems.

indeed attempt to redress the balance by humiliating you in turn. She notes that anger is frequently tangled up with this concern for status – a preoccupation that is unhelpful, and serves only to impede our pursuit of other human goods. For example, if a man decided to murder his neighbour's cat, the neighbour would be justifiably outraged. Part of this outrage would be tangled up in status ("How dare you!"). In an attempt to regain lost status, the neighbour might decide to take revenge, for example by murdering the man's cat in turn.

Looking beyond anger

Retaliation might solve the status problem (the neighbour proving that he is a person to be reckoned with, thus regaining "equal" status), but it does not solve the other major problem of the dead cat (there are now two dead cats) and has most definitely escalated the thorny issue of neighbourhood disharmony. Nussbaum is not claiming that we should not experience anger, but that we should see it as a transitional phase, and should then move as quickly as possible to attempt to remedy the situation in a spirit of "generosity and forward-looking reason". She cites Nelson Mandela (see box, right) as someone who was able to look beyond anger.

In 2017, Nussbaum was invited to give the Jefferson Lecture by the National Endowment for the Humanities, one of the highest honours in US academia.

IN CONTEXT
Apartheid and anger

For Nussbaum, Nelson Mandela (1918–2013) is an example of a public figure who managed to overcome anger in pursuit of building a better future. Imprisoned on Robben Island for 27 years under South Africa's apartheid regime, Mandela wrote about his own struggles with anger. While he was in prison, he read the Stoic philosopher Marcus Aurelius, and trained himself to move beyond rage, seeing that there could be no possibility for nation-building when resentment was rife. Mandela's overcoming of anger was not an attempt to overlook the wrongs of the past, but instead was a positive attempt to move to a brighter future.

NELSON MANDELA REVISITING HIS CELL ON ROBBEN ISLAND, 1994

Nussbaum has written about many aspects of human emotional life, including disgust, shame, desire, and anger. In her work on anger, she dismantles our beliefs in anger as justified or even useful. "If we think closely about anger," she writes, "we can begin to see why it is a stupid way to run one's life." Nussbaum argues that the desire for payback or retaliation is central to anger. However, this desire for retaliation is deeply flawed, according to the philosopher. It does nothing whatsoever to restore the previous wrong, nor does it make the world a better place. The only way in which it makes sense, Nussbaum argues, is in terms of status. If you humiliate me and lessen my status then I can

> " There's **no emotion** we **ought** to **think harder** and **more clearly about** than **anger**. "
>
> MARTHA NUSSBAUM, "BEYOND ANGER"

Slavoj Žižek

BORN 1949, SLOVENIAN

Hailed as one of the most brilliant philosophers of his generation, Žižek has used his prominent media profile to present a complex mixture of high and popular culture, philosophy, psychology, and politics.

After World War II, Slovenia was a part of communist Yugoslavia under the leadership of Josip Broz, known as Tito, the "benign dictator", who allowed greater freedom and a more relaxed attitude to Western culture than was permitted in other communist states. Slavoj Žižek was born in the Slovenian capital, Ljubljana, in 1949, and grew up in a period of gradual liberalization and relatively high prosperity.

Slavoj's father was an economist and civil servant, and his mother an accountant in a state-owned company. When he was a child, they moved to the seaside town of Portorož, where Slavoj was educated at the local primary school. As he grew up he developed a love of the cinema – and particularly Hollywood films – which provided an escape from the dull, officially approved entertainment available on state television. An only child, Žižek spent much of his time alone, consuming what he could of Western culture, and when the family returned to Ljubljana he dreamed of becoming a film director.

Žižek's discovery of philosophy, and especially his reading of Hegel's *The Phenomenology of the Mind* (1807), set him on a different path, towards the Structuralist and Poststructuralist French thinkers such as Foucault, Derrida, and Lacan. Possessed of a fierce intellect and fluent in several languages, Žižek displayed his remarkable precocity when he published the first ever Slovene translation of Derrida while still a student at Bežigrad High School.

Political philosophy

After graduating in 1967, Žižek enrolled at the University of Ljubljana to study philosophy and sociology – a course heavily weighted towards a Marxist interpretation; he was strongly influenced by Božidar Debenjak, his professor of philosophy. One incident that illuminates Žižek's political stance at the time occurred during a visit to Czechoslovakia in 1968. This was after the "Prague Spring", when the Czechs had achieved reforms that freed them from the control of the Soviet Union. As the Soviet troops invaded the capital to quell the rebellion, Žižek watched, eating strawberry cakes at a café in the central square. Although no supporter of totalitarian

△ **TITO STAMP, 1967**
A Yugoslav stamp, printed in 1967, bears the image of Josip Broz Tito, who served as president in 1953–80. He promoted a route to socialism independent of Soviet hegemony.

IN CONTEXT
The collapse of communism

A groundswell of anti-communist feeling in Central and Eastern Europe during the 1980s came to a head in the (largely nonviolent) revolutions of 1989, which led to the eventual dismantling of the Soviet Union. The trade union Solidarity came to power in Poland in June, and this had a domino effect, with Hungary and then East Germany tearing down the Iron Curtain later that year. This was followed by the dissolution of the USSR in 1991, and the abandoning of communism in Albania and Yugoslavia in the early 1990s.

THE FALL OF THE BERLIN WALL, NOVEMBER 1991

> " **Beyond** the **fiction** of **reality**, there is the **reality** of the **fiction**. "
>
> SLAVOJ ZIZEK, *LESS THAN NOTHING: HEGEL AND THE SHADOW OF DIALECTICAL MATERIALISM*

▷ **SLAVOJ ZIZEK**
Žižek has popularized philosophy, but is never less than controversial. He holds many of his contemporaries in contempt, and has been variously described as the "Elvis of cultural theory"and the "Borat of philosophy".

KEY WORKS

1989
Gains international recognition for his first book in English, *The Sublime Object of Ideology*.

1991
Publishes *Looking Awry: An Introduction to Jacques Lacan Through Popular Culture*.

1993
Publishes a study of German Idealism, *Tarrying With the Negative: Kant, Hegel, and the Critique of Ideology*.

2002
Responds to the 11 September attack in New York with a collection of essays, *Welcome to the Desert of the Real!*

2008
The failure of the left, a recurrent theme for Žižek, is the subject of his *In Defense of Lost Causes*.

2010
In *Living in the End Times* Žižek explores the consequences of the death of global capitalism.

∇ **END OF THE PRAGUE SPRING**
From April 1968, Czechoslovakia enjoyed four months of freedom from oppressive Soviet rule. This brief period – which is known as the Prague Spring – ended on 20 August, when 500,000 Warsaw Pact troops invaded the country. Here, on the streets of Prague, a young Czech woman and other protesters register their opposition to the invasion.

communism, he declared that he was also suspicious of the liberalism that it was trying to suppress.

At university in Ljubljana he became deeply involved with several groups of student activists and political dissidents, writing articles for various progressive magazines. He also followed up his studies of French philosophers, whose ideas – although left-leaning or even Marxist – were very different from the Hegelian

Marxism being taught at the university. He graduated in 1971 and was offered a job as an assistant researcher in order to continue his postgraduate studies. Unfortunately, this coincided with an official crackdown on politically suspect activities; and when he submitted his master's thesis it was rejected for diverging from Marxist theory. Žižek then lost his job at the university and was forced to resubmit his thesis with an appendix

explaining how his ideas were at odds with approved theory. There was, however, no doubting the brilliance of his work, and Žižek was eventually awarded his master's degree in 1975, but by this time he found himself virtually unemployable as an academic because of his unorthodox brand of philosophy.

Over the next few years, Žižek worked as a freelance translator, but after he married fellow philosopher

◁ **UNIVERSITY OF LJUBLJANA**
Throughout his life, Žižek has been closely associated with Slovenia's oldest university, where he is now professor of philosophy and theoretic psychoanalysis.

Renata Salecl and started a family, he sought a less precarious way of making a living. Swallowing his pride, he joined the Communist Party. This allowed him to find a job as a researcher in the Institute for Sociology and Philosophy at Ljubljana University. Here he returned to his earlier interest in the psychologist and philosopher Jacques Lacan (see box, right).

Lacan was by then an old man, so Žižek was unable to achieve his dream of meeting his hero. Nevertheless, he made his way to Paris, where he took a course in psychoanalysis and studied under Lacan's son-in law, Jacques-Alain Miller. He completed his thesis on Lacan in 1981, and was awarded a doctorate by Ljubljana University, which by then had softened its attitude towards ideas that were previously considered subversive.

With his doctorate complete and now in a research post with no teaching responsibilities, Žižek began to write prolifically, elaborating on his theme of reconciling Hegelian Marxism with Lacanian psychology, and branching out into the theory of literary and film criticism.

▷ **DOCUMENTARY WORK**
Žižek worked with British director Sophie Fiennes on the 2012 documentary *The Pervert's Guide to Ideology*, which explored prevailing ideologies through popular film.

Media stardom

Žižek developed his own distinctive writing style, making frequent references to popular culture, juxtaposing seemingly contradictory arguments, and being deliberately provocative. This was a reflection of his manner of speaking: he has a slight speech impediment, and gives the impression that he cannot speak fast enough to keep up with thoughts; and his animated, quick-fire delivery is accompanied by nervous tics, such as pulling his nose and tugging at his shirt. Combined with his unkempt appearance, he comes across very differently from the conventional idea of an academic philosopher.

In 1989 Žižek published his first book in English, *The Sublime Object of Ideology*, which catapulted him into the international limelight. He was by this time far more actively involved in politics in Yugoslavia, as many intellectuals were pushing for a more democratic Slovenia following the death of Tito in 1980.

Žižek was also a contributor to left-liberal magazines in Slovenia, and stood for election as a Liberal Democratic candidate in the country's first free elections in 1990; he was narrowly beaten for a place as one of the four-person joint presidency.

Žižek became a media personality, touring, appearing on television and radio, and even featuring in films. He raised some eyebrows with his second marriage, to a 27-year-old model, the daughter of an Argentinian Lacanian psychologist. His fame has undoubtedly popularized philosophy, showing it to be exciting and relevant in the modern world.

Žižek remains a familiar face (and voice) in television and radio discussions, and he is sought out for his views on current affairs as much as on philosophy and culture.

His books, sometimes appearing at the rate of three or four a year, have been published worldwide from the 1990s onwards, and he has spent much of his time as a visiting academic in the US and across Europe, while still holding his post as a researcher at Ljubljana. At the time of writing, Žižek is living in Ljubljana with his third wife, the journalist Jela Krečič, and their son.

IN PROFILE
Jacques Lacan

The psychoanalyst and psychiatrist Jacques Lacan (1901–81) was a prominent thinker in the Structuralist movement that became popular in the 1960s, particularly among French intellectuals. He presented a radically new interpretation of Freud's theories, taking the view that the unconscious is linguistic in its structure, and best understood by deconstruction, a method derived from linguistics. Lacan's ideas had major implications, not only for psychotherapy, but also more widely in the analysis of philosophical, political, and cultural discourse.

JACQUES LACAN

"We **feel free** because **we lack** the very language to articulate our **unfreedom**."

SLAVOJ ZIZEK, "INTRODUCTION: THE MISSING INK"

▷ **BELL HOOKS, 1980**
bell hooks's writing includes poetry and texts on gender, spirituality, race, class, and education – works that continue to enlighten and empower a global readership.

bell hooks

1952–2021, AMERICAN

A feminist, scholar, social critic, and activist, hooks was one of the US's leading intellectuals, and a powerful and important commentator on race, gender, and class.

One of seven children, Gloria Jean Watkins was born in a rural, racially segregated town in Kentucky in 1952. Her father worked as a caretaker and her mother was a part-time maid in white households. She later took her great-grandmother's name, Bell Hooks, as a pen name – although using lowercase to prioritize her message over her personality.

Her childhood was traumatic: she witnessed numerous violent attacks on her mother by her abusive father, and was frightened of most white people. She described her world as one in which the women "dug fishing worms, set traps for rabbits, made butter and wine, sewed quilts, and wrung the necks of chickens". She attended a segregated primary school, but was later sent to an integrated high school, which exposed her to acute differences in race and class.

Academic achievement

hooks escaped from working-class Kentucky to take up a place at Stanford University – a prestigious white college. Despite her parents' hostility to her study, in 1973 she graduated with a degree in English. As an undergraduate, she began a stormy, 12-year relationship with a poet, Mack, whom she wrote about in her memoir, *Wounds of Passion* (1997), a text that also expounds on race and gender. After being awarded an MA and then a doctorate, for a thesis on the writer Toni Morrison, she committed to teaching and writing, recognizing both as crucial forms of political resistance.

Her career began in 1976 as a professor in ethnic studies at the University of Southern California. She went on to hold several academic posts, including at Yale University, City University of New York, and Berea College, Kentucky.

" **Most men** find it **difficult** to be **patriarchs...** but they **fear letting go** of **the benefits.** "

BELL HOOKS, *FEMINISM IS FOR EVERYBODY*

Prolific writing

hooks wrote her first book at the age of 19, but her first major work, *Ain't I a Woman*, was published 10 years later, in 1981. In it, she emphasized that the struggle for Black liberation had always been defined as the liberation of Black men, and feminism as the liberation of white women – ideas that she developed in *Feminist Theory: From Margin to Center* (1984).

In *The Will to Change*, she explained, with characteristic razor-sharp perception, the complex, interlocking forms of oppression that uphold political and social systems. Extending Kimberlé Crenshaw's concept of intersectionality (see box, below), she identified the complex mechanisms of power that oppress individuals under "imperialist white-supremacist capitalist patriarchy".

hooks published more than 30 books. A highly charismatic speaker, she lectured and gave talks on social and cultural issues, including the Black Lives Matter movement.

In her acceptance speech at the Kentucky Writers Hall of Fame ceremony in Lexington in 2018, she said that her presence there to receive an award was a victory: having moved from a childhood defined by racial apartheid and by schools that told her that Black people do not write books, it was "wonderful to return home to Kentucky, to be the Kentucky writer... to be a person of courage, to be self-determining, and to be a person of love". However, she also called for resistance to those who, in the era of the Trump administration, had attempted to return people to the "culture of fear". hooks died in 2021.

△ **BLACK LIVES MATTER**
Black American women were instrumental in establishing Black Lives Matter, a movement that campaigns against racism and racial inequality. bell hooks engaged with the issue of how such social activism can be channelled to create lasting change.

IN CONTEXT
Intersectionality

The term "intersectionality" was coined in 1989 by Black US lawyer Kimberlé Crenshaw to explain how forms of oppression, such as racism and sexism, overlap and reinforce one another, creating multiple levels of injustice. She introduced the term in response to a case of a Black woman whose claim for discrimination against a company who refused to hire her was dismissed by a court because the employer did hire Black men and white women. Crenshaw maintained, however, that as a Black woman the claimant was doubly discriminated against, but fell through a legal loophole as the law could only address each form of discrimination separately. The term intersectionality is now more widely used to include LGBTQ+ issues, among others.

INTERSECTIONALITY IS THE MEETING OF TWO OR MORE STREAMS OF PREJUDICE

Judith Butler

BORN 1956, AMERICAN

Butler is a radical cultural theorist who has been at the forefront of feminist and LGBTQ+ issues since 1990. Their work has helped to reshape how we think about gender and sexuality in the modern world.

IN PROFILE
Monique Wittig

Monique Wittig (1935–2003) was a radical French feminist, theorist, avant-garde writer, and co-founder of *Psychoanalyse et Politique*, a group established in 1969 to fight for women's rights from a psychoanalytic and political perspective. She viewed heterosexuality as a sexual and labour contract. Her fiction was a major source of inspiration to Butler.
  In Wittig's *Les Guérillères* (1969), female warriors overthrow patriarchy to create a new, free state; and in *The Lesbian Body* (1973) she avoids masculine pronouns and jettisons gender binaries to suggest, in Butler's own words, "a being whom neither man nor woman truly describes". Wittig's fiction, explains Butler, offers "an experience beyond the categories of identity".

◁ **MARCH FOR RIGHTS**
Prejudice against the LGBT+ community prompted the Stonewall riots in New York in 1969; the riots are commemorated here in a march some 25 years later.

Søren Kierkegaard and Baruch Spinoza. However, as a teenager, what really sparked their passion for philosophy was a rabbi at their synagogue, an outstanding intellectual, according to Butler. They bombarded him with questions about German idealism and existential theology.

The price of seriousness

Thereafter, they read widely, and at the age of 18, in 1974, set off to Bennington College, Vermont, a place where – as a young queer person – they felt they could survive (they knew bisexuals who studied there). Two years later, they transferred to Yale University in Connecticut to read philosophy; this included a Fulbright scholarship in 1979 to study with Hans-Georg Gadamer in Heidelberg, Germany.
  Butler became absorbed in Hegel's exploration of the relationship between desire and recognition, which was the springboard for their focus on feminism and gender, and the basis of their doctoral thesis.

POSTER FOR A FEMINIST DEMONSTRATION IN PARIS, 1971

▷ **JUDITH BUTLER, 2010**
Butler is active in gender politics, human rights, and anti-war campaigns, and is currently serving on the board of the Center for Constitutional Rights in New York.

When asked in an interview, at the age of 12, what they would like to do when they grew up, Judith Butler replied that they wanted to be either a philosopher or a clown: "I understood," they explained, "that much depended on whether or not I found the world worth philosophizing about, and what the price of seriousness might be."
  Butler was born in Cleveland, Ohio, and attended the local Hebrew school: their parents were of Russian and Hungarian Jewish descent. Their father was a dentist; their mother's

family owned several cinemas. "I grew up," they say, "with a generation of American Jews that understood assimilation meant conforming to certain gender norms that were presented in the Hollywood movies."
  Nonetheless, Butler says they were a "problem child": rebellious, defiant, unhappy; their school warned that they may become a criminal. They were also precocious, and would lock themselves in their parents' basement to read their books – dense works by philosophical heavyweights, such as

> " **Gender** is the **repeated stylization** of the **body**... over **time** to **produce** the appearance of **substance**, of a **natural** sort of **being**. "
>
> JUDITH BUTLER, *GENDER TROUBLE*

△ **QUESTIONS OF GENDER**
Butler's theories and activism have brought questions of gender into the heart of US national debate and have also sparked a broader awakening of identity politics.

Their first published work, *Subjects of Desire: Hegelian Reflections in Twentieth-Century France*, was a revision of their thesis on Hegel. It appeared in 1987 (three years after Yale awarded them a PhD) and remains an important contribution to French Hegelianism. Other thinkers who were crucial to the development of Butler's work include Freud, Althusser, de Beauvoir, Foucault, Derrida, Sartre, Kristeva, Irigaray, and Wittig (see box, p.348).

Denaturalization of gender

Butler's groundbreaking work *Gender Trouble: Feminism and the Subversion of Identity* (1990) evolved out of their readings of these major thinkers, and also reflected their critique of dominant forms of late 20th-century feminism. The text poses immense challenges to traditional ideas of

gender by suggesting that gender is not simple, or fixed and stable – it reflects what we do, not what we are. Their key concept is that of "performativity": the repetition of rituals and behaviours, which, over a long period of time, constructs and reinforces our identities according to norms and expectations. These "gender acts", performances of "being a man" or "being a woman", include, among many other things, a person's mannerisms, how they talk, look, dress, and act.

Butler argues that we can destabilize these supposedly fixed identities and challenge or subvert the man/woman gender binary by performing in different ways (through cross-dressing and drag, for example), so that "cultural configurations of sex and gender might then proliferate". A German journalist once said that

Butler resembled "a young Italian man" – an observation that they apparently found amusing.

Gender Trouble rocketed Butler to celebrity status. It also sparked controversy in both academic and non-academic circles, to which they responded, three years later, in *Bodies That Matter: On the Discursive Limits of "Sex"* (1993). They emphasized that performativity is involuntary and not equivalent to performance or a question of personal choice; they also broadened the boundaries of gender and sexuality and opened the door to the development of queer theory in the following decade (see box, right).

Academic career

Butler held posts at a number of US universities before their appointment in 1993 at the University of California, Berkeley. It was here, five years later,

KEY WORKS

"**Gender** is a kind of **imitation** for which there is **no original**."

JUDITH BUTLER, "IMITATION AND GENDER INSUBORDINATION"

that they took up the prestigious post of Maxine Elliot Professor in the Department of Comparative Literature and Critical Theory, where they still teach. Other notable positions held by Butler have included the Hannah Arendt Chair and Professor of Philosophy at the European Graduate School in Saas-Fee, Switzerland, and chair of the board of the International Gay and Lesbian Human Rights Commission in New York.

In the late 1990s, in their book *Excitable Speech*, Butler angled their theory of performativity to address injurious or hate speech (which includes, for example, racial and sexual taunts and pornography). Since then, they have revisited their theories on gender, power, and sexuality – in, for example, *Undoing Gender* (2004) – and, more recently, written on a wide range of topics that align with their involvement in human rights organizations and their political activism. These range from the idea of the nation-state, the media's portrayal of armed conflict and war, and domination and servitude, to issues surrounding Jewishness and Zionism, vulnerability, dispossession, and the events of 9/11.

Awards and honours

In 2012, Butler received the Adorno Prize for their outstanding contributions to feminist and moral philosophy, amid considerable controversy linked to their criticism of Israeli policy in the Middle East. Three

years later, they were made an "honorary geographer" by the American Association of Geographers and were elected as a corresponding fellow of the British Academy. They have received nine honorary degrees and many other awards and prizes.

Butler lives in Berkeley with their partner Wendy Brown, also a prominent political philosopher, and their son, Isaac, a musician.

Criticism and legacy

Despite a generally popular academic and public profile (a 1993 fanzine, *Judy!*, dedicated itself to the gender superstar), Butler has been subject to various critiques. The controversial social critic Camille Paglia, for example, has referred to them as a "slick, super-careerist Foucault flunky", while the feminist philosopher Martha Nussbaum claims their work is " not directed at a non-academic

audience eager to grapple with actual injustices". Critics have also often argued that their writing is theoretically obtuse and that their use of language is unnecessarily convoluted and complex.

It is undoubted, nonetheless, that Butler is a key philosopher of the modern age whose work, widely acknowledged and frequently cited, has introduced new ways of thinking about and engaging with the world. They have not only challenged accepted definitions of gender and sexuality and the notion of two "ideal" bodily forms, but have contributed to the gradual dismantling of reactionary models and frameworks of oppression. The fact that the key ideas expressed in their early work are now considered mainstream, as opposed to radical or marginal, is thought by many to be a measure of their impact and influence.

△ **THE PSYCHIC LIFE OF POWER**
In their 1997 work, Butler brings together psychoanalytical principles with the ideas of Foucault, Lacan, Nietzsche, and others, to argue that we are all subject to identity struggles as a result of the ideological constructs of power.

IN CONTEXT
Queer theory

Queer theory is an expanding field of study that challenges conventional ideas of 'normality" and fixed sexual identities. It suggests that sexuality is a social construction and that in fact very few people fit into the binary oppositions, such as male and female, gay and straight.

Although Butler was one of the earliest theorists of queer theory, Foucault's work in the 1970s on the enforcement of behavioural norms, regulatory regimes, and sex, power, and sexuality is very often seen as pioneering. Other notable theorists include the US academic Eve Kosofsky Sedgwick, whose work in the field is considered groundbreaking, and the US scholar Steven Seidman, who has examined the sociological implications of queer theory.

MARRIAGE PROPOSAL INVOLVING FOUR WOMEN; PHOTOGRAPH, c.1912

Directory

Sylvia Wynter

BORN 1928, JAMAICAN

One of the most influential Caribbean thinkers alive today, Sylvia Wynter is a playwright, novelist, and philosopher whose work challenges underlying assumptions in Western ontology and epistemology. Born in Cuba in 1928, Wynter grew up in Jamaica and went on to earn undergraduate and postgraduate degrees in modern languages from King's College London. She taught at the University of the West Indies, the University of California, San Diego, and Stanford University before retiring in 1997.

Wynter is known for her claim that Western concepts of the human "overrepresent" white bourgeois perspectives. Drawing on the natural sciences, the arts, literature, and philosophy, her provocative essays outline a theory of culture that unsettles and re-imagines humanism and modernity in anti-racist and anticolonial terms.

KEY WORKS: "The Ceremony Must Be Found: After Humanism", 1984; "Unsettling the Coloniality of Being/Power/Truth/Freedom: Towards the Human, After Man, Its Overrepresentation" 2003

▷ Judith Jarvis Thomson

BORN 1929–2020, AMERICAN

Thomson, whose work focused primarily on moral theory and metaphysics, was born in New York. She received her PhD in philosophy from Columbia University in 1959. In her most famous article, "A Defense of Abortion" (1971), she argued that "the right to life consists not in the right not to be killed, but rather in the right not to be killed unjustly".

The article sparked important debates about the morality of abortion. She also made a major contribution to development of the "trolley problem", which addresses the moral dilemma of whether, given specific circumstances, it is justifiable to save the lives of several people by killing one person.

Thomson taught at Barnard College, New York, Boston University, and, after 1964, at Massachusetts Institute of Technology (MIT), where she was professor emerita. She died in 2020.

KEY WORKS: "A Defense of Abortion", 1971; "The Trolley Problem", 1985; *Normativity*, 2008

Alasdair MacIntyre

BORN 1929, BRITISH

MacIntyre is one of the modern world's most influential thinkers on community, moral philosophy, and "virtue ethics" (which places character and virtue above duty).

The son of two physicians, he was born in the city of Glasgow, and educated at the universities of London, Manchester, and Oxford. After receiving his doctorate, and before moving to the US in 1970, he taught at the universities of Leeds, Essex, and Oxford. He then held posts at various leading universities throughout the US, including Princeton, Vanderbilt, Duke, and Notre Dame.

MacIntyre's work emphasizes the role of history in philosophical theorizing and also engages with Aristotelian ethics. He is best known for his highly acclaimed *After Virtue*, a major study in moral and political theory. This was followed by two other influential books on the formation and transformation of rival traditions of moral reasoning: *Whose Justice? Which Rationality?* and *Three Rival Versions of Moral Enquiry*.

Although he retired from teaching in 2010, MacIntyre continues to write and publish; he also holds various distinguished posts at universities in the UK and US.

KEY WORKS: *After Virtue*, 1981; *Whose Justice? Which Rationality?*, 1988; *Three Rival Versions of Moral Enquiry*, 1990; *Ethics in the Conflicts of Modernity*, 2016

Carol Gilligan

BORN 1936, AMERICAN

A feminist and a psychologist, Gilligan is famous for her work on the moral development of women and girls, and for offering new perspectives on gender, education, and mental health. Born in New York, she completed her PhD in social psychology at Harvard in 1964, then taught at the University of Chicago for two years and had three children. In 1967, she returned to Harvard, where she later became its first professor of gender studies.

In her hugely influential work *In A Different Voice* (1982), which secured her reputation, she argues that females approach moral decisions differently from males. A decade later Gilligan won the Grawmeyer Award in Education and, in 1996, she was listed as one of *Time* magazine's 25 most influential people. Her first novel, *Kyra* – which challenges the discourses of patriarchy and domination – was published in 2008. Gilligan is currently Professor of Humanities and Applied Psychology at New York University.

KEY WORKS: *In A Different Voice*, 1982; *Between Voice and Silence*, 1997; *The Birth of Pleasure*, 2002; *Kyra*, 2008

△ JUDITH JARVIS THOMSON, 2016

▷ Alain Badiou

BORN 1937, FRENCH

Badiou was born in Rabat, Morocco, the son of a mathematician. In the 1950s, he studied at the École Normale Supérieure in Paris, France, to which he later returned to take up the chair in philosophy, and where he remains to this day.

A fierce and vocal opponent of the war in Algeria (1954–62), Badiou also participated in the protests in Paris in May 1968 – indeed, much of his later work was informed by these events. The communist philosopher – intellectual hero of the far left from the 1960s – was influenced by the work of France's major radical thinkers, including Sartre, Althusser, and Lacan.

Badiou has written on a wide range of topics, from Marxism, ontology, psychoanalysis, and mathematics to literature and love. He is a frequent, and always controversial, contributor to modern political debate. His landmark text, *Being and Event*, is a radically interdisciplinary work that combines readings of poets and philosophers with complex mathematical formulae.

KEY WORKS: *Theory of the Subject*, 1982; *Being and Event*, 1988; *The Meaning of Sarkozy*, 2007; *In Praise of Love*, 2009

Thomas Nagel

BORN 1937, AMERICAN

A prominent philosopher and professor of law, Nagel was born in Belgrade, Yugoslavia (modern-day Serbia), to a Jewish family. He studied philosophy at the universities of Cornell and Oxford and then went on to complete his doctorate, under the supervision of the eminent philosopher John Rawls, at Harvard University in 1963.

Nagel is a professor emeritus of philosophy and law at New York University, where he taught from

△ **ALAIN BADIOU, 2011**

1980 to 2016; previously he held posts at the universities of California, Berkeley, and Princeton.

He is notable as a philosopher of ethics, politics, and the mind. In what is considered by many to be his most influential work, *The View From Nowhere*, he addresses the mind-body problem, ethics, free will, and the meaning of death.

Nagel has received three honorary doctorates and numerous prestigious awards and prizes in philosophy, including the Mellon Distinguished Achievement Award in the humanities, the Rolf Schock Prize in logic and philosophy, and the Balzan Prize in moral philosophy.

KEY WORKS: *The Possibility of Altruism*, 1970; "What is it Like to be a Bat?", 1974; *Mortal Questions*, 1979; *The View from Nowhere*, 1986; *Mind and Cosmos*, 2012

Robert Nozick

1938–2002, AMERICAN

Born in Brooklyn, New York, Nozick was the son of Russian immigrants. He graduated from Columbia College and, in 1963, was awarded his doctorate from Princeton University, where he was appointed as an assistant professor. He then taught at Harvard and Rockefeller universities, before becoming a full professor at Harvard at the age of 30.

Nozick rose to prominence with his first, and what turned out to be his most influential, work *Anarchy, State, and Utopia*, published in 1974, which draws on the work of John Locke. In it, Nozick launches a powerful defence of libertarianism, advocating minimal intervention by the state in the citizen's right to life, liberty, and property. Although he was later critical of the radical stance he adopted in the book, it marked a significant shift in his thinking from his earlier socialist beliefs.

Nozick's intellectual interests were broad: as well as being a leading political philosopher, he was influential in epistemology, decision-making theory, ethics, and philosophy of mind. He died of stomach cancer, aged 64.

KEY WORKS: *Anarchy, State, and Utopia*, 1974; *Philosophical Explanations*, 1981; *The Nature of Rationality*, 1993; *Invariances: The Structure of the Objective World*, 2001

Saul Kripke

1940–2022, AMERICAN

Kripke was considered by many to be a modern genius. He was the world's leading philosopher of modal logic and arguably best known for developing Kripke semantics, the standard semantics for modal logic. He also made outstanding contributions to the philosophy of language, theories of truth, and the work of Wittgenstein.

Born into a Jewish family in Long Island, New York, Kripke was a child prodigy who is said to have taught himself Hebrew, and read Descartes and the complete works of Shakespeare by the age of nine. In 1957, while still at school, he wrote a highly influential paper on modal logic.

Kripke studied mathematics at Harvard and taught graduate courses in logic before having graduated himself. He went on to teach at Rockefeller and Princeton universities. His most famous book is *Naming and Necessity* – a work that created an entirely new language of logical necessity. Before his death in 2022, he was distinguished professor of philosophy at the Graduate Center of the City University of New York and emeritus professor at Princeton.

KEY WORKS: *Naming and Necessity*, 1980; *Wittgenstein on Rules and Private Language*, 1982; *Philosophical Troubles, Volume 1*, 2013

Gayatri Chakravorty Spivak

BORN 1942, INDIAN

Born in Calcutta, West Bengal, to middle-class parents, Spivak received her education at the universities of Calcutta, Cambridge, and Cornell. She stepped into the limelight in 1976 as the first translator in English of Jacques Derrida's deconstructive work *Of Grammatology*. But it was the appearance of her dense and eloquent essay "Can the Subaltern Speak?" in 1988 – a piercing analysis of colonialism and marginalization – that sealed her global reputation.

Spivak, who now teaches at Columbia University in New York, went on to become one of the world's foremost thinkers in postcolonial studies and "third-world feminism", although she is hugely critical of "essentialist" categories such as these. She is known for her radical, "interventionist" readings of literary and other texts, in which she presents formidable challenges to colonial and patriarchal discourse.

KEY WORKS: *In Other Worlds*, 1987; "Can the Subaltern Speak?", 1988; *A Critique of Post-Colonial Reason*, 1999; *Other Asias*, 2005

Patricia Churchland

BORN 1943, CANADIAN–AMERICAN

Churchland was born in British Columbia, the daughter of a nurse and a newspaper worker; the family also ran a small farm. In 1965, she graduated from the University of British Columbia, and then took higher degrees at the universities of Pittsburg and Oxford. Since then she has been influential in the philosophy of neuroscience and of the mind as well as in neuroethics – the ethical issues arising from our increased understanding of the human brain.

Several of her key works examine the interface between neuroscience and philosophy. Her book *Touching a*

Nerve, examines issues of identity, free will, and consciousness. She is professor emeritus of philosophy at the University of California, San Diego, and adjunct professor at the Salk Institute. Her husband and both her children are neuroscientists.

KEY WORKS: *Neurophilosophy: Toward a Unified Science of the Mind-Brain*, 1986; *Braintrust: What Neuroscience Tells Us About Morality*, 2011; *Touching a Nerve: The Self as Brain*, 2013

Susan Haack

BORN 1945, BRITISH

Haack's contribution to philosophy has been wide-ranging and includes legal philosophy, the philosophy of logic and language, epistemology, metaphysics, the philosophy of science, pragmatism, feminism, social philosophy, the law of evidence, and the philosophy of literature.

Born in Buckinghamshire, she was awarded her PhD from the University of Cambridge; her dissertation was published two years later as *Deviant Logic* (1974), her first book. She is best known for "foundherentism", her theory of justification, which takes a middle ground between the schools of coherentism and foundationalism. Haack has lived in the US since 1990, and is a professor of philosophy and law at the University of Miami.

KEY WORKS: *Philosophy of Logics*, 1978; *Evidence and Inquiry*, 1993; *Defending Science*, 2003; *Putting Philosophy to Work*, 2008

Charles W. Mills

1951–2021, JAMAICAN

One of the most influential thinkers of the late 20th century, Charles Mills challenged the central assumptions of Western political philosophy. Born in London, Mills was raised in Jamaica and attended the University of the West Indies. After receiving his PhD

△ **MICHAEL SANDEL, 2018**

from the University of Toronto, he moved to the US, and worked at the University of Illinois Chicago, the City University of New York Graduate Center, and Northwestern University.

In his groundbreaking book *The Racial Contract* (1997), Mills argues that the liberal political tradition of the social contract is built on racism. Instead of being a neutral agreement among free political actors, it is a racial contract that establishes white supremacy. Mills's other essays and books explore how this deep history of racial domination shapes life and philosophy into the present day. Mills died of cancer in 2021 at the age of 70.

KEY WORKS: *The Racial Contract*, 1997; *Blackness Visible: Essays on Philosophy and Race, Contract and Domination* (with Carole Pateman), 2013.

△ Michael Sandel

BORN 1953, AMERICAN

A moral and political philosopher, Sandal was born into a Jewish family in Minneapolis, and received his PhD from the University of Oxford. He has been teaching at Harvard University since 1980.

Sandal has become famous for his pioneering BBC programme *The Global Philosopher*, which brings together participants in a video-linked "global conversation" on the most pressing ethical and civil issues of the modern age – from the state of democracy and climate change to immigration and national borders. A charismatic, superstar intellectual, dubbed the "rockstar moralist", he has attracted audiences of tens of millions to his shows. Sandel is also well known for his first book, *Liberalism and the Limits of Justice* (1982), which challenges John Rawls's *A Theory of Justice*. Several of Sandel's other works are bestsellers, including *What Money Can't Buy*, which examines the effect of the free market on our everyday lives. In 2010, *China Newsweek* proclaimed Sandel the "most influential foreign figure of the year".

KEY WORKS: *Liberalism and the Limits of Justice*, 1982; *Justice: What's the Right Thing To Do?*, 2009; *What Money Can't Buy: The Moral Limits of Markets*, 2012

▷ Cornel West

BORN 1953, AMERICAN

The son of a Baptist minister, West was born into a middle-class family in Oklahoma. His great-great uncle was lynched in Texas and his body wrapped in the US flag. Unsurprisingly, it was an incident that came to haunt West; at the age of nine he refused to stand for the US pledge of allegiance. By the age of 27, in 1980, he had become the first Black American to be awarded a PhD in philosophy from Princeton.

Since then West has become famous for his hugely influential publication *Race Matters* (1993), and as one of the US's most powerful voices in civil rights, race, gender, and class issues. He sees himself as contributing to the struggle to empower everyday people to "shape their own destinies".

A self-proclaimed "prominent and provocative democratic intellectual", West is chair of the Democratic Socialists of America and professor of the practice of public philosophy at Harvard University. He has appeared in films and television programmes, and has made spoken-word albums.

KEY WORKS: *Race Matters*, 1993; *Democracy Matters: Winning the Fight Against Imperialism*, 2009; *Brother West: Living and Loving Out Loud*, 2010

Kwame Anthony Appiah

BORN 1954, AMERICAN

Appiah was born in London. His father was a Ghanaian lawyer and statesman, his mother a member of the British landed gentry. After receiving his doctorate in philosophy from the University of Cambridge in 1982, he moved to the US, where he has since taught at major universities, including Yale, Princeton, and Harvard.

His *Necessary Questions* was a groundbreaking text on analytical philosophy, while *Thinking It Through* (2003) is seen as a key analysis of modern philosophy. It was, however, *In My Father's House* that established Appiah as a leading scholar in African studies. Here, as in other works, he

△ **CORNEL WEST, 1994**

urges the abolition of the concept of race. He is also famous for his deconstruction of the concepts of identity and selfhood (race, nationality, gender, sexuality, and class). Appiah is professor of law and philosophy at New York University.

KEY WORKS: *Necessary Questions: An Introduction to Philosophy*, 1989; *In My Father's House*, 1992; *Color-Consciousness*, 1996

Anne Dufourmantelle

1964–2017, FRENCH

Dufourmantelle, a philosopher and psychoanalyst, was born in Paris and completed her PhD at the Sorbonne on Kierkegaard, Nietzsche, Lévinas, and Patočka. She later lectured in the US and Switzerland, and wrote for the socialist newspaper *Libération*.

Dufourmantelle was influenced by Lacan and collaborated with several leading radical thinkers, such as Derrida and Butler. Her interests were wide-ranging and included love, sex, God, faith, and the idea of the foreigner. But it was the concept of risk that was also central to her work: "When there is really a danger to be faced," she said, "there is a very strong incentive to... surpassing oneself." In a tragic postscript to this philosophical preoccupation, she died in a courageous bid to rescue two children from drowning in the sea near Saint-Tropez in southern France.

KEY WORKS: *Of Hospitality* (with Derrida), 1997; *Blind Date: Sex and Philosophy*, 2003; *Praise of Risk*, 2011

David Chalmers

BORN 1966, AUSTRALIAN

Chalmers – who was born in Sydney and brought up in Adelaide – is one of the world's foremost philosophers of mind and consciousness. He teaches at New York University, US, and is the lead singer of the Zombie Blues band.

As a boy Chalmers was brilliant at mathematics and went on to receive a degree in the subject from the University of Adelaide. He was, however, awarded a PhD from Indiana University Bloomington, US, in philosophy and cognitive science.

Chalmers is most famous for what he defines as the "hard problem" of consciousness – the explanatory gap between how physical processes in the brain give rise to subjective experience. In 1996, he outlined these complex ideas in his influential *The Conscious Mind*, which remains a key work on consciousness and the mind–body problem.

KEY WORKS: *The Conscious Mind*, 1996; *The Character of Consciousness*, 2010; *Constructing The World*, 2012

Glossary

the Absolute
Ultimate reality conceived of as an all-embracing, single principle. Some thinkers have identified this principle with God; others have believed in the Absolute but not in God; others have not believed in either. The philosopher most closely associated with the idea is Hegel.

analytic philosophy
A view of philosophy that sees its aim as clarification of concepts, statements, methods, arguments, and theories by carefully taking them apart, especially influential in Britain and the US.

atomism
In Ancient Greece, the theory put forward by Democritus that all matter is composed of tiny, indivisible, differently shaped particles, or atoms, and empty space, or void.

Buddhism
Philosophy/religion founded by Siddhartha Gautama around the 6th century BCE in India that aims to achieve liberation (*nirvana*) from the cycle of rebirth (*samsara*) via **ethics**, meditation, compassion, and wisdom.

Confucianism
A **humanistic** philosophy/religion developed from the teachings of Confucius that emphasized duty, family, and social harmony, one of the major official ideologies of China over millennia.

Cynicism
A philosophy popularized in Ancient Greece by Diogenes in the 4th century BCE that urged its followers to achieve the virtuous life via asceticism, known for its ridiculing of conventional pretensions and its mockery of socially acceptable behaviour.

Daoism
Chinese philosophy/religion founded by Laozi in the 6th century BCE that stresses the unity of humanity and the universe, based on the *dao* (way) and the seeking of *wu wei* (freedom) from desires.

determinism
The view that nothing can happen other than what does happen, because every event is the necessary outcome of causes preceding it – which themselves were the necessary outcome of causes preceding them. *See also* free will.

dialectic
(i) Skill in questioning or argument. (ii) A technical term used by followers of Hegel or Marx for the idea that any assertion, whether in word or deed, evokes opposition, the two of which then become reconciled in a synthesis that includes elements of both.

dualism
A view of something as made up of two irreducible elements, usually taken to be material and immaterial, or physical and spiritual. *See also* mind–body dualism.

empiricism
The view that all knowledge of anything that actually exists must be derived from experience and mediated through the senses. It grew from the establishment of experimental science.

Epicurianism
A philosophy proposed by Epicurus around the 4th century BCE, based on the pursuit of modest pleasures and freedom from desire, fear, and pain, which would lead to the attainment of happiness.

epistemology
The branch of philosophy concerned with what knowledge is, what we can know, and how we can know what we know. *See also* ontology.

ethics
The study of right and wrong human behaviour and the moral principles that govern that behaviour. Also known as moral philosophy.

existentialism
An approach that arose in 20th-century philosophy that focuses on human existence and the search for meaning or purpose in life.

free will
The possibility of being able to freely choose between different courses of action; linked to such concepts as responsibility, guilt, sin, and so on. *See also* determinism.

German idealism
A form of **idealism** evolving with and after Kant in the late-18th and 19th centuries in Germany, influenced by Romanticism and the Enlightenment.

humanism
A philosophical approach based on the assumption that humankind is the most important "anything" that exists, and that there can be no knowledge of a supernatural world, if any such world exists.

idealism
The view that fundamental reality consists of something non-material, whether mind, our minds and mental contents, or spirits, or one spirit.

linguistic philosophy
Also known as linguistic analysis. The view that philosophical problems arise from a muddled use of language, and are to be solved, or dissolved, by a careful analysis of the language in which they have been expressed.

logic
The branch of philosophy that makes a study of rational argument itself – its terms, concepts, rules, methods, and so on.

logical positivism
The doctrine that the only **empirical** statements that are meaningful are those that are verifiable.

materialism
The doctrine that all real existence is ultimately of something material.

mechanism
Doctrine especially prevalent in the 17th century that held that the universe could be reduced to mechanical principles; in other words, that all **phenomena** could be explained through the motion and collision of matter according to the laws of physics.

metaphysics
The branch of philosophy concerned with the ultimate nature of what exists. It questions the natural world "from outside", as it were, and its questions therefore cannot be dealt with by the methods of science. Philosophers who take the natural world to be all there is use the term metaphysics for the broadest, most general possible frameworks of human thinking.

mind–body dualism
The view that mental things and physical things are fundamentally distinct, arising especially with Descartes in the 17th century as a solution to the "mind–body problem" (how to understand the place of mind in nature), though originally a far older belief.

moral philosophy
See ethics.

naturalism
The view that reality is explicable without reference to anything outside the natural world.

natural philosophy
The study of nature and the physical universe from Ancient Greek times to the 19th century; considered the precursor to natural science.

nature
The empirical world as given to humankind.

Neo-Confucianism (*daoxue*)
A **rationalist** ethical philosophy that flourished in Tang dynasty China, largely secular though borrowing concepts from **Buddhism** and **Daoism**, and seeing a return to **Confucian** ideas as a reaction against those two schools of thought.

nihilism
Complete rejection of the idea that life has any meaningful value or purpose; or that life contains any intrinsic morality.

nominalism
Belief that a general name or word applies to specific objects or individuals without reference to an independently existing **universal**. *See also* realism.

noumenon
As posited by Kant, the unknowable reality behind what presents itself to human consciousness. A thing as it is in itself, independently of being experienced, is said to be the noumenon. "The noumenal" has therefore become a term for the ultimate nature of reality. *Compare* **phenomenon**.

ontology
A branch of philosophy that asks what actually exists, as distinct from the nature of our knowledge of it, which is covered by the branch of **epistemology**. Ontology and epistemology taken together constitute the central tradition of philosophy.

paradigm
A typical example of something, a pattern or model; a set or framework of underlying assumptions about a situation or the world.

phenomenology
An approach to philosophy that investigates objects of experience (known as **phenomena**) only to the extent that they manifest themselves in our consciousness, without making any assumptions about their nature as independent things.

phenomenon
An experience that is immediately present. If I look at an object, the object as experienced by me is a phenomenon. Kant distinguished this from the object as it is in itself, independently of being experienced: he called the object in itself the **noumenon**.

philosophy of religion
The branch of philosophy that looks at human belief systems and the real or imaginary objects, such as gods, that form the basis of these beliefs.

philosophy of science
A branch of philosophy concerned with the nature of scientific knowledge and the practice of scientific endeavour.

Platonic Forms or Ideals
According to Plato, ideal forms of things are contained in a world separate from the world we live in. We only ever see imperfect reflections of these perfect forms. Forms are the essences of objects: for example, all chairs are different from each other but all contain the Form, or essence, of chairness.

political philosophy
The branch of philosophy that questions both the nature and the methods of the state and deals with such subjects as justice, law, social hierarchies, political power, and constitutions.

positivism
A philosophy put forward by Comte that the whole of human knowledge comprises only what can be verified with scientific, mathematical, or logical proof, therefore rejecting **theology** and **metaphysics**. *See also* logical positivism.

poststructuralism
A movement disagreeing with **Structuralist** ideas and binary oppositions and emphasizing plurality of meaning. Associated with French philosophers and critical theorists of the 1960s and 70s.

pragmatism
A theory of truth. It holds that a statement is true if it does all the jobs required of it: accurately describes a situation, prompts us to anticipate experience correctly, fits in with already well-attested statements, and so on.

rationalism
The view that we can gain knowledge of the world through the use of reason, without relying on sense-perception, which is regarded by rationalists as unreliable. The opposite view is known as **empiricism**.

realism
In opposition to **nominalism**, the belief that **universals** exist independently of the specific objects or individuals that exemplify or embody them.

scepticism
The view that it is impossible for us to know anything for certain; that we do not or cannot have knowledge in a particular area. For example, sceptics about the external world say that we cannot know about the world outside our own minds.

Scholasticism
Philosophical study as practised by Christian thinkers in European universities in the medieval period, combining religious doctrine and study of Greek philosophers such as Aristotle.

semantics
The study of meanings in linguistic expressions.

semiotics
The study of signs and symbols, in particular their relationships with the things they are meant to signify.

social contract
An implicit agreement among members of a society to cooperate in order to achieve goals that benefit the whole group, sometimes at the expense of individuals within it.

sophist
Someone whose aim in argument is not to seek the truth but to win the argument. In Ancient Greece, young men aspiring to public life were taught by the Sophists to learn the various methods of winning arguments.

Stoicism
A school of thought that flourished in Ancient Greece and Rome, in which virtue, or **ethics**, is the basis of knowledge, and the goal of humans is to live a life of self-control and morality in accordance with the nature of the world.

Structuralism
Initiating in the field of linguistics and later applied to other disciplines in the human sciences, a method of interpreting social phenomena and human behaviours in the context of the interrelationships between them. It sees an overarching network, or structure, underlying all human behaviour, beliefs, perceptions, products, and so on. *See also* post-structuralism.

tabula rasa
The human mind having no innate ideas, such as at birth; a clean slate.

theology
Enquiry into scholarly and intellectual questions concerning the nature of God. Philosophy, by contrast, does not assume the existence of God, though some philosophers have attempted to prove his/her existence.

transcendental
Outside the world of sense experience. Someone (for example Wittgenstein) who believes that **ethics** are transcendental believes that ethics have their source outside the **empirical** world. Thoroughgoing empiricists do not believe that anything transcendental exists, and nor likewise do Nietzsche or **humanist existentialists**.

Übermensch
Nietzsche's "Superman" or "Overman", a superior human who will transcend conventional morality by creating value and morality for himself that is not based on superstition; he will overcome the herd instinct and live purely by the will to power, though not necessarily power over others.

universal
A concept of general application, like "red". It has been disputed whether universals have an existence of their own. Does "redness" exist, or are there only individual red objects? In the Middle Ages, philosophers who believed that "redness" possessed real existence were called **realists**, while philosophers who maintained that it was no more than a term or word were known as **nominalists**.

utilitarianism
A theory in **moral** and **political philosophy** that judges the morality of an action by its consequences, and regards the most desirable outcome as that which achieves the greatest good for the greatest number.

virtue ethics
Various theories of **ethics** in which morality is considered with reference to the virtues and character intrinsic to the individual rather than reflecting the individual's actions or behaviour.

Index

Acknowledgments

Toucan would like to thank Dr Alan Schrift for advice on content, Julie Brooke for proofreading, and Vanessa Bird for indexing. The publisher would like to thank the following for their kind permission to reproduce their photographs:

(Key: a-above; b-below; c-centre; l-left; r-right; t-top)

1 Getty Images: PHAS / Contributor (c). **2 Alamy Stock Photo:** Artexplorer (c). **3 Getty Images:** Science & Society Picture Library / Contributor (c). **5 Getty Images:** Fine Art / Contributor (c). **12 akg-images:** (tr). **13 Bridgeman Images:** Freer Gallery of Art and Arthur M. Sackler Gallery, USA / Gift of Eugene and Agnes E. Meyer (tr). **13 Getty Images:** Burstein Collection / Contributor (tl). **13 Alamy Stock Photo:** Dan Hanscom (br). **14 Alamy Stock Photo:** agefotostock (tr). The History Collection (br). **15 Alamy Stock Photo:** IanDagnall Computing (c). **16 akg-images:** Roland and Sabrina Michaud (tr). **16 Getty Images:** Bettmann / Contributor (bc). **17 Cobalt ID:** (tr). **17 Alamy Stock Photo:** Design Pics Inc (b). **18 Alamy Stock Photo:** Danita Delimont (b). **19 Alamy Stock Photo:** The Picture Art Collection (tl). **19 Bridgeman Images:** British Library, London, UK / © British Library Board. All Rights Reserved (cr). **19 Getty Images:** Werner Forman / Contributor (bl). **20 Alamy Stock Photo:** R.M. Nunes (c). **21 Getty Images:** Heritage Images / Contributor (cl). **21 Alamy Stock Photo:** Dinodia Photos (cr). **22 Getty Images:** Universal History Archive / Contributor (cl). **22 Alamy Stock Photo:** World Religions Photo Library (br). **23 Alamy Stock Photo:** imageBROKER (t). **24 Alamy Stock Photo:** The Picture Art Collection (c). **25 Getty Images:** Heritage Images / Contributor (b). **25 Alamy Stock Photo:** Artokoloro Quint Lox Limited (tr). **26 akg-images:** Erich Lessing (tr). **27 Alamy Stock Photo:** QUANTUM PICTURES (tl). **27 Bridgeman Images:** De Agostini Picture Library (br). **28 Alamy Stock Photo:** The Picture Art Collection (tr). Vito Arcomano (bl). **29 Getty Images:** Fine Art / Contributor (t). **30 Alamy Stock Photo:** MuseoPics - Paul Williams (tl). The Picture Art Collection (br). Zoonar GmbH (bl). **31 akg-images:** (c). **32 Getty Images:** DEA / G. NIMATALLAH / Contributor (cl). **32 Bridgeman Images:** Alinari (br). **32 akg-images:** Album / Oronoz (c). **34 Dorling Kindersley:** Rob Reichenfeld / National War Museum (tl). **34 Getty Images:** Heritage Images / Contributor (b). **35 Alamy Stock Photo:** Walker Art Library (tr). Angus McComiskey (b). **36 Alamy Stock Photo:** Hemis (t). **36 Bridgeman Images:** Prismatic Pictures (b). **37 Getty Images:** Leemage (b). **38 Getty Images:** Print Collector / Contributor (c). **39 Alamy Stock Photo:** Hercules Milas (tl). **39 Bridgeman Images:** Fitzwilliam Museum, University of Cambridge, UK (br). **40 Alamy Stock Photo:** imageBROKER (t). **40 Getty Images:** Universal History Archive / Contributor (br). **41 Alamy Stock Photo:** Specialpictures.nl (tr). **41 Getty Images:** Print Collector / Contributor (bc). **42 akg-images:** (tr). **42 Bridgeman Images:** Biblioteca Medicea-Laurenziana, Florence, Italy / De Agostini Picture Library / Pinaider (bl). **43 Getty Images:** Stock Montage / Contributor (tl). UniversalImagesGroup / Contributor (br). **44 akg-images:** (tr). **45 Dorling Kindersley:** Gary Ombler / Durham University Oriental Museum (tr). **45 Alamy Stock Photo:** Xinhua (bl). **46 Alamy Stock Photo:** The History Collection (bc). **46 akg-images:** Pictures From History (crb). **47 Getty Images:** VCG / Contributor (l). **48 Alamy Stock Photo:** Artokoloro Quint Lox Limited (bl). The Picture Art Collection (r). **49 Bridgeman Images:** Photo © Christie's Image (t). **50 Getty Images:** Print Collector / Contributor (c). **50 Bridgeman Images:** Archives Charmet (bl). **51 Getty Images:** ullstein bild Dtl. / Contributor (c). **52 Getty Images:** Mondadori Portfolio / Contributor (tr). **53 Getty Images:** DEA / A. DAGLI ORTI / Contributor (tl). **53 Alamy Stock Photo:** The Picture Art Collection (cr). MuseoPics - Paul Williams (br). **54 Alamy Stock Photo:** The History Collection (c). **55 Alamy Stock Photo:** imageBROKER (br). **56 Getty Images:** DEA / G. DAGLI ORTI / Contributor (bl). **56 Alamy Stock Photo:** Peter Horree (br). **57 Getty Images:** Leemage (c). **58 Alamy Stock Photo:** The Picture Art Collection (cl). **58 Bridgeman Images:** De Agostini Picture Library (tl). **59 Alamy Stock Photo:** Ivan Vdovin (b). **59 Bridgeman Images:** The University of St. Andrews, Scotland, UK (tr). **60 Alamy Stock Photo:** Science History Images (tr). **61 Alamy Stock Photo:** The Picture Art Collection (ca).

61 akg-images: Hervé Champollion (bl). **61 Getty Images:** adoc-photos / Contributor (br). **62 Alamy Stock Photo:** Craig Lovell / Eagle Visions Photography (bc). PRISMA ARCHIVO (tr). **64 Getty Images:** Heritage Images / Contributor (tc). **65 Bridgeman Images:** Pictures from History (bl). **68 Getty Images:** Heritage Images / Contributor (c). **69 Bridgeman Images:** Museo Civico Cristiano, Brescia, Italy (bl). **69 Alamy Stock Photo:** The Picture Art Collection (tc). Granger Historical Picture Archive (br). **70 Bridgeman Images:** (br). **71 Getty Images:** Mondadori Portfolio / Contributor (c). **72 akg-images:** (bl). **73 Getty Images:** Roger Wood / Contributor (br). **73 Alamy Stock Photo:** INTERFOTO (tl). Science History Images (r). **74 Alamy Stock Photo:** PjrWindows (c). **75 Alamy Stock Photo:** Historic Images (cl). **75 Getty Images:** Heritage Images (cr). **75 Alamy Stock Photo:** Andia (br). **76 Alamy Stock Photo:** FALKENSTEINFOTO (c). **77 Alamy Stock Photo:** The Picture Art Collection (bl). Heritage Image Partnership Ltd (br). **78 Getty Images:** Heritage Images / Contributor (bl). **78 Bridgeman Images:** Church of St. Johannes, Cappenberg, Germany (crb). **79 Alamy Stock Photo:** Zvonimir Atletić (c). **80 akg-images:** Pictures From History (tr). **81 Alamy Stock Photo:** Sorin Colac (bl). **81 Getty Images:** Universal History Archive / Contributor (tr). **82 akg-images:** Roland & Sabrina Michaud (c). **83 Alamy Stock Photo:** The History Collection (br). **83 akg-images:** Pictures From History (tr). **84 Alamy Stock Photo:** The History Collection (bl). **84 Bridgeman Images:** Pictures from History (tr). **85 Bridgeman Images:** FuZhai Archive (l). **85 Alamy Stock Photo:** John Warburton-Lee Photography (br). **86 Alamy Stock Photo:** The Picture Art Collection (c). **87 Getty Images:** Fine Art / Contributor (bl). Print Collector (tc). **87 Alamy Stock Photo:** Lanmas (br). **88 Getty Images:** Heritage Images (c). **89 Getty Images:** Science & Society Picture Library / Contributor (tr). **89 Alamy Stock Photo:** The Granger Collection (br). **90 Getty Images:** Library of Congress / Contributor (tr). Heritage Images / Contributor (br). **91 Alamy Stock Photo:** Art Collection 2 (c). **92 Alamy Stock Photo:** RM Images (t). **93 Getty Images:** UniversalImagesGroup / Contributor (tl). adoc-photos / Contributor (bl). **93 Bridgeman Images:** Museo Campano, Capua, Italy / Roger-Viollet, Paris (cr). **94 Bridgeman Images:** culture-images/Lebrecht (c). **95 Getty Images:** Angelo Hornak / Contributor (bl). **95 Alamy Stock Photo:** INTERFOTO (tr). **96 Alamy Stock Photo:** Art Collection 3 (bc). **97 Alamy Stock Photo:** The Picture Art Collection (tr). **98 Getty Images:** Stefano Bianchetti / Contributor (bl). **99 Getty Images:** DEA / G. DAGLI ORTI / Contributor (br). **102 Alamy Stock Photo:** Stuart Black (bl). The National Trust Photolibrary (tc). **102 Getty Images:** PHAS / Contributor (br). **103 Getty Images:** (c). **104 Getty Images:** Imagno / Contributor (tr). **105 akg-images:** Erich Lessing (tl). **105 Getty Images:** DEA PICTURE LIBRARY / Contributor (bl). **106 Getty Images:** DEA / G. DAGLI ORTI / Contributor (br). **106 Mary Evans Picture Library:** Iberfoto (tr). **107 Getty Images:** Heritage Images / Contributor (c). **108 The British Museum:** ©Trustees of the British Museum (cl). **108 Getty Images:** Heritage Images / Contributor (br). **109 Alamy Stock Photo:** age fotostock (t). The Picture Art Collection (br). **110 Bridgeman Images:** Private Collection (c). **111 Alamy Stock Photo:** Pictorial Press Ltd (tr). PvE (br). **112 Alamy Stock Photo:** The Picture Art Collection (c). **113 Getty Images:** Print Collector / Contributor (bc). Culture Club / Contributor (tr). **114 Alamy Stock Photo:** IanDagnall Computing (cl). **114 Getty Images:** Print Collector / Contributor (tr). Kean Collection / Staff (bc). **115 Getty Images:** National Galleries of Scotland / Contributor (br). **116 Bridgeman Images:** (c). **117 Alamy Stock Photo:** Oldtime (c). **117 Bridgeman Images:** Photo © Christie's Images (br). **118 Alamy Stock Photo:** FALKENSTEINFOTO (b). **119 Bridgeman Images:** Archives Charmet (tl). **119 Getty Images:** Photo 12 / Contributor (tr). **119 Bridgeman Images:** Photo © Philip Mould Ltd, London (br). **120 Alamy Stock Photo:** Pictorial Press Ltd (tl). **120 Getty Images:** Heritage Images / Contributor (bl). **120 Bridgeman Images:** Archives Charmet (tr). **121 Getty Images:** UniversalImagesGroup / Contributor (t). **122 Getty Images:** Imagno / Contributor (c). Science & Society Picture Library / Contributor (tr). **123 Alamy Stock Photo:** PRISMA ARCHIVO (bc). **124 Alamy Stock Photo:** The Picture Art Collection (tr). **125 Alamy Stock Photo:** Lebrecht Music & Arts (br). Painters (tr). **126 Alamy Stock Photo:** The

Picture Art Collection (bl). The History Collection (tr). **127 akg-images:** Erich Lessing (t). **128 Getty Images:** UniversalImagesGroup / Contributor (tr). Culture Club / Contributor (br). **129 Getty Images:** Heritage Images / Contributor (c). **130 Alamy Stock Photo:** GL Archive (c). **131 Getty Images:** Science & Society Picture Library / Contributor (bc). **132 Alamy Stock Photo:** Chronicle (cr). The Picture Art Collection (bl). **132 Getty Images:** Paul Popper / Popperfoto / Contributor (tl). **134 Alamy Stock Photo:** Heritage Image Partnership Ltd (c). age fotostock (bl). **135 Alamy Stock Photo:** The Picture Art Collection (c). **136 Alamy Stock Photo:** GL Archive (c). **137 Getty Images:** Epics / Contributor (tr). Hulton Archive / Handout (br). **138 Alamy Stock Photo:** Art Collection 2 (t). **139 Alamy Stock Photo:** The History Collection (b). **139 Getty Images:** Print Collector / Contributor (tr). **140 Getty Images:** Photo Josse/ Leemage / Contributor (c). **141 Getty Images:** AFP / Stringer (br). **141 Alamy Stock Photo:** The Picture Art Collection (cr). **142 Alamy Stock Photo:** GL Archive (c). **143 Bridgeman Images:** Photo © Christie's Images (cr). **143 Alamy Stock Photo:** Claudine Klodien (br). **144 Getty Images:** Print Collector / Contributor (bl). **144 Alamy Stock Photo:** Antiqua Print Gallery (br). **146 Alamy Stock Photo:** PRISMA ARCHIVO (tr). **147 Getty Images:** Imagno / Contributor (bc). **148 Alamy Stock Photo:** History and Art Collection (tc). **149 Getty Images:** Photo Josse/Leemage / Contributor (tr). **149 Getty Images:** Print Collector / Contributor (t). **152 akg-images:** Erich Lessing (bl). **152 Alamy Stock Photo:** Historic Images (br). **153 Getty Images:** Heritage Images / Contributor (c). **154 Getty Images:** Photo Josse/Leemage / Contributor (bl). **154 Alamy Stock Photo:** Lebrecht Music & Arts (br). **155 akg-images:** Erich Lessing (t). **155 Getty Images:** Photo Josse/Leemage / Contributor (br). **156 Alamy Stock Photo:** GL Archive (tr). **157 Getty Images:** Print Collector / Contributor (tl). **157 Bridgeman Images:** The Hunterian, University of Glasgow, Scotland (br). **158 Alamy Stock Photo:** Josse Christophel (tl). Gerry McCann (br). **159 Getty Images:** Photo Josse/Leemage / Contributor (tr). **159 Alamy Stock Photo:** Jeffrey Blackler (bl). **160 Getty Images:** Alinari Archives / Contributor (bl). Science & Society Picture Library / Contributor (crb). **161 Getty Images:** Heritage Images / Contributor (c). **162 Alamy Stock Photo:** Chronicle (tr). **162 Bridgeman Images:** De Agostini Picture Library (clb). **163 akg-images:** (b). **164 Bridgeman Images:** Royal Albert Memorial Museum, Exeter, Devon, UK (tr). **165 Bridgeman Images:** Courtesy of the Warden and Scholars of New College, Oxford (tl). **165 Alamy Stock Photo:** ART Collection (bc). The Picture Art Collection (cr). **166 Getty Images:** Print Collector / Contributor (b). Leemage / Contributor (tr). **167 Bridgeman Images:** Photo © Christie's Images (c). **168 Bridgeman Images:** Underwood Archives/UIG (t). **168 Alamy Stock Photo:** The Picture Art Collection (cl). **169 Alamy Stock Photo:** Joana Kruse (b). **169 Getty Images:** Universal History Archive / Contributor / Universal Images Group Editorial (t). **170 Getty Images:** Fine Art / Contributor (c). **171 Getty Images:** Heritage Images / Contributor (c). United Archives / Contributor (bl). **171 Alamy Stock Photo:** The Picture Art Collection (br). **172 Getty Images:** Photo Josse/Leemage / Contributor (br). **172 Alamy Stock Photo:** The Picture Art Collection (tr). **173 Alamy Stock Photo:** Pictorial Press Ltd (c). **174 Alamy Stock Photo:** Heritage Image Partnership Ltd (c). **175 Getty Images:** Culture Club / Contributor (tl). Culture Club / Contributor (tr). **175 akg-images:** (br). **176 Alamy Stock Photo:** The Picture Art Collection (br). **177 Getty Images:** DEA PICTURE LIBRARY / Contributor (c). **178 Getty Images:** Heritage Images / Contributor (tr). **179 akg-images:** (bl). (br). **180 Getty Images:** Arkivi / Contributor (bl). **180 Alamy Stock Photo:** The Picture Art Collection (br). **181 Alamy Stock Photo:** The Picture Art Collection (c). **182 Bridgeman Images:** Bristol Museum and Art Gallery, UK / Given by Miss A. Kiddell to the Bristol Institution (forerunner of the City Museum), 1841, and transferred to Bristol Art Gallery, 1905. (tr). **183 Alamy Stock Photo:** Dinodia Photos (tc). **183 Getty Images:** Universal History Archive / Contributor (bl). Mansell / Contributor (cr). **184 Getty Images:** ullstein bild Dtl. / Contributor (bl). **184 akg-images:** (tc). **184 Alamy Stock Photo:** John Glover (br). **185 Getty Images:** Culture Club / Contributor (c). **186 Alamy Stock Photo:** Art Library (bl). INTERFOTO (tr). **187 akg-images:** (b). **188 akg-images:** Pictures From History (c). **189 Alamy Stock Photo:** Chronicle (bl). UtCon Collection (br). **190 Getty Images:** Imagno / Contributor (c). **191 Getty Images:** Boston Globe / Contributor (bl). **191 Alamy Stock Photo:** Granger Historical Picture Archive (tc). **191 Getty Images:** Bettmann / Contributor (br). **192 Getty Images:** adoc-photos / Contributor (c).

193 akg-images: (tl). (tr). **193 Getty Images:** Time Life Pictures / Contributor (br). **194 Getty Images:** DEA PICTURE LIBRARY / Contributor (c). **195 Bridgeman Images:** British Library, London, UK / © British Library Board. All Rights Reserved (tr). **195 Alamy Stock Photo:** Ian C Dagnall (br). **196 Alamy Stock Photo:** Granger Historical Picture Archive (tl). **196 Getty Images:** Photo 12 / Contributor (br). **197 Getty Images:** London Stereoscopic Company / Stringer (tl). **197 Alamy Stock Photo:** Historic Images (br). **198 Getty Images:** Bettmann / Contributor (tr). **199 Alamy Stock Photo:** The Picture Art Collection (cr). **199 Getty Images:** Print Collector / Contributor (br). **200 Getty Images:** Heritage Images / Contributor (bl). **200 Alamy Stock Photo:** Granger Historical Picture Archive (br). **201 Getty Images:** Bettmann / Contributor (tl). **201 Alamy Stock Photo:** INTERFOTO (br). **202 Alamy Stock Photo:** Granger Historical Picture Archive (tr). **203 Bridgeman Images:** New York Public Library, USA (br). Granger (tc). **203 Getty Images:** GraphicaArtis / Contributor (cr). **204 Alamy Stock Photo:** imageBROKER (cl). World History Archive (cr). **205 Getty Images:** Bettmann / Contributor (c). **206 Alamy Stock Photo:** Granger Historical Picture Archive (t). **206 akg-images:** Fototeca Gilardi (bl). (br). **207 Bridgeman Images:** Sputnik (b). **208 Alamy Stock Photo:** INTERFOTO (cl). **208 Getty Images:** View Pictures / Contributor (t). **209 Getty Images:** Photo 12 / Contributor (b). **209 Alamy Stock Photo:** Historic Images (tr). **210 National Portrait Gallery, Smithsonian Institution**. **211 Alamy Stock Photo:** GRANGER - Historical Picture Archive (l). Collection of the Smithsonian National Museum of African American History and Culture: (tr). **211 Getty Images:** Fotosearch / Stringer / Archive Photos (br). **212 Alamy Stock Photo:** Artokoloro Quint Lox Limited (tc). Ian Dagnall (br). **213 Alamy Stock Photo:** Granger Historical Picture Archive (c). **214 Alamy Stock Photo:** Chronicle (bl). Granger Historical Picture Archive (bc). **215 Bridgeman Images:** De Agostini Picture Library / G. Dagli Orti (tl). **215 Alamy Stock Photo:** Granger Historical Picture Archive (cr). **216 akg-images:** (tr). **216 Getty Images:** Imagno / Contributor (br). **217 Getty Images:** Universal History Archive / Contributor (c). **218 Getty Images:** DEA / A. DAGLI ORTI / Contributor (bl). **219 Alamy Stock Photo:** Niday Picture Library (t). **219 akg-images:** (br). **220 Alamy Stock Photo:** Michelangelo Oprandi (br). **221 Alamy Stock Photo:** The History Collection (tc). **221 Bridgeman Images:** British Library, London, UK / © British Library Board. All Rights Reserved (br). **222 Getty Images:** Heritage Images / Contributor (bl). **223 Getty Images:** Culture Club / Contributor (tc). **224 Alamy Stock Photo:** The History Collection (tc). **225 Alamy Stock Photo:** FLHC 80 (bc). **228 akg-images:** (tl). **228 Alamy Stock Photo:** The History Collection (br). **229 Getty Images:** adoc-photos / Contributor (c). **230 Cobalt ID:** (tl). **230 Getty Images:** United Archives / Contributor (tr). Hulton Archive / Stringer (bl). **231 Getty Images:** Historical Picture Archive / Contributor (br). **232 Getty Images:** Bettmann / Contributor (c). **233 Getty Images:** Chicago History Museum / Contributor (cr). **233 Bridgeman Images:** Newberry Library, Chicago, Illinois, USA (bl). **234 Mary Evans Picture Library:** J. Bedmar/Iberfoto (c). **235 Getty Images:** Fine Art / Contributor (bl). Print Collector / Contributor (br). **235 Bridgeman Images:** Musee des Beaux-Arts, Rouen, France (tr). **236 Getty Images:** JHU Sheridan Libraries/Gado / Contributor (c). **237 Getty Images:** Rykoff Collection / Contributor (tl). **237 Alamy Stock Photo:** The Granger Collection (br). **238 Getty Images:** George Silk / Contributor (tr). **239 Alamy Stock Photo:** Roman Babakin (tl). **239 Getty Images:** Bettmann / Contributor (crb). **240 Alamy Stock Photo:** GRANGER - Historical Picture Archive (cl). The New York Public Library: (br). **241 Getty Images:** AFP. **242 Getty Images:** Bettmann / Contributor (c). **243 Alamy Stock Photo:** Rolf Richardson (tl). Pictorial Press Ltd (br). **244 Getty Images:** Universal History Archive / Contributor (t). Imagno / Contributor (bl). **244 Bridgeman Images:** Private Collection (br). **245 Getty Images:** Jeremy Fletcher / Contributor (tr). **245 Alamy Stock Photo:** Chronicle (br). **246 Alamy Stock Photo:** Heritage Image Partnership Ltd (c). **246 Getty Images:** Culture Club / Contributor (cr). **247 akg-images:** (c). **248 Getty Images:** ullstein bild / Contributor (c). **249 Getty Images:** Galerie Bilderwelt / Contributor (c). DEA / A. DAGLI ORTI / Contributor (br). **250 Bridgeman Images:** Prismatic Pictures (tr). **251 Getty Images:** Bettmann / Contributor (tr). ullstein bild Dtl. / Contributor (bl). **252 Alamy Stock Photo:** Archive PL (t). **252 Getty Images:** Imagno / Contributor (bl). **253 Alamy Stock Photo:** allOver images (tl). **253 Getty Images:** UniversalImagesGroup / Contributor (cl). **253 Alamy**

Stock Photo: Science History Images (cr). **254 Getty Images:** ullstein bild / Contributor (tr). **255 Alamy Stock Photo:** The Picture Art Collection (cla). **255 Getty Images:** Culture Club / Contributor (br). **256 Bridgeman Images:** Musee de Tesse, Le Mans, France (t). **257 Bridgeman Images:** Joerg Hejkal; Martin Heidegger, Being and Time, Max Niemeyer Verlag, 1927, title page (tr). **257 Getty Images:** Keystone / Stringer (br). **258 Getty Images:** Mondadori Portfolio / Contributor (c). **259 Getty Images:** Heritage Images / Contributor (bl). **259 Getty Images:** Janet Fries / Contributor / Hulton Archive (br). **260 Alamy Stock Photo:** Jochen Tack (bl). Peter Horree (tc). **260 Getty Images:** Nina Leen / Contributor (br). **261 Alamy Stock Photo:** The Picture Art Collection (c). **262 Alamy Stock Photo:** dpa picture alliance (tr). **263 Alamy Stock Photo:** Galina Samoylovich (tr). **263 akg-images:** picture-alliance (bl). **264 Bridgeman Images:** © SZ Photo / Ingrid von Kruse (c). **265 Alamy Stock Photo:** Chronicle (cl). **265 Getty Images:** Heritage Images / Contributor (br). **266 Getty Images:** Imagno / Contributor (tl). **266 Alamy Stock Photo:** Austrian National Library/Interfoto (bl). **267 Getty Images:** API / Contributor (tl). **267 Dorling Kindersley:** NASA (cr). **268 Getty Images:** Imagno / Contributor (c). **269 Getty Images:** Photo 12 / Contributor (cla). Fred Stein Archive / Contributor (crb). **270 Getty Images:** Lambert / Contributor (tr). DEA / A. DAGLI ORTI / Contributor (clb). **271 Getty Images:** Imagno / Contributor (cra). Gjon Mili / Contributor (bl). **272 Getty Images:** Loomis Dean / Contributor (cr). **273 Getty Images:** Dominique BERRETTY / Contributor (c). **274 Getty Images:** Lipnitzki / Contributor (bc). **275 Getty Images:** Michael Nicholson / Contributor (tl). **275 TopFoto:** © Le Livre de Poche (tr). **275 Getty Images:** Michel Ginfray / Contributor (br). **276 Bridgeman Images:** (tr). **277 Alamy Stock Photo:** Chronicle (bl). **278 Getty Images:** Heritage Images / Contributor (cl). **279 Getty Images:** Handout (bl). **279 Alamy Stock Photo:** Granger Historical Picture Archive (cr). **280 Getty Images:** Roger Viollet Collection / Contributor (c). **281 Getty Images:** ND / Contributor (bl). **281 Bridgeman Images:** Archives Charmet (br). **282 Alamy Stock Photo:** Keystone Pictures USA (tc). **282 Cobalt ID:** (bl). **283 Getty Images:** Hulton Archive / Stringer (tr). Alain Nogues / Contributor (b). **284 Bridgeman Images:** Tallandier (tr). **285 Getty Images:** Keystone-France / Contributor (tl). **285 Alamy Stock Photo:** Granger Historical Picture Archive (bl). **285 Getty Images:** Apic/RETIRED / Contributor (br). **286 akg-images:** (c). **287 Alamy Stock Photo:** David Robertson (c). **287 Cobalt ID:** (br). **288 Getty Images:** Heritage Images / Contributor (bl). **288 Dorling Kindersley:** William Reavell (tr). **289 Getty Images:** Ulf Andersen / Contributor (c). **290 Getty Images:** Alain MINGAM / Contributor (tr). **291 Cobalt ID:** © Bloomsbury Publishing Plc (tr). **291 Alamy Stock Photo:** Photo 12 (br). **292 Alamy Stock Photo:** age fotostock (c). **293 Alamy Stock Photo:** Ben Ramos (c) / From *A Severed Head* by Iris Murdoch published by Chatto & Windus. Reproduced by permission of The Random House Group Ltd. ©1961. Jonathan Player (br). **294 Cobalt ID:** (tr). **294 Alamy Stock Photo:** Jinny Goodman (br). **295 Getty Images:** Steve Pyke / Contributor (c). **296 Getty Images:** Frederic REGLAIN / Contributor (tr). **297 Getty Images:** Keystone / Stringer (tl). Dan Kitwood / Staff (b). **298 Alamy Stock Photo:** Pictorial Press Ltd (tl). **299 Getty Images:** Bill Pierce / Contributor (c). **300 Getty Images:** ND / Contributor (b). **301 Getty Images:** Fine Art / Contributor (tr). **301 Bridgeman Images:** De Agostini Picture Library / J. E. Bulloz (br). **302 Aurimages:** Ulf Andersen (c). **303 Getty Images:** UniversalImagesGroup / Contributor (bl). Ulf Andersen / Contributor (crb). **304 Alamy Stock Photo:** Everett Collection Historical (tr). **305 Getty Images:** Photo 12 / Contributor (tr). **305 Alamy Stock Photo:** Peter Vallance (br). **306 akg-images:** UIG / Godong (bl). **307 Rex Features:** Sipa/REX/Shutterstock (c). **308 Getty Images:** UniversalImagesGroup / Contributor (tr). **309 Getty Images:** United Archives / Contributor (bl). Urbano Delvalle / Contributor (cr). **310 Getty Images:** Antonio RIBEIRO / Contributor (c). **311 Alamy Stock Photo:** Everett Collection Inc (tr). **311 Getty Images:** JACQUES MARIE / Contributor (br). **312 Dorling Kindersley:** (tr). **312 Getty Images:** David Goddard / Contributor (br). **313 Getty Images:** Louis MONIER / Contributor (c). **314 Alamy Stock Photo:** fullempty (tl). Granger Historical Picture Archive (br). **315 Getty Images:** PHILIP LITTLETON / Staff (tl). Ulf Andersen / Contributor (br). **316 Getty Images:** Marty Katz / Contributor (tr). **317 Getty Images:** Construction Photography/Avalon / Contributor (bl). Araldo De Luca / Contributor (cr). **318 Getty Images:** Photo 12 / Contributor (bc). **319 Getty Images:** Bettmann / Contributor (tc). **320 Getty Images:** Ulf Andersen / Contributor (bl). **321 Bridgeman Images:** Gilles Deleuze / PVDE (br). **324 Getty Images:** Lee Lockwood / Contributor (tr). **325 Getty Images:** Frederic Lewis / Staff (cla). Ralph Freso / Stringer (bl). **326 Alamy Stock Photo:** Sueddeutsche Zeitung Photo (cl). **326 Getty Images:** Richard Baker / Contributor / In Pictures (b). **327 Shutterstock.com:** SIPA. **328 Bridgeman Images:** Photo © Christie's Images (bl). **328 The Metropolitan Museum of Art:** Purchase, Lila Acheson Wallace Gift, 2001 (br). **329 Alberto Ramella/SYNC. 330 Hall Family Archive. 331 Getty Images:** Eamonn McCabe / Popperfoto. **332 Getty Images:** George Rose / Contributor (c). **333 Alamy Stock Photo:** Universal Art Archive (bc). **333 Getty Images:** Paul Bergen / Contributor (br). **334 Getty Images:** James Andanson / Contributor (tr). **335 Getty Images:** Time Life Pictures / Contributor (tc). **335 Alamy Stock Photo:** AGB Photo Library (cr). Mehdi32300 (bl). **336 Getty Images:** Patrick BOX / Contributor (c). **337 Cobalt ID:** (ca). **337 Getty Images:** Sunset Boulevard / Contributor (bl). **337 Alamy Stock Photo:** The History Collection (br). **338 Getty Images:** The AGE / Contributor (c). **339 Alamy Stock Photo:** Geoff A Howard (br). **340 Getty Images:** Florilegius / Contributor (cl). **340 Alamy Stock Photo:** Serhii Chrucky (br). **341 Bridgeman Images:** Gabinetto dei Disegni e Stampe, Galleria Degli Uffizi, Florence, Tuscany, Italy (tl). **341 Getty Images:** Louise Gubb / Contributor (cr). **341 Alamy Stock Photo:** Sergey Komarov-Kohl (tr). **342 Getty Images:** GERARD MALIE / Staff (br). **343 Bridgeman Images:** © Basso Cannarsa/Opale/Leemage (c). **344 Getty Images:** Bettmann / Contributor (b). **345 Alamy Stock Photo:** Eric Nathan (tl). Everett Collection Inc (cb). **345 Bridgeman Images:** Collection Bourgeron (crb). **347 Getty Images:** Anthony Barboza / Contributor (tr). **347 Alamy Stock Photo:** Shawn Porter (tr). Joshua Davenport (br). **348 Getty Images:** Barbara Alper / Contributor (cl). **348 Bridgeman Images:** Bibliotheque Marguerite Durand, Paris, France / Archives Charmet (cr). **349 Alamy Stock Photo:** Agencja Fotograficzna Caro (c). **350 Getty Images:** mark peterson / Contributor (t). **351 Alamy Stock Photo:** Jonny White (tr). **351 Getty Images:** Kirn Vintage Stock / Contributor (br). **352 Getty Images:** Paul Marotta / Contributor (bc). **353 Getty Images:** Eric Fougere / Contributor (tc). **354 Getty Images:** Ethan Miller / Staff (tr). **355 Getty Images:** Anthony Barboza / Contributor (bc).

All other images © Dorling Kindersley. For more information see: **www.dkimages.com**

What will you discover next?

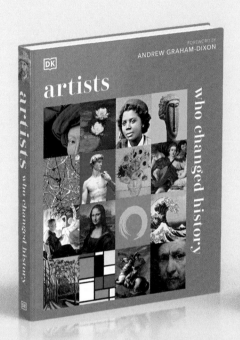

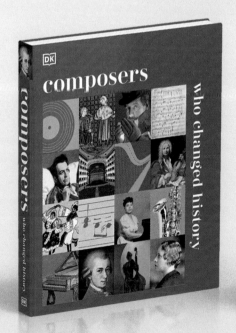

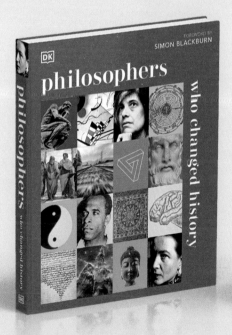

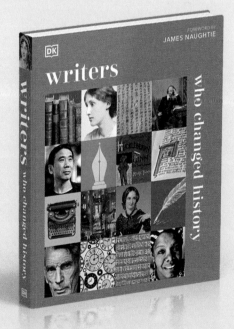